EDUCATING LATINO STUDENTS

Educating Latino Students

A GUIDE to SUCCESSFUL PRACTICE

Edited by

María Luisa González
Educational Management and Development Department
New Mexico State University

Ana Huerta-Macías
Department of Curriculum and Instruction
New Mexico State University

Josefina Villamil Tinajero
College of Education
University of Texas at El Paso

TECHNOMIC
PUBLISHING CO., INC.
LANCASTER · BASEL

Educating Latino Students
a **TECHNOMIC** publication

Published in the Western Hemisphere by
Technomic Publishing Company, Inc.
851 New Holland Avenue, Box 3535
Lancaster, Pennsylvania 17604 U.S.A.

Distributed in the Rest of the World by
Technomic Publishing AG
Missionsstrasse 44
CH-4055 Basel, Switzerland

Printed in the United States of America
10 9 8 7 6 5 4 3 2 1

Main entry under title:
    Educating Latino Students: A Guide to Successful Practice

A Technomic Publishing Company book
Bibliography: p.
Includes index p. 377

Library of Congress Catalog Card No. 97-60883
ISBN No. 1-56676-568-4

Contents

PART V—EXEMPLARY PRACTICES FOR LATINOS IN MIDDLE SCHOOLS

12. Middle Schools for Latinos: A Framework for Success   239
REBECCA BENJAMIN—*University of New Mexico*

13. Literacy Instruction for Middle-School Latinos   269
KARIN M. WIBURG—*New Mexico State University*

PART VI—EXEMPLARY PRACTICES FOR LATINOS AT THE HIGH-SCHOOL LEVEL

14. Transforming High Schools to Meet the Needs of Latinos   291
JULIA ROSA EMSLIE—*Eastern New Mexico University*
JUAN A. CONTRERAS—*Ysleta Independent School District*
VIRGINIA R. PADILLA—*Ysleta Independent School District*

Acknowledgements

THIS book would not have been possible without the unfailing support of Dr. Cynthia Ann Bell dos Santos and Ms. Kiran Katira. Their dedication in seeing that all the details were done and that all of the tasks were coordinated among the editors and multiple chapter authors was a feat in itself. We would also like to thank Karen Wilbanks, April Padilla, Anthony Marin, and Lisa Gamboa. We are thankful for the long hours spent on this project and their true commitment to the purpose of this endeavor.

Introduction

As Latino numbers increase nationally, moving from minority to majority status, many public school systems are still struggling with the challenges of serving these linguistically and culturally different students. *Educating Latino Students: A Guide to Successful Practice* addresses this major concern of schools in the United States. Latinos comprise the largest group of high-school dropouts, as well as the group most affected by poverty. As schools attempt to meet the needs of Latino children throughout the United States, less than inviting attitudes are present in many educational communities, due to frustration in not knowing what to do and how to deal with Latinos. Confusion and fear often lead to detrimental policies and practices that affect these students, their families, and ultimately society as a whole. Therefore, this book attempts to assist readers in expanding their knowledge base in the area of quality practices for Latino students. The chapters contain many examples of successful educational practices that can be implemented in other educational settings. As educators grapple with issues of schooling Latinos, little is available that meets the needs of educators across the broad educational spectrum. This book is a response to this need.

Educating Latino Students: A Guide to Successful Practice covers the areas of best practices in terms of educating Latinos at all levels of the educational system, from preschool to secondary school. Most books with a focus on Latinos provide much theory but rarely combine theory with practice. Others are written with solely the bilingual educator in mind, taking for granted that only bilingual personnel "deal with Latinos," which is definitely not the case. Thus, our intention is to be inclusive of the educational personnel, who often are major decision makers and who must also attend to the Latino student without having had any prior training or experience.

This volume serves as a guide and resource not only for teachers but for those beyond the classroom walls. Included herein are the different roles community, parents, teachers, and administrators, as well as all stakeholders play in providing the educational leadership for successful practice in educating Latino students. This volume represents a comprehensive collection of work by recognized authors and successful practitioners who are able to explain theory with actual examples of application. These examples demonstrate where and how education is successfully working for Latinos.

One note to the reader is in order. The federal and some state governments have elected to use a single term, Limited English Proficient (LEP), to describe individuals with varying degrees of proficiency in English who are not native speakers of English. In this volume, the reader will find that the term LEP is not used. The editors, in keeping with a philosophy that sees the linguistically and culturally different as students full of potential and talent, decided to utilize the term Potentially English Proficient (PEP) instead of LEP.

Overview

THE first nine chapters discuss successful practices from early childhood through elementary schooling and are divided into three parts—Part I: Creating a Supportive School Culture in Serving Latinos; Part II: Successful Practices for Latinos in Early Childhood Programs; and Part III: Exemplary Practices for Latinos at the Elementary Level.

In Part I several perspectives are discussed that focus on a positive school climate for serving Latinos. This part sets some of the foundations for the additional discussions of quality schooling in succeeding chapters. In Chapter 1, María Luísa González addresses the issue of the principal's role by presenting sketches of three culturally competent leaders who are exemplary by way of the supportive atmosphere that they promote in their schools for Latinos. In Chapter 2, Ana Huerta-Macías provides an in-depth discussion of the sociocultural aspects of working with linguistically and culturally different students. In Chapter 3, Alma Flor Ada and Nancy Jean Smith describe exemplary parent-involvement projects developed around a participatory and critical framework that involves Latino parents as true educational partners.

In order to provide a comprehensive picture of positive educational practices that meet the needs of Latinos, we must look across all grade levels, beginning with preschool. This journey is begun in Part II, which discusses early childhood education for young bilingual children. In Chapter 4, Elizabeth Quintero writes about the importance of looking at young preschoolers as children, first and foremost. Then an explanation follows on what educators can do to meet the needs of children in the early stages of life. She additionally describes practices that make the curriculum culturally and linguistically appropriate for these young Latinos. In Chapter 5, Maria Cristina González continues the discussion by providing an in-depth review on literacy development among Latinos in a kindergarten setting. In Chapter 6, Irene Serna, Cecilia Espinosa, and Karen Moore illustrate the variety of literacy experiences that occurred in a bilingual classroom as children worked on a project focusing on a relevant theme.

Part III focuses on elementary curriculum by looking at the language arts, math, and science areas. In Chapter 7, Josefina Tinajero, Sandra Hurley, and Elizabeth Varela Lozano discuss a variety of activities that can be implemented to assist the language development processes among bilingual students. In Chapter 8, Yolanda de la Cruz provides examples of classroom projects and activities that help develop concepts in the areas of math and science. In Chapter 9, Jozi De León and Linda Holman discuss an issue that is critical to Latinos at all levels—the impact of standardized testing. The inappropriate placement of Latinos in special education programs is given particular attention in this chapter.

In brief, the first nine chapters will provide the reader with a discussion of sound administrative and pedagogical practices for young Latinos and their families. Readers will find the information to be highly accessible and useful across a variety of educational settings.

Chapters 10–17 provide the reader with demographic information on the Latino population, take the reader to the middle and secondary levels of schooling, and consist of four sections—Part IV: Leadership Practices for Success among Diverse Latino Populations; Part V: Exemplary Practices for Latinos in Middle Schools; Part VI: Exemplary Practices for Latinos at the High-School Level; and Part VII: Responsible Assessment for Latinos and Their Schools. Part IV begins with a chapter by Alicia Sosa where she discusses the diversity of the Latino population in terms of their origin, describes some of the bilingual education models that are currently being implemented for Latinos, and provides some statistical information related to the schooling success of Latinos. In Chapter 11 María Luísa González and Ana Huerta-Macías describe successful schools with an emphasis on the role of the principal. In Part V Rebecca Benjamin leads the reader into the middle school with a discussion on the importance of looking at the whole middle-school student and addressing the specific physical and emotional as well as academic needs of Latino adolescents. In Chapter 13, Karin Wiburg discusses an integrated literacy curriculum for middle schoolers with an emphasis on technology. In the following chapter (Part VI), Juan Contreras, Virginia Padilla, and Julia Rosa Emslie focus on specific features that are characteristic of an exemplary program for Latinos at the high-school level. In Chapter 15, Nancy Lucas addresses programs for newly arrived unschooled Latinos. Part VII addresses the issue of assessment. Ann Del Vecchio, Cyndee Gustke, and Judith Wilde describe several alternative assessment measures that can be used to evaluate student work in the various content areas and that are responsive to the linguistic and cultural needs of Latinos. Finally, Cecilia Navarrete, Christopher Nelson, and Paul Martínez provide a "capstone" discussion by describing a systemic assessment instrument that can be used to evaluate the school climate as well as to place priorities for improvement in schools that serve Latinos.

PART I

CREATING A SUPPORTIVE SCHOOL CULTURE IN SERVING LATINOS

CHAPTER 1

Successfully Educating Latinos: The Pivotal Role of the Principal

MARÍA LUÍSA GONZÁLEZ—*New Mexico State University*

INTRODUCTION

IN schools serving Latinos the principal sets the tone of respect, acceptance, and knowledge of sound instructional practice that results in high expectations. It is the principal who must exhibit a combination of skills and knowledge to effectively lead a school in providing the quality education legally guaranteed to Latinos, in order for them to become successful, productive citizens in the twenty-first century. At a minimum, the principal must ensure that the school's language response program addresses the following points (Sosa, 1993, p. 28):

- teaching English language learners the degree of fluency in English that they need to be successful in an all-English classroom
- ensuring that the English language learners receive understandable instruction in the content areas, using the native language or ESL to teach the content areas during the time they are learning English
- providing catch-up assistance through tutoring, homework assistance, and accelerated learning that will enable students to keep up with their school work

Presently, many administrators find themselves challenged by their lack of understanding and knowledge of the particular needs of Latinos. Much of the current, mainstream literature, especially over the last decade, has focused on the pivotal role that a principal plays in school success. However, little research, even in the area of bilingual education and second language acquisition, has focused on the role of the principal in the education of Latino students. Nonetheless, demographers continually remind us that (Howe, 1994, p. 42):

- Latinos remain the most undereducated major segment of the U.S. population.

3

- One of twelve persons living in this country can trace their roots to Latin America.
- Latinos have increased at a rate five times that of non-Hispanic whites, African Americans, and Asians combined.
- The number of Spanish-speaking Latinos will increase to over 22 million by the year 2000.

Despite these statistics, little is being done to prepare principals for success with school populations that are culturally diverse (Reyes and Valencia, 1993; Smith and Greene, 1990). However, there are principals who engage in leadership practices that lead to successful educational attainment for all their students. These principals serve as models in promoting the education of culturally, ethnically, and linguistically diverse students.

SKETCHES OF SUCCESSFUL PRINCIPALS

Administrators who understand the issues connected with schooling Latino students, including the needs of the poor as well as those of English language learners, work on changing attitudes and practices that create incompatibilities between home and school. These incompatibilities are caused by the unreal expectation that every student should function as a middle-income, English-speaking monolingual child (González, 1992).

Competent educators find students' cultural and linguistic differences rewarding and feel a moral commitment toward their education (Sergiovanni, 1992). This philosophy is exemplified throughout the sketches of three elementary school leaders described in subsequent sections of this chapter. These principals "are living examples of success" (Carter and Chatfield, 1986) and were selected based on informal feedback from central office administrators, university professors, teachers, parents, and students themselves. All three principals are located in the border Southwest with one leading a school in an urban area, another in a rural vicinity, and the last one in a multilingual school. Each sketch was gleaned from interviews with the principals and other school personnel, as well as observations of the principals. The sketches provide a short background on the school and its principal, describe some actions taken by the principals in transforming their schools, discuss how they demonstrate advocacy for Latino students, parents, language, and culture, and include their leadership plans for the future.

A Principal Serving Latinos in a Successful Urban School

Ysleta Elementary is my school where I am given a chance to be unique, to display my talents in a variety of ways, and to feel special. I believe that I will always be learning with my friends, teachers, parents, school helpers, and community. I am inspired to be better, to be a skilled, useful member of my community, and to follow my dreams! I know that I am expected to be responsible, to be respectful, and to do my best at all times. I am expected to help and to be helped. Ysleta Elementary is a place for people to find happiness, knowledge, and success! (Ysleta Elementary Self-Study, 1994)

Background on School and Principal

The vision statement included in the school's campus improvement plan fully describes the commitment that the entire school holds for the education of its students. Ysleta Elementary has approximately 700 students enrolled in its programs. The campus consists of a main building, which is nearly forty-five years old, along with two large parking lots and several small buildings covering an entire block. One building houses a police center that provides decentralized and personalized police services to the community. The school is located close to an international border crossing with Mexico, and serves a population of first and second generation immigrants. Over 90 percent of the students are on free or reduced lunch, with fewer than 20 percent of the students coming from homes where one or both parents hold a high-school diploma. The majority come from single-parent families with a high mobility rate due to the availability of low-rent properties in the area. However, when the families do move they usually remain in the same school zone.

The principal, Ms. Dolores De Avila, has led the school over the past six years and has much to do with why parents and students choose to stay at Ysleta Elementary. The school offers a rich educational experience to children and their families. Her school is a far cry from the school she attended as a child where she was punished for speaking Spanish. In spite of her own negative educational experiences, De Avila continued her formal education and taught for nine years. Once she received her master's degree, she worked at central office as an instructional supervisor and a lead teacher. All of her experiences have led her to believe that people are important and should be treated with dignity and respect. She has internalized this concept and models this in her school and its community. Although unfairly treated in school as a child, she loves learning and has vowed to provide the best education for every child, thus embracing the culturally and linguistically different.

Transforming the School

Major challenges faced De Avila as she was assigned to Ysleta Elementary. Initially there were few parents working with the school; there was a climate of complacency among the faculty and a negative feeling toward administration. Teachers had a very narrow view of instruction. The focus was on discipline, with study carrels lined up and down a hallway to isolate "problem children." De Avila moved the school from its former reactive stance to education, where punitive measures were sought, to one that is proactive. Her vision is for a school that is child- and learner-centered. This includes working within a holistic view of education—by focusing on the whole child while involving the entire community.

Upon her arrival, the principal asked herself how she could impact instruction at this school. She began by encouraging teachers to read professional journals. She also lowered teacher per pupil ratio by adding a teacher to each grade level. Currently, in the lower grades there are about eighteen students per class; in the upper levels there are approximately twenty-two per class. The principal took full advantage of the flexibility in current Title I schoolwide funding as well as the district's school-based budgeting to accomplish these additions and shifts in personnel.

Furthermore, she realized the need for parent involvement and sought central office support to hire a social worker and a parent educator. Through long hours of discussion with central office and the schoolwide committee, she convinced them of the need to follow the Comer Model of schools working with parents and families (ASCD Advisory Panel on Improving Student Achievement, 1995). This model is based on the work of the psychiatrist, James Comer, from the Yale Child Study Center. The model includes a process of fostering strong relationships among children, teachers, and parents or guardians. Parents or guardians are encouraged to be an active presence in the school, where social activities bring families and school staff together to gain trust in the school.

Her commitment to the Comer Model was further evidenced as successful grants were obtained for the different projects that have improved education at Ysleta Elementary. One grant provided funds to establish a parent center within the school. When the center was first established, parents were satisfied with creating handcrafts. Through the principal's insistence, training for parents began to take deeper meaning when parents became involved in understanding the school's curriculum. The parent involvement component has reached new heights. For example, after meeting directly with Howard Gardner, who visited the school as part of his ongoing research, parents became interested in the Multiple Intelligences Theory. They became engaged in the design and implementation of an arts enrichment program based on the Multiple Intelligences Theory (Gardner, 1993). Parents now feel empowered to also assume civic responsibilities. For example, they successfully lobbied city hall for better traffic control on the dangerous streets surrounding the school, which were creating safety concerns.

Ysleta Elementary is lauded as one of the most innovative schools in the area. Among the school's highlights is an accelerated school model that involves all stakeholders in decision making. This approach involves the philosophy and systematic process for providing the best possible education for each child (Hopfenberg and Levin, 1993). The instructional approach is not fast-track but designed to enrich students' experiential learning through higher expectations, relevant content, and stimulating instruction. It involves schoolwide principles that are based on the belief that expertise is found within the school community and must be built on the strength of its entirety. The model calls for a unified focus by all involved. Empowerment is evident as important educational decisions are made and responsibility is accepted by school personnel, as well as parents and students (Keller, 1995). Initially, for instance, teachers and parents expected De Avila to take care of all problems. They now feel enough ownership to seek solutions together whenever problems do arise.

In order to serve the needs of PEP students, this school follows a late-exit transitional bilingual model adopted by the district. This model offers students a minimum of 40 percent of total instructional time in Spanish language arts, mathematics, social studies, and science. Although students may be reclassified as fluent English proficient, they remain in the late-exit program through the sixth grade (Díaz-Rico and Weed, 1995). Research on late-exit bilingual programs has shown greater achievement gains in comparison to early-exit models, as well as a positive impact on self-esteem and cultural pride (Ramírez, 1992). Collier (1995a) goes on to explain that in:

> late-exit bilingual education programs that continue through the upper elementary grades to provide first language academic instruction, along with balanced second language academic instruction, language minority students can also maintain their academic success at the secondary level,

even when the instruction in middle and high school is delivered exclusively through second language. Academic knowledge gained in first language transfers to the second language. Thus, the more students have received high quality education in the first language, the deeper their knowledge base across the two languages. Even though language minority students may be segregated from English speakers in this type of program, they are able to build the self-confidence and academic skills needed to succeed in secondary school contexts all in the second language. (p. 36)

To further strengthen the program for PEP students, the school has started an instructional initiative that espouses a whole language philosophy to address reading, writing, problem solving, and technology. Within this framework the school also established multiage classrooms combining two grade levels from kindergarten through the sixth grade. This practice involves grouping children so the age span of the class extends beyond the homogeneity principle. Multiage grouping attempts to maximize the benefits of interaction and cooperation among children of different experiences and stages of development in all classroom activities, including the mastery of basic literacy and numeracy skills (Privett, 1996).

Advocacy for Latino Students, Parents, Language, and Culture

Ms. De Avila's philosophy with respect to education is one that avoids seeing children as deficient in any way. Her philosophy looks at strengths and possibilities by focusing on the "big picture." In advocating for students and parents, Ms. De Avila believes that educators need to learn who their children are and to see them as assets. They further need to understand what their own beliefs are concerning children. Educators, she feels, often respond to stereotypes, whereas they need to counteract these stereotypical responses by understanding who the customer is. The quality of instruction is also central to her philosophy of education. She adds, "Instruction never leaves me nor does what happens with parents."

Parents are not restricted to the parent center. They are also welcome in what used to be known as the teachers' lounge. Now both parents and teachers eat side by side in the school. To further promote this partnership between school and home, a community-based project offers training for both teachers and parents. Through this training they get to know each other well, outside their traditional roles. This was accomplished by teachers and parents traveling together to professional conferences and even sharing rooms. Now every training session has a mix of teachers, parents, and different community people coming together.

Thus, professional development is one of the major thrusts of the school. Teachers share in the innovations to which they are committed. When they meet to select presenters they collectively decide who will be invited. The undergirding theme is that there is no sole expert, and the group must pool its knowledge to obtain the staff development they need and desire in their school. Another area where Ms. De Avila has introduced change is in teacher appraisals. Teachers at her school construct a portfolio by setting their own goals and by selecting an academic area that will be their focus for the year. They include how they plan to involve parents in their selected area and describe how they will also integrate technology. If, for example, they were to select writing as an academic area, their portfolio would address the following questions: Who will work on the writing process? How will parents become involved? How will parents understand the writing process and how will they, in turn, support the teacher's efforts?

Ms. De Avila, as a principal, sees the educational system in its entirety and has been able to move the school's culture from a bureaucratic model to a collaborative-relational one. She builds on connecting to the whole rather than seeing the educational system as a series of fragmented pieces. She finds that building relationships and trust at all levels must be established for stakeholders to speak honestly with one another. Her expectations of staff and faculty are as high as those she holds for children and parents.

Dolores De Avila never leaves her sense of instructional leadership. By looking at the whole, she constantly reflects on the reasons for her actions. Reflection, she feels, is also important in order for teachers to gain ownership and understand the "whole process." Therefore, the principal, along with teachers, holds reflective sessions where the reasons for certain methods, activities, and lessons, as well as their impact in the areas of reading, writing, and mathematics are analyzed. These sessions are held with the five vertical teams that comprise the instructional format at this school.

At large schools such as Ysleta Elementary, vertical teaming is a vehicle to provide safety nets for children by allowing them, their teachers, and their parents the opportunity to know each other well throughout their duration at the school. Each vertical team at Ysleta Elementary is comprised of a teacher representing each grade level from kindergarten through sixth grade. Teams meet regularly to resolve problems and create new teaching strategies. Each group of teachers and their classes is assigned to its own part of the building. This concept enhances the sense that the teachers and their students are part of one unit, one "family." As students advance from grade to grade, they are taught by the same "family" of teachers who take a personal interest in each student's progress.

Another aspect of De Avila's leadership that promotes positive change is her involvement in major community reform efforts. Though these efforts impose tremendous demands on her time because they involve research and grant writing, she feels that they are well worth the time and energy expended because the students benefit directly from these activities. The school has been able to obtain up to $200,000 in grant monies. Much of the grant money received is a result of the school's involvement with the Alliance Schools Initiative. This project is dedicated to developing a strong community-based constituency of parents, teachers, and community leaders who are working to dramatically improve student achievement in low-income communities throughout Texas. This project has helped De Avila in her vision of building a community of learners and creating a democratic school.

One grant that has had a tremendous impact at Ysleta Elementary involves an enrichment through the arts after-school program. This program integrates learning activities through the arts with lessons stimulating creativity. The program currently employs five professional artists who offer instruction in chess, drama, video production, painting, drawing, and music. Five parents have taken the leadership by coordinating the program, which takes place after school on a daily basis. Additional assistance is provided by high-school and college students acting as tutors. This program addresses a very important need in the Ysleta community—the supervision of latchkey children. It has also assisted students in their academic achievement. This program has helped raise math scores among the chess-playing students and has given parents an added opportunity for true partnership with the school. It has further provided students with a more positive outlook related to the school, their own abilities, as well as their academic achievement.

Leadership into the Future

Ms. De Avila feels that a principal is not going to transform a school in a low socio-economic area unless the community learns the importance of academics and what gets in the way of academic attainment.

There are barriers to knowledge and concerns for educational issues that must be addressed through continued dialogue with parents. Concerns must be more than school driven; community concerns must be included.

The principal further believes that school administrators should be cognizant of their own belief systems and from where these arise. Each must have a sense of community and know how to work where they serve; public relations skills are not enough. Most of these understandings must begin in university preparation programs—for both administrators and teachers. Here questions can be addressed as to why so many administrators and teachers cannot articulate their own beliefs about education, children, and learning. Educators also need earlier experiences in the field. Her collaboration with a university renewal project places education majors in the classroom at an early stage in their teacher preparation program. This type of program has allowed her to see the impact that early field experiences have on prospective and practicing teachers.

Dolores De Avila aptly summarizes her philosophy by explaining the educator's role in the education of all students: "One has to become real with people, understand them, and develop relationships with them. There is a moral obligation to the community. It is not only about test scores, there are moral dimensions to stewardship. We need to educate teachers and principals related to this. One must improve the art of teaching to work and succeed with the 'whole child.' When this occurs there will be hope for all families and young people."

A Principal Serving Latinos in a Successful Rural School

Originally La Union (the name of the school) signified "La Union de las dos naciones"—the joining of two nations. Today the name is meaningful because it signifies the union of all school personnel, parents, community, and students towards the common goal of preserving our culture and values while providing educational excellence for our future. It is also meaningful because it signifies the union of diverse communities: the stable rural, land-grant village of La Union and its agricultural environs and the new, suburban area of Santa Teresa. (La Union Elementary Self-Study Report, 1994)

Background on School and Principal

The above description from La Union's self-study clearly points out the respect and commitment to preserving two cultures. The school that began in 1883 serves a student population representing a diversity not expected in such an isolated community. The principal and teachers describe their student population as one that is "diverse academically, ethnically, and socio-economically." With a student enrollment nearing 500, student needs are addressed through various programs. Over 100 students are served by the bilingual program. Chapter I engages ninety students in its reading and language arts program. Special education serves a proportionate number of Latinos with a total of sixty-three students enrolled in the program. Students who live in the immediate school vicinity represent a low socio-economic status; however, 30 percent of the students are bussed in from a suburban, country-club area.

Isela Jáquez, the principal of four years, along with the school secretary and several other staff members attended this same elementary school as children. At the time they were children, the majority of the teachers were Latinas, although the student population was mixed with a 50/50 break between the Anglo and Latino ethnic groups. During this period the school mainly served the children from community families who made their living from farming.

Transforming the School

Over the past two years the school has been undergoing a process of yearly self-analysis under Isela Jáquez's direction. Meetings are held to set long- and short-range goals. The school improvement team is involved in a process of recommending proposals, policy revisions, and goal setting. They have also established a conflict mediation program involving trained student mediators and a related classroom curriculum. This program has resulted in a significant reduction in disciplinary referrals.

The accomplishments at La Union are many. Even though the results come from the coordinated and sustained effort of all—students, parents, faculty and staff—the principal is the person who has promoted innovations and offered the continuing support to all the stakeholders in the school. In this way she models a respect for the contributions of each. The principal's educational philosophy echoes that of Ron Edmonds (1979)—"I believe that everyone can learn." Further, she believes that her role as principal is to impact the greatest number of lives, and this she feels can be accomplished by impacting the teachers who in turn will affect the students.

Advocacy for Latino Students, Parents, Language, and Culture

The principal is vocal about her beliefs regarding the education of Latinos. She feels that a school for Latinos or a school with Latinos should always offer the same quality programs found in other exemplary schools. Foremost, the children are to be valued for their background, language, and culture. Teachers' professional development includes an in-depth understanding of the strengths that cultural and linguistic differences bring to a school. Differences are recognized as benefits, not as an aggregation of deficits. Latino students are not foreign elements. Every attempt is made not to assign Latinos into separate classes. The children are seen as resources, not problems. Ms. Jáquez plainly states: "Never use their language against them, as has been done in the past; this only erodes who they are."

Advocacy for Potentially English Proficient (PEP) students is further shown through her beliefs, practices, and policies that include:

- continuous communication with students and families
- conducting home visits along with teachers
- investigating and asking questions related to program placement
- providing more flexibility and adapting the curriculum and instruction to meet the needs of Latino students
- attending every referral and Individual Educational Plan (IEP) meeting in order to understand the problems involved

Because Ms. Jáquez serves as a model, the teachers also advocate for the students. Teachers conduct home visits on a weekly basis. Teachers at this school model respect for one another and in turn show respect for the students. They focus on the student and consider the community to be an integral part of their long-range plans. Teachers constantly spend time in planning and assessing instruction to see what works in the best interest of the students.

One of the best measures of a successful school is the testimony that students themselves offer. One child, Carlos, a fifth grader, has been living with his grandparents to be able to attend school at La Union. At a young age he has chosen to live away from his parents and home in Mexico, to remain in the school he has grown to love. Carlos describes his principal as caring and "always there." Fourth grader José, opted to remain with relatives when his mother and young sisters moved to a larger town, 250 miles away. José, who receives special education services, has blossomed at the school. This young boy, who had habitual discipline problems the previous year, now has the maturity to attend his own special education IEP meetings. The mother and student attribute his progress to the principal. Repeatedly, the principal's sense of caring describes her leadership style as well as her constant visibility. Many Latino parents claim that they never saw any of the previous principals, yet they always see this principal. She attends every school function as well as all community events.

Students are an essential part of the school community. They feel at ease in dropping by to see the principal and elicit her help. All groups feel that she is responsive to their needs. Students are active in student council and begin the day with morning announcements, which are conducted in both English and Spanish.

Many parents spend hours each week assisting with tutoring. This project will be extended to the community, where parents will open up their homes and become homework partners for students in the bilingual program. The principal believes that parents help their children as long as the instruction is in the language they understand. Neighbors will be taught to cooperate with each other's children when help is needed. This is also part of the principal's strong belief that educational ownership should be given to the community.

Another recommendation that the principal makes in dealing with parents from different socio-economic strata is to not keep the Latino parents and/or those from low socio-economic status preparing ethnic foods in the back kitchen. She strongly believes in paying attention to the needs of all families and in valuing the suggestions and contributions of all parents equally. One of her biggest accomplishments has been the collaborative relations she has established among the families of diverse students. An example of positive change that has been implemented as a result of parent suggestions deals with the format for PTA meetings. After sitting through many long, boring meetings, where parents had to listen to others talk, the principal consulted with parents and teachers. The decision was to institute a change. The parent-teacher meetings are now considered fellowship meetings with different activities connected with the meetings. The focus is to get the parents to engage in activities with their children. Contrary to the common practice of asking parents to leave their children at home, La Union welcomes parents with their children. Thus, the school embraces Latino culture. Latinos are generally family centered and believe that they should spend as much time as they can with their young children. This she finds as a strength and has shaped school practice to meet the needs of her community. A typical meeting might include a short introduction presented in both languages, then the families work in groups, and sessions end with a translated discussion held by the participants. The message of respecting linguistic diversity is clear at these meetings.

To further parental commitment to their children's education, Ms. Jáquez sees that her parents become involved at the district level. She is especially proud of parent involvement on district bilingual/ESL committees. She feels that the school's expectations of parents and a commitment to make parents feel genuine ownership have promoted their involvement. For example, specific meetings are held to build awareness of what parents should expect of a school. She feels that this is the ultimate form of accountability. Meetings are held to explain the different stages of the bilingual program. Some meetings cover curriculum and programmatic requirements to better assist the parents as their children move into English language instruction. At meetings, explanations are provided on how parents can promote the use of the primary language and the conceptual development of their children. Parents are given the knowledge and tools to demand from the school what they want for their child. In this way the parents can hold other schools accountable as well.

It is evident that advocacy for language and culture abounds. Even the school community has moved to formally express this advocacy. According to their five-year plan, the school will become a dual language school in the near future. The principal is a critical part of this movement, since she would like to expand the type of program that is currently offered for PEP students. The district has adopted an early-exit transitional bilingual model where there is some initial instruction in the primary language with all other instruction conducted in English; the primary language is used only for support. By third grade it is district policy that bilingual education students should be transitioning in the all-English curriculum. Ms. Jáquez clearly understands that by the third grade students in the bilingual program may not be able to carry out cognitively demanding tasks in English and subsequently are labeled "subtractively bilingual" (Díaz-Rico and Weed, 1995). To address the inherent weaknesses in this type of program, part of her solution is for all parents, students, and teachers to become involved in learning a language they do not speak, either English or Spanish. In the future, the choice will be expanded to as many languages as volunteers are willing to teach. The staff has already planned for the dual language program, conducted research, and sought district resources; implementation is ready to begin. The program will be adapted to meet the needs of this particular setting. The school and its principal stand firm in its mission that "preservation of culture and values is preparation for the future."

Leadership into the Future

Isela Jáquez finds her greatest sense of satisfaction from the dedication of the teaching staff. She feels the school is successful in no small sense because of the quality of her staff. She relates that meetings often last beyond school hours and teachers remain without ill will. This is the price that educators pay for shared decision making and especially site-based management, which is an ongoing process at La Union. She promotes the idea of teachers as "reflective practitioners" and the process of action research in an effort to better serve their students.

To remunerate teachers for the extra time that is required to plan collaboratively, Jáquez has written grants that provide funding for meetings held on Saturdays and for staff summer camps. Topics that are covered are music, science, language arts and second language acquisition, appropriate discipline techniques, writing, alternative assessment, and learning about cultural diversity. Experts are brought from neighboring districts, as part of staff development, to engage the group in meaningful activities. However, staff development can include something as different as a guided bus tour of the school community and its vicinity. The principal has made a commitment to see that her staff has the expertise to accomplish its mission.

One way to summarize this principal's style of leadership would be to describe her as one who empowers others. Isela Jáquez understands her role as leader of leaders, largely because of her knowledge of curriculum and strong bilingual/ESL foundation. She believes that good leaders prepare others to take over and lead on when she states: "I want the school to be able to continue on this path even if there are personnel changes. Then, as new personnel arrive they will rise to meet the challenge of who and what we are: a bilingual, bicultural community."

A Principal Serving Latinos in a Successful Non-Traditional School

The Multilingual Magnet School is an innovative elementary school concept for students focusing on language and cultural development, and producing students who are multilingual, highly motivated, contributing members of a global society. (Mission Statement of Alicia R. Chacón International School)

Background on School and Principal

This statement exemplifies Bob Schulte's passion for multilingualism. As the principal he leads a kindergarten through third grade magnet school that sits in the middle of a neighborhood with well-kept homes and a mobile home park, in a lower-income area of this border community. The gray brick building with blue trimming is newly constructed, housing two educational programs. One program is the district's pre-kindergarten program; the other is the multilingual program that is unique to the border Southwest and is in its first year of operation. The day begins by honoring the multilingual approach that is the school's focus; students take turns relating announcements in Spanish and the Pledge of Allegiance in English.

The main program is a dual language immersion program in Spanish and English. The program was modeled after its mentor school in California that has consistently outperformed its counterparts in both English and Spanish norm-referenced tests. At Chacón International all incoming kindergarten children receive instruction mostly in Spanish with the exception of ESL/English language arts and selective third languages. Instructional time in English will be gradually increased as students progress through the grade levels. The plan is that by sixth grade students will be receiving instruction in Spanish and English in equal amounts of time.

One additional and major difference that marks the International School from other dual language programs is the inclusion of a third language, where students may select one of four language choices and an accompanying culturally specific activity. For example, if the parents opt for Russian, then the children take ballet, if German then German dancing, if Chinese then Kung Fu, if Japanese then Karate. Each third language and its activity is totally taught in that language by native speakers who are also certified teachers. The concentration of the target language is on oral language development. The target language teacher is a native speaker of this language who goes into the classroom daily for an hour of language instruction. Evening classes are also offered for the parents in each language.

Because the school is a magnet attracting nearly 300 children from diverse homes and different incomes, it was decided to open this year with a dress requirement—the use of uniforms. The principal wears the uniform proudly with one minor modification—the use of a tie. For the principal this school is a dream come true. According to Schulte, being raised in a border community calls for the use of both English and

Spanish. He felt cheated when he was not given the opportunity to learn Spanish at home or at school. As a principal in a former school he began researching dual bilingual programs and designed a program that proved successful. This gave him the impetus to apply for a school opening that called for a totally new concept, one that provides instruction in three languages.

Transforming the School

The school is under constant transformation and development, since it is undergoing its first year of operation. The building is still under construction and students travel from classroom to classroom while workers go about the business of sealing walls and finishing hallways. The construction will be completed this year, and the school will cycle through its first experience with year-round schooling. Plans are to add a new grade level per year, with its first group of sixth graders graduating in 1999.

The principal and teachers continually work on creating the instructional program that will accentuate languages and build on cognition. The principal firmly believes that children should be given choices when it comes to classroom activities. He adds that "there are no limits to what children can do given multiple opportunities, proper support, and an appropriate environment." Teachers are to serve as facilitators of knowledge and teach children to be independent learners. A mentorship program helps the newer teachers work with more experienced ones. The teaching of concepts in two languages plus oral language development in a third is a heavy load, but faculty meet regularly for grade-level planning and to solve problems collectively. All staff came to this school voluntarily. They underwent an intensive interview in applying for this job that queried them on their philosophy of bilingual education, language acquisition, and teaching methods for bilingual students. Even at this early stage, faculty are integrally involved in the decision making at the school. For example, priorities for staff training are set in the campus action plan, which represents the collective decisions of representatives from the school community. In addition, whenever possible, staff training is conducted for all faculty and staff at the school. If the training is not available for all, then representatives are determined democratically so that all will have equal opportunity. Individual training needs are considered through discussion between principal and teachers. Shared decision making and open communication provide the basis for campus decision making. Teachers are given leadership roles in all aspects of campus activities. This is reinforced by weekly meetings where a democratic environment exists in that all ideas and opinions can be freely expressed and discussed. Once decisions are made, committees and sub-committees are formed to get the job done.

Advocacy for Latino Students, Parents, Language, and Culture

The population of the school is 95 percent Latino—however, the majority of the students (70 percent) are English dominant. Although their linguistic strength lies in English, many of them hear some Spanish spoken in the home. The role of advocate is evident when Bob Schulte discusses the importance of speaking at least two languages. While other bilingual programs teach Spanish as a secondary language, Schulte's stand is that both English and Spanish hold equal status in school and in society as a whole. Schulte's program is supported through such research as that conducted by Thomas and Collier in 1995. The researchers found that two-way bilingual education at the elementary level is the most promising program model for the long-term academic success of language minority students. Collier (1995a) concluded that:

> as a group, students in this program maintain grade-level skills in their first language at least through sixth grade and reach the 50th percentile or normal curve equivalent (NCE) in their second language generally after 4–5 years of schooling in both languages. They also generally sustain the gains they made when they reach secondary education, unlike the students in programs that provide little or no academic support in the first language. (p. 4)

At this school, from kindergarten through third grade 80 percent of the instruction is conducted in Spanish with the remaining 20 percent evenly split between English and the targeted third languages. The rationale for this format and its benefits are succinctly stated by Saravia-Shore and Garcia (1995):

> In dual language programs students proficient in languages other than English learn more effectively. They continue to learn content in their native language while learning English as a second language by interacting with monolingual English speaking students who are also learning a second language. This model affirms and respects young people's native language when it becomes a subject taught to English-speaking peers.

Second, potentially bilingual students can share their native-language expertise as peer tutors to English-speaking students who are learning a second language for enrichment. Third, the long-term gains are greater since, in this additive bilingual strategy, students proficient in languages other than English become bilingual and biliterate. Fourth, students are not segregated into classes for potentially bilingual students or monolingual English-speaking students; all are integrated and become bilingual over a period of five or six years. (pp. 62–63)

Schulte initiated planning for the program with his faculty of sixteen bilingual English and Spanish teachers, together with the four native speakers who teach the target languages and are also fluent in English and Spanish. The instructional design of the program demands that all content areas be taught in Spanish through such methods as the natural approach and total physical response. The two-way immersion model as implemented calls for team teaching for English language development (ELD). Students exchange classrooms by going to an adjoining class for ELD. This makes it convenient for children to develop both languages as they primarily identify their homeroom teacher with the Spanish language and the team teacher with ELD.

The principal models commitment to language and culture through his actions. He is highly visible throughout the day interacting with students, staff, and parents on the playground, in classrooms, or in the cafeteria, using his Spanish freely with all. He feels if children experience the use of Spanish among adults at the school in both formal and informal situations they will not see the language as an inferior one.

Parents are key players in the success of this school. Since they end up selecting this school, parents are expected to play an integral role in their child's education—more so than what is normally expected in other educational settings. Parents sign a contract committing themselves to provide a minimum of four hours of volunteer work per month. This contract is a commitment for at least four years if their child begins this school at grade three, or seven years if their child enters at kindergarten. Parents agree to cooperate with the completion of homework and are also required to support the school by communicating the importance of the program to their children. They also ensure that students attend school on a regular basis.

For parents without full-time jobs, a parent center is housed in an adjoining portable building where it is not uncommon to find parents and/or relatives helping teachers with class projects. The parent center has been fully furnished by parents with school assistance. In the future, funding will be sought to have a full-time parent specialist. This is only one step in promoting a feeling of acceptance that all parents are welcome, and Schulte's attitude emphasizes this point. His plans for the near future include engaging parents in curricular decisions.

Parents who are involved at the International School point out that, in other schools, they did not feel validated. In fact, as they compare their involvement in this school and a former one, the only time they visited the other school was when a problem arose. They relate that when they walked into other schools, administrators asked them to state their business. A totally different atmosphere exists at this school where parents are always welcome.

Parents also play a critical role in the positive discipline approach adopted at this school. When a problem first appears the principal lets the teacher try out any necessary correctives. If the problem continues, parents are asked to help. Once the principal meets with a parent over a discipline matter, the principal assumes a counseling stance. He does not propose actions. Choosing to ask parents as to how they might deal with the problem, he then invites them to suggest alternative measures if corporal punishment is suggested. The principal feels that this helps parents search for means away from corporal punishment, which is not an acceptable practice at this school. One solution is to have a parent spend one to two days following her/his child from class to class and observing the child's behavior. This has worked on several occasions, thus bringing school and home together for a child's benefit. The Alicia Chacón International School discipline plan also includes conflict resolution for all students, where class meetings focus on this concept. The main rule at this school is respect.

Parent meetings also strive to bring all parents together. During these evening meetings children are given an opportunity to become involved in outdoor activities, and special opportunities are open to keep the children busy while their parents are involved in school decisions. All meetings are conducted in both English and Spanish.

The principal shows a strong interest in opening the school to the community. For example, he insisted that four basketball courts be fitted with automatic lighting that community members could turn on and off. This encouragement of community to use school facilities is different from the attitude that one finds in other schools, where tall chain linked fences are built to keep people out. There are evening classes that bring community members interested in GED and ESL training to the building. Plans are being formulated to expand course offerings to include opportunities for technology use after school hours.

Bob Schulte is well recognized for his egalitarian treatment of all the stakeholders in the school. He models this by treating the county commissioner and his family in the same manner that he would the full-time single parent who may not have a formal education. All parents, he feels, share the same interest in their children's education. His school will offer the best education to all children. The principal further models equity by helping clean cafeteria tables and doing other "housekeeping" as needed, during his daily walks throughout the school.

He is described as being "democratic" and permitting teachers to take risks. His teachers feel they are treated as colleagues. For example, the teachers decided on a more formal uniform as opposed to a T-shirt uniform. He supports and encourages them to involve parents in the ultimate decisions. He believes in participatory management and does not hesitate in taking a back seat when decisions are in process.

Mr. Schulte is a life-long and independent educator. He keeps current by reading and participating in professional development activities. In this way he keeps on equal footing with the most innovative teachers on his faculty. Since he wants teachers to capitalize on what the students bring with them from home, he advocates for the teaching of culture along with language. One way of doing this is through the integration of history to go along with the celebration of special holidays to teach the children pride in their own heritage.

Leadership into the Future

Bob Schulte's dream is for students to eventually be given educational choices. He sees technology as a means to help students become independent learners. Therefore, each classroom has four computers with a CD-ROM and scanner. Interactive software is available in Spanish. They also belong to a network that provides customized curriculum research that can be faxed to the school within minutes. It is important to note that although Alicia R. Chacón International School received a slightly higher than average funding for startup costs (due to increases in technology needs), it currently does not receive more funding than other schools to purchase their hardware and software.

Bob Schulte has been able to begin building a model program that brings in all aspects of successful practices for Latino students. His advice to other principals of schools with Latino students is to: "Open your mind, be receptive, listen to the opportunity for multilingualism. Don't limit yourself and don't limit the children."

WHAT THESE PRINCIPALS TEACH US ABOUT SUCCESSFUL PRACTICES

This chapter has described principals' leadership in elementary schools successfully serving Latino populations. A sketch for each principal included a background on the school and principal, their efforts to transform their schools, and the advocacy they demonstrate for Latino students, parents, language, and culture. It further presented their plans for leading the school in the future.

Each school was in a different area of the border Southwest. One school was located in a rural area, while the other two were located in urban areas near an international border crossing. In all schools the majority of the children were Latinos of Mexican descent. Whereas all schools served predominantly lower SES populations, two of the schools also enrolled Latino children of parents with high-economic status and parents with an education equal to their non-Latino counterparts. Each school had a different program to address its Latino populations who were English language learners. However, even within the different bilingual/ESL programs present at each school, these programs were part of the core curriculum. It is interesting to note that, in one of the schools whose program was of a transitional nature, the principal was expecting to serve her Latino English language learners in a more effective manner by eventually adopting a dual language program. This, she felt, would better serve the needs of her students regardless of English language ability and would further promote the Latino language and culture. It is important to note here that dual language programs must be implemented as "magnet" or voluntary programs in the schools; because of this characteristic they are impossible to provide in all settings. Another characteristic is that in schools where the vast majority are PEP students, such as at Ysleta Elementary, a dual language program may be very difficult to implement. If the school does not have a substantial number of monolingual English-speaking students, the program cannot work.

The three schools are considered innovative and successful by educators in their area because of their principals. These principals manifest a knowledge and commitment to instruction and learning. Two of them represent part of that small percentage—3 percent—of Latino principals found in the nation (Reyes and Valencia, 1993). These same two principals basically transformed their schools from the archaic practices that existed to the successful ones that are now present. The other principal is creating a new brand of dual language program. All three are trailblazers. The three principals enhance their knowledge about curriculum and instruction through the study of research. They are avid readers of professional literature—a quality also found to be present in the study done by Nieto (1986). The principal in her case study on self-renewal in a Title VII school was a "voracious reader and always tested the ideas on his staff " (p. 221). Furthermore, all three principals value the sharing of research with the faculty as part of their school activities. In fact, two of the principals are engaged in a more formal process of sharing.

In the Ysleta District a "bilingual education study group" was originated, and Bob Schulte was part of this group. The study group met weekly, read research, and discussed its proper use in the schools. Currently both Ysleta Elementary and Chacón International have implemented study groups that are an outgrowth of the district group. The facilitators are teachers who were in the original group. Having teachers study research is crucial, for it treats them as intellectuals by adding the responsibility of keeping abreast of the most current research, and charges them with the duty of implementing it in their classrooms. This aspect of teachers studying alongside principals is important as it places them in situations where they are learning together. Both principals are supportive of this process and their active participation is evidence of this. The central budget is used to pay facilitators for their work and teachers are paid a voluntary staff development stipend.

All three see the education of Latinos as an integral part of the school's program. Instead of leaving this responsibility solely in the hands of the ESL or bilingual education teachers, they take full responsibility in seeing that the programs are implemented and integrated into the academic program of the school. These principals are masters of instruction, and they have ample experience in bilingual/ESL education. Whereas two hold graduate degrees in instruction with additional certification or licensure in educational administration, the other has studied the research on dual language programs on his own and implemented a similar program at his former school. Batsis (1987) also found this background knowledge present in his study of principals in language minority schools. He found that good principals had "a commitment to bilingual and multicultural education as an integral part of the school's curriculum and an understanding of the technical and complex issues in language minority schools" (p. 9). To further promote their commitment to serving their Latino populations with the most successful practices, all three principals are actively involved in writing grants to seek external funding. The exemplary practices at all three schools are due to the extra time, involving long hours, that principals and teachers are willing to give. Although some of this time may be remunerated, the majority is voluntary.

They are engaged in professional ongoing staff development activities for themselves and their teachers. All three are fully cognizant of the integration of technology to strengthen the skills of children and their families. Their creativity in terms of instructional innovations is fueled by their ability to manipulate school finances to provide the necessary resources for the programs Latinos need. Regular funding patterns benefit only the "regular" students. While they spend time writing grants for additional funds, they find it extremely valuable to work on the regular ongoing funding to make marked differences in the education of Latinos, especially in the areas of personnel and technology.

The principals' philosophy is apparent in all that they do. They honor and capitalize on the Latino language and culture. Instead of seeing differences as deficiencies, they have a passion for high expectations and hold those involved in the schooling process—from staff to students and their families—to this tenet. The successful instructional programs at their schools are evidence of this belief. In addition, these principals further demonstrate that the Spanish language can be used formally and informally to bridge the home-school partnerships that they so aptly have created, regardless of their own Spanish language ability.

All three have instituted high levels of parent engagement at their schools. They have understood that the traditional Parent Teacher Associations of the past do not necessarily address the needs of Latino communities of the present. Therefore, they have enlisted support from the home by having all their families become an essential part of the school community. They have created a school atmosphere of belonging and acceptance for all families. They feel quite comfortable in taking the school to the community by avidly conducting home visits and actively engaging in community events.

They are clearly the primary instructional leaders in their schools. However, their leadership is one that creates a sense of empowerment among the faculty. They permit risk taking as long as it is based on sound principles. They create venues for parents and teachers to collaborate in the design of instruction. They recognize and respect teacher autonomy, seeing themselves as educators first and managers last. The terms "shared decision making" and "collaboration" are not empty phrases.

These are continuing practices at their schools. This same practice was evident in the research of several bilingual schools conducted by García (1987).

Although all three principals elicit a strong sense of professional satisfaction, they feel other major accomplishments must be made in their schools. They eagerly discuss plans to change their bilingual programs, carry parental engagement to new heights, and provide the staff with more in-depth professional opportunities. These principals never stop imagining what better practices they and their staff can provide. Their visions are ever changing; as they accomplish preset goals, other goals rise to take their place. They see their jobs as never-ending, yet look forward to meeting new challenges that they set for themselves. They are models for children, staff, and community— never expecting more of others than they do for themselves. They are able to establish a climate where Latino students and parents flourish. This issue is mentioned as an effective management practice by Collier (1995b) when she summarizes the research related to positive school climate for English language learners:

> In schools with strong support for language minority students, researchers have found that administrators and all school staff have a commitment to empowering language minority students through providing bilin-gual/bicultural role models, serving as community advocates, providing bicultural counseling support with knowledge of post secondary opportunities, being available after school and organizing meaningful extracurricular activities, and creating a school climate that values cultural and linguistic diversity. (p. 39)

SUMMARY

In their long-term case study of a bilingual school, Carter and Chatfield (1986) found that there is a "dynamic nature of the effective school and the mutually reinforcing interaction between bilingual programs and school context that produces high levels of student achievement" (p. 200). The sketches of the three principals found in this chapter seem to support these findings. If one tries to look at their schools' success alone one would be leaving out the major player in this outcome—the principal's leadership. These are successful schools that are educating Latino students to reach their full potential from the 1990s into the twenty-first century. The main ingredient to their school success is the culturally competent principal. Pedroza (1993) clearly defines the principal's role in a school serving Latinos as one which focuses and builds on the diversity of the community. She explains that:

A culturally competent administrator is a school leader who has clarified his/her own values and thinking regarding cultural incorporation, who has taken steps toward understanding the community culture, who has examined the relationships between his/her own cultural identity and that of the community, and who is willing to acknowledge that conflict can arise from a misalignment of perceptions or miscommunication or misunderstanding of cultural norms. Recognizing the richness of diversity and a willingness to act as a culture broker between the school and the community defines the culturally competent administrator. (p.13)

REFERENCES

ASCD Advisory Panel on Improving Student Achievement. 1995. "Barriers to Good Instruction," in *Educating Everybody's Children: Diverse Teaching Strategies for Diverse Learners*. R. W. Cole, ed. Alexandria, VA: Association for Supervision and Curriculum Development.

Batsis, T. M. 1987. *Translating the Task: Administrators in Language Minority Schools*. Washington, D.C.: ERIC Clearinghouse on School Administration, pp. 1–10.

Carter, T. P. and M. L. Chatfield. 1986. "Effective Bilingual Schools: Implications for Policy and Practice," *American Journal of Education*, 95(1):200–232.

Collier, V. P. 1995a. "Acquiring a Second Language for School," *Directions in Language and Education*, 4(1): 1–6. Washington, D.C.: National Clearinghouse for Bilingual Education.

Collier, V. P. 1995b. *Promoting Academic Success for ESL Students*. Elizabeth, NJ: New Jersey Teachers of English to Speakers of Other Languages—Bilingual Educators.

Díaz-Rico, L. T. and K. Z. Weed. 1995. *The Crosscultural Language and Academic Development Handbook*. Needham Heights, MA: Allyn & Bacon.

Edmonds, R. 1979. "Effective Schools for the Urban Poor," *Educational Leadership*, 37(1):15–24.

García, E. E. 1987. "Effective Schooling for Minority Students," *New Focus*, The National Clearinghouse for Bilingual Education Occasional Papers, Winter 1987–88, 99:1–11.

Gardner, H. 1993. *Multiple Intelligences: The Theory in Practice*. New York, NY: Basic Books.

González, M. L. 1992. "Educational Climate for the Homeless: Cultivating the Family and School Relationship," in *Educating Homeless Children and Adolescents*. J. H. Strong, ed. Newbury Park, CA: Sage Publications, pp. 194–211.

Hopfenberg, W. S. and H. M. Levin. 1993. *The Accelerated Schools Resource Guide*. San Francisco, CA: Jossey-Bass Publishers.

Howe, C. K. 1994. "Improving the Achievement of Hispanic Students," *Educational Leadership*, 51(8): 42–44.

Keller, B. M. 1995. "Accelerated Schools; Hands-On Learning in a Unified Community," *Educational Leadership*, 52(50):10–13.

Nieto, C. 1986. "Title VII in the Hands of a Principal: Strategy for Change," *NABE Journal,* Spring, pp. 213–223.

Pedroza, A. 1993. Ethnic and Racial Conflict in Schools: Implications for School Administration, Paper Presented at University Council for Educational Administration Annual Conference, October 29-31, 1993, Houston, TX, pp. 14–15.

Privett, N. B. 1996. "Without Fear of Failure: The Attributes of an Ungraded Primary School," *The School Administrator,* 53(1): 6–11.

Ramírez, J. 1992. "Longitudinal Study of Structured English Immersion Strategy, Early Exit and Late Exit Transitional Bilingual Education Program for Language-Minority Children," *Bilingual Research Journal ,* 16(1,2):1–62.

Reyes, P. and R. R. Valencia. 1993. "Educational Policy and the Growing Latino Student Population: Problems and Prospects," *Hispanic Journal of Behavioral Sciences,* 15(2): 258–283.

Saravia-Shore, E. and E. Garcia. 1995. "Diverse Teaching Strategies for Diverse Learners," in *Educating Everybody's Children: Diverse Teaching Strategies for Diverse Learners.* R. W. Cole, ed. Alexandria, VA: Association for Supervision and Curriculum Development.

Sergiovanni, T. J. 1992. *Moral Leadership: Getting to the Heart of School Improvement.* San Francisco, CA: Jossey-Bass Publishers.

Smith, D. C. and E. E. Greene. 1990. "Preparing Tomorrow's Principals Today," *The Principal,* 28(2):20–24.

Sosa, A. 1993. *Thorough and Fair: Creating Routes to Success for Mexican-American Students.* Charleston, WV: ERIC Clearinghouse on Rural Education and Small Schools.

Thomas, W. P. and V. P. Collier. 1995. "Language Minority Students Achievement and Program Effectiveness," Manuscript in Preparation.

CHAPTER 2

Learning for Latinos: The Sociocultural Perspective

ANA HUERTA-MACÍAS—*New Mexico State University*

INTRODUCTION

HAYES et al. (1991) present a dismal portrait of a classroom as it existed in a small, rural community. This classroom had children ages 10–16, some being recent immigrants from Mexico, many having been retained at least one year, and others not having attended school for one or two years. All of the students would return to the fields with their parents at the end of the school year to live in shacks with no running water and to work from sunup to sundown. Yet, at the end of the year, these children, well-accustomed to failure, had experienced success in their day-to-day learning activities. They left the school with high educational aspirations and a more positive outlook on life. The authors write that "the children gained control over their learning. Their world widened and expanded. These sons and daughters of migrant workers, in this rural South Texas agricultural community, had discovered how to incorporate their linguistic and cultural heritage in the world of school" (pp. 136–137).

Such is the ending for a success story as it unfolded in a fifth-grade classroom in a small agricultural community in South Texas. What was the secret? No doubt there were several interplaying factors that had a role here. Researchers have found that success among students from linguistically and culturally diverse backgrounds cannot be attributed to any one factor—that would be simplifying what in essence is a complex process involving personal, societal, and political factors (Nieto, 1992; Ogbu and Matute-Bianche, 1989). Nonetheless, there is agreement that the social context plays a major part in the multidimensional model of success for culturally and linguistically different students (Delgado-Gaitán and Trueba, 1991).

The social context in which the learning took place certainly made a difference in this particular classroom. The teacher created a positive

29

context by drawing on the sociocultural experiences and background knowledge of his students as he went about the teaching and learning process. He built on this knowledge as he facilitated their literacy development in both English and Spanish.

LEARNING AS A SOCIOCULTURAL PROCESS

Much has been written about the importance of incorporating culture into the classroom, particularly where the students are nonmainstream (Alverman and Phelps, 1994; Hadley, 1993). Yet this is often misinterpreted by teachers who feel that the celebration of holidays, for instance, or cooking ethnic foods or talking about traditional dress fulfills this cultural mandate. These things certainly constitute a part of culture; however, the concept of culture goes much beyond that to include a total way of life. Culture includes the customs, beliefs, values, religion, and patterns of behavior of members of a given society (Delgado-Gaitán and Trueba, 1991; Heath and Mangiola, 1991; Trueba, 1990), all of which constitute what is generally referred to as their sociocultural knowledge. Thus, our sociocultural knowledge is something that is constructed, from the time we are born and throughout our lives, through social interactions with members of a group. These cultural experiences, which include childrearing practices, socialization patterns, and sociolinguistic patterns, provide us with a lens through which we perceive and interpret the world. It is in this sense that our sociocultural knowledge is intimately related to literacy development and to the learning process in general.

Trueba (1990) writes:

> Language and culture are inseparable in the process of mediation between social and mental processes that constitute the instructional process. . . . Language and culture play a key role in the organization of cognitive tasks, the development of critical thinking skills, and the process of creative thinking. (pp. 2–3)

Giroux (1992), in his discussion of the language of possibility within critical literacy, elaborates on the relationship between curriculum and student experience: "schools are not merely instructional sites designed to transmit knowledge; they are also cultural sites" (p. 16). He adds that, as cultural sites, schools more often than not legitimate the dominant culture. This is evidenced, for example, by their support for specific ways of speaking, by legitimizing only certain forms of knowledge, and by confirming particular ways of seeing and experiencing the world.

Schools, in essence, do not meet the needs of culturally different students because they do not provide a social context for learning that allows them to access knowledge in ways that are comfortable and familiar to them.

Thus, it becomes critical that the learning environment be a supportive one if children are to reach their full potential as learners. This does not imply that all classrooms are to be socioculturally congruent for all children, for that would be a nearly impossible task given the diversity that is found in our nation's classrooms and the extreme shortage of bilingual/bicultural teachers that currently exists (Macías, 1989; Sosa, 1993). However, we can develop a learning context that is multiculturally sensitive, where differences are acknowledged and appreciated and where opportunities do exist for learning in nonmainstream patterns. This means one must create classrooms that are comfortable, where tasks that are meaningful to the students are implemented, where activities draw on their background knowledge and experiences, where students can participate in activities in ways that are familiar to them, and where the teacher presents new and different experiences in an additive and not a subtractive way. What does all of this translate to in the case of Latinos? In what follows I will provide some answers to this question by presenting some sociocultural information about Latinos and discussing the application of this information to the classroom.

PATTERNS OF INTERACTION

Communication and interaction with others are the basis for learning. It is through discussions, reading, writing, viewing, and listening that we construct ideas about the world around us and our place in it; these activities provide access to knowledge. Yet, while this is a distinctly human behavior, not all of us communicate and interact in the same way. Distinct patterns of communicative behavior are found within different cultural groups (Casanave, 1992; Heath, 1983; Philips, 1993; Vásquez, 1992; Wong-Fillmore, 1988). Different aspects of these communicative patterns are discussed in what follows.

Participation Structures

The concept of participation structures refers to the ways in which different types of interactions are structured between teachers and students. Research with culturally and linguistically different groups (Au,

1980; Philips, 1993; Watson-Gegeo and Boggs, 1977) has found that communication in the classroom can be either enhanced or impeded to the point of silence, depending on the cultural congruence of participation structures used in the classroom with those that students use in their homes and communities. Additional research by McCollum (cited in Au and Kawakami, 1994) found that a Spanish-speaking Puerto Rican teacher and an English-speaking Anglo teacher displayed distinct patterns of conducting lessons in their classrooms. The Puerto Rican teacher facilitated conversation in her classroom by inviting students to respond and by allowing students to develop the discussion in different directions, even though digressions that included personal information went on for a while before she steered them back to the topic. This was in contrast to the Anglo teacher who called on individuals and controlled the conversation closely by ignoring student attempts to initiate conversation. In sum, the research in this area indicates that students' willingness to participate in lessons will be enhanced and thus learning will be improved if teachers structure interactions in the classroom in ways that are culturally congruent with students' experiences outside the classroom. The following presents some additional insights into patterns of classroom interaction.

Modeling and Hands-on Activities

Educational research on Latinos has demonstrated that certain styles of interaction are prevalent within the family. Wong-Fillmore (1988), in her work in early childhood education, reports on some of this research. Mexican American children learn through observation and practice. This is a process that takes much time and patience to learn. In doing tasks around the home, for example, family members provide guidance but do not generally give verbal explanations nor ask questions of the kind that are typical in mainstream Anglo culture. A Mexican parent would not typically ask the child in a learning situation questions such as "Now, can you tell me what the first two steps are?" or "What's the first thing you do . . . and next . . . and then?" Heath (1989) adds that question patterns in Mexican American families are unlike questioning patterns found in mainstream classrooms in that parents do not ask for known information: "If parents know what has happened, they feel they do not need to ask a child who also knows to recount the event. . . . Adults rarely request recounts of children" (p. 173). She also confirms the importance of learning through observation in the home. "Modeling and close observation, supplemented by reinforcement through praise or caution, surround the teaching of most tasks in the home" (p. 173).

Children learn by taking on specific tasks of varying complexity, as they are deemed ready by the parents. Those individuals who do acquire specific skills are respected and looked up to by their apprentices. *"Respeto,"* or respect, particularly for adults, is highly promoted within the family, as are patience, responsibility, cooperation, and interdependence. Nieto (1992) also points out that *"respeto"* is highly valued among Puerto Ricans. This respect in the classroom is inclusive to teachers' behavior towards their students. She reports that Latino teachers "were much more apt to use less brusque means than European American teachers to control student behavior" (p. 118). This was achieved by an increased use of conditional tenses, personal appeals, and more polite forms such as "please" and "thank you."

This translates to greater use of modeling and hands-on experiences for Latino students, particularly for recent immigrants who are just beginning to learn about and adapt to the more verbal style of learning that is typical of mainstream society. Hands-on activities have traditionally been emphasized in early childhood curriculum; however, they are important for older children as well. Rather than talking about science, history, or writing, for example, we need to actually engage students in scientific, historical, and writing processes. Hayes et al. (1991) provide us with a good example of this in the area of biliteracy development. The curriculum for this group of bilingual fifth graders evolved around the publication of a series of books that focused on varying topics in the areas of health, science, and language arts. The students not only selected the themes for the books but also wrote, edited, and did all of the art work (including book covers) and binding for the books that they published. Thus, several of the topics discussed in class in the different areas led to a hands-on project in the form of a book where all children were involved in a variety of tasks individually and in groups.

Torres-Guzmán et al. (1994), in writing about their Intercambio Research Project, provide us with additional examples of projects that provide students with actual hands-on learning experiences. Students, for instance, looked at individual and community rights to a healthy environment as they investigated, discussed, analyzed, and wrote about a toxic waste storage facility near their school. In another school, students became involved in ethnographic research in a surrounding community, the Barrio Obrero Community, which was overridden with socio-economic problems but which also had a rich popular culture. Beginning by looking at the life of a popular salsa musician who had died and who had been raised in that community, the students then proceeded to do additional research by way of readings, interviews, and discussions with members from the community. The project not only provided valuable reading and writing experiences, but also engaged students in a reflection and appreciation of the culture within their own communities. These types of projects involve a great deal of peer group interaction, a subject to which we now turn.

Collaboration

The issue of interdependence and collaboration was mentioned above. The Latino family and the socialization practices that children are reared into within the family are central to Latino culture. Writing on the topic of the family among Latinos, Heyck (1994) writes "Though the Latino family is under great pressure today—generational, cultural, and economic—still it represents the most basic source of cultural values for Latinos in the United States and their major source of strength" (p. 19). These family ties, moreover, focus on cooperation rather than competition, a fact that remains true even though traditional Latino families are becoming less common (Nieto, 1992; Saracho and Hancock, 1983). This same observation has been generally made of all Latinos by other researchers and educators who stress the importance of cooperative learning practices for Latinos and language minority students of differing backgrounds (Garcia, 1994; Kagan, 1989; Tinajero et al., 1993). Tharp and Gallimore (1988) contrast this with the typical North American classroom with rank-and-file seating and a teacher-leader who gives demonstrations and gives assignments—the latter being some form of individual study or practice. They acknowledge that group work does exist, but with much less frequency, and urge us to make the organization of teaching, learning, and performance compatible with the social structures in which students are most productive.

Cooperative learning is currently defined by many educators as a system of very specific and systematic practices that are implemented by teams of students in a classroom. Kagan (1989), for instance, discusses various cooperative learning structures such as jigsaw, roundtable, and numbered heads together. However, what is of significance here is the philosophy of cooperative learning, rather than the elaborate system of rules and practices that has been put together in a variety of ways by different educators. That is, students should be given the opportunity to work collaboratively in order that they may utilize each other as resources and take a more active part in their own learning. Working in groups provides a structure that promotes more effective interaction and communication among students and that also draws on a learning pattern that is familiar to Latino families. An added and highly significant benefit, particularly for recent immigrants who look to friends for helping them adapt to their new world, is the "peer-bonding" (Igoa, 1993) that results when students work together on projects.

Another significant issue with respect to the use of cooperative learning deals with the role of the teacher rather than the students. This concerns the teacher's belief systems about cooperative learning; simply putting students into groups and asking them to work together does not provide for a positive social context in the classroom. As Meloth (1991) has pointed out, teachers need to carefully plan and organize the activities to maximize the cognitive as well as the social benefits. That is, putting students together for rote practice drill or memorization of facts is not an effective use of cooperative learning. Simply answering the who, what, when, and where questions to a story is also not an appropriate task. Rather, teachers must believe in the effectiveness of collaborative learning to achieve the higher-order critical skills and use it as such, for example, by asking students to organize into small groups to discuss different strategies for understanding stories in general. Teachers must create appropriate tasks and then monitor the group interactions to make sure that students are engaged in the essential parts of cooperative learning.

An important caveat discussed by Nieto (1992) is relevant here. Cooperative learning must not be used as a discriminatory practice. It must not be used as a rationale for excluding Latinos from certain activities or limiting the use of resources for them. Nieto writes that cooperative learning must not be used as rationale for

> not granting Hispanic students solo performances in plays or leadership activities in other situations; placing them in activities they had not themselves chosen, whereas other children were allowed choices; and having them share books when there were not enough to go around, whereas the non-Hispanic students could have individual copies. (p. 113)

Teachers must be careful not to reinforce negative notions about Latinos by misinterpreting the research. While cooperative activities should be provided in the classroom in order to enhance learning among Latinos, this should not be at the exclusion of opportunities for individual work. The latter is clearly discriminatory in that it would prevent students from developing an individual style of learning that is imperative for success in mainstream society.

Cross-Age Tutoring

Another form of collaborative learning, although mentioned much less often in the literature, is cross-age or cross-peer tutoring. This involves older students meeting regularly with younger students in order to engage in learning activities of varying kinds (for example, discussion, reading, writing, interviewing, etc.). Cross-age tutoring provides an opportunity for Latinos to engage in a social pattern of learning that is quite familiar and comfortable for them, being that the Latino family is quite cohesive and emphasizes cooperation among siblings as well as among all family members. Another practice among Latino families that makes cross-age tutoring particularly relevant is that some older siblings are often specifically responsible for the care and general well-being of younger brothers and sisters.

Rintell and Skovholt (1990) implemented a cross-age tutoring project with great success in a bilingual program. In this case, fifth graders who were in transition to all English instruction met with younger students whom they had chosen as partners to read aloud with and reflect on stories and to do journal writing. The meetings occurred twice a week and were preceded by a training where the older students were exposed to different reading models and taught varying types of questioning techniques to use with the younger students.

Heath and Mangiola (1991) report on the successful use of cross-age tutoring with Mexican American as well as with other groups (black, Laotian, Cambodian) of students. Projects in California and Texas involved fifth- and sixth-grade students working on reading and writing activities with younger students. The success of their work, they feel, rests on the sharing of group knowledge and resources—the experiences that the students already had. The sociocultural basis for this practice also goes back to the concept of apprenticeship discussed earlier, where children learn from older and skilled individuals by observing and practicing with them, thus making the learning process a more active one. Some of the benefits of cross-age tutoring projects include: (1) teachers spending less time disciplining and more time in individual consultation, (2) the opportunity for extensive and highly motivated student writing in authentic situations (as students analyzed and reported on their tutoring sessions), and (3) an opportunity for teachers to act as "facilitators" rather than "directors" in the classroom and thus more easily help students build on their prior experiences and background knowledge (Heath and Mangiola, 1991, p. 25).

What is involved in implementing a cross-age tutoring project? The following are some of the suggestions provided by educators who have implemented these types of projects (Heath and Mangiola, 1991, pp. 52–53):

(1) Allow a preparation period of a month to six weeks for the student tutors. This allows them to learn about the tutoring process itself and to familiarize themselves with the materials they will be using with their tutees.

(2) Use as much writing as possible in the context of tutoring from the very beginning. This may include letters, texts for picture books, written conversations worked out together, and transcriptions of stories told by the tutees.

(3) Provide time for students to write field notes after every tutoring session.

(4) Provide students with supportive models of open-ended questioning as well as with ways in which they can expand tutees' responses and also expand on the content of the book in order to relate it to tutees' experiences.

(5) Provide opportunities for tutors to prepare for their sessions.

(6) Develop real audiences for students' written work.

(7) View the tutoring experiences as one of academic language study for the tutors, one in which they use language both as the instrument and focus of study.

SOCIOLINGUISTIC PATTERNS

Language and culture are intimately related. Our knowledge of the ways in which language(s) are used in different communities has expanded recently as researchers study language variation both within and across linguistic groups. While the above focused on variation in socialization with respect to learning patterns within Latino families, the following will discuss the role of oral and written language in creating a positive social context for learning and specifically for literacy development. Different patterns exist with respect to how language is used in

Latino versus mainstream culture. Escamilla (1993) points out the differences in text structure, for example, between story grammar in English prose and that of Spanish and other Romance languages. While in English, stories progress from point A to point B in a linear fashion, much more digression is allowed in Spanish—digression that would be considered superfluous in English, which stresses "getting to the point." A discourse event in English, for instance, might read as: "I need a pair of shoes. I'm going to the store. I'll buy running shoes"; while the Spanish version might read more like the following: "I need a pair of shoes. I'll get some running shoes. You know my sister, she got some running shoes a while ago at the corner store. They gave her blisters, but they were cheap. Maybe we should go there to look for shoes" (p. 229).

Thus, the Spanish-speaking student needs to be made aware of such differences in text discourse as part of the teaching strategies for literacy development in English. Taking the issues of culture and meaning construction a step further, Lucas (1992) discusses how students' sociocultural experiences influenced their classroom journal writing. In her study of eight students from six different countries she found that each student approached writing differently with respect to organizational features, linguistic features, and content; their individual background knowledge and experiences influenced the degree to which they followed the journal writing genre that they were taught in English. Alicia, a student from El Salvador, for example, wrote pieces that "tended to consist of strings of loosely connected events, none of them developed. . . . She engaged in the personal and representational elements of the writing, but did not engage in the reflective elements" (p. 220). While this is *not* to be misinterpreted as "Latinos cannot reflect in their writing," it does point to the complexity of the situation that involved an interplay between (1) the role of this individual's past experiences in war-torn El Salvador, (2) the lack of writing instruction in her schooling in her home country, and (3) her socialization patterns with respect to appropriate and inappropriate content for writing, which influenced her own personal agenda for writing. Lucas writes that, "From the teachers' points of view, all of the writers were presented with the same writing tasks, but by the time the tasks were in the hands of the writers, they were not the same anymore" (p. 228). The suggestion, then, is to not make assumptions about what will make sense to the students, but rather to first inquire about their past with respect to opportunities that they have had to acquire formal and informal knowledge relevant to what the teacher is trying to teach, and then to use that information to help the task make sense to them. This study also points to the importance of considering each student as an individual and not assuming that all Latinos, or even Puerto Ricans or Mexicans, for instance, will consistently exhibit the same behavior. Culture is not monolithic nor is it static, for it is constantly being made and remade within given communities. While we can discuss certain sociocultural influences on a student's schooling we must emphasize that these are general patterns; every human being is uniquely impacted by a multiplicity of factors in his/her life that ultimately make this person different from everyone else.

Literacy is often interpreted within the classroom in the narrow sense of reading and writing skills. It is further limited in mainstream classrooms to specific types of reading and writing (emphasizing, for instance, the linear "straight to the point" type of writing mentioned above). However, if we broaden our vision of literacy to include all uses of language that are meaningful and purposeful within a given sociocultural context, we find that Latinos who are often labeled as "illiterate" are indeed quite literate—although in ways that may be unfamiliar to us. In order to familiarize ourselves with these "literacies" we must again inquire and make bridges between the family and school (to be elaborated on below) in order to build on that knowledge that our students bring to the classroom in the area of literacy. Barrera (1992) addresses some critical questions relevant to this issue in her discussion of cross-cultural dimensions of literacy and literature instruction. She questions the definition of "literature" as well as who defines it, who mediates it, and who decides what are acceptable responses to the literature (pp. 237–239). It is the latter that I wish to focus on here, not solely in the area of responding to literature but in literacy development in general.

The Latino culture is rich in different genres of oral and written language, all of which constitute part of a student's sociocultural knowledge. Children grow up listening to, relating, and writing language in its different forms. *"Cuentos"* (stories in the oral tradition) and *"dichos"* (proverbs), for example, are told and retold within the families and through the generations, often to reinforce a moral lesson both for children and adults. *"Corridos"* (ballads) are a very popular form of song lyrics, often telling tales of the romantic as well as the tragic. Games often focus on the use of language. One of the most popular of these is a game called *"Secretos y Voces"* (Secrets and Voices). The game revolves around how language can be distorted in the oral communication process and involves a form of metalinguistic analysis as players reflect on and are amused by the linguistic output at the end of the game. These genres, which Latino children are familiar with, are typically ignored in the mainstream classroom; yet, they present a tremendous opportunity for students to demonstrate their literacy competence and for teachers to use as a springboard for further literacy development in both English and Spanish. Learning how to analyze the different parts of a story in English, for instance, might be facilitated by first having the student reflect on a familiar *"cuento"* and its different components and then proceeding to an analysis of a story in English while referring back to the *"cuento"* for conceptual support.

Vásquez (1992) discusses other aspects of the linguistic repertoire that Latinos come to school with but that are also often ignored. In her study of conversations of four working-class Mexican families residing in the east side of the San Francisco Bay area in California, she found discursive patterns that were not unlike those used in the analyses of text in typical classrooms. That is, these families were using analytical strategies in their conversations to analyze text (including print, photographs, traffic symbols, and phonetically interesting words) that mirrored the literate behaviors conventionally associated with print analysis in typical classrooms. This study, then, underscores the necessity of looking at and validating children's oral as well as written competencies in order to design instructional strategies that build on what they already have in terms of literacy and biliteracy development. This can be done by conversing with the student as well as the family about activities within the home—a topic to be discussed later in this paper.

The use of both Spanish and English in discourse is another sociolinguistic pattern that we need to be sensitive to and appreciate in our work with Latinos. The literature has identified the alternate use of Spanish and English by bilinguals as being purposeful and meaningful in both oral and written forms (Huerta-Macías and Quintero, 1993). Teachers must appreciate this form of linguistic behavior as one which again demonstrates literacy, rather than illiteracy, in either language. Edelsky (1986), in her study of bilingual children's writing, found that the use of two languages was not a limitation but rather increased the writers' options for interpreting and signaling meaning. She writes, "By using two codes in writing, the children effectively communicated certain added meanings" (p. 69). Thus, an effective strategy for building on this competence would be to present opportunities for the student to use each of his/her languages to enhance communication and/or expression in classroom activities. These activities might include, for example, journal writing, poetry, role-playing, story writing, and music—all of which will help develop each of the student's two languages in both oral and written form.

COMMUNITY AND FAMILY AS INSTRUCTIONAL RESOURCES

The need to be aware of the Latino's sociocultural experiences and to use that knowledge to inform instruction has been emphasized in the above. This appears not to be an easy task among teachers. How does one go about gathering both the factual and sociocultural information that is necessary to design appropriate instructional strategies? The answer can be found by looking at the immense success of family literacy programs throughout the country (Barbara Bush Foundation for Family Literacy, 1989; Brizius and Foster, 1993; McIvor, 1990; Quintero and Huerta-Macías, 1991). The connection to the family and the community is the key to the success of these programs; parents as well as children are involved in projects that integrate community resources. This strategy builds on the binding ties that the community has among Latino culture: "in their family practices, Latinos exhibit an organic view of life, one that sees the basic interconnectedness of the individual to the family, to God, and to the community" (Heyck, 1994, p. 162). These same linkages to the family and the community must be built in the classroom in order to utilize parents and other community members as resources that can inform instruction. Ada and Smith (Chapter 3, this volume) provide examples of some model programs that have successfully built these bridges. How does the classroom teacher initiate this bidirectional learning?

Students, themselves, will provide much information when given the opportunity to demonstrate knowledge and/or talk and write about experiences. Classroom discussions can and should allow for multiple perspectives to be heard. Students can be asked to provide input that draws on their background knowledge and experiences through questions relevant to the topic at hand such as: "What might someone from your family/country do in this situation?" "What would be the response from your parents if you were to make this choice?" "Who are some of the most popular heroes from your homeland?" or "Tell us about your family gatherings. When do you get together? How do you celebrate?"

Children can also bring sociocultural and factual information into the classroom if they are given assignments that involve their families.

Teachers, for instance, can ask students as part of a social studies lesson to go home and ask their parents about their childhood memories (a favorite story, activity, family/home descriptions) or about their activities at work, and report back to the class. A lesson on health or science might involve the children going home to ask their parents about home remedies, such as medicinal herbs, to incorporate into a classroom report or demonstration. This type of activity not only provides useful information for the teacher but also validates the experiences and knowledge of the family as multiple perspectives are integrated into the lesson. Informal communication with parents is a highly effective strategy for getting to know the families and their children. Formal letters sent out from the school usually do not work. However, research has shown that Latino parents do respond to other more personal strategies where parents feel more comfortable (Garcia, 1986; Quintero and Huerta-Macías, 1991) such as: (1) invitations to informal "*cafe y pan dulce*" (coffee) gatherings before school, (2) lunch invitations in the school cafeteria so that parents can eat with the teacher and students, (3) after-school classroom demonstrations put on by the students, (4) phone calls, (5) home visits, (6) after-school conversations in the school yard with parents who pick up their children, and (7) informal schoolwide "*charlas*" (discussion groups) for parents on topics of their choice. Communication that occurs in such settings as the above can provide information that is critical in helping Latino children achieve schooling success (Quintero and Huerta-Macías, 1993).

Parents as well as community members can also be invited to the classroom to share their knowledge and expertise with students. These invitations should not be restricted to the doctor or lawyer, but must also involve community members in other professions or vocations, including, for example, construction workers, plumbers, electricians, secretaries, dietitians, and nurse's aides—all of whom provide critical services to the community. Moll (1990) in his work on community-mediated instruction writes that such classroom visits by community workers "created new instructional routines . . . that helped the teacher and students exceed the curriculum, stretch the limits of writing, and expand the knowledge that formed lessons" (p. 12).

SUMMARY

The teaching and learning process in our work with Latino students must go beyond the frameworks established by mainstream society for academic achievement. Treating all students equally does *not* provide equal access to education. Latino children bring with them a multitude of experiences that are different from the experiences of mainstream Anglo children. Thus, we cannot expect that the same instructional treatment is going to produce the same results in culturally and linguistically different groups. We must meet these students where they are at, for as Sowell (1981) writes, "We do not live in the past, but the past in us" (p. 273). We cannot ignore the past in our students; we must acknowledge it, be sensitive to it, and appreciate it. Only then can we provide an education where all children are given equal opportunities to learn, to excel, and to reach their full potential while still maintaining their sociocultural pride and integrity.

REFERENCES

Alverman, D. E. and S. Phelps. 1994. *Content Reading and Literacy: Succeeding in Today's Diverse Classrooms.* Needham Heights, MA: Allyn & Bacon.

Au, K. 1980. "Participation Structures in a Reading Lesson with Hawaiian Children," *Anthropology and Education Quarterly*, 11:91–115

Au, K. and A. J. Kawakami. 1994. "Cultural Congruence in Instruction," in *Teaching Diverse Populations: Formulating a Knowledge Base.* E. Hollins, J. King, and W. Hayman, eds. Albany, NY: State University of New York Press, pp. 5–25.

Barbara Bush Foundation for Family Literacy. 1989. *First Teachers: A Family Literacy Handbook for Parents, Policy-Makers, and Literacy Providers.* Washington, D.C.: Barbara Bush Foundation for Family Literacy.

Barrera, R. 1992. "The Cultural Gap in Literature-Based Literacy Instruction," *Education and Urban Society*, 24(2):227–243.

Brizius, J. A. and S. A. Foster. 1993. *Generation to Generation: Realizing the Promise of Family Literacy.* Ypsilanti, MI: High Scope Press.

Casanave, C.P. 1992. "Cultural Diversity and Socialization: A Case Study of a Hispanic Woman in a Doctoral Program in Sociology," in *Diversity as Resource: Redefining Cultural Literacy.* Denise E. Murray, ed. Alexandria, VA: Teachers of English to Speakers of Other Languages, pp. 90–112.

Delgado-Gaitán C. and H. Trueba. 1991. *Crossing Cultural Borders: Education for Immigrant Families in America.* New York, NY: The Falmer Press.

Edelsky, C. 1986. *Habia una Vez: Writing in a Bilingual Program.* Norwood, NJ: Ablex Publishing Corp.

Escamilla, K. 1993. "Promoting Biliteracy: Issues in Promoting English Literacy in Students Acquiring English," in *The Power of Two Languages: Literacy and Biliteracy for Spanish-Speaking Students.* J. V. Tinajero and A. F. Ada, eds. New York, NY: Macmillan/McGraw-Hill Publishing Company, pp. 220–233.

Garcia, D. 1986. "Parents Assisting in Learning," in *Issues of Parent Involvement and Literacy: Proceedings of the Symposium.* Washington, D.C.: Trinity College Department of Education & Counseling, pp. 93–95.

Garcia, E. 1994. "The Education of Linguistically and Culturally Diverse Students:

Effective Instructional Practices," in *Compendium of Readings in Bilingual Education: Issues and Practices.* R. Rodriguez, N. J. Ramos, and J. A. Ruiz-Escalante, eds. Austin, TX: Texas Association of Bilingual Education, pp. 87–94.

Giroux, H. A. 1992. "Critical Literacy and Student Experience: Donald Graves' Approach to Literacy," in *Becoming Political: Readings and Writings in the Politics of Literacy Education.* P. Shannon, ed. Portsmouth, NH: Heinemann, pp. 15–20.

Hadley, A. O. 1993. *Teaching Language in Context.* Boston, MA: Heinle & Heinle Publishers.

Hayes, C. W., R. Bahruth, and C. Kessler. 1991. *Literacy con Cariño.* Portsmouth, NH: Heinemann.

Heath, S. B. 1983. *Ways with Words: Language, Life, and Work in Communities and Classrooms.* Cambridge, MA: Cambridge University Press.

Heath, S. B. 1989. "Sociocultural Contexts of Language Development," in *Beyond Language: Social & Cultural Factors in Schooling Language Minority Students.* Los Angeles, CA: California State University, pp. 143–186.

Heath, S. B. and L. Mangiola. 1991. *Children of Promise: Literate Activity in Linguistically and Culturally Diverse Classrooms.* Washington, D.C.: National Education Association.

Heyck, D. L. 1994. *Barrios and Borderlands: Cultures of Latinos and Latinas in the United States.* New York, NY: Routledge.

Huerta-Macías, A. and E. Quintero. 1993. "Teaching Language and Literacy in the Context of Family and Community," in *The Power of Two Languages: Literacy and Biliteracy for Spanish-Speaking Students.* J. V. Tinajero and A. F. Ada, eds. New York, NY: Macmillan/McGraw-Hill Publishing Company, pp. 152–157.

Igoa, C. 1993. "Second Language Literacy and Immigrant Children: The Inner World of the Immigrant Child," in *The Power of Two Languages: Literacy and Biliteracy for Spanish-Speaking Students.* J. V. Tinajero and A. F. Ada, eds. New York, NY: Macmillan/McGraw-Hill Publishing Company, pp. 84–99.

Kagan, S. 1989. *Cooperative Learning: Resources for Teachers.* Riverside, CA: University of California.

Lucas, T. 1992. "Diversity Among Individuals: Eight Students Making Sense of Classroom Journal Writing," in Diversity as Resource: Redefining Cultural Literacy. D. E. Murray, ed. Alexandria, VA: Teachers of English to Speakers of Other Languages, pp. 202–229.

Macías, R. 1989. *Bilingual Teacher Supply and Demand in the United States.* University of Southern California, Center for Multilingual, Multicultural Research and The Tomás Rivera Center.

McIvor, M. C. 1990. *Family Literacy in Action: A Survey of Successful Programs.* New York, NY: New Readers Press.

Meloth, M. S. 1991. "Enhancing Literacy through Cooperative Learning," in *Literacy for a Diverse Society.* Elfrieda H. Hiebert, ed. New York, NY: Teachers College Press, pp. 172–183.

Moll, L. C. 1990. "Community-Mediated Instruction: A Qualitative Approach." Paper presented at National AERA Conference, Boston, MA.

Nieto, S. 1992. *Affirming Diversity.* New York, NY: Longman Publishing Group.

Ogbu, J. U. and M. A. Matute-Bianche. 1989. "Understanding Sociocultural Factors: Knowledge, Identity, and School Adjustment," in *Beyond Language: Social &*

Cultural Factors in Schooling Language Minority Students. Los Angeles, CA: California State University, pp. 73–142.

Philips, S. 1993. *The Invisible Culture: Communication in Classroom and Community on the Warm Springs Indian Reservation.* Prospect Heights, IL: Waveland Press, Inc.

Quintero, E. and A. Huerta-Macías. 1991. "Learning Together, Sociocultural Issues in Literacy," *The Journal of Educational Issues of Language Minority Students: Special Issue—Real Issues in the Classroom,* 10:71–156.

Quintero, E. and A. Huerta-Macías. 1993. "Whole Language: Critical Curriculum for Family Literacy," *The School Community Journal,* 3(2):45–62.

Rintell, E. and M. E. Skovholt. 1990. "First We Were Like Kind of Scared: A Read Aloud Project for Bilingual Children," *National Clearinghouse for Bilingual Education Forum,* 13(5):6.

Saracho, O. N. and F. Martinez Hancock. 1983. "Mexican-American Culture," in *Understanding the Multicultural Experience in Early Childhood Education.* O. N. Saracho and B. Spodek, eds. Washington, D.C.: National Association for the Education of Young Children, pp. 3–15.

Sosa, A. 1993. *Thorough and Fair.* Washington, D.C.: ERIC Clearinghouse on Rural Education and Small Schools.

Sowell, T. 1981. *Ethnic America: A History.* New York, NY: Basic Books, Inc.

Tharp, R. and R. Gallimore. 1988. *Rousing Minds to Life: Teaching, Learning, and Schooling in Social Context.* Cambridge, MA: Cambridge University Press.

Tinajero, J. V., M. Calderón, and R. Hertz-Lazarowitz. 1993. "Cooperative Learning Strategies: Bilingual Classroom Applications," in *The Power of Two Languages: Literacy and Biliteracy for Spanish-Speaking Students.* J. V. Tinajero and A. F. Ada, eds. New York, NY: MacMillan/McGraw-Hill Publishing Company, pp. 241–253.

Torres-Guzmán, M., C. I. Mercade, A. H. Quintero, and D. R. Viera. 1994. "Teaching and Learning in Puerto Rican/Latino Collaboratives: Implications for Teacher Education," in *Teaching Diverse Populations: Formulating a Knowledge Base.* E. R. Hollins, J. E. King, and W. C. Hayman, eds. Albany, NY: State University of New York Press, pp. 105–129.

Trueba, H. 1990. "The Role of Culture in Literacy Acquisition: An Interdisciplinary Approach to Qualitative Research," *International Journal of Qualitative Studies in Education,* 3(1):1–13.

Vásquez, O. 1992. "A Mexicano Perspective: Reading the World in a Multicultural Setting," in *Diversity as Resource: Redefining Cultural Literacy.* D. Murray, ed. Alexandria, VA: TESOL, pp. 113–134.

Watson-Gegeo, K. A. and S. T. Boggs. 1977. "From Verbal Play to Talk Story: The Role of Routine in Speech Events among Hawaiian Children," in *Child Discourse.* S. Ervin-Tripp and C. Mitchell-Kernan, eds. New York, NY: Academic Press.

Wong-Fillmore, L. 1988. "Now or Later? Issues Related to the Early Education of Minority Group Children." Paper presented to the Council of Chief State School Officers. Boston, MA.

CHAPTER 3

Fostering the Home-School Connection for Latinos

ALMA FLOR ADA—*University of San Francisco*
NANCY JEAN SMITH—*Title VII Resource Center for Bilingual Education San Joaquin Valley*

INTRODUCTION

I tried to cultivate my own self, by reading. It was something that was born from inside of me, from watching my father work from dawn to dusk seven days a week. Sometimes he would not eat so that we could eat. It was his wish that one day I would have a better life. (Translation by Valerie Andriola Balderas)

—Roberto Arreguin, Migrant Parent
Watsonville, California

ONE of the most disempowering and disenfranchising aspects of our contemporary technological society is the emphasis on knowledge as a commodity. Through the process of schooling, this knowledge is purchased or acquired by those who understand or are guided to understand mainstream codes and thus make these codes their private property. For Latino students and their families who are either outside the understanding of mainstream codes or who have been systematically excluded, this translates many times into closed doors. Linguistically and/or culturally many Latino students and their families find themselves outside these gates, without keys.

PARENTS AS A SOURCE OF KNOWLEDGE

Certain types of knowledge are systematically devalued by schools—especially that knowledge which arises from the experiences, lives, and reasoning of many Latino students and their families. Students are rarely asked to reflect upon what they already know, or to ask themselves what they can find out with the resources they have available. As students go through the schooling process, validity is attached only to learning and knowledge that has been written in books and presented by recognized authorities. The result is that people who have had limited

47

or no opportunity for schooling will tend to devalue their own knowledge and even their language. They tend to accept that they are ignorant. Frequently they arrive at the false conclusion that not only do they not know, but that they are incapable of knowing. The ensuing low self-esteem further perpetuates a feeling of insecurity towards schooling along with a sense of helplessness.

An acknowledgment of the consequences of traditional schooling is indeed needed to create new ways of teaching. By recognizing that schooling is only one part of the children's lives, one can begin to face the multitude of challenges that lie outside the classroom. The educational process must extend beyond the classroom and the school walls. It must also include a frank reexamination of the prestige granted to formal education and the printed word, and how, in a highly literate society such as the United States, Latino family knowledge has almost no status in the established curriculum. For many Latino parents, the story of their life in the United States is a story of overcoming many difficult obstacles, and that in itself is filled with learning and knowledge. We must begin to counteract pervasive societal forces that disenfranchise people by qualifying knowledge as private property belonging only to some and not to others.

Family Knowledge as Curriculum

The challenge is to conceive of projects in which the knowledge that the parents already have, or can generate and reflect upon, will be valued in and out of class, and will then become an integral part of the curriculum. All parents have a life story with a wide repertoire of anecdotes about events and experiences. Teachers can encourage students to ask parents about their childhood and their process of growing up. What was life like when they were young? How was it different from what it is today? What lessons about life have they learned from their experiences?

Parents can also be asked to talk about their work. What happens in their work and how is it useful? How is it regulated and organized? Who controls it? How does it contribute to the well-being of society? Farm workers can talk about agriculture and the work in their fields. Immigrant parents can be asked to talk about their lives, which reflect both the history of this country and the history of their country of origin.

When carried out with sincere respect and appreciation, these kinds of activities model the belief for parents that they themselves possess valid forms of knowledge. As a result, students will appreciate their parents as a source of knowledge and information, and parents will begin to see themselves in the same light. Families can bring a wealth of values, traditions, and wisdom to the classroom, including extensive oral literature composed of legends, folktales, songs, poems, games, and stories. They can also provide practical everyday experiences and an awareness of the processes by which people interact and learn, verbalize how they have been systematically excluded, and, most importantly, have ideas about creating a more equitable situation. We as a society can be greatly enriched and learn from this knowledge.

The plea to teachers, administrators, teacher educators, and curriculum and material developers is to ask themselves every day, in each educational act, for each lesson:

- What am I doing to ensure the development of each student's first language, whether I can speak that language or not, as the vehicle for home interaction?
- What am I doing to acknowledge parents' lives, experiences, and knowledge and their ability to construct knowledge?
- What am I doing to foster communication at home between parents and children?
- What am I doing to use the printed word as a means of validating and celebrating parents?
- What am I doing to encourage parents and students to act as agents of their own liberation?

These are not questions posed in a vacuum; rather, they are concerns that have been successfully implemented into practice. Let's turn our focus to four specific programs that have made these concerns and questions concrete.

PROJECTS THAT ILLUSTRATE A VISION FOR PARENT INVOLVEMENT

The following describes successful parent involvement projects that incorporate family knowledge into their curriculum.

The Pajaro Valley Project

A young mother, somewhat intimidated in front of a group of nearly a hundred people, is about to read a story written by her daughter. She hesitates, unsure whether the story is appropriate, and apologizes because it contains words which she considers unseemly.

At last, she holds up the title page. It shows a man in field workers' clothing, wearing boots and a hat and holding a long whip in his hand. A small girl is standing next to him, reaching barely to his knee. The mother begins to read: "I am going to tell you a story about a father who returned home from work very angry," and here the mother interrupts the story to explain: "All of this is true. My husband is much older than me, and he comes from work very tired. And if the children are talking very loudly or making noise he gets upset and," adding with obvious pain, "he sometimes scolds and even punishes them."

She continues reading the story and it is here that the miracle occurs. The story tells us that when the father returned home upset, his daughter asked him what was the matter. Upon finding out that he was tired, she continues: "The old man received a big surprise." His little daughter told him: "Look, father I have a cure for your tiredness . . . I will tell you a very pretty story that mother read me from a book . . . and the story was so amusing that the father forgot how tired he was and he laughed and hugged his little daughter and gave her a kiss." (Ada, 1988, p. 223)

Through the process of dictating this story to her older sister, Araceli, a five-year-old author has come to understand her personal ability to effect change in her daily family life. She is a heroine who confronts various difficulties and finds a way to guide the situation to an ending that is healing for her family as well as validating for her personally. What is clear in this little story is how literature can be a powerful model for both parents and children in rethinking their interactions and providing creative alternatives to experiences they may be living. It is precisely this type of interaction that this project creates—where children and adults are analyzing their reality and applying new ideas to that analysis.

The Pajaro Valley project has been an inspirational springboard for a myriad of parent projects (Igoa, 1995; McCaleb, 1994; Patrón, 1988; Reichmuth, 1988) that work towards bridging the gap between home and school. The goals for the project were to increase parental consciousness concerning relationships between parents and their children's schooling. Parents investigated and reflected on how that relationship affected their children's future. Interwoven into this process was the critical goal of helping "parents recover their sense of dignity and self-identity" (Ada, 1988, p. 224). One mother's words illustrate these goals: "Ever since I understood I had no need to feel ashamed of speaking Spanish, I have become stronger. Now I feel I can speak with the teachers about my children's education and I can tell them I want my children to know Spanish. I have gained courage" (Ada, 1988, p. 235).

Overview of the Project

This intergenerational project involving parents, children, and grand-parents evolved in cooperation with the bilingual program of the Pajaro Valley School District near Watsonville, California. The mostly rural population is more than half Latino with over one third of the children receiving migrant services. The parents were born into primarily low socio-economic families in Mexico, where they received limited formal schooling, and have immigrated to this country seeking a better life for themselves and their family. The project is still functioning with continuing success.

Sessions were held in the high-school library, the high school being the most recent and formidable barrier to institutional learning that many Latino parents had experienced. This location was specifically chosen to neutralize tensions parents might have felt related to past experiences, and to reinforce the literary aspect of the project through the environment. All meetings received top billing as special events. In addition, parents were contacted and offered transportation if needed. Special support was also instituted through separate children's activities, which allowed the parents to concentrate on the meeting they were attending.

Approximately 75 percent of the entire group would attend monthly meetings. Small group dialogue sessions emphasized critical issues and personalized discussion, at the same time bringing forth reflections on the parents' condition in life. One parent observed the importance of critically discussing their lives: "In these meetings we can learn to talk without feeling embarrassed or shy; it is very important to get rid of our inhibitions, because it is very difficult to talk in public" (Ada, 1988, p. 234). By conducting the sessions in the home language of the participants, parents were encouraged to view their language as both a vehicle for communication as well as a means of creating greater possibilities for the academic success of their children. Encouraging parents to verbalize and write about their reality was at the heart of each meeting. Writing and illustrating their own stories helped families discover hidden abilities and opened new windows of shared pride, as this father illustrates: "We discovered that our son has a talent for drawing . . . maybe some day he will become an artist" (Ada, 1988, p. 234).

The Creative Reading Methodology

The creative reading methodology (Ada, 1991) employed in this project links literature to participants' lives through a gradual progression of naming, personal interpretation, personal and collective multicultural/critical reflection, and action. The story Araceli wrote at the beginning of this section beautifully illustrates the possibility that this methodology holds out for looking at our lives through new lenses. Araceli was able through this process to relate literature to her personal experience, move to a more critical analysis integrating lived experience, and finally apply the information to a real-life situation. This allowed her to recreate her lived reality and reconcile it to match new understandings.

Outcomes of the Project

Videotapes of the sessions were borrowed by the educators and viewed in homes throughout the community. It was powerfully validating for many children to see their parents on TV, watching them read stories they and their parents had written. The parents, in turn, were able to critically watch themselves and gain strength from personal and family critiques. Directly related, as an outgrowth of the video viewing, these same parents displayed self-confidence in acts like petitioning the district school board for a meeting to talk about the academic future of their children and presenting on children's literature at a Regional Migrant Education Conference.

What is tremendously powerful about this project is that not only did the parents come to believe in themselves, but they also began to reassess their abilities and the impact they could exert with their voice in the familial and community arenas. Special care was taken in choosing literature that held the possibility of being culturally relevant and having potential for investigating culture in context. Relating her experience to the book *Arturo and Clementina*, a story in which the protagonist learns to be independent, one mother shared that, although her husband had not believed in her abilities in the past, she now saw that: "Nonetheless, I am not remaining silent like Clementina did, but instead, I make him (the husband) see that I can get things done" (Ada, 1988, p. 232).

Family History Writing Project

At that time, we slept on the cold floor on a mat, I didn't wear shoes until I was ten years old. Almost everyone went to school without shoes. . . .

Now we live like kings because we have a house, a bed and running water
when before it came from a spring in the ground.
                                                    —J. Chávez, participating parent

The profound and deeply moving words found above and at the
beginning of this chapter were spoken during a dialogue session as part
of a parent writing project in Watsonville, California. Parents and children from Valerie Andriola-Balderas's (1993) kindergarten class in the
Pajaro Valley were engaged in an intergenerational process of conscien-
tization (Freire and Faundez, 1989). The dialogue brought forth written
stories of pain, nostalgia, humanity, and hope for the next generation.
The parents were invited to write and illustrate their life story, which they
shared with other parents. As they continued to dialogue about what they
were thinking, their writings and illustrations became increasingly more
voluminous and detailed.

Overview of the Project

Parents' childhood memories were audiotaped, transcribed, and translated. Upon seeing their first dialogue in written form, the parents were
surprised at how beautiful their words looked in black and white. A
parent, A. Chávez, said that she "felt very emotional to see the summary
of my life story on paper, that my children would read it and know the
effort I have made in order for them to live better." Parents were deeply
moved when they saw their oral words in text form and expressed
admiration and pride in themselves. Most dramatically, they began to
take ownership of the process. This was critical as they embarked upon
writing and illustrating personal family histories.

Through orally sharing their histories at monthly childrens' literature
workshops (Ada, 1988), parents bonded in a common bicultural, binational struggle. Many parents and their teachers were moved to tears as
personal accounts of suffering and common experiences communicated
a profound sense of community among the participants. Children also
learned more about their parents' childhood: "Ofelia Villegas's son was
surprised to know that his mother sold *nopales* (an edible cactus) all day
at the flea market when she was his age."

Parents' Lives Reflected as History

There exists a great need for these stories to be told and written because many other people share these same struggles. Children must see both their lives and their parents' lives located in books so that they can place themselves in history, and in doing so, connect their struggles to the larger society. This is what L. Arreguín had to say when she saw her words included in the school library: "I feel very fortunate to know that this project was accomplished and that in one small corner of the school (and the world) a small part of our lives is available to all children who might wish to know about it. Hopefully it will serve as an example for them to continue with their education." One of the most powerful uses of these publications is making them available to others through placement in class libraries, schools, public libraries, and also public places.

Outcomes of the Project

Parents will embrace partnerships and work wholeheartedly with teachers when they are respected for whom they are and what they know, and when faith is demonstrated in their abilities. Parent involvement programs must raise consciousness in a way that can be translated into action, so that parents can become advocates for their children. Programs that provide a platform for parental voices will undoubtedly benefit children.

In the discussion groups and illustrations of their family histories, parents found a common interest in the hope for a better life for their children. L. Arreguín's words give us much to reflect on: "Even though they talk about it (United States) over there (Mexico), they can't imagine how hard it is and all that goes on here." None of the participants ever imagined how difficult life would be for them in the United States and how much they would miss what they left behind. Parents' words, once bound and published, give us insight and guidance for a better, more caring society.

This project encourages inclusive policies of curriculum development by fomenting artistic growth and validates the collective knowledge of a historically marginalized people. This is an example of how parents and educators together can initiate new ways of creating materials that emerge from the soul of family experience. When children see themselves and their parents in books, they begin to see themselves as part of history, and in doing so, connect their struggles to the struggles of others, and thus find the strength, inspiration, and courage to live as protagonists of a transformative process.

Project L.I.B.R.E.: Family Literacy

Mr. Dolores, a single father, is a 33-year-old trying to raise two children. While he tries to be involved in his children's school work, he finds single parenting overwhelming. In spite of this, he attends the L.I.B.R.E. (Literacy Improvement by Reading Enjoyment) parent program to help improve his English. At the beginning he could not participate in class, "No teacher, I really don't have anything to add." Then one day as we discussed a multicultural book which dealt with plants, he lit up. "This is what I did back home, I had a plot of land and grew lots of food." He spent the next 1/2 hour explaining it to the class. Other families told him they enjoyed his explanation and he continued to participate. For a person who thought he had nothing to offer, he had arrived. He now participates in all parent meetings in the school. (Gómez-Valdez, 1993, p. 74)

Overview of the Project

Project L.I.B.R.E., an acronym meaning "free" in Spanish, was conceived as a Title VII Family Literacy Project by Cristina Gómez-Valdez (1993) with a group of parents at Ditmar Elementary School in Oceanside, California. Gómez-Valdez documented, transcribed, and translated the project. As is so beautifully illustrated in the previous quote, L.I.B.R.E.'s framework was built on the belief that parents hold valuable knowledge. Validating these experiences increases the parent's self-confidence, which in turn increases participation and involvement in their children's schooling. In this case, when the parent had a chance to share his prior knowledge and the experience he had actually lived, he was able to take ownership of the process and felt like part of the program. This is the beginning of parent partnerships.

Latinos account for 85 percent of the student body at Ditmar Elementary; yet one Mexican man describes his experience as follows: "We are like ghosts here, transparent, as if we didn't exist." Once a month culturally relevant genres are investigated and translated into classroom curriculum. They are explored in association with parent expectations of their children's future and their role as advocates in the educational institution, thus uniting informal with formal education and making school knowledge an extension of family knowledge.

The dual program structure focuses on strengths of adult learners to break down barriers such as this parent expressed: "They [the school system] left me without language. I can't do it in Spanish or English.

People look at me funny." Biweekly meetings are two hours: one hour of intergenerational Spanish children's literacy development (Ada, 1988) and the other hour of English language literacy based on individual need. During the English component, a parallel program is provided for children, which allows the parents freedom to concentrate. Additionally, on a monthly basis there are three hour institutes that deal with culturally specific literacy practices. The program's theoretical framework is grounded in the work of Freire and Faundez (1989), who teach critical dialogue as a basis for understanding that reading and writing can be extensions of the act of knowing as a subject.

Outcomes of the Project

One parent saw the connection between her child's class and her own learning by explaining that in the future she would "observe what the child likes and help him so that he flourishes." Literacy programs have proven successful in situations where parents see literacy as a vehicle to parent involvement and action. As one parent explained, "I believe we are all intelligent but education moves us along. We all have good things but education helps to lead it towards the positive. Education is a guide for people to excel in all aspects: the way we live, the way we govern. A person with an education can do many things. Both forms of education; formal and informal go hand in hand" (Gómez-Valdez, 1993, pp. 103–104).

Praxis: Putting Theory into Practice

If children at any grade level are encouraged to return home daily with something to share with their parents and/or questions to ask of them, communication at home is bound to increase. And if the information requested from the parents encourages them to revisit their own childhood, they will in the process develop a greater understanding of their own children. Thus, inviting parents to share childhood memories with their children not only provides a framework for communication, but also promotes better parenting.

When contributions offered by the parents are recorded on charts or collected in classroom books, an interest and appreciation of the parent's thoughts and experiences is shown, and this encourages children to continue asking for their parents' input and perspectives. Parent-child interaction encourages not only the maintenance and development of the home language but also communication in the home.

Children and parents can also participate jointly in co-authoring a book on a subject of mutual interest. Writing a book together allows parents and children to learn about each other's worlds. It provides an opportunity for children to have a greater sense of their own identity through self-reflection, a sharing of their insights, thoughts, and childhood experiences. By engaging in the process of co-authoring a book, parents and children have a chance to share moments of mutual understanding that might not otherwise take place.

Children can also author books in which they are the protagonists, using information they have first obtained from their parents. For example: "How I got my name," "My autobiography," "The day I was born," or "Something big that happened when I was little." They could also interview and dialogue with their parents to write books where their parents are the protagonists, such as: "My father's (mother's) childhood friends," "To make the world a better place, my mother (father) suggests . . . ," "A day that changed my father's (mother's) life," "My mother's (father's) best advice for life." Of course, all of these could be extended to other members of the family, godparents, and family friends. These kinds of activities are not costly. They require no outside assistance nor special permission, and all parents and children can participate.

Participation of All Teachers Is Essential

It is important to re-emphasize that all teachers, regardless of ethnicity or language skill, can function as powerful allies for children and their families by providing strong support. Of course it is essential for children to have strong role models of their own ethnic heritage, and of course it is vital for them to have their home language validated in schools and other loci of social prestige. Yet teachers who have true respect and appreciation for their students' lives, families, language, and cultures can, as a consequence, benefit the students, even when they do not share the same ethnic heritage or do not speak the student's home language.

While it is ideal that the home language be used in the classroom, all of the activities described here can take place at home, in the home language, and their results can be shared in the classroom in English. In this way, the home language can be honored and encouraged along with validation of parents' lives, experiences, and knowledge. Communication among family members is developed and fostered regardless of the teacher's linguistic repertoire. What is important is the teacher's integrity and commitment to serve all children.

Teachers can also model their willingness to take on a certain amount of risk by sharing their personal stories. Children and their families must see the teacher take that risk first—writing a book about her or his own life, family, or children, and then sending the book home with the students so that they can share it with their families. The students and their parents are more likely to open up and share their personal stories as well. For a teacher to model this process is not necessarily easy but certainly worthwhile.

Often teachers at conferences and workshops have expressed how, after hearing these ideas, they have begun the process of applying these ideas into practice. They have written books themselves, shared the books with students' families, and successfully encouraged many parents and children to begin writing books of their own that reflect their lives, their histories, and their experiences. They also report that their teaching and lives have taken on a new, deeper meaning.

Authoring Our Lives

As parents and children engage in writing books of their own, the process of producing a book is demystified. Perhaps one day they will conceive and produce their own books, independently of the classroom. Writing from their own life experience contributes to and strengthens parents' and children's self-esteem and self-identity. This is an example of what is meant by "finding one's own voice." Having someone listen to us, someone who believes that we have something worthwhile to say, is fundamental to the process. And the more that our experience is denied or deemed worthless by others, the more important that single experience becomes.

No one becomes an author unless he/she feels that there is something significant and valuable to say. Teachers need to communicate to children and parents that their stories and voices are important and meaningful. By producing books, we provide a constant validation of the parents' thinking, language, and history. Thus parents are helped to realize the valuable role they have as educators and teachers of their children. They are encouraged to recognize that, regardless of their own level of schooling, they have important contributions to make to their children and to the learning process. They are persuaded by our actions that their personal history is important and worth sharing. In many instances they may have painful memories and scars connected to their schooling experience. It will be extremely significant for them to discover that the school values and recognizes what they have to say.

SUMMARY

For these ideas to have authentic value, the ultimate goal of all of these practices must not be forgotten. What is presented here are not activities to be carried out for activity's sake, nor for the sake of the final material product. The aim is not to have a lot of "cute family books" to show and tell, but instead for students and parents to recognize themselves as authors not merely of books and texts, but of their own lives; to recognize themselves as protagonists not only of stories of their past, but also of their present day struggles.

What is essential is for parents and students to be able to analyze their reality, to understand the structures and forces that constrain them, to feel strong enough to question the world around them, and to feel free enough to engage in solidarity with others in order to shape and transform the world. In order for our work to have meaningful effect, we need to be continuously cognizant of our main purpose. We need to adapt these activities and undertake them in a way that is authentic and meaningful to us, in order that they become authentic and meaningful for parents and families. We need to be aware of our own attitudes and assumptions in order for us to not be patronizing towards the parents we are working with; instead, we should communicate a deep respect for whom they are. We need to model the kind of risk taking and self-development we want to facilitate in others.

REFERENCES

Ada, A. F. 1988. "The Pajaro Valley Experience: Working with Spanish Speaking Parents to Develop Children's Reading and Writing Skills through the Use of Children's Literature," in *Minority Education: From Shame to Struggle.* T. Skutnabb-Kangas and J. Cummins, eds. Philadelphia, PA: Multilingual Matters, pp. 223–238.

Ada, A. F. 1991. "Creative Reading: A Relevant Methodology for Language Minority Children," in *Literacy as Praxis.* C. Walsh, ed. Norwood: Ablex Publishing Corporation, pp. 89–102.

Andriola-Balderas, V. 1993. "Reclaiming and Affirming Voice and Culture: Family Contributions through Book Creations of Lived History and Experience—A Participatory Study," Unpublished diss., University of San Francisco.

Freire, P. and A. Faundez. 1989. *Learning to Question: A Pedagogy of Liberation.* New York: Continuum.

Gómez-Valdez, C. 1993. "The Silent Majority Raise Their Voices: Reflections of Mexican Parents on Learning and Schooling, A Participatory Research," Unpublished diss., University of San Francisco.

Igoa, C. 1995. *The Inner World of the Immigrant Child.* Hillsdale, New Jersey: Lawrence Erlbaum Associates, Inc.

McCaleb, S. P. 1994. *Building Communities of Learners: A Collaboration Among Students, Teachers, Families and Community.* New York, NY: St. Martin's Press.

Patrón, R. 1988. "Promoting Family Interaction and Literacy through Children's Literature in Spanish with Spanish-Speaking Parents," Unpublished diss., University of San Francisco.

Reichmuth, S. 1988. "Hispanic Parent Empowerment through Critical Dialogue and Parent-Child Interaction within the School Setting," Unpublished diss., University of San Francisco.

PART II

SUCCESSFUL PRACTICES FOR LATINOS IN EARLY CHILDHOOD PROGRAMS

Developmentally Appropriate Practice: Rethinking the Preschool Curriculum with Latino Families

ELIZABETH QUINTERO—*University of Minnesota at Duluth*

INTRODUCTION

Angel es mi amigo.
(Angel is my friend.)

Quiero a mi maestra.
(I love my teacher.)

Soy contento cuando me dejan ir al rio.
(I am happy when they let me go to the river.)

THESE words written by 5- and 6-year-old Mexican American children are vibrant voices of socially and cognitively competent children telling us about their worlds. These children and their parents participated in a bilingual, family literacy project operating in seven schools in a border area in the Southwest for three years. Parents and their 4-, 5-, and 6-year-old children attended class, once a week after school in their neighborhood school, to participate in small group sessions. As the families worked on literacy activities based on informational themes they had requested, the literacy staff learned much about rethinking preschool curriculum. Attention was given to the worlds of these children and their families, their hopes and dreams. These hopes and dreams serve as the point of departure for authentically appropriate curriculum.

The first section of this chapter discusses what was learned from the families regarding four particular areas of redesigning preschool curricula for Latino children: (1) rethinking Developmentally Appropriate Practice, (2) giving importance to the context of family, (3) valuing bilingualism, (4) and valuing alternative ways of knowing. The second section presents practical ways of implementing supportive preschool environments for Latino children that encourage child-centered activities. The third section presents activities that are teacher-directed but child-centered and developmentally and culturally appropriate.

REDESIGNING PRESCHOOL CURRICULA FOR LATINO CHILDREN

The following discussion presents some insights on rethinking Developmentally Appropriate Practice, examining the interpretation of "family," and valuing bilingualism. There is a growing body of information (Lubeck, 1994) that explores the limitations of previous Developmentally Appropriate Practice guidelines. Many of the critical questions around this topic are posed intending to rethink the guildlines so that they will be more appropriate for many culturally and linguistically diverse groups. Furthermore, a related issue that is important to Latino families is the interpretation of "family" by student groups and their communities. The classroom and activities must reflect and be inclusive of the families represented by the preschool children. Finally, if the students are bilingual and from bilingual communities, this use of two languages must be apparent in the physical environment and in the programming of activities.

Rethinking Developmentally Appropriate Practice

There are various issues to consider when developing preschool curricula for bilingual children. The National Association for the Education of Young Children (NAEYC) has developed a position statement regarding appropriate learning contexts and methods for young children regarding cognitive, social, emotional, and physical development (Bredekamp, 1987). However, early childhood educators do not all agree on the emphases of the Developmentally Appropriate Practice especially regarding sociocultural development and learning for groups of children from diverse backgrounds in the United States (Bloch, 1991; Kessler, 1991; Swadener and Kessler, 1991; Walsh, 1991). For the most part, Developmentally Appropriate Practice is based upon the premises of developmental psychology and constructivism (McLaughlin, 1992). Constructivism is generally considered to be the theory that humans learn through creating cognitive structures from interaction with the environment. Lubeck (1994) discusses ways in which reliance on these theoretical perspectives becomes problematic, especially for culturally diverse children.

To further question these assumptions, specific cultural norms and family child-rearing preferences among many Latino groups come to mind. Parental authority is an important value in Latino culture. Latino parents inculcate in their children a profound respect for teachers and for school. As Reyes (1993) reports, Latinos hold high regard for teachers as authority figures; thus it is her opinion that direct instruction or active, direct interaction from the teacher is expected. This direct interaction does not necessarily have to take away from a goal of learning to be an independent thinker on the part of the child, but the path leading to the goal is more familiar with a respected guide. Mexican American parents believe that children learn by observing people who have the skill or knowledge that is being learned (Briggs, 1984). They also believe that people learn through practice. Skills and knowledge aren't acquired immediately, and anyone who thinks he can be an expert overnight will not become competent. According to Briggs (1984), precocious behavior is viewed as a sign of disrespect to those who have earned their expertise the hard way. "*Respeto*" (respect) is a central cultural value and requires deference to older and more skilled individuals who have a greater command of the skills being learned. Furthermore, group-centered activities are very common in Latino families. According to Valdés (1986), the family unit takes precedence over all else in Mexican culture, and the socialization of children is seen as preparing them to become contributing members of the family and community. Cooperation of group members, whether in family or community, is a significant part of children's experiences before exposure to schools.

A complex example of sociocultural family interactions that intertwined with cognitive teaching issues was seen in the story of Diana, one of the family literacy project participants. Diana, a kindergarten student, lived with both her parents in a lower-middle-class neighborhood. She was an only child. The family spoke only Spanish at home. Her father attended two years of high school in Mexico and her mother went to a business school in Mexico and subsequently took two years of English as a second language classes in the United States. The mother, Ms. García, stated in the first parent interview that her greatest desire was for her daughter to study and to have a professional career that she would enjoy. Ms. García clearly indicated that she wanted to participate in her daughter's education and clearly took pride in what she was able to teach her daughter. During the first interview, for example, she said that one of her greatest accomplishments was having taught Diana her letters and colors.

Diana was just beginning to learn English as the literacy groups started in September. Diana exhibited familiar patterns of behavior for a five-year-old at the beginning of the literacy sessions. She spoke little at first, mostly in Spanish, often answering the instructor's questions with a "yes," "no," or short phrase. When the teacher asked her a question in English that she did not seem to understand, she looked to her mother for the Spanish translation. She often waited for a response from her mother, even when she understood the language used. For example, during the first session when the children were drawing a picture of the home where their family lived, she started drawing, hesitated, looked at her mother. Her mother then asked, "Diana, qué sigue?" (What's next?) Diana answered, "Las ventanas." (The windows.) She then drew the windows.

Regarding the mother/daughter interactions in the literacy class, at first the observers perceived that Ms. García was apparently impatient with her daughter and had a persistent tendency to dominate the interactions. For example, during a lesson on the seasons, the following exchange took place:

> *Ms. G.:* ¿Qué vas a pintar en este árbol de winter? (What are you going to paint on this tree in winter?)
>
> *Diana:* "Hojas." (Leaves)
>
> *Ms. G.:* No, no, no. ¿Qué es eso? . . . toma . . . no tienes ganas o sí. No, Diana! ¿Qué tienes? ¿Dime qué tienes? Espérate para que hagas bien y no cochinadas" (No, no, no. What's that? Do . . . you want to or not? No, Diana! What's the matter with you! Wait so you'll do it right and not make a mess.)
>
> *Diana:* ¿Qué parezcan leaves? Acá, necesita más brown. (They need to look like leaves? Here, they need more brown.)

The observer noted "This was a complex interaction; Mom cueing but not always appropriately."

In the case of Diana and her mother, appropriate practice for mother and daughter appears to differ dramatically from the guidelines for Developmentally Appropriate Practice. The mother is not abusive, but definitely authoritative. Developmentally Appropriate Practice guidelines fail to take account of cultural differences in child-rearing practices, or the negotiation of the tension that results between differing child-rearing assumptions at home and at school. Diana respects her mother's strong personality and interactive style, yet maintains her own willful intentions when it is important to her. Her mother is adamant about being a part of her daughter's education—directly—even when she is given information about the importance of her daughter's independence in learning and literacy events. Ms. García was realistic to insist that her daughter write well and correctly in both her mother tongue and English. She had had experiences in both Mexican and American society, both of which had stressed the relationship between success and hard work to conform to form—in this case—writing. She was determined to insure that her daughter succeed in learning English and she believed strongly that adhering to correct form at school is important. At the same time, she was strong in her conviction, which is supported by much recent research (Genishi et al., 1994) as promising practice to promote bilingualism, that her family speak exclusively Spanish in the home. This is favorable in that current research shows that adults speaking Spanish at home support the children's English development at school.

Using the Language of Family

Trueba et al. (1990) point out:

Educators, especially teachers, need to become aware of the contributions of immigrants and refugees to America in order to inculcate in all students genuine appreciation for the richness of American culture and of immigrants' commitment to the continued existence of democratic institutions. (p. 1)

In other words, developmentally and culturally appropriate curriculum values the sociocultural background of children's families and the resulting interpretations of their worlds. True, all children consider their families as the center of their world, but their worlds are often different from what is portrayed in many storybooks or on television. In many Latino communities, friends and community members are "family." Many children live with extended family, thus a grandparent is not someone to write letters to once a year, but someone in the next room. Many children live with aunts, cousins, or friends who aren't blood relatives—but who are "family" just the same. For example, Antonio, a five-year-old child participating with his mother in a family literacy class, often mentioned activities that he enjoyed doing with his brother and sisters. He made valentine cards for his mother and father and often spoke of his close friends and the things they did together. His family and friends should be the point of departure for all curriculum development, just as is the case for all preschool children. If his experiences, family members, and living situation differ from what teachers' story-books or "curriculum kits" portray, it is the teachers' responsibility to include the world of Antonio and his friends.

Another child, Vicente, demonstrated by both conversation and written work that his world is closely tied to his family. During a lesson about "sharing" the teacher asked, "What do you share with friends?" Vicente answered, "Legos." During a writing exercise he wrote, "I share with my brother the truck" [sic]. On another occasion, the teacher asked, "Why do we have Valentine's Day? What do we get? Who do you love?" Vicente answered, "My mom, my brother, my dad, my grandma." Yet, during one family literacy class, which Vicente's family attended, the theme of the class was community helpers, and the teacher missed the opportunity to tie a cognitive activity to Vicente's sociocultural need to connect with his family. The teacher opened the lesson by asking questions about community helpers such as:

   T: "Vicente, how does a bus driver help you?"

   T: "What would you like to be Vicente?"

   V: "A Ghostbuster . . . a cuidar mi hermano." (A Ghostbuster so I can take care of my brother.)

   T: "Is a Ghostbuster a community helper? No. What about a fireman, a policeman, or something like that?"

Both Piagetian and Vygotskyan researchers have taught us that child cognition is nurtured by imagination and meaningful social relationships. Cazden (1981), Cummins (1989), Gonzalez-Mena (1981), Goodman (1986), and others have pointed out that young children learn a second language through rich, interactive language environments. In the previous example the teacher missed an opportunity to build on Vicente's creativity about community helpers and his desire to care for his brother.

This information speaks directly to curriculum planning, both in terms of activity development and in terms of the social environment in the classroom. It is appropriate to plan activities that center on "The Family"—the children's families, including all varieties and configurations of "family."

Valuing Bilingualism

Conversations for many bilingual children often take place in both languages. For example, during a lesson in which the theme was "friends," the family literacy teacher asked Antonio, "What is a friend? Do you have a friend?" Antonio answered in English, "Next door house. Ruly." His mother explained, in Spanish, that Ruly is Raúl, a neighbor. When the children were asked to draw a picture of their friend, Antonio's mother commented with a laugh to Antonio as he drew, "No lo está viendo con mucha misericordia." (He's not seeing him with much mercy.) She then guided, "No, Antonio, con un sólo color." (No, Antonio, with one color only.) Antonio asked his mom, "The shirt?" His oral code-switching (language alternation) ability occurred naturally in his interactions with his mother. While his mother is not fluent in English, she does understand the language well enough to interact with her son and provide support for his Spanish language development. This mother is an example of a valuable resource person to visit the early childhood classroom. Her ability to understand both Spanish and English and her native fluency in Spanish is an asset to the language development of all her children. The school's inviting her into the classroom gives a strong message about valuing bilingualism.

Children write naturally, in two languages, in ways that are meaningful to them. Work samples from the family literacy project provide evidence of this. Bilingual children must be given the freedom to use code-switching, oral and written, in their developmental writing (Quintero and Macías, 1995), as in the following examples:

- Angel es m fnd [sic]. (Angel is my friend.)
- doy gracias por la comida milk meat juice apple doy gracias por mis papás mom dad doy gracias por mis juguetes bear pollito bike cup ball ice cream (I give thanks for the food, milk, meat, apple juice. I give thanks for my parents, mom, dad. I give thanks for my toys, bear, little chick, bike, cup, ball, ice cream.)
- Me alegro mucho de estar en la escuela. (I am very happy to be in the school.)
- Quiero aprender muchas cosas. (I want to learn many things.)
- Gracias a mi maestra que la quiero mucho. (Thanks to my teacher whom I love very much.)
- Quiero mucho a mis amigos de la escuela. (I love my friends at school very much.)

These children show literacy development in two languages as explained by Tinajero and Huerta-Macías (1993). Their written language is integrally tied to their social lives and thus to their communication.

Including Alternative Ways of Knowing

Alternatives to Euroamerican mainstream cultural norms are persevering in some contexts through the practice of raising children and passing on family cultural traditions. While anthropologists have sought to understand alternative ways of knowing for decades, educators have more recently given attention to this:

> Knowledge can come from many sources, and alternative ways of knowing can only add to our vision of issues, influences on development and schooling, and understanding of curriculum and pedagogy. It is useful to hear different voices tell their stories about how they experience education or schooling. (Bloch, 1991, p. 106)

Alternative ways of knowing that are represented by parents and children must be included in the preschool curricula for the sake of both Latino children and the sake of other children. I have found that students will tell us, as Sleeter and Grant's (1991) students told them "what concerned them, interested them, motivated them. They could tell us in rich detail about their world and their dreams" (p. 67). Soto (1991) says that "part of our role as researchers is to educate individuals not cognizant of the issues faced by diverse families which on the surface appear to overshadow enriching and positive contributions" (p. 159).

Examples of parents sharing alternative forms of factual knowledge in classrooms were evident in the family literacy classes. For example, one parent, Ms. Ibarra, was always eager to share information about her personal background knowledge. She asked and answered questions during the family literacy lessons and contributed comments that expanded on the theme. She consistently talked about her family's personal experiences including comments about plants, music, construction, cooking, and crossing the international bridge at rush hour. One lesson, for example, was about cotton—something which Ms. Ibarra knew a lot about from working in the cotton fields. During that lesson, she "taught" the group about the different stages in the growth of the cotton plant, and at one point, she even corrected the teacher. In this particular instance, the teacher was explaining the process of plant growth:

> *Teacher:* Sale una flor amarilla . . . después se seca la flor. (A yellow
>   flower blooms . . . then it dries.)
>
> *Ms. Ibarra:* No. Se hace verde. (No, it turns green.)
>
> *Teacher:* ¿Se hace verde? (It turns green?)

Ms. Ibarra: Sí, sí, . . . se va abriendo y luego se seca (Yes, yes, . . . it blossoms, and then it dries).

Another mother shared with the staff that she tells stories to her son *every* morning. She also shared with us that she reads aloud from the Bible on a daily basis and that her home is *"una biblioteca"* (a library). Her comments about being an avid reader indicate that, while she is a monolingual Spanish speaker, she is quite literate in her native language. In the family literacy class, she calmly and consistently prompted and encouraged her son and appropriately explained things to him in Spanish. The boy would then explain the issue or story to the class in perfect English. He often wrote in English. Thus, while the mother didn't consider herself bilingual or biliterate, she was an effective leader of this bilingual, biliterate family team with much important background knowledge.

Thus, the parents and their children in the family literacy project taught the staff many things about what is appropriate, what is preferred, and what is needed for preschool environments for Latino preschool children. This information has been useful in designing child-centered environments and child-centered activities for Latino children. In the following section this information is combined with information about quality programming for all children in the field of early childhood education.

CREATING SUPPORTIVE, CHILD-CENTERED PRESCHOOL ENVIRONMENTS FOR LATINO CHILDREN

What is the learning environment like in a preschool? By observing and listening to children—especially in the context of play, which is the most natural context of childhood—much is learned about their families, culture, and language. This context provides an ongoing, authentic guide for planning the children's learning environments.

Where does play happen at preschool? Virtually everywhere. The early childhood classroom learning environment can easily include the special aspects needed to help Latino children feel at home and thrive. The physical space can take many forms, and arrangements are made according to program philosophy, licensing regulations, room configurations, and availability of equipment and materials. In spite of these variations, there are a few overall "musts" for preschool environments. Some teachers call these arrangements "centers." It doesn't matter what they are called, but they must be present in early childhood classrooms. Centers are used by children during "choice time," free play time, or all the time during the school day depending upon the design and schedule of the program. The following are the most common: a dramatic play area, a block center, a book center, a manipulative toy area, a large motor rumpus area, a science area, a sand and water play area, and an art area. Various research studies (Spodek and Saracho, 1994) in early childhood education have discussed the importance of providing varied learning environments for early cognitive and socioemotional development. Other research has specifically documented the development of emergent literacy and enhanced positive sociocultural interactions in responsive preschool environments (Harste et al., 1984; Quintero, 1986).

Ramsey (1987) discusses requirements for the physical environment that focus on culturally sensitive, concrete ways in which to meet children's developmental needs. For example, in the case of environments for Latino children, are Latinos represented by the pictures and photographs currently displayed in the classroom? How authentic are these displays? Do they represent real individuals or more stereotyped images? Similarly, are Latinos represented in the doll collection? Do they represent a more differentiated range of racial groups than simply black and white dolls? Are Latinos' cultural traditions represented in the equipment in the housekeeping area? What lifestyles are children being encouraged to represent in the block building center? What is made available as stimulus materials? What props are available for them to use? Do storybooks represent Latino ethnic, racial, occupational, regional, linguistic, and socio-economic groups?

It should be noted as the preschool environment is set up that children enjoy and use materials, tools, and props that are catalysts to intellectual and sociocultural experiences. In order to engage children actively, there needs to be a balance between familiarity and novelty—children thrive through a combination of repetitious routine and new variety in terms of materials and activities. Children use props and materials to reenact their own experiences. If confronted by a completely unfamiliar scent or tool, they may simply ignore it. If the unfamiliar is woven into familiar activities, however, children can blend the known and unknown in their play. Materials are introduced deliberately in the preschool classroom. Remember it can be dangerous, or at the very least frustrating, to overstimulate young children with too many new materials. Introduce only a few materials at the beginning of the year and gradually add others as time goes on to maintain a comfortable, challenging environment.

The Centers

As mentioned previously, the physical space includes "centers" that must be present in all preschool environments. These centers, used by children during "choice time," free play time, or all the time during the school day depending upon the design and schedule of the program, represent quality programming for all young children. These centers may include: a dramatic play area, a block center, a book center, a manipulative toy area, a large motor rumpus area, a science area, a sand and water play area, and an art area. These centers can be enhanced with Latino cultural materials and Spanish language print materials to make them even more appropriate for Latino children.

Dramatic Play Area

The dramatic play area, sometimes called the "home area" or "pretend play" center, is a favorite of many children throughout their preschool experience. Boys and girls construct elaborate play here, based on their own reality and their combined imaginations. As stated before, it is important to include in this center familiar items that the children see and use at home and also to introduce some items that are new to the children. A list of possible materials follows:

- stoves, sinks, refrigerators, dishes, and an *alternative* set of props for food storage and preparation [barbecues, campfires (pretend), and cookstoves]. These should be labeled in Spanish and English to encourage biliteracy development and show that both languages are valued.
- house-making materials such as boxes, cloths, blankets (cloth from indigenous groups in Latin America is colorful, durable, and may be familiar to the children). Photographs of many types of alternatives in housing—mobile homes, tents, apartments, houseboats—may be included.
- utensils for cooking—standard discount versions and other versions from the children's families such as lemon juicers and *"flan"* molds. Even *"comale"* for heating tortillas and *"molcajetes"* for grinding corn or dried herbs, which are only used rarely in some households today, are still an enjoyment for the children. These utensils are presented in stories of elders and in literature and history books, if not present in children's homes.

- food props—cereal boxes, food containers, canned and packaged goods (again, use empty boxes with print in Spanish and English). Include packages of "*atole*" (corn starch) and "*sopa*" as well as jello and noodles.
- clothes props—costumes, scarves, hats, long pieces of material from as many cultures as you can find, and many photos to observe and copy and discuss
- caring-for-children props—cribs, high chairs, cradles, backpacks, carrying slings, etc.
- dolls and puppets with a variety of skin tones, hair colors, eye color, and modes of dress
- "work" props—clothes and tools, from typewriters to fishing poles to computers to lunch boxes to portfolios (briefcases)
- teacher-made "telephone books," in Spanish and English, of the children's names, pictures, and telephone numbers
- teacher-made (or child-made) menus, in Spanish and English, with cut-out pictures of the pretend food that is actually in the house-keeping corner, with the name of the particular food next to it
- newspapers and magazines in both Spanish and English. (When the teacher or the children's families don't have access to a Spanish language newspaper, subscribe to one. It will be supply money well spent!)
- children's recipe books, in two or more languages
- sports section and food section of both a Spanish language and English language newspaper
- storybooks in both languages to be read to the "dollies"
- paper and pencils near the telephones

The dramatic play center is one of the most active in the preschool environment. With a few simple props, many child-initiated literacy development activities begin here (Quintero, 1986). Children exhibit daily many instances of cognitive development while playing here (Kamii, 1991). Also, social development is always at the forefront in the pretend play evolving at this center (Lubeck, 1994).

Block Center

The block center is another favorite, active center for the children to experiment with, combining previously known information and newly experienced information. Most children come to preschool with the skill of building some structures for the purposes of their play. Certainly, most children, of both genders, like experimenting with new materials here. Some of the equipment is standard—wooden unit blocks, for example—yet, a few simple additions enhance Latino culture. Materials for this center could include:

- wooden blocks of various sizes and shapes
- cardboard blocks
- plastic blocks
- photographs of many different types of constructions—apartments, hogans, pagodas, adobe houses, mobile homes, lighthouses
- cloth, egg cartons, straw, pipe cleaners, stones
- trains, boats, planes, cars, bicycles, space vehicles
- books (in Spanish and English) about construction and architecture
- magazines (in Spanish and English) about cars

Often block center play and dramatic center play can lead to projects in other centers. For example, at the writing center, maps can be made and directions written for people to travel on the constructed roads to the new "buildings" in the block center. Especially when children need to give others a turn to play in the block center, or if a group gets a little too loud, a teacher can request that the children move to another center and suggest an extension of the play begun in the block center in the new center.

Writing Center

The writing center can be a flourishing, busy center that enhances projects begun in other centers or simply a continuously "open" center for children to experiment with their own versions of literacy and biliteracy. If a new project in the dramatic play center involves a need for writing letters, writing directions for a recipe, or making signs, the writing center becomes an important part of the preschool environment. Some suggested materials might include:

- paper hole-punches
- stapler
- teacher-made *Name Book, Words of the Month Book* (in Spanish and English) or other collections of words around a particular theme that children discuss
- picture dictionaries in both languages
- a "book" of children's favorite labels in both languages

Parents and families of the children are valuable resources for the writing center. Old greeting cards, letters, and lists for the children to play with and use as models are always popular.

Book Center

The book center is an obvious, effective center in which to include many examples of Latino culture and Spanish language books and magazines and bilingual Spanish/English books. More Spanish language children's books are available in bookstores and through publishing houses. Also, magazines, recipe books, and technical manuals that families have at home and are willing to loan or give to the school are always useful. A few specific suggestions are:

- storybooks in Spanish, bilingual Spanish/English storybooks, and storybooks in English
- storybooks depicting cultural groups represented by the children in the class must be available to the children. It is very important to do this because all bilingual or Spanish language storybooks are not the same. Some books are printed (and translated accordingly) in Spain, some are written and printed in Puerto Rico, while others are written and printed in New York. Some are written and printed in Mexico, and some represent Chicano experience and language use. This variation in language use, if represented by the children in the class, must be represented. Use parents as resources, call librarians, call historians who study the different groups. This is important.

Teachers should constantly acquire new materials for the book center and constantly observe the children using the books. What do they seem the most interested in? What stories do they come back to over and over again? Their preferences show us what they know and what they would like to know.

Manipulative Toy and Game Center

The manipulatives and game center is an integral part of all quality early childhood programs. Obviously, when the teaching staff is able to purchase or make puzzles with Latino culture represented and printed in Spanish, this is especially good for children. The following suggested materials represent items that are important for the development of all young children, including Latino children:

- legos
- bristle blocks
- tinkertoys
- small blocks
- bendables
- puzzles
- dressing frames

These items can also be enhanced by teacher-made materials such as lotto games with pictures labeled in Spanish. Memory games can be purchased with some print in Spanish. Children can make constructions with tinkertoys or small blocks that represent their experiences.

Rumpus Area

All preschool staff recognize the importance of this center for active preschoolers to interact and expend their overabundant energy. This center often takes the tone of "pretend play" begun in other centers. For example, if a group had been pretending to be participants in a "Quinceñera" (a sweet sixteen party) in the dramatic play area, they will probably go to the rumpus area to dance. This area should include areas for crawling through small passages, climbing ladders, and jumping down elevated forms, cardboard boxes, packing crates, and blankets (for tent and hide-out making).

Some teachers have enough space in the preschool classroom to set up this center in the same room. Other preschool rooms are too small so an adjoining room is needed. In warm climates, depending upon the layout of the building, this center could even be outside.

Science Center

The science center, sometimes called the "discovery center," can be set up on a table or in the corner of the room on some available counter space. This is another center that is important for all preschoolers, including Latino children. Some ideas for materials at this center are things to classify or put in groups, styrofoam packing pieces, old mismatched toys or game pieces, magnets, sink and float equipment, plants, animals, stones, feathers, and seashells.

Teaching staff should observe the children and build on their interests as they play here and adjust the materials accordingly. A helpful hint to consider is to locate this center near a water faucet, if possible.

Sand and Water Center

Another center that is imperative for cognitive and social development is the sand and water center. Research (Spodek and Saracho, 1994) has consistently shown that all children thrive developmentally by interacting with materials such as a sand table or washtub filled with sand or mud or snow or styrofoam packing pieces, shovels, spoons, play people, animals, and toy cars. Likewise, a water table or washtub or baby bathtub may be filled with water and bubbles, and food coloring. Measuring cups, spoons, cooking utensils, eggbeaters, squirt bottles, and pump bottles add to the excitement and learning opportunities at the water table.

Art Center

Early childhood art is another positive activity for all preschoolers. Most art specialists suggest providing materials and encouraging creativity on the part of the children rather than insisting that young children follow "models." Some suggested materials are paper of all types including manila paper, drawing paper, construction paper, poster paper, butcher paper, and wrapping paper. Free sources of paper are newsprint, newspaper, wallpaper, print shop end rolls, magazines and catalogs, wrapping paper, boxes, shopping bags, and carpet covers. The art center should also include crayons, chalk (thick and thin), markers of primary colors and wild colors, pencils, and pens. Additional materials to make available are paint, sponges, rollers, cotton swabs, paste and glue, cornstarch paste, wheat paste, white glue, liquid starch, scissors, and clay.

The art center should be surrounded by posters, paintings, and photographs representing Latino culture. This is considered good preschool practice valuing culture. While teachers should never tell preschoolers to "copy" an art form, the cultural examples should be available for them to appreciate and to show that the school values the cultural contributions.

What do all these centers have to do with language and culture? As early childhood teachers know, language permeates all planned and unplanned activities. If children are encouraged to communicate about real events with real people their languages will develop and their cultural preferences will be integrated into virtually every activity, planned and unplanned. By encouraging interactions in the early childhood classroom, child-centered language development will be occurring every moment of every day. If there are questions about the nature of the language development or ways in which to enhance this development, there are several ways to evaluate the situations. For example, a tape recorder placed near the center where the children are playing is useful. Record and transcribe the tapes and analyze them. To what extent and in what ways did the children get involved in exploring and expressing their play through language? What new directions did the children think of in their encounter with the experience, and how could the teacher help them follow their new-found interests in subsequent experiences? What could be done differently if the children were involved in this experience or sequence of experiences again?

These suggestions for center development are integral to a quality program for Latino preschoolers. As explained earlier, they enhance the child-initiated activities in a program. Next, some activities that are more teacher-directed are presented.

TEACHER-DIRECTED, CHILD-CENTERED, CULTURALLY APPROPRIATE LANGUAGE DEVELOPMENT ACTIVITIES

Teacher-directed literacy/language activity ideas that can be implemented with any age group and language group are another source of support for Latino children. These activities are designed according to a five-step model that encourages language development, literacy development, critical thinking, and cooperative and individual work on the part of the children. The five steps are as follows:

(1) Initial Inquiry: During this oral language activity, the teacher leads a large group discussion, while introducing information about the theme of the lesson, stressing open-ended questioning, expanding vocabulary and elaborating, and valuing mutual respect for each learner's opinion and contribution to the discussion.

(2) Concrete Learning Activity: During this hands-on experience, the children do an activity (in a small group or individually) that relates

to the theme of the lesson. This may be an art activity, a construction activity, or virtually any project that helps the child *actively* construct knowledge about the theme and literacy involved in a holistic manner.

(3) Language Experience Activity: During this activity the teacher encourages either writing with each child or using and becoming confident in invented spelling and his/her own version of developmental writing. Also, any type of group language experience story writing is appropriate.

(4) Storybook Activity: During this activity the teacher brings all the children back to a large group to do an interactive storybook reading relating to the theme of the lesson.

(5) Home Activity: The teacher suggests activities for each child to do with a parent, other family member, or the whole family at home.

Teacher-Directed Literacy Activities

These activities can be done in the preschool classroom in a variety of ways. The children can be grouped in pairs or cooperative groups of four, the children can be paired with older mentors (upper-grade students who come into the classroom to work with the children), or the children can be paired with parent or adult community volunteers. A theme is chosen for the activity and then the five steps defined previously serve as the framework guide for the activity. A few examples of activities are:

Activity #1 Theme: Families/ What Do We Treasure?

Step 1

(1) What is something that you have and love that belongs only to you? (a toy, a bike, etc.) Why?

(2) What is something that you love to do alone? With others? Why?

(3) What things belong to your family communally? Which things are the most dear to you, your mother, your sister, etc.? Do you like to share some things? Why or why not?

(4) How do you feel when someone takes your things without permission? Why do you feel this way? What do you tell them?

(5) How do you take care of your treasure? How does your mother/grandmother/brother/father/uncle take care of her/his treasure?

Step 2

(1) Have a sheet of construction paper with the name of one family member (one for each member) for personal treasures and one sheet with all the names (the whole family) for communal treasures.

(2) Cut out pictures from magazines of household items and paste them appropriately in the respective owner's paper or the community property family paper.

Step 3

(1) Write a sentence (in English or Spanish) describing the treasures pictured from Step 2.

OR

(2) Label the collected pictures (in Spanish or English) collected.

Step 4

(1) Possible storybooks: *Mi Casa* by Francisca Altamirano, *Diego* by Jeanette and Jonah Winter, *The Legend of Food Mountain* by Harriet Rohmer and Graciela Carrillo, *Soy Náhuatl* by Rosa Román Lagunes and Jesús Vitorino Dolores, *Triste Historia del Sol con Final Feliz* by Elena Climent, *Bety y su Ratón* by Elena Climent.

Step 5

(1) Invent a game at home. Play the game. Draw or write the instructions.

OR

(2) Write a letter to a favorite relative.

OR

(3) Have the family divide into two teams to form a scavenger hunt. Each team must get one item belonging to each different family member and one community property item.

Activity #2 Theme: Families/Family Chores

Step 1

(1) What are some things that you do together, as a family? Outside the home? At home? What about household chores? Does your family do that together?

(2) Who does what in your family? What is your job? How do you feel about this? Do you think that should change? Why? How? How can you bring this change about?

(3) What would happen if you didn't do your chores one day? for two days? for three? What if a family member is not doing her/his part and this is making you upset—what can you do? What if they react negatively? How do you deal with that? What do you think is a good way to get everyone to cooperate and do their job?

Step 2

(1) Suggest that the children draw a "floorplan" of their home and draw the person responsible for various chores doing that job.

OR

(2) Distribute a box to each child with "chore pictures" (and labels?) inside the box. Encourage them to sort these pictures according to who is doing what (i.e., according to chore assignments).

Step 3

(1) Begin to write a family plan by listing all the things that need to be done on a weekly basis. List who might do what. Use the floorplan done in step 2 if appropriate.

OR

(2) Think about your home. Select a treasured object or set of objects and describe how you, personally, are taking care of that.

OR

(3) Write or draw a set of family guides/rules that will explain what to do when you are sick or can't do your chores for whatever reason.

Step 4

(1) Possible storybooks: *The Cat in the Hat Comes Back* (Bilingual Spanish/English version) by Dr. Seuss, or any storybook that relates to chores and family responsibilities, such as *The Little Red Hen, La Gallinita Roja.*

Step 5

(1) Design a family poster for illustrating and/or listing each member's household duties by the day. Leave space for stars or other symbols, if desired.

OR

(2) Begin carrying out your family plan for household duties. Write about your experiences.

OR

(3) Talk with a friend about your plan. Ask your friend for reactions or ideas. How does your plan compare with what your friend's family does?

SUMMARY

There are many ways the preschool environment can support Latino children cognitively, socially, and culturally. As explained here, the environment in terms of materials, supplies, and activities presented is important. Preschoolers thrive best with a mixture of child-initiated and teacher-directed activities. It is important to remember that the field of early childhood education has a rich history of quality practice out of which teachers are guided to serve the needs for all children. These aspects of programming should be provided for Latino children. In addition, it is also important to pay attention to what Latino families and the children themselves need and prefer to make the preschool culturally and linguistically supportive.

As Lilly Wong Fillmore (1990) maintains,

> The teachers are cultural and linguistic bridges connecting the worlds of the home and the classroom; they facilitate the children's entry to school by building on what the children have learned in their homes. The family is drawn into the life and work of the Center rather than dismissed as irrelevant. (pp. 5–6)

Teachers participating with Latino children in preschool classrooms must help to be the cultural and linguistic bridges between the children, their families, and the outside world. The preschool teachers' dreams are that the children will benefit and be enriched by their preschool experiences.

REFERENCES

Bloch, M. N. 1991. "Critical Science and the History of Child Development's Influence on Early Education Research," *Early Education and Development,* 2(2): 95–108.

Bredekamp, S. 1987. *Developmentally Appropriate Practice in Early Childhood Pro-

grams Serving Children from Birth through Age 8. Washington, D.C.: National Association for Education of Young Children.

Briggs, C. L. 1984. "Learning How to Ask," *Language in Society,* 13:1–28.

Cazden, C. 1981. *Language in Early Childhood Education.* Washington, D.C. :NAEYC.

Cummins, J. 1989. *Empowering Minority Students.* Sacramento, CA: CABE.

Genishi, C., A. H. Dyson, and R. Fassler. 1994. "Language and Diversity in Early Childhood," in *Diversity & Developmentally Appropriate Practices: Challenges for Early Childhood Education.* B. L. Mallory, and R. S. New, eds. New York, NY: Teachers College Press.

Gonzalez-Mena, J. 1981. "English as a Second Language for Preschool Children," in *Language in Early Childhood Education.* C. Cazden, ed. Washington, D.C.: NAEYC.

Goodman, K. 1986. *What's Whole in Whole Language.* Portsmouth, NH: Heinemann.

Harste, J., V. Woodward, and C. Burke. 1984. *Language Stories and Literacy Lessons.* Portsmouth, NH: Heinemann.

Kamii, C. 1991, February. "How Children Construct Knowledge." Paper presented at the Illinois State Bilingual Education Conference, Chicago, IL.

Kessler, S. A. 1991. "Early Childhood Education as Development: Critique of the Metaphor," *Early Education and Development,* 2(2): 137–152.

Lubeck, S. 1994. "The Politics of Developmentally Appropriate Practice: Exploring Issues of Culture, Class, and Curriculum," in *Diversity & Developmentally Appropriate Practices: Challenges for Early Childhood Education.* B. L. Mallory, and R. S. New, eds. New York, NY: Teachers College Press, pp. 17–43.

McLaughlin, M. 1992. "Appropriate for Whom?: A Critique of the Culture and Class Bias Underlying Developmentally Appropriate Practice in Early Childhood Education." Paper presented at the *Conference on Reconceptualizing Early Childhood Education: Research, Theory and Practice*, Chicago, IL.

Quintero, E. P. 1986. "Preschool Literacy: The Effect of Sociocultural Context." ERIC # ED282181.

Quintero, E. P. and A. H. Macías. Spring/Summer, 1995. "Bilingual Children's Writing: Evidence of Active Learning in Social Context," *Journal of Research in Childhood Education.* Wheaton, MD: ACEI.

Ramsey, P. G. 1987. *Teaching and Learning in a Diverse World: Multicultural Education for Young Children.* New York, NY: Teachers College Press.

Reyes, M. de la Luz. 1993. "Challenging Venerable Assumptions: Literacy Instruction for Linguistically Different Students," *Harvard Educational Review,* 62(4):427–446.

Sleeter, C. and C. Grant. 1991. "Mapping Terrains of Power: Student Cultural Knowledge versus Classroom Knowledge," in *Empowerment through Multicultural Education.* C. Sleeter, and C. Grant, eds. New York: SUNY, pp. 49–68.

Soto, L. D. January, 1991. "Understanding Bilingual/Bicultural Young Children," *Young Children,* 46(2):30–36.

Spodek, B. and O. N. Saracho. 1994. *Right from the Start.* Boston, MA: Allyn and Bacon.

Swadener, E.B. and S. Kessler. 1991. "Introduction to the Special Issue," *Early Education and Development,* 2(2):85–94.

Tinajero, J. V. and A. Huerta-Macías. 1993. "Enhancing the Skills of Emergent Writers Acquiring English," in *The Power of Two Languages: Literacy and Biliteracy for*

Spanish-Speaking Students. J. V. Tinajero and A. F. Ada, eds. New York, NY: Macmillan/McGraw-Hill Publishing Co., pp. 254–263.

Trueba, H. T., L. Jacobs, and E. Kirton. 1990. *Cultural Conflict and Adaptation: The Case of Hmong Children in American Society.* New York, NY: Falmer Press.

Valdés, G. 1986. "Brothers and Sisters: A Closer Look at the Development of 'Cooperative' Social Orientations in Mexican-American Children." Paper presented at the 37th Annual Convention of the California Association of School Psychologists, Oakland, CA.

Walsh, D. J. 1991. "Extending the Discourse on Developmental Appropriateness: A Developmental Perspective," *Early Education and Development,* 2(2):109–119.

Wong Fillmore, L. 1990. *Latino Families and the Schools. California Perspectives: An Anthology.* Los Angeles, CA: The Immigrant Writers Project.

CHAPTER 5

Emergent Literacy: Implications for Kindergarten Settings

MARIA CRISTINA GONZÁLEZ—*El Paso Community College*

INTRODUCTION

MUCH attention has been given to restructuring early childhood education programs for Latino children through the enhancement of learning environments (see Quintero, Chapter 4). This chapter will focus on learning and teaching strategies in the enhancement of spoken language, reading, and writing in kindergarten, for Spanish-speaking Latino children. Attention will be given to teacher practice in literacy development with this age group.

It is important to begin by accentuating what is known about young children. Much of what is known about young children and their knowledge of literacy comes from research on child development drawn from multiple disciplines. These basic principles of early childhood apply to Latino and all other children as well. However, the role that culture and language play in development must not be overlooked. Recent research on emergent literacy informs educators about the critical role that language and culture play in the construction of literacies (Anthony et al., 1991; Boyarin, 1992; De La Luz Reyes, 1992; Delgado-Gaitan and Trueba, 1991; Edelsky, 1991; Ferdman et al., 1994; Nieto, 1992; Taylor and Dorsey-Gaines, 1988). An important aspect of literacy to note is that Latino children traverse through their development in essentially the same fashion as their non-Latino counterparts. However, from the research we are becoming acutely aware of just how the peculiarities of the children's social context play upon their growing awareness of literacies. Therefore, it is incumbent upon educators to pay close attention to the different cultural codes (those particular behaviors, gestures, and linguistic signs and symbols) upon which Latino children and families operate.

Latino children, for the most part, are keen observers, needing time for reflection as learning materials and instructions for their use are given. Culturally, they have been socialized in the family to listen attentively and respectfully to adults. Another particular cultural characteristic for Latino children is that parents tend to assist their children in routine grooming, eating, and dressing activities. Parents will dress, bathe, feed, and carry their children until they consider them able to do this on their own. The criteria for when to stop these parenting activities may not meet the same time frame as that for non-Latino children. This does not mean that children who have been assisted in this manner are not competent, but rather, they have had a different parenting experience at home. Other evidence of intervening occurs when older siblings are asked to assist younger children in the acquisition of a skill such as putting on shoes or in the elaboration of a task such as assisting with homework. In addition, older siblings may be asked to help feed, bathe, and dress younger children until it is considered appropriate for the younger children to do so independently. These practices of assisting younger children are socially accepted in many Latino families. Children who are five or six years of age may still be considered in need of assistance. This may contrast with what is considered appropriate child guidance practices. The National Association for the Education of Young Children (NAEYC), in its guidelines for appropriate practice, advocates for developing independence in young children as young as two years of age (Bredekamp, 1987).

Children in cultural settings such as those in Latino families, who depend on older children and their parents for assistance in their developmental trajectory, are seen as different from non-Latino children (Eisner, 1985; Heath, 1983; Wong Fillmore, 1990). Therefore, educators must be sensitive to Latino children's unique and particular needs in the acquisition of literacy skills, which may include direct instruction or assistance. Reading appropriate practice involves teachers critically reflecting on their practices, which may be culturally incongruent with Latino families. One of the most obvious codes to consider is language. For many Latino children, Spanish is the dominant language and one they bring with them into the school setting. While many teachers may not be fluent in Spanish, they should have command of the language in order to help Latino children make the transition from the home to the school. This is one way that teachers can create an environment of care and support (Heath, 1983).

Four- and five-year-olds have developed a keen awareness of print and its uses and to some degree gained the skills necessary to use it (Edelsky, 1991; Eisner, 1985; Ferreiro and Teberosky, 1979; Goodman et al., 1989; Goodman, 1990; Kamii et al., 1991; Manning et al., 1987). If we observe children for any length of time, we will invariably find them scribbling, using a variety of sources such as pens, pencils, markers, and crayons. Outdoors they may use sticks or their fingers in an effort to write. In a kindergarten classroom, the sources for print are plentiful, given the right combination of materials, time, and encouragement necessary for children to practice (see Quintero, Chapter 4). Another important aspect to consider is how the teacher selects the medium of instruction. In a developmentally appropriate classroom, the teacher acts as facilitator and resource for students, rather than as disseminator or transmitter of information. In other words, the work of the teacher is marked by careful planning, observing, and assessing the relative effectiveness of lessons and materials selected. Learning to observe children takes time, skill, and practice. These observation events are ways of "reading" the child. The next section discusses this concept.

"READING" THE CHILD

An essential aspect of teaching, regardless of cultural, social, and linguistic differences, is the skill that teachers must have to know individual children's developmental level and abilities (Anthony et al., 1991). Without this knowledge, teachers cannot adequately plan and effect curriculum that is developmentally appropriate. Whenever possible, it is a definite plus to know the children prior to their coming to kindergarten. This means that teachers need to visit the families and become aware of the community from where the children will come. By gathering information about the children's home, their families, and their communities, teachers are at a great advantage when they start their school year. Another advantage to this kind of activity is that the teachers may develop good rapport with the families and engage them as partners in their children's education. As the year begins, the teacher keeps notes, anecdotes, and other documentation on the children's work, noting progress and growth. This information is a valuable tool to describe children's progress to parents, administrators, and the children themselves. In addition, this type of information gathering is essential in planning the curriculum, for the teacher is acutely aware of each child's development.

To maintain good recordkeeping, the teacher should:

- Develop a file on each child.
- Keep the files within easy access, adding notes that document children's growth, children's own constructions (drawings, print, other scribbles, etc.) and other sources that reflect their progress.
- Review the information in the files periodically, writing down an analysis or profile of children's progress as evidenced through their work and teacher's notes.
- Keep a running list of skills (illustrating growth and development) the child has mastered to be shared with parents.

This type of recordkeeping assists the teacher in the development of lessons, in the search for materials, in the elaboration of "experiences" that are meaningful to her children, and in curriculum building.

Another important area that needs attention is the structuring of the learning environment. The following section discusses the importance of language in its many forms via the environment.

THE LEARNING ENVIRONMENT

A developmentally appropriate environment is key in the promotion of literacy. The most arduous task in designing appropriate curricula is the fostering of good learning environments. Since our goal is to provide effective literacy development opportunities for Latino children, we need to consider the nature of literacy, which is described as follows. Literacy is not *just* learning how to read. Literacy, as educators have come to know it, is a complex, multivaried process. It involves all the senses and is tied to a cultural schemata. It also occurs simultaneously as other processes are beginning to emerge including spoken language, thought and awareness of thought, reading, writing, and fine and gross motor development. Because of all these reasons, the way in which teachers structure learning environments will provide a strong foundation in which literacy can continue to flourish. To be able to model literacy, teachers themselves must be sensitive to the ways they effect reading, writing, and speaking.

For Latino children, this means labeling the environment with Spanish words when their first language is Spanish. This provides for congruency between spoken and written language as children begin to perceive print and its meaning in their environment.

The environment should reflect a rich print source:

- Using either sentence strips, index cards, construction colored paper, or just plain white paper, the furniture should be labeled, probably in Spanish at first and gradually introduce the English.
- Shelving where the materials are stored should have pictures with the words themselves describing the material. This serves both to introduce reading, but also as a management tool.
- Kindergarten appropriate print from the children's own home and community should be reflected in the environment. This promotes an understanding and acceptance of the child's language and culture.

Writing in English and Spanish should be everywhere, whether it be to label the children's work or the teacher's. It should be a natural part of the everyday life of the children. Examples of writing events are capsulized in the following ways:

- Teachers need to write out and post the rules the class has designed as a community of learners, write out routines for toileting and for movement around the different learning centers, and write out other information that communicates important events that occur in the course of a child's time in the classroom.
- Teachers need to explain the reading and writing tasks they are involved in such as: taking attendance, writing out memos to the office, writing notes to send home, taking a lunch count, reading the menu, speaking with children and with colleagues, etc.

A print-rich learning environment is an excellent strategy teachers can use to encourage reading and writing. Modeling from teachers is critical, as is the provision of a wide assortment of materials that encourage children's reading and writing throughout the day.

SPEAKING AND LISTENING

Many opportunities for children to talk throughout the day must be provided, preferably in unstructured time blocks, where children can converse with one another in meaningful ways. Children need to practice their primary language since it will be through language that they will incorporate and make sense of their world and acquire concepts. Hence, it follows that teachers need to speak to and respond to children in that primary language. Learning centers should be designed for children to have easy access to materials and other children. They will construct meaning and understand ideas through their interaction with these materials and with each other. Children have many things to talk about when given the opportunity to express themselves. The creative teacher adds material in the different learning centers that motivates and stimulates questioning and dialogue among the children. She is alert to children's language while engaged in different tasks with them in each of the learning centers. She enhances, expands, and questions children in an effort to foster growth in understanding and skill-building.

Every routine throughout the day should include opportunities for interactions. Examples of these are the handwashing and toileting activities that should include discussions on a number of topics, either selected by the children themselves or planned by the teacher. Regardless of one's cultural traditions, eating is still an important part of our socialization process. Therefore, while at lunch, the teacher also engages in dialogue with children, and children are allowed to talk to one another freely and comfortably. Talk should be a natural part of the everyday life of children and adults in the kindergarten classroom.

An important strategy teachers need to practice is questioning. Through questioning, the teacher elicits the development of critical thinking by helping children coalesce ideas. What follows is an example of a teacher working with very young children. Notice that the questioning is open-ended and encourages divergent thinking that in turn promotes learning.

> At the water table, three children (two boys and a girl) play using water wheels, funnels, jugs, measuring cups, straws. The water has been tinted yellow and has soapy suds. As one child pours water onto the water wheel, a child exclaims "Look, more suds!" The careful teacher comes over and asks: "What made those suds?" One of the children says, "The water wheel!" Another child says, "No, it was my jug!" As the children enter into a dialogue on the phenomena being experienced, the teacher guides, probes, questions and children are allowed to wander into a myriad of possibilities on the events occurring at this water table.

Teachers whose command of Spanish is strong have the ability to pursue conversations with children in these natural settings. The teacher is able to harmoniously interact at a very precise moment when learning can occur. Incidental learning provides for much of what children take into more formalized instructional arenas later on in their school experience. For this reason, it is imperative that teachers be in tune with their children's conversations.

In order to capitalize on the incidental learning that occurs on a regular basis in their classrooms, questioning strategies require that the adult be alert, informed, and knowledgeable about child development. In this manner, the teacher knows when to interfere to create a learning moment, and when to let the event unfold on its own as children make discoveries about people and the world around them. In any event, the teacher, to a great extent, controls the pulse in the classroom.

Other forms of language interaction can occur when the teacher directs the learning. In the following scenario, the teacher has *planned* the event.

Margaret, the teacher, has noticed much discussion among the children about the giant turtles they saw on a field trip to a special zoo exhibit. She decides to bring her three pet turtles from home and let the children experience them during circle time. She brings in the turtles and permits the children to touch and pet them as they gather early in the morning for group time. Margaret always allows children to wander in and warm up to the day at the very beginning of the school day. Children are moving about, talking with one another in small groups, or by themselves in the different learning centers. However, when Margaret begins to answer questions about the turtles, several of the children are drawn to the large carpet area. An exciting and stimulating conversation begins, with teacher and children asking such questions about the turtles as "What do they eat? Why do they hide inside? Why are their shells so hard? Where do they sleep? Are there boy turtles and girl turtles?"

This kind of discussion fuels interest in many of the children and a research project begins: a unit on turtles, reptiles and crustaceans. Discussions/conversations are a wonderful way that children discover their world of people and things. With this rich background, children are better able to link these real things with print. Literacy, seen in this way, helps teachers gain a greater sense of the holistic nature of one's communicative ability. Reading, then, is one of the forms of communication that children learn to understand at a very early age.

READING IN KINDERGARTEN

A reading area should be carefully selected so that it is accessible to every child. The area should be well lit, colorful, and have comfortable chairs or pillows in which children can sit by themselves or with others and enjoy books, audiotapes, and other reading material, such as newspapers, magazines, comic books, maps, and telephone directories.

The selection of the books and the materials for this area should be done in a very careful and thoughtful manner. For the most part, kindergartens have good literature. There is a wide assortment of children's literature in English that provides readers with hours of enjoyment in many areas of interest. Unfortunately, books in Spanish are difficult to obtain, especially those written about Latino children in multiple settings—rural, urban, and from different ethnic identities. Latinos comprise a diverse population of Spanish-speaking people. The teacher must know the population of children in the community and the peculiarities of that variety of Spanish. This knowledge helps the teacher select books and other reading material that celebrate their culture by including familiar ideas and themes with which the children can relate. Teachers should also select books and other printed material with themes and geography that mirror the children's lived experiences.

It is not enough to simply buy or select books that have pictures of brown or black faces, but rather, the story lines and their implications to the unique cultures represented in the classroom must be considered. In addition, teachers should be aware that translated versions of the widely accepted "classics" in children's literature may not adequately reflect the culture, language, and histories of the Latino children being served. For these reasons, the teacher has a challenging task ahead when selecting the reading materials that will comprise her reading corner. Because of the dearth of materials of this type, the creative teacher may have to search for sources outside the classroom and into the community that adequately reflect children's lives. Many Latino communities across the United States already have a viable network of printed material accessible to their members. There are, for instance, "*fotonovelas*," books with pictures and print, similar to comic books. It may be important to scrutinize the content of these "*fotonovelas*" for appropriateness before selecting these for the classroom. Other sources are magazines, newspapers, and books in Spanish being sold in local stores and newspaper vending places. These are rich sources of print to be used in the reading corner. The teacher must promote reading in conjunction with writing (see Espinosa et al., Chapter 6). However, in the daily routines, reading must be central. Storytime with one or two children provides children with opportunities for a teacher to read to the children. We know that when small groups are engaged in reading, much interaction can happen. Children ask questions, remark on the story line, and share personal and familiar experiences with each other and the teacher. This does not happen in large groups where ideas, comments, and questions are swallowed up in the crowd. These kinds of experiences in reading provide an excellent avenue for children to interact with print in supportive ways. They also allow teachers opportunities to assess the knowledge of the children in their care. Through individual and small group interactions, teachers become familiarized with the unique and special capabilities of each child, not to mention the richness in literacy enhancement provided during these short episodes. This type of reading activity is critical in kindergarten. However, it should be mentioned that much reading also occurs in the course of the day as children read the environmental print and their own writing constructions. Reading and writing go hand in hand. For this reason, writing should be on a level of priority with reading. Providing children with writing experiences on a daily basis helps the connection of writing to reading and reading to writing in a natural way. The following discusses how teachers can posture the writing curricula in their classrooms.

WRITING IN KINDERGARTEN

Two areas that should be positioned side by side that complement one another are the writing corner and the art center. Children's beginning experimentation with print is in the art center, although children will experiment with other writing tools as well if given the opportunity. Below is a sample of the kinds of things one must consider when setting up a writing corner as well as an art center. These two areas are mediums for communication that should serve to assist a child in her/his interpretations of ideas in written form.

The Art Center

Children at this age enjoy art media, and their experiences are richly rewarded when there is immediate feedback upon completion of an art project. This area needs to be totally open, free of "patterns" and teacher-directed art projects. The center should be user-friendly with much creativity being encouraged. Children are at a level where they are experimenting with form, texture, color, design, and other aesthetic qualities as they attempt to represent their image of the world. Another consideration is that, at this age, it is the process and not the product that is important. Therefore, children should be allowed to express that natural desire to involve themselves in these sensorial experiences. This period is marked by attempts at the representation of abstract ideas and physical things in the children's realm of experiences. The teacher's role is to label these for the children in a print form. By doing so, the teacher connects the image children represent with another symbolic form, that of writing. Because children are sharing materials and the tables in which they work, they too are sharing ideas and their images of the world, as they negotiate, compromise, and share different points of view. The value of these encounters is immense as children learn to value another's perspective, as well as enriching each other with language. There are similar encounters that children will gain as they use other more "writing-specific" material in the construction of writing. A more deliberate attempt to imitate writing for communication purposes is made by children as they encounter writing sources. The following section suggests how teachers may utilize another learning center in their classrooms to maximize this metacognitive awareness of writing as communication in their children.

The Writing Corner

At the writing corner, many of the children will have access to material from the art center. It is not uncommon for children to move from the art center or other centers with material from those centers as they engage in a different activity. Their thinking is holistic and therefore they tend to move freely from the different areas in the classroom as they elaborate their ideas. Consequently, the creative teacher seizes many opportunities to observe and follow up what the children are constructing. The following are possible suggestions for reading and writing activities.

READING AND WRITING ACTIVITIES

There should be a natural connection for the children between the reading and the writing. For example, children who have been engaged in the drawing of an event should be encouraged to talk about it with the adults and the other children in the group. Similarly, children's stories should be written down, signed, and displayed. Children should be able to share these stories with the class. While the teacher writes down the stories for the children as they complete their drawings, the teacher then consults with them about the accuracy of their stories. The teacher can then have children read their stories back. Children already have a keen sense of the writing that is taking place. However, it is incumbent upon the teacher to encourage literacy in the children. It is important for the children to understand that they need to start writing on their own, at the first opportunity, whether it is only letters that they have configurated or the connection of letters in the beginning of writing "real" words. Teachers can be catalysts to children's attempts at writing. Reading and writing must occur in the child's first language in order that it enhances knowledge construction. Activities must be connected to a natural progression of the curriculum in ways that are concrete and familiar to each student. The exercises must have meaning to the learner, otherwise they become useless and meaningless. The following is a set of activities that will enhance and promote reading and writing in the classroom, throughout the course of the day.

Taking Attendance

The teacher writes out the name of each child (first and last name) on a large poster board, vertically on the left hand side of the board. Across the top, the teacher writes the names of the school days of the week, starting with Monday, ending on Friday. With a marker connected to the poster board the teacher asks each child to write *in* at the beginning of each day, for the entire class to know who is present that day. A child is assigned on a daily basis to fill in those blank spaces next to each child who is absent with the word *out*. In this manner, the teacher has a record of daily class attendance and the children learn each other's names, the days of the week, as well as a ritual process in school. Through modeling, encouragement, and support, children become keenly involved in the reading and writing events that accompany these seemingly mundane tasks. Another writing/reading event, which is carefully planned and carried out, with the children taking charge of their daily tasks, entails a ritual of check and review in the completion of tasks agreed upon at the beginning of the week between learners and teachers.

Completion Tasks

The teacher assigns the children a clipboard at the start of each school year. Children write their name on it. At the start of the week, the teacher passes out a sheet to each child with the different lessons developed for that week. Each child puts this sheet on the clipboard. Across the top are written the names of the days of the school week. For each day, the child will read the lesson and complete it. Pictures are useful to clue children to the writing. After the lesson, the child will write "completed" after it has been done for each day required. At the end of each day or at the end of the week, the child sits with the teacher and goes over each of the lessons giving and receiving feedback. These self-regulating tasks assist children in becoming more independent with regard to their own learning. The next activity allows children to communicate desires in writing to the teacher.

Journals in Kindergarten

The teacher gives each child a spiral notebook or a bound notebook with blank pages inside. Sometime during the day, the child draws or writes something important for the child on that day. At first the teacher leaves the activity relatively open, giving children many opportunities for reflection on their experiences. Later on, the teacher may want them to focus on some experience or concept that was elaborated with the children that week. At first children may need encouragement since the writing experience may be unfamiliar to them. However, eventually the children will begin to have more to say in their journals. Each of the journals should be read on a daily basis and teachers should share their views with the children, asking them questions and giving them feedback on their ideas. Journal writing has been found to be a positive incentive for sharing ideas between teacher and children and among the children as well. Letter writing, which follows, is a similar tool for writing and sharing, providing avenues for the development of social and communication skills.

Writing Letters

Teachers can select another kindergarten classroom in their school or at another school and develop a letter-writing activity among the two kindergarten groups. Children can begin by drawing pictures that represent ideas of common interest. Those children who are already writing can be encouraged to use invented spelling as they construct letters for their pen pals. Children can use envelopes and "make-shift" stamps to be delivered to the kindergarten pen pals, and letters can be collected from the other kindergarten for their group. Teachers can use time during the day when children can read each other's letters/drawings. They can assist and facilitate this process. Other forms of writing are included in the activities that follow. The skills gained are reinforced through the practice of these activities on a regular basis.

Thank-you Notes

After a guest speaker or a field trip, teachers can have the class (individually or in groups) write a letter of thanks to these community people. They should read to the class any note or letter that is sent to their group, whether by the principal, another teacher, parents, or other community people. Children learn the value of writing for special purposes through this kind of activity. The next activity is one that involves a higher level of understanding of symbolic printed material such as maps, directories, recipe books, and how-to manuals.

Planning Trips

In planning field trips, teachers can bring in maps (pictorial ones are best) that give a representation of where the children will be going, labeling the streets, main signposts, and the place itself. Many of these places already have maps that describe their location. In small groups, the teacher goes over the map, identifying the important route that takes them to that site. During the trip, the children can recall different streets they have traversed and how these are in relation to the map activity in class. Through the use of maps and other symbolic material related to topography, children learn the value of these printed materials in contextually related situations. What follows are simple activities that further awareness of resource materials such as cooking experiences and composing a directory.

Cooking Experiences

Parents can send in recipes of dishes cooked at home that may be done in the classroom. With the help of the children, the teacher puts together a recipe book from these and has it bound, then gives each child a copy. During the cooking activities, the teacher or the children select a recipe from the book. Children may then work in small groups to prepare the dish. It may be necessary to rewrite these recipes using pictures (sequentially) to represent the steps in putting together each dish. The teacher may later add more recipes. These activities encourage the sharing of family and cultural backgrounds among the children. Children will be able to understand differences in the types of foods and their preparation in ways that celebrate diversity. The following activity allows for the sharing of personal information and at the same time promotes social interaction among children outside the classroom.

Composing a Directory

Children write their names, addresses, telephone numbers on an index card. The teacher copies each index card, or has the children make enough index cards to go around to each of the children in the group. Using a hole punch, each child punches two to three holes on the left hand side of the index card. In small groups, the teacher gathers the index cards and begins to arrange them alphabetically. By the end of a month, each child should have a set of cards that includes every child. Each child ties her/his cards into a class directory and takes them home giving them the opportunity to call each other throughout the year. Invariably, not all children will have a phone, but each child will learn each other's names and where they live. There is a metacognitive awareness about space and place that is gained as children are able to understand the meaning of directories. They can locate their friends from the lists in these directories and where they live. It helps children see themselves outside of the classroom and in the communities in which they reside. Another important area in literacy development is parental involvement. The following section provides teachers with ideas on incorporating the support of parents in the kindergarten.

PARENTS AS PARTNERS

The creative teacher knows that even with all the effort and work that is undertaken in the classroom, nothing is complete without the professional commitment to work in unison with parents and families. For this reason, from the very beginning, the teacher must build rapport with parents. Once the teacher has achieved a working relationship with parents, their support and advice is invaluable. Understanding the parents' language is critical if one is to achieve the kind of relationship where sharing and dialogue occur. In addition, there needs to be a feeling of openness and care on the part of teachers in order to engage parents. Attitudes are reflected in the way that parents are physically approached, as well as in the way voice tone and language is projected. Teachers need to reflect on knowledge of self in order to identify what strategies they already possess that enables this kind of dialogue or to identify what kinds of strategies they need to acquire in order to achieve it. Primarily, teachers need to ask themselves whether they want parents involved in the curriculum planning of their classrooms. This question is central and at the heart of building partnerships with parents. What follows are suggestions for building these partnerships. It should be noted that the suggestions emphasize two-way communication for curriculum building. In other words, it is not only the teacher sending parents things to do that expand the work in the classroom, but rather it is collaboration between teachers and parents on what is important to be taught and experienced at home and at school. This is a powerful tool and serves to give voice to families in ways that are empowering to them. The following activities are suggestions for the kindergarten. They should be adjusted and modified to fit the style of teacher and students when needed.

"Notitas" to the Home

Teachers can establish a forum for communicating with parents on an ongoing basis. Teachers give children a 3-1/2" x 5" notepad. Children then write their full name on it (front cover). On a regular basis, the teacher writes something about the child to the parent on a notepad and has the child take it home. The parent reads it to the child and then has the child write a response to be read the next day by the teacher. It could be a question about the child, the assignments in school, or a remark on how well the child has mastered certain skills. These *"notitas"* (little notes) serve to maintain a closeness between home and school and add to the attitude of care and concern on the part of the teacher.

Suggestions from Parents

At the beginning of the year, teachers should sit down with their kindergarten parents and families to discuss the agenda for the year. Parents can share their goals and expectations for their children. Teachers share their own, based on their experience and training. Together, teachers and parents can come up with the year-long goals for learning. As teachers write curriculum, they invite parents to give suggestions on materials or experiences that they may have to augment the curriculum, particularly those reflective of their culture. Adding suggestions from parents into the curriculum serves a dual purpose. First, it celebrates the child's home and culture. Second, it affirms the belief that parents have important information to share with the schools.

"Cuentos" as Part of the Curriculum

A vital part of many Latino families is sharing *"cuentos"* with young children. Teachers can request that parents write these *cuentos* down in order to share them with the rest of the class. These *cuentos* serve as excellent reading material for the reading corner. They are real-life experiences of parents and other family members. Some may be folktales that have been handed down from generation to generation. It is equally effective to invite parents to come into the classroom and share the *cuentos* in an oral fashion. This is only one of the ways that parents serve as resources in building curriculum. Below are other examples of parents as resources.

Parents as Resources

Parents can serve as excellent resources in the classroom. Some parents have skills or specialized knowledge that may enhance the curriculum. It is probable that teachers may be able to have parents assist them as partners in the classroom in the different learning areas. Involving parents takes a certain amount of skill and tact. Many Latino parents are not accustomed to involving themselves in school as collaborators in the classroom. For many parents the idea of assisting with teaching may be foreign and perhaps intimidating. To involve parents in the classroom, therefore, it is necessary to have workshops with these parents to orient them with the routines and the culture of the classroom. In addition, these workshops set the tone for the working relationship necessary that teachers need to have with parents. Topics should center around the philosophy of the program, curriculum issues, instructional strategies, and instructional material. These collaborative efforts invite parents to participate and create avenues for communication throughout the school year. The rapport that is developed makes it easier for teachers to gain the partnership status in the education of the child. One of the ways a partnership can succeed is in the continuity of learning that teachers try to achieve through homework.

Homework That Promotes Literacy

While it is not desirable for kindergartners to have homework, this kind of home activity is appropriate for young children in that it gets them involved in projects with their families. For instance, we know from the literature that much of what children know about literacy comes directly from the home. Children's experiences with their own parents, their other relatives, and other people in their lives can help promote literacy. For this reason, the teacher should capture and capitalize on these experiences by providing suggestions for fostering these relationships. Follow-up discussion at home on concepts discussed at school is an example of this. The teacher provides reading material, or discusses with parents the concepts covered in class. Concomitantly, the parents can send notes (on the notepad) of special events that are occurring in the home such as weddings, baptisms, death of pets or relatives, birth of new brothers, sisters, etc. These provide information to the teacher that will be useful in building language topics in the class. If the child has learned a new skill at home, such as plumbing, carpentry, saddling a horse, making "*tortillas*," using a computer, etc., these can be shared with the teacher as the partnership evolves between teachers and parents. Writing about these events is important in that it promotes a complete circle of literacy: from the lived experience, the sharing of the experience, to the drawing of it, and finally, the writing and reading of it. These are all meaningful interactions that occur between parents and their children, as well as between parents and teachers. Another example of partnership-building between home and school is illustrated in this next section.

Writing Letters

Teachers can assist parents in understanding the modeling that is going on at home related to literacy. For instance, the teacher explains the importance of having parents answer children's questions about reading and writing. Examples abound in many homes as parents write relatives living far away, or when they read the newspaper, or follow a recipe, or follow a map, or select items from a menu, etc. One of the roles that teachers play as partners is to help parents understand the direct influence they have on their children's education. Thus, greater communication is enhanced among children, parents, and teachers. Through these types of literacy events, children are socialized into the many ways that families connect with relatives as well as with the broader society. The teacher who engages in this type of teaching/learning is able to help families make these important connections.

SUMMARY

The key to working with Latino families is a deliberate and concerted effort with a desire to involve them in the classroom. A concern for many teachers may be an unfamiliarity with the family's language and culture. This entails, then, a purposeful acquainting of the teacher with the family and the community. It also means that the teacher may have to gain a minimal mastery of Spanish. All families aspire to similar goals for their children. Latino parents are no different. Most parents want what is best for their children and need the teacher's collaboration to achieve their goals. Therefore, if teachers of Latino children and young children in general want to be effective, they need to affirm and validate the culture, language, and traditions of the families with which they work (Garcia and Donato, 1991). There must be a bridge that connects educators to the families they serve in order to promote congruency between what happens at home and what happens in our classrooms. Learning is occurring all the time. However, when the culture of the home comes into direct opposition or clashes with the culture of the school through our classrooms, learning is hampered. Making smooth transitions between the home and the school should be a goal of every kindergarten educator and those in the business of early childhood education. It is imperative that teachers and the educational personnel develop processes in schools to facilitate home and school transitions. These transitions should be easy and painless, regardless of the family's language, race, or culture. This exemplifies the attitude of care and respect that should be present in each classroom throughout every school. It also exemplifies the commitment to the celebration of diversity.

This chapter has made important suggestions for the involvement of parents and families in the teaching/learning processes inherent in schools. With the addition of valuable information about the child, the family, and the community, teachers are able to enhance their own teaching while honoring the children's rich histories. The celebration of diversity implies an attitude of acceptance, inclusion, and respect for difference. It implies a departure from traditional modes of teaching/learning that suggest standardization to a prescribed model of curriculum development. The broad domains in language and literacy development are meant as points of reference for the teacher. While in the classroom, the teacher needs to maintain an alert and intellectual stance that is keenly tied to the understanding of the children in the classroom and their unique characteristics. It should be noted that these activities can be modified, changed, and adapted to the specific needs of the children being served. Ultimately, it is the teacher who makes important choices and decisions about the teaching/learning process.

Equally important is the point that it is the intelligent and critical teacher who makes these choices and decisions based on theories that provide for critical thinking and respect for diversity.

REFERENCES

Anthony, R. J., T. D. Johnson, N. I. Mickelson, and A. Preece. eds. 1991. *Evaluating Literacy: A Perspective for Change.* Portsmouth, NH: Heinemann, pp. 15–24.

Boyarin, J. ed. 1992. *The Ethnography of Reading.* Berkeley, CA: University of California Press, pp. 139–155.

Bredekamp, C. 1987. *Developmentally Appropriate Practice for Children Birth through Eight.* Washington, D.C.: National Association for the Education of Young Children.

De la Luz Reyes, M. 1992. "Challenging Venerable Assumptions: Literacy Instruction for Linguistically Different Students," *Harvard Educational Review,* 62(4):427–446.

Delgado-Gaitan, C. and H. Trueba. 1991. *Crossing Cultural Borders: Education for Immigrant Families in America.* New York, NY: The Falmer Press, pp. 1–38.

Edelsky, C. 1991. *With Literacy and Justice for All: Rethinking the Social in Language and Education.* New York, NY: The Falmer Press, pp. 29–43.

Eisner, E. ed. 1985. *Learning and Teaching the Ways of Knowing.* Washington, D.C.: NEA, pp. 97–115.

Ferdman, B. M., R. M. Weber, and A. G. Ramirez. eds. 1994. *Literacy across Languages and Cultures.* Albany, NY: State University of New York Press, pp. 3–29.

Ferreiro, E. and A. Teberosky. 1979. *Literacy before Schooling.* Portsmouth, NH: Heinemann, pp. 1–26.

Garcia, H. S. and R. Donato. 1991. "Language Minority Parent Involvement within Middle-Class Schooling Boundaries," *Community Education Journal,* 12(9).

Goodman, K. S., Y. M. Goodman, and W. J. Hood. 1989. *The Whole Language Evaluation Book.* Portsmouth, NH: Heinemann.

Goodman, Y. M. ed. 1990. *How Children Construct Literacy: Piagetian Perspectives.* Newark, DE: IRA.

Heath, S. B. 1983. *Ways with Words: Language, Life and Work in Communities and Classrooms.* Cambridge, MA: Cambridge University Press.

Kamii, C., M. Manning, and G. Manning. eds. 1991. *Early Literacy: A Constructivist Foundation for Whole Language.* Washington, D.C.: NEW.

Manning, M. M., G. L. Manning, R. Long, and B. J. Wolfson. 1987. *Reading and Writing in the Primary Grades: A Whole Language View.* Washington, D.C.: NEW Professional Library.

Nieto, S. 1992. *Affirming Diversity: The Sociopolitical Context of Multicultural Education.* White Plains, NY: Longman, pp. 109–120.

Taylor, D. and C. Dorsey-Gaines. 1988. *Growing up Literate: Learning from Inner-City Families.* Portsmouth, NH: Heinemann.

Wong Fillmore, L. 1990. "Families and the Schools," *California Perspectives: An Anthology from the Immigrant Students Project* [not numbered], Winter.

CHAPTER 6

Learning Environments Supportive of Young Latinos

CECILIA ESPINOSA—*Creighton Elementary School District, Phoenix, AZ*
KAREN MOORE—*Creighton Elementary School District, Phoenix, AZ*
IRENE SERNA—*Scottsdale School District*

INTRODUCTION

THREE weeks into the study of the Sonoran Desert, kindergarten children had already examined books and posters, and preserved specimens of animals and plants. They had examined physical characteristics of plants and animals, life cycles, food and shelter, predatory/prey relationships, and how an animal or plant protects itself in its habitat. The next task was for the children to classify their animal as a bird, reptile, mammal, fish, or amphibian based on the information they had collected. A chart developed from a previous study on animals was available as a resource to facilitate the children's identification of the class to which each animal belonged. The group studying scorpions had the following dialogue as they tried to classify their animal by looking at this chart:

Fernando: Cecilia, we don't understand. It doesn't make any sense.

Teacher: I don't know. Let's look at the chart and let's look at some of the books and think about what we know about this animal. Describe the scorpion to me. How are the babies born?

Fernando: They're born out of eggs. And the mother keeps the eggs in her mouth, and spits the babies out of her mouth, and then they're born alive.

Teacher: Does it shed its skin?

Fernando: Oh, it's a reptile.

As they continued to read, discuss, and question their assumptions about the scorpions, the children recalled a prior study of insects. The children began to compare and contrast scorpions to what they already knew about insects, not just reptiles.

107

Teacher: Let's look at the body parts. Does it have an abdomen? A head? A thorax? How many legs does it have?

Joey: They have eight legs.

Fernando: So a scorpion can't be an insect.

Having already compared spiders to insects in previous studies, the children knew that a spider was not an insect because it has eight legs and two main body parts. Fernando was getting very frustrated because he observed that other groups were readily classifying their animals and were able to explain why each fell in a particular category, but his group was struggling. Somehow he knew their task was more complex. At this point his teacher realized that the resources the children were asked to use were limited and had been exhausted, so she and the children decided to explore the books again to find out what kind of animal the scorpion really was.

In rereading the book on scorpions, they discovered that the scorpion was a member of the arachnid family. Fernando cued into the language of the book that said, "Scorpions are relatives of the spiders." From the word "relative," Fernando understood the idea that animals could be classified by specific characteristics. He led the group in continuing to examine how scorpions are related to spiders. What does this example demonstrate about the bilingual classrooms described in this chapter and how children learn and use language?

THEORETICAL FRAMEWORK FOR LANGUAGE AND LITERACY DEVELOPMENT AND LEARNING

This conversation demonstrates how children engage in dialogue with each other and adults as they actively explore and try to make sense of their environment. All children want to make sense of their world. They do this by engaging in inquiry. This inquiry process involves: observing, asking questions, manipulating the physical environment, making predictions, experimenting, making generalizations, hypothesizing, and making mistakes. In reviewing old and new information young children revise their thinking based on what they have discovered. They pose new questions that drive subsequent observations, experimentation, generalization, etc. They process their learning continuously in this cyclical, spiral way (Bredekamp and Rosegrant, 1992; Harlen, 1985; Katz and Chard, 1989; Piaget, 1952, 1954; Vygotsky, 1978, 1986). Their thinking about the world drives their learning and their language acquisition.

Young children use their own language and knowledge that they bring with them from home as their tools for learning in school. Furthermore, language development emanates from children's active engagement in learning about their world rather than as isolated language lessons. First and second language acquisition and literacy development are contextualized within young children's desire to learn about their world as they engage in investigations with others and utilize an inquiry process. In bilingual settings, children are engaged in dialogues in which they have to make sense of what they hear in two languages and express their ideas so that speakers of either language will understand. Their language acquisition is both authentic and purposeful because it stems from their experiences and interactions with others. Thus, children's learning and language acquisition are both social and constructive processes (Bruner, 1983; Chamot and O'Malley, 1989; Edelsky et al., 1991; Goodman, 1986; Halliday, 1975; Heath, 1983; Lindfors, 1987, 1989). These assumptions about language development and learning serve as the foundation for the work children undertake in the two bilingual classrooms described in this chapter.

MACHAN'S BILINGUAL PROGRAM

The classrooms described in this chapter are part of the bilingual program located at Wm. T. Machan Elementary School, a K–5 public elementary school in the Creighton Elementary School District in Phoenix, Arizona. Machan's student population is approximately two thirds Latino; about half of the children are speakers of English as a second language; and over two thirds of the children, according to the Arizona Department of Education criteria, have been designated as "at-risk for school failure."

The bilingual program is based on a whole language philosophy of education. Additionally, in this program Spanish literacy abilities are valued and serve as the foundation for learning and acquiring English literacy abilities. One of the bilingual program's goals is to help all the children become bilingual and biliterate. In order to achieve this, children's first language is used; for some that is Spanish and for others it is English. The children's first language literacy is maintained as they move toward acquiring literacy abilities in the second language, from kindergarten through fifth grade. This program decision was based on research evidence that indicates that first language and literacy abilities support bilingual/biliteracy development and academic achievement (Barrera,

1981; Collier, 1992; Edelsky, 1986; Franklin, 1989; Garcia, 1991; Hudelson, 1981, 1984, 1987, 1989; Lindfors, 1989; Montiel, 1992; Ramirez, 1992; Serna and Hudelson, 1993; Urzúa, 1989).

The children, who implemented the study of the Sonoran Desert described in this chapter, range in age from five to eight years old, spanning kindergarten through second grade. They remained in the same multiage bilingual classrooms for three years. Approximately twenty-five children participated in each of the two classrooms. Each classroom was staffed by one teacher and a teaching assistant. When this particular study of the Sonoran Desert occurred, a student teacher had also been assigned to each classroom. All six teachers were bilingual in Spanish

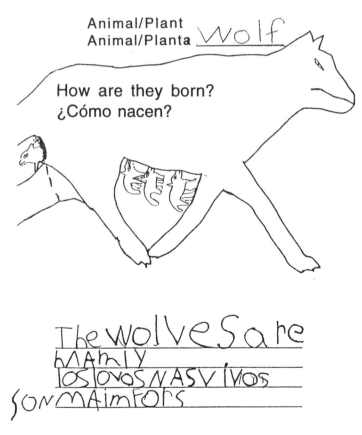

The wolves are mammals.
Los lobos nacen vivos.
Son mamíferos.

FIGURE 1 Method of reproduction for wolves.

Animal/Plant
Animal/Planta Coyote

What kind of animal is your animal? Why?
¿Qué clase de animal es? ¿Por qué?

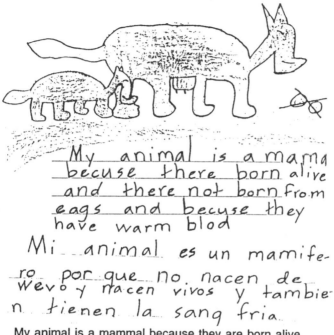

My animal is a mamma becuse there born alive and there not born from eags and becuse they have warm blod

Mi animal es un mamifero por que no nacen de wevo y nacen vivos y tambien tienen la sang fria

My animal is a mammal because they are born alive
and they are not born from eggs and because they
have warm blood.
Mi animal es un mamífero porque no nacen de huevo
y nacen vivos y también (no) tienen la sangre fria.

FIGURE 2 Animal classification for coyotes.

and English. Though the children were officially classified as English or Spanish speakers, there were in reality multiple levels of bilingualism present. Children were encouraged to use their first language and literacy abilities as they made sense of the second language. For example, in Figures 1 and 2, Lenny, José, and Luis wrote their explanations bilingually because they saw their audiences as either Spanish- or English-speaking. These children wrote initially in their first language and then either collaborated with another child to write in the second language or individually translated the text. Their literacy abilities in the first language helped them to write in the second language. Teachers' expectations were that everyone: (1) would attend to and respect each other's first language and cultural background; (2) would be engaged in the process of learning a second language and gaining cross-cultural knowledge; and (3) would be responsible for assuring mutual understanding.

Conducting the Sonoran Desert Study

Rather than implementing district-mandated curriculum or utilizing a textbook-driven curriculum, the study of basic science and social studies concepts is based on children's interests. Utilizing an inquiry process, children are developing a way of thinking about science and social studies from a critical perspective. They are learning to use investigative methods and to think, talk, and write like scientists from various disciplines. By implementing the project approach (Katz and Chard, 1989), children are developing a disposition to continuously inquire and to explore their world in many ways. The following section describes how the children identified a topic for extended inquiry and how teachers supported their investigation of the Sonoran Desert ecosystem and peoples.

Organizing and Managing the Learning Environment to Support Children's Research Projects

To enable children to do their research as independently as possible they must have access to the tools and materials they need. Teachers used the wall space to hang posters with photographs and text from which the children could gain information. For the Sonoran Desert study it made sense to first organize the books and reference materials by the categories of plants, animals, and people. Later, when the small groups were formed and the topics chosen, books that would not be useful were removed from the collection, and books very specific to each topic were sought and added. Whenever possible the teachers used single topic books, i.e., a book only about gila monsters was selected, rather than a more general book about reptiles. When resources were limited and information on a specific topic was difficult to find, the teachers marked specific pages of books with "post-it" notes so that the children could easily find the page or paragraphs pertaining to their topic. The books for each group were bundled together with heavy rubber bands and stored in a box labeled for that group. This decreased the amount of time the children had to spend searching for their books each day. Other resources were brought into the classrooms to facilitate the children's research, the gathering of information. For example, there were many types of cacti for the plant groups to study. Other groups saw videos, interviewed experts, examined scientific diagrams, etc.

As children became more immersed in their study, they began bringing in artifacts and materials that they would use for their projects. Each group chose or was assigned a box, shelf, or closet where materials could be stored as the group members' work progressed. Each group had a folder in which members kept their notes and learning logs. The children referred to their collective notes as they prepared reports and three-dimensional displays.

As their work became more intense, students and teachers negotiated time slots each day when certain groups could work on their projects. The hour a day in the afternoon that had originally been designated as research time was not enough. More than one hour was needed to get children into their groups, to set up their materials, and to engage in their work. Many times an hour had passed just as the children had become intensely involved in their project. Children wanted and needed two or three hours at a time to work, depending on the status of their projects. Thus, the schedule and routine had to change as the children's research projects progressed. Some groups were independent enough to work on their own throughout the day as they chose. For those groups who needed more assistance, a teacher or parent volunteer worked with them for an extended amount of time while the rest of the class went on with the business of the day. Because the teachers and children arranged the schedule to allow for large blocks of time without frequent interruptions or transitions, the children were more self-directed and engaged in their research projects. The atmosphere of the room was also less chaotic because the work in small research groups was staggered throughout the day; this allowed teachers to work more extensively with each group.

Selecting the Topic for Inquiry

Many of the children went on weekend outings to the desert, nearby river, or mountains with their families. Often they would bring artifacts they had collected from their excursions and had stories to tell about what they had seen and what had happened to them. We were able to observe from their comments, journal entries, artwork, and dramatic play both their knowledge and curiosity about the Sonoran Desert. Given that the children had interests in desert animals and plants, and were posing many questions, the teachers decided that a study of the desert was appropriate. The study of the desert was feasible because the natural desert environment was close enough to the metropolitan Phoenix area to provide the children with primary resources (i.e., plants, experts, field trips, animal skeletons, and live animals), not just secondary resources (i.e., books, pictures, and films). Young children need to be able to actively manipulate materials as they investigate. They do not learn enough conceptually from just gathering information by examining print media. Thus, by examining real objects children can begin to generate questions for investigations that guide subsequent activities. Curricular decisions were based on the children's questions and teachers' thinking about the potential for investigations, as described in the following sections.

Brainstorming Ideas and Questions

The teachers began the study of the Sonoran Desert by developing a web as a way of seeing and planning the possibilities for the study (see Figure 3). This provided a mental framework of where the study of the Sonoran Desert might go, suggested resources to be gathered, identified multiple entry points for children and adult participants, and identified possible ways of organizing small and large study groups. The web was not designed to be the lesson plan for the study but was to serve as a resource, to be referred to as teachers, parents, and children began their investigations. By thinking through the possibilities for the Sonoran Desert study in this way, teachers could also be sure to provide for multisensory experiences and to integrate curricular areas.

Determining the Children's Prior Knowledge

The next step was to web with the children to determine their prior knowledge and interests about the topic. As seen in Figure 4, this web visually represented what the children already knew about desert animals and plants. It also displayed what the whole class knew about the Sonoran Desert. The children's web modeled: (1) information organized into categories; (2) interconnections among categories; (3) descriptive language labeling categories; and (4) ways of exploring topics. In their attempts to talk about what they already knew about the Sonoran Desert the children also raised questions. Questions were also generated from the discussions children had about particular topics. Sometimes dis-

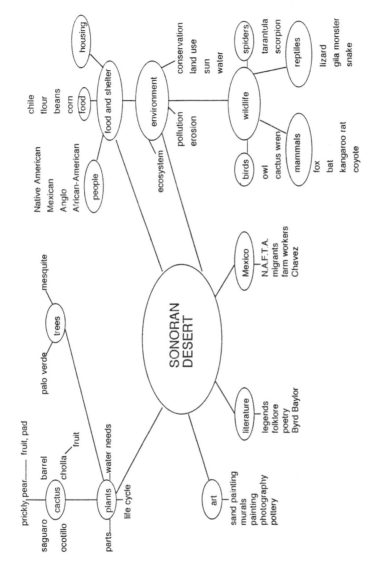

FIGURE 3 Teachers' web for the Sonoran Desert study.

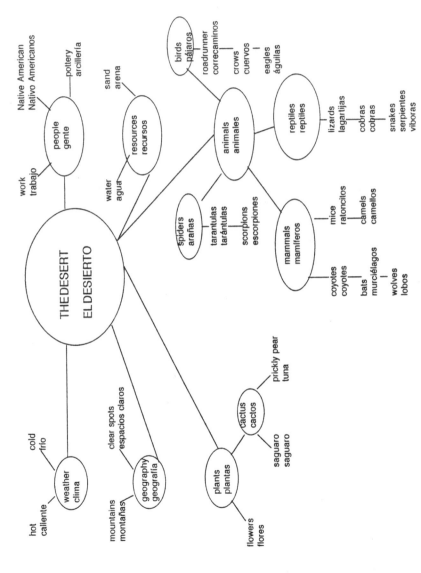

FIGURE 4 Children's web for the Sonoran Desert study.

agreements over information generated questions to be resolved with further investigation. The questions asked by the children at the beginning of the Sonoran Desert study were:

- How many different kinds of animals are there in the desert?
- What are the reasons animals die in the desert?
- Why is the desert so dry? and hot?
- Are all the plants called cactuses?
- ¿Qué clase de animales hay en el desierto? (What kinds of animals are there in the desert?)
- ¿Cómo nacen las plantas del desierto? (How do plants germinate in the desert?)
- ¿Qué clase de flores hay? (What kinds of flowers are there in the desert?)
- How do the animals find water?
- How does the cactus find water?
- How does the cactus grow when it doesn't rain?
- ¿Cúantas personas viven en el desierto? (How many people live in the desert?)
- ¿Porqué se mueren los animales? (Why do the animals die?)
- When a cactus dies how does another one grow?
- How many kinds of cactuses are there?
- Why do they pollute the desert?
- ¿Cómo se sabe cúantos años tienen los cactus? (How do you know how old a cactus is?)
- When two plants are too close to each other how do they survive if there is little water?
- ¿Dónde toman agua las víboras? (Where do snakes drink water?)
- ¿Cómo pican las víboras? (How do snakes bite?)
- ¿Cómo florecen los cactus? (How do cactuses bloom?)
- What happens to the flowers when there is no water?
- ¿Cómo cambian de piel las víboras? (How do snakes shed their skin?)
- ¿Cómo nacen las víboras? (How are snakes born?)
- How does the cactus hold the water for a long time?

This list of questions captured what the whole class wanted to know about the plants and animals that live in the Sonoran Desert and how they survive in such a harsh environment. Thus, the children's web and questions, as well as the teachers' web, guided the investigation of the Sonoran Desert ecosystem.

Gathering Resources

After webbing with the children to determine their knowledge base, teachers spent the next few days gathering resources, contacting experts, planning outings, and informing the parents through a letter about the upcoming study. The letter had a dual purpose. One was to inform the parents about the content of the study and about the activities being planned around it. The other purpose was to encourage the parents to participate by lending their expertise to the classroom and field experiences. For example, during the desert study one parent shared the medicinal uses of the aloe vera plant and another parent cooked *nopales* (prickly pear cactus pods) with the children. While this study focused on the Sonoran Desert, similar environmental studies can be conducted within any natural setting.

Examining Resources

The classrooms were filled with primary resources (natural specimens, experts, models, etc.) and secondary resources (books, posters, film, etc.), and children were given large blocks of time to explore them. Teachers used this time to interact with the children to facilitate exploration and description of artifacts and specimens, to record observations, and to read fiction and nonfiction books aloud with the children in both languages. For instance, the day one parent brought in *nopales* (cactus pods) the teacher and children brainstormed ways to examine the cactus pods. They decided to cut them and study the inside. Children then chose the tools they would need to examine the cactus pods more closely. They gathered knives, scissors, toothpicks, magnifying glasses, and tweezers. Children worked in small groups to examine the cactus and record their findings. As this example illustrates, the teacher's role was not to direct but to become a co-participant in the investigation. Then in a whole group, with the teacher acting as a scribe, the children dictated what they discovered about the prickly pear cactus. Some of their comments were:

- The skin is like tape.
- It has a skin, it is slimy.
- It keeps water in.
- Se siente mojado por dentro. (It feels wet inside.)
- Es resbaloso. (It's slippery, meaning slimy.)
- Tiene un cuerito duro. (It has thick skin.)

- It has a skin, sort of like people's.
- Es grueso para protegerse y para retener el agua. (It is thick for protection and to retain water.)
- Se protegen del calor del sol. (They protect themselves from the heat of the sun.)

The children's comments reflect that they did not just report what the cactus looked like, but that they used higher-level thinking to make inferences about how the thick outer layer serves as protection against the heat of the desert and helps the plant retain water. They implied that its thorns are also protective and that other living things, i.e., people, also have skin that protects them. The dictation did not include direct translations either of Spanish or English, and the teacher wrote the children's language verbatim. The written comments reflected the conversation among the children where they built upon each other's knowledge. The teacher's role was to facilitate the conversation in such a way that the sharing of ideas and knowledge was what was important. Recording children's thinking was the focus, rather than engaging children in the activity of merely creating a language experience chart and/or modeling conventional writing.

It was important to give the children ample time to explore the materials in order for them to consider and prioritize what they might be interested in studying. Once they had time to make their decisions about what they wanted to study, they were more committed to pursuing the topic they had chosen to research.

Organizing Small Groups

The teachers often team taught, thus the children participated in projects which combined both classrooms. In a whole group discussion, children indicated and teachers charted possible topics of study. The whole group negotiated how individual choices could be organized, so that topics could be merged to meet the organizational demands without compromising someone's interest. In other words, when it made sense some topics could be combined to reduce the total number of groups so that time, materials, and adult assistance could be better managed as the study of the Sonoran Desert progressed. For instance, three children individually interested in bats, owls, and night animals worked together. A total of fourteen topics was identified, such as tarantulas, lizards, snakes, foxes, coyotes, scorpions, owls, and saguaros. Based on the children's interest some of the groups included Spanish-speaking, English-speaking, and bilingual children. Likewise, some of the groups were comprised of only Spanish-speaking or English-speaking children. The children's language background was not a factor in how the groups were organized.

Since these were kindergarten through second-grade multiage classrooms, each study group could be led by a second grader. The second graders, who were more literate, responsible, experienced with collaborative group work, and in most cases bilingual and biliterate, facilitated a small group of three or four children. During the study of the Sonoran Desert two teachers, two teaching assistants, and two student teachers worked with the two classrooms of approximately fifty children. Parent volunteers were also recruited. (In addition to parents, teachers could also seek the assistance of middle-grade students as facilitators.) The adults (teachers and parent volunteers) rotated among the groups to facilitate the children's investigations. Leading a group was a responsibility shared by children and adults. At any given time, the majority of the study groups worked independently. No study group was solely directed by an adult throughout the entire study of the Sonoran Desert. Whether an adult participated with a study group or not, children understood that every member was responsible for ensuring that each person in the group felt safe and included, and was able to contribute to the group's success (Peterson, 1992).

Getting Each Group to Generate Questions and List Necessary Resources

Children met in the small groups they had chosen. Each group generated its own questions to begin the research. For example, the following questions were generated by the group studying scorpions:

- How do they get poison?
- How do they lay eggs?
- How do they age?
- How do they find a house?
- Where do they live?
- How do they get teeth?
- Do they have ears?
- How do they get skin?

- How do they grow up?
- How many legs do they have?

The groups then went to the resources the teachers had gathered for them and looked at what was available to get started. Each group informed the teachers of any other resources that were needed, such as getting nonfiction books on a particular topic in Spanish.

Identifying Universal Themes

At this point the teachers met to identify some universal themes that would guide the entire Sonoran Desert study and help each group organize its information. Themes could also be used to make connections to previous and perhaps future studies. The suggested themes for each group to explore included: the physical characteristics of a plant or animal; shelter, food, and water requirements; predator and prey relationships; life cycles; and plant and animal classifications. To help the children begin to observe more closely and to record their observations, one of the teachers demonstrated how she would observe and record the physical characteristics of one of the children in the classroom.

Subsequently, children were encouraged to record information that they found interesting throughout their research. As they worked together daily children were observed talking with each other, sharing information, comparing notes, reading together from books, and translating information as needed. The teachers used this time to conference with each group. They read, rephrased text, facilitated finding other resources, answered questions, and helped the children assess their own work to assure that everyone had contributed information. Although working together in a small group, each individual member was responsible for keeping notes in his/her learning log. The children developed their own diagrams and explained in writing what they had learned about an animal or plant within their small groups. Entries from the children's learning logs, Figures 5–12, illustrate the themes all groups were examining: physical characteristics of the plant or animal; how the plant or animal obtained food and water; how it sought shelter; how it reproduced; predator-prey relationships; how the plant or animal protected itself from predators; the plant or animal's life cycle; and lastly, the plant or animal's classification.

Animal/Plant
Animal/Planta RABBITS

Physical Characteristics
Características Fisicas

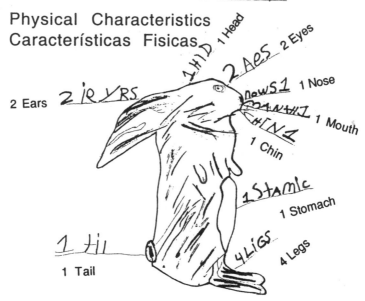

2 Ears
1 Head
2 Eyes
1 Nose
1 Mouth
1 Chin
1 Stomach
4 Legs
1 Tail

FIGURE 5 Physical characteristics of rabbits.

Animal/Plant
Animal/Planta *Fox*

Food/Comida

They eat mice, eggs, fruits, insects, and worms,
and other small animals

Water/Agua

They drink from rivers and lakes and puddles

FIGURE 6 How a fox obtains food and water.

Animal/Plant
Animal/Planta Fox

Shelter/Refugio

they Live in caves.
The Re peRRected By There MoMsDad
And By cLiMing TRees. And BY
TheRe Teeth.

They live in caves.
They're protected by their mom & dad
and by climbing trees. And by their teeth.

FIGURE 7 A fox's shelter.

Animal/Plant
Animal/Planta _T a r o N ĩ u l a_

How are they born?
¿Cómo nacen?

_T h i r B o r N i N e g g s S a k s_

They're born in egg sacks.

FIGURE 8 Method of reproduction for tarantulas.

Animal/Plant
Animal/Planta <u>Fox</u>

Predator/Predador

The predator is dogs and hunters.

Prey/Presa

They eat all kinds of small animals. Like chickens, meat, mice, rabbits, and fruit.

FIGURE 9 A fox's predator/prey relationships.

Animal/Plant
Animal/Planta _cacTos_

How does the animal or plant protect itself?
¿Cómo se protege el animal o la planta?

lo   cacTos   se
Protegenconlas
esPinas.

Los cactos se protegen con las espinas.
(The spines of cactus protect them.)

FIGURE 10 Protective adaptation of a cactus.

Animal/Plant
Animal/Planta *Tecotes* Tecolotes/Owls

Life Cycle
El Ciclo de la Vida

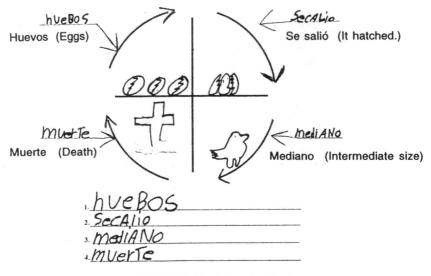

huEBoS

Huevos (Eggs)

SecALio

Se salió (It hatched.)

muerTe

Muerte (Death)

mediANo

Mediano (Intermediate size)

1. *huEBoS*
2. *SecALio*
3. *mediANo*
4. *muerTe*

FIGURE 11 The life cycle of owls.

128

Animal/Plant   Vultures
Animal/Planta Vultures Buitres
                Bultre

What kind of animal is your animal? Why?
¿Qué clase de animal es? ¿Por qué?

Son aves porque tienen alas
y plumas. Y tienen sangre
caliente. Nacen de huevos.

They are birds because they have wings and feathers.
And they are warm-blooded.
They are born from eggs.

FIGURE 12 The animal classifications of vultures.

Developing Reports

Once the notes in learning logs were completed the teachers asked the members of each group to pull their information together to develop one report. At first the children generated lists of facts that were unconnected and unorganized. By reviewing the learning logs the teachers noticed that the children's knowledge about the plant or animal was not lacking; they had understood how the physical characteristics of an animal or plant helped it to adapt to the desert environment. For example, Angelica explained: El saguaro se protege con sus espinas y el saguaro es muy duro. (The saguaro protects itself with its spines and the saguaro's [skin] is very hard.) Thus, they did not organize the information as isolated facts, but related the information. Connecting facts to explain relationships demonstrated a higher level of thinking. The teachers realized that the children were inexperienced in their ability to organize and present the information in a summary report. Moving from stating relationships in the learning logs to writing a report, summarizing how the plant or animal survives in the Sonoran Desert environment, was difficult for the children. They found it very challenging to integrate the factual knowledge in their writing in a way that made sense to them and to the reader. They did not understand the mechanics of writing a coherent report that summarized what they had learned. All of the children's first attempts to write rough drafts were lists of facts. Presenting the information in list form made sense to them. For example, in Jessica's first attempt to summarize the information on foxes, she wrote:

(1) They are born live.
(2) They are warm-blooded.
(3) They live in caves.
(4) They drink from the mom.
(5) They aren't born from eggs.
(6) They aren't reptiles.
(7) They eat fruits.
(8) The predator is dogs and hunters.
(9) They are protected by their teeth.
(10) They eat mice, eggs, and chickens.
(11) They live close to food.
(12) They aren't just brown.

Her list demonstrated that she understood the fox's classification, its predator-prey relationships, how it protects itself, and where it seeks shelter.

Realizing that the children were having difficulty moving from lists of factual information to a summary relating the facts, the teachers returned to reading and talking about how expository texts were written. Teachers observed that some of the children were then verbally able to summarize with great detail their knowledge about their animal or plant. For some children writing a summary was the context for lessons on the mechanics of writing a report. However, students struggled in their efforts to transfer what they knew into a written summary. For example, in her second attempt to write a summary Jessica revised her list, rich with factual information, into a less informative, repetitive, and disjointed approximation of a summary. She embellished the text with language that she thought would make it more interesting to read:

> Although there aren't many foxes left, we'll always seem to like them even when there aren't any which will never happen. What I like about them is that they're nice to some animals and they have babies which will make more foxes. Foxes aren't like most other animals because most people don't like them because they eat their chickens and then the people kill them. But we just think the people just don't think at that time. The foxes protect themselves by their teeth and by climbing.

While the written content lacked clarity the teachers could see that she understood the themes that had been explored. Jessica knew how the fox reproduced, how it protected itself, its predator-prey relationships, and why it is endangered. The teachers thought that her ability to verbally explain her thinking and the depth of her knowledge of this topic would allow her to continue to revise and improve her written summary. They asked Jessica to return to her questions as a way of organizing the information. Jessica could have considered explaining why the foxes are mammals, how they obtain food and water, where they seek shelter, and how they protect themselves. Jessica still needed assistance from a teacher to relate the information by category into separate paragraphs that were logically sequenced.

Nonfiction Literature as a Model for Revising Reports

In order for children to be able to write coherent reports they need more experience with reading and examining expository texts as another genre for their writing. For example, Luis, who was a very fluent reader and writer in both languages, was able to revise and produce a more coherent summary after he read and examined expository texts, which served as models for his writing. Luis explained how the coyote had adapted to the desert environment:

> Los coyotes tienen dientes filosos y no matan a la gente porque le tienen miedo. Hacen una cueva para esconderse de la gente y para que no les de calor. Aunque la gente los mata y nacen más en el desierto porque son muy inteligentes. Los coyote se comen a los ratones, pájaros y a los conejos. Casi no se ven porque tienen la piel como la tierra. Comen fruta.

> [The coyotes have sharp teeth and they do not kill people because they are afraid of them. They make caves to hide from people and so they won't get too hot. Even though the people kill them and more of them are born in the desert because they are very smart (i.e., they are born in remote areas of the desert away from populated cities and that's why more of them are born and why they are smart). Coyotes eat rats, birds, and rabbits. They can hardly be seen because their fur is the same color as the sand. They eat fruit.]

He reported that the coyote is protected by its physical characteristics, sharp teeth, and by the color of its fur, a natural camouflage. He also stated that the coyote seeks shelter in caves to hide and to escape the desert heat. Lastly, the coyote is a predator of small animals, and also eats fruit to obtain nutrient food and water.

Why was Luis able to write a more coherent report than Jessica? Luis was observed reading nonfiction literature quite often, and from these models he was able to construct a report that related physical characteristics and behaviors to the coyote's habitat, which enabled it to survive. Jessica, on the other hand, read mostly fictional and poetic literature and did not have a good sense of what an expository text was like. This was her first experience with report writing and she needed assistance with examining nonfiction literature in order to connect her ideas coherently. To help the children write reports the teachers read aloud and examined more nonfiction literature with the children so that they had models for composing their own expository texts.

Culminating the Sonoran Desert Study with a Multimedia Exhibit

The research phase of the Sonoran Desert study took four weeks. As a culminating activity for reporting their research projects, each group prepared a formal presentation. The purposes for presenting the information more publicly were: (1) for each group to share with the other groups what they had learned, to get a sense of the whole Sonoran Desert study; (2) to share their studies with other classes; and (3) to share with parents what they had been doing. Sharing their work with others through presentations not only provided opportunities for the children to recognize what they had accomplished, but also allowed parents, teachers, and other students to acknowledge and celebrate their learning. The process of developing reports, models, and presentations involved self-assessment, group assessment, and informal assessment by teachers and peers.

As the groups were working on their research projects they began to generate ideas and discuss possible options for how they would present their information. When it was time to prepare for presentations, the groups had already decided how they wanted to proceed. They developed plans for how they would show each animal or plant in its habitat, through the use of posters, dioramas, sculptures, or models. Teachers conferenced with each group to determine if the method for showing the animal or plant in its habitat had been well thought out. For instance, the group studying bats had planned to develop a poster. When they conferred with one of the teachers and looked at the notes describing the animal's habitat, they decided that a two-dimensional poster would not be the most realistic model they could build, since bats live in caves, which would require a three-dimensional construction. The teachers encouraged each group to consider a variety of possibilities in order to select the most realistic depiction. Once each group's plan was ready, members of the groups had to develop a list of materials they needed to construct their projects. With lists in hand, teachers and children gathered the necessary materials to construct their exhibits.

In preparation for the exhibit, the teachers spent the first few days helping the children visualize what the project would look like once completed. They needed to help the children slow down to recognize the steps involved in constructing a poster, diorama, model, or sculpture. Some children could integrate what they knew about scale, size, and perspective, while others were learning about these concepts for the first time. Teachers observed and facilitated the groups' construction of their projects by continuing to emphasize that group members needed to work together and share responsibilities. The teachers also helped children work through the struggles they had in accepting each other's work and opinions. Many times teachers mediated for group members so that all members of the group would continue to work together. The tension for some children was their intense need to have ownership and control over how the project should look, making it difficult for them to accept ideas and work with others. It was a time of stress for the children and teachers as they searched for ways to keep each group intact, and for each group member to feel respected and that his/her contribution was valued.

The teachers tried to schedule at least an hour daily for two weeks to allow the children ample time to complete their projects. At times, those who needed to could work beyond an hour if they could not find a place to stop, while the rest of the class moved on to something else. With two teachers, two teaching assistants, and two student teachers, and occasional parent helpers for fourteen groups, the adults were able to move through the groups at the beginning of the hour to help them get started. Beyond the first fifteen minutes, teachers could concentrate on those groups that needed more help, depending on what the children needed to accomplish that day. Each group was seen by an adult daily during the last two weeks to finalize the projects for exhibition.

The entire Sonoran Desert study had taken six weeks. In the final meetings the groups worked together to design the space for their exhibit, planned, practiced, and revised their presentations. Teachers listened to the groups' plans and oral presentations. They gave feedback to help the groups arrange their exhibits and offered suggestions to improve the organization and clarity of their presentations.

The groups used their summaries to write poster-size reports to supplement their models and oral presentations. The reports were written by group members collaboratively in both languages. The summary written by the group studying coyotes is a good example of a bilingual report:

Los Coyotes

Los coyotes comen fruta conejos y animalitos. Le tienen miedo a la jente y Nacen vivos. Casi no se pueden ver porque tienen la piel como la tierra y son mamifero porque toman leche de su mamá y son como la jente y tienen sagre caliente porque no tienen sagre fria como los reptiles y tienen los dietes grandes y los tienen filosos pero les tienen miedo a la jente y el prededor es la jente.

[Conventional Spanish spellings: Los coyotes comen fruta conejos y animalitos. Le tienen miedo a la gente y nacen vivos. Casi no se pueden ver porque tienen la piel como la tierra y son mamíferos porque toman leche de su mamá y son como la gente y tienen sangre caliente porque no tienen sangre fria como los reptiles y tienen los dientes grandes y los tienen filosos pero les tienen miedo a la gente y el predador es la gente.]

The Coyotes

The coyotes eat frut rabbits & animals. They are afrad of people & they are born alive & You almost cant see deme becuse dey have the skin like the sand & they are mamal becuse the babys drik milk from the mom & they are like people & they have there blood hot becuse they are not reptiles & they have sharp tith but they are scare of people and the preditor is the people. They shut coyotes.

[Conventional English spellings: The coyotes eat fruit rabbits and animals. They are afraid of people and they are born alive and you almost can't see them because they have the skin like the sand and they are mammal because the babies drink milk from the mom and they are like people and they have their blood hot because they are not reptiles and they have sharp teeth but they are scared of people and the predator is the people. They shoot coyotes.]

It should be noted that the Spanish version of this report, which was written first, appears more coherent and contains more conventional forms than the English version, which is the children's second language. The coherence of the English text was dependent upon the children's ability to express their ideas initially in Spanish. This writing sample again demonstrates that writing abilities in Spanish, the children's first language, facilitated their attempts to write in English, their second language. Furthermore, the children in this group were willing to try writing in English because they were able to write in Spanish. Their purpose for writing in both languages was probably due to their desire to have accessible reading material for English and Spanish speakers. These poster-size reports were hung next to or above the corresponding models, to be read by those who toured the exhibits.

The teachers were impressed throughout the study of the Sonoran Desert with how self-directed the children were, especially in the days of preparation for the public presentations. They had learned to divide the work that needed to be done, to delegate and accept responsibility, and to work towards a common goal. Rather than anticipating needs, the teachers increasingly responded to requests made by the children, such as identifying resource people who could provide materials (cardboard boxes, butcher paper, papier-maché, wire, wood, etc.), share ideas, or show examples of models for presenting their projects.

When the actual day came for the children to give their formal presentations in front of an audience, they were very excited and confident. The classrooms had the feel of an exhibition hall, with all the projects displayed throughout and the children standing beside their creations eager to present orally to anyone who approached them. Other classes and community members were invited to tour the exhibits, listen to the presentations, ask questions, and give feedback to the presenters.

As the teachers walked through the rooms they were immersed in the buzz of conversation. One could easily tune into a group's "conversation" and the rest of the noise would disappear. They heard questions and explanations such as: "Mom, do you know why a fox is a mammal?" And the same child explaining, "A fox is a mammal because the babies drink milk from the mother." And a parent asking a child, "What does nocturnal mean?" And that child responding, "Nocturnal means the owl wakes up at night and sleeps during the day." No one child was designated as the sole presenter of a group's project, nor were the sections of a report assigned. What naturally occurred were conversations in which group members took turns sharing what they knew collectively.

To add to the feel of a celebration, teachers and children hosted a reception, complete with authentic southwestern *aperitivos* (appetizers), like *nopalitos con huevos* (scrambled eggs with prickly pear), crackers with prickly pear jelly, *tortillas* and *salsa*, and *tostaditas*. Teachers and children felt a sense of accomplishment and delight.

Assessment

At the time of the celebration and for several days following, teachers could sense how proud the children were of the work they had completed. The children could look back with nostalgia at all the weeks of collaborative work. Children recollected how they simultaneously struggled to make their own contributions and to accept those of others. They explained how they had gathered information, reviewed their notes, generated new questions, searched further to collect additional information, organized the information to describe the themes that were examined, and summarized their findings, which were presented as reports and multimedia projects. Having presented, to several audiences and having received responses from those who heard their presentations, the children were able to reflect and assess how effectively they had displayed and explained what they had learned about a desert animal or plant.

Teachers also met with each child for a final assessment of his/her work. During these conferences children were given opportunities to review and describe their process for creating reports and models from their learning log entries. The teachers noted each child's ability to describe his/her plant or animal and its habitat coherently. Teachers also noted in which language each child wrote, the production of conventional and invented forms, and evidence of editing invented spellings, letter forms, capitalization, punctuation, spacing, grammar, and syntax. The children were also asked to evaluate their own work and the work of the group as a whole. The teachers gave feedback to the children about how they observed their effort and participation in the study. These conferences not only served as a way to assess children's learning and literacy, but also provided opportunities for teachers to evaluate their own work, i.e., planning, gathering of resources, facilitating investigations, responding to children's work, and reflecting on their practice. For instance, they learned that children were having difficulty writing reports because of their lack of experience with reading and writing expository texts. They concluded that in subsequent studies more time would be spent reading expository texts with the children, modeling and discussing report writing, and having the children work through drafts to compose more coherent reports.

At the conclusion of the Sonoran Desert study the children recognized that no matter how much one learns through investigations, there are always more questions that could be pursued, and that with each study one is always constructing meaning and making new connections. Everyone knew that this was a time to celebrate that the desert study had come to some closure, and also recognized that what had been learned would continue to be studied in all its possibilities again and again. Throughout the Sonoran Desert study the teachers had been making connections and noticing possibilities for related projects. For example, in subsequent studies teachers and children examined environmental as well as social issues faced by people living in the southwest region of the United States and Mexico. Specifically they looked at the plight of migrant farm workers, the life and work of Cesar Chavez, and at other issues of human and civil rights. Some social issues were even explored through the music of the singer Tish Hinojosa.

SUMMARY

The teachers involved in the study of the Sonoran Desert were bilingual and biliterate. The type of inquiry described can still be executed even when the teachers do not share the children's language. First, children should be encouraged to use their first language as a means of processing information presented to them in their second language. Working ideas out in the first language will help children express themselves verbally and in written form in English. To do so, however, requires fluency as a reader and writer in the first language. Second, older and more bilingual students or parent volunteers, who speak the child's language, can help the child read and write to gather, record, and report information. These more bilingual and biliterate persons can help young children access and report information in the first language as well as the second language, English. Third, monolingual teachers should not be afraid to let children use their first language as a resource for reading, writing, and as they interact with other second language learners in small groups in the classroom. It is more important for the children to understand what they are learning than for the teacher to understand everything that is being said among children. Teachers need to trust that speaking, reading, and writing in the first language will support learning as well as language and literacy development in English as a second language. As the children reported in this chapter have demonstrated, literacy abilities in the first language facilitate second language learners' understanding of content and acquisition of English literacy abilities.

As stated previously, it is not enough to be knowledgeable about theory, nor is it enough to be creative in planning lessons and to be resourceful in gathering materials. Teachers need to take time to step back, observe, interact, and reflect on their own practice. One's practice, like the children's work, is not linear and does not have an ending point; it continues to evolve and change as one gains a deeper understanding about children and the teaching-learning cycle.

REFERENCES

Barrera, R. B. 1981. "Reading in Spanish: Insights from Children's Miscues," in *Linguistics and Literacy: Learning to Read in Different Languages*, S. J. Hudelson, ed. Washington, D.C.: Center for Applied Linguistics, pp. 1–9.

Bredekamp, S. and T. Rosegrant. 1992. *Reaching Potentials: Appropriate Curriculum and Assessment for Young Children, Vol. 1.* Washington, D.C.: National Association for the Education of Young Children.

Bruner, J. 1983. *Child's Talk: Learning to Use Language.* New York, NY: Norton.

Chamot, A. and J. M. O'Malley. 1989. "The Cognitive Academic Language Learning Approach," in *When They Don't All Speak English: Integrating the ESL Student into the Regular Classroom.*, P. Rigg and V. G. Allen, eds. Urbana, IL: National Council of Teachers of English, pp. 108–125.

Collier, V. 1992. "A Synthesis of Studies Examining Long-Term Language-Minority Student Data on Academic Achievement," *Bilingual Research Journal*, 16(1 & 2):187–212.

Edelsky, C. 1986. *Writing in a Bilingual Program: Había Una Vez.* Norwood, NJ: Ablex.

Edelsky, C., B. Altwerger, and B. Flores. 1991. *Whole Language: What's the Difference?* Portsmouth, NH: Heinemann.

Franklin, E. 1989. "Encouraging and Understanding the Visual and Written Works of Second-language Children," in *When They Don't All Speak English: Integrating the ESL Student into the Regular Classroom*, P. Rigg and V. G. Allen, eds. Urbana, IL: National Council of Teachers of English, pp. 77–95.

Garcia, G. E. 1991. "Factors Influencing the English Reading Test Performance of Spanish-speaking Hispanic Children," *Reading Research Quarterly*, 26(4):371–392.

Goodman, K. 1986. *What's Whole in Whole Language?* Portsmouth, NH: Heinemann.

Halliday, M. A. K. 1975. *Learning How to Mean.* London, England: Edward Arnold.

Harlen, W. 1985. *Teaching and Learning Primary Science.* New York: Teachers College Press.

Heath, S. B. 1983. *Ways with Words: Language, Life and Work in Communities and Classrooms.* New York, NY: Cambridge University Press.

Hudelson, S. J. 1981. "An Investigation of the Oral Reading Behaviors of Native Spanish-speakers Reading in Spanish," in *Linguistics and Literacy: Learning to Read in Different Languages*, S. J. Hudelson, ed. Washington, D.C.: Center for Applied Linguistics, pp. 10–21.

Hudelson, S. J. 1984. "Kanyu Ret and Rayt en Ingles? Children Become Literate in English as a Second Language," *TESOL Quarterly*, 18(2):221–238.

Hudelson, S. J. 1987. "The Role of Native Language Literacy in the Education of Language Minority Children," *Language Arts*, 64(8):827–841.

Hudelson, S. J. 1989. "Teaching English through Content-Area Activities," in *When They Don't All Speak English: Integrating the ESL Student into the Regular Classroom*, P. Rigg and V. G. Allen, eds. Urbana, IL: National Council of Teachers of English, pp. 139–151.

Katz, L. and S. Chard. 1989. *Engaging Children's Minds: The Project Approach.* Norwood, NJ: Ablex Publishing Co.

Lindfors, J. 1987. *Children's Language and Learning.* Second edition. Englewood Cliffs, NJ: Prentice-Hall.

Lindfors, J. 1989. "The Classroom: A Good Environment for Language Learning," in *When They Don't All Speak English: Integrating the ESL Student into the Regular Classroom*, P. Rigg and V. G. Allen, eds. Urbana, IL: National Council of Teachers of English, pp. 39–54.

Montiel, Y. 1992. "Spanish-Speaking Children's Emergent Literacy During First and Second Grades: Three Case Studies," Ph.D. dissertation, Arizona State University.

Peterson, R. 1992. *Life in a Crowded Place: Making a Learning Community.* Portsmouth, NH: Heinemann.

Piaget, J. 1952. *The Origins of Intelligence.* New York: International Universities Press.

Piaget, J. 1954. *Construction of Reality in the Child.* New York, NY: Free Press.

Ramirez, J. D. 1992. "Executive Summary of Volumes I and II of the Final Report: Longitudinal Study of Structured English Immersion Strategy, Early-Exit and Late-Exit Transitional Bilingual Education Programs for Language Minority Children," *Bilingual Research Journal*, 16(1 & 2):1–62.

Serna, I. and S. J. Hudelson. 1993. "Emergent Spanish Literacy in Whole Language Bilingual Classrooms," in *At-risk Students: Portraits, Policies, and Programs*, R.

Donmoyer and R. Kos, eds. Albany, NY: New York State University Press, pp. 291–321.

Urzúa, C. 1989. "I Grow for a Living," in *When They Don't All Speak English: Integrating the ESL Student into Regular Classrooms*, P. Rigg and V. G. Allen, eds. Urbana, IL: National Council of Teachers of English, pp. 15–38.

Vygotsky, L. S. 1978. *Mind in Society: The Development of Higher Mental Processes*. Cambridge, MA: Harvard University Press.

Vygotsky, L. S. 1986. *Thought and Language*. Cambridge, MA: Massachusetts Institute of Technology Press.

PART III

EXEMPLARY PRACTICES FOR LATINOS AT THE ELEMENTARY LEVEL

CHAPTER 7

Developing Language and Literacy in Bilingual Classrooms

JOSEFINA VILLAMIL TINAJERO—*The University of Texas at El Paso*
SANDRA ROLLINS HURLEY—*The University of Texas at El Paso*
ELIZABETH VARELA LOZANO—*The University of Texas at El Paso*

INTRODUCTION

OVER the past two decades literacy and language arts educators have revolutionized the way they think about children's reading and writing development (Goodman 1986; Martinez and Teale, 1993a; Teale and Sulzby, 1989). As a result of new understandings, a learner-centered, holistic perspective on language learning and teaching has emerged (Teale and Martinez, 1988). Educators have become increasingly interested in developing language and literacy skills in an integrated, holistic manner, providing children with numerous opportunities for functional and meaningful experiences with literature. The result is a "new literacy" defined by Willinsky (1990) as "those strategies in the teaching of reading and writing which attempt to shift the control of literacy from the teacher to the students" (p. 8). This new view of language and literacy development includes interactive practices like storybook reading, literature-based instruction using big books and predictable/pattern stories, integrated language arts, journal writing, and cooperative group activities. These practices have had an impact in the language arts curriculum in mainstream classrooms as well as in bilingual classrooms where instruction is provided for Latino students in both Spanish and English.

The instructional practices and strategies discussed in this chapter reflect these and other paradigm shifts in the language arts that provide children with literacy events that are holistic and authentic. That is, they engage children in meaningful uses of written language and promote proficient uses of all language modes. Most of the chapter is devoted to exemplary practices for Latino students in elementary bilingual education classrooms where they receive instruction in both the native language (Spanish) and English as a Second Language (ESL); nevertheless, many of the instructional strategies suggested are equally relevant to mainstream classrooms that also serve large numbers of Latino students.

143

The chapter begins with a discussion of several new perspectives in the teaching of literacy, followed by a rationale for literacy development in the native language. Next is a discussion of exemplary practices derived from a holistic perspective to the teaching of the language arts in both the native language and English. The chapter closes with ways to nurture second language development.

It is important to keep in mind that, ideally, the content and skills presented in the literacy/language arts curriculum in bilingual classrooms match or parallel those being presented at a comparable age and grade level in the mainstream English language arts program. The difference is that in bilingual classrooms, instruction is provided in the native language and English (using ESL methodology). It is also important to keep in mind that many of the strategies and techniques suggested in the chapter for teaching literacy can be applied in both languages.

NEW PERSPECTIVES IN THE TEACHING OF LITERACY/LANGUAGE ARTS

Current understandings of how children learn have had an impact on instruction in the beginnings of reading and writing, known as emergent literacy. Instead of treating skills and objectives (which teachers feel are important to language and literacy development) as discrete entities, these skills are now developed in an integrated, holistic manner through content themes identified as appropriate by teachers (Strickland, 1989). From the beginning of school, children now participate in genuine reading and writing activities in ways that help them not only to be able to read and write but also to want to read and write as they go through life (Martinez and Teale, 1993a). Instructional practices and materials for young children are based on a set of beliefs that according to Martinez and Teale (1993a) are the foundations of emergent literacy: (1) learning to read and write begins very early in life as children participate in activities in the home, community, and school that involve literacy; (2) reading and writing develop concurrently and interrelatedly rather than sequentially; (3) the functions of literacy are a critically important part of learning to read and write; (4) in becoming literate, young children develop knowledge and strategies in many different aspects of reading and writing; and (5) although early literacy learning can be described in terms of generalized benchmarks of progress, children become literate at different rates and take a variety of different paths to literacy.

Literacy Instruction in the First and Second Language

As a result of these new understandings, literacy instruction in both the first language (L1) and the second language (L2) has gone through a paradigm shift in which instruction has shifted (1) from a focus on teaching isolated basic skills in the belief that the accumulation of these skills will result in comprehension, to a focus on teaching the what, how, and when of comprehension through holistic and strategic approaches; (2) from a focus on using reading skills after reading to analyze text to the skills being recast as part of the strategies employed during meaningful reading contexts; (3) from teacher-directed instruction, with the students as passive recipients of knowledge, to instruction involving student-teacher dialogue and interaction with the students actively engaged; (4) from instruction focused on helping students discover the author's meaning in the text to instruction focused on the reader—on his/her constructing meaning by interacting with text; (5) from an emphasis on assessing the products of comprehension (accuracy and correctness being important) to an emphasis on modeling the process of comprehending where risk taking and learning from mistakes are encouraged; and (6) from strategies taught using contrived text and adapted literature to strategies taught using authentic text and original, unadapted literature (Goodman, 1986; Roser and Hoffman, 1993).

Writing Instruction

Similar paradigm shifts have impacted the teaching of writing. Instruction has moved from the use of highly structured exercises to the development of writing skills through rich, exciting, and purposeful writing opportunities in the classroom. These include hands-on activities, creative dramatics and art activities, content area experiences, explorations beyond the classroom, and opportunities to write about personal experiences beyond school (Martinez and Teale, 1993b). Most importantly, writing instruction has become part of the literacy process.

Martinez and Teale (1993b) contend that central to these efforts to ignite children's writing are rich literature experiences that lead to activities such as journal writing. In such literacy-focused environments, children naturally follow a progression from scribbling to writing in both the first and second languages. Text produced by students acquiring English look very much like those produced by young native writers. These texts demonstrate that all young writers make predictions about how the written language works. As their predictions change, their texts change (Hudelson, 1988). As children's language proficiency increases, so do their writing skills. This progression is not always smooth. The writing of students acquiring English often reflects elements from their first language. This is expected and is part of the natural process of acquiring a second language.

The teacher's role in promoting writing is to arrange the environment so that it both supports second language acquisition and motivates students to express themselves through print. Moreover, students need to be engaged in writing activities that allow them the freedom to manipulate and invent meaningful written language. They should also be free to experiment with print and to take risks as they use newly acquired skills. Children develop as writers when they have frequent opportunities to write and when they perceive the content of their writing to be meaningful—that is, when they write for a purpose. Thus, students should have opportunities to write every day about subjects that are real and important to them. Culturally related experiences are often good starting points.

ESL Instruction

In ESL, traditional techniques that focus on discrete units of language that are taught in a structured, sequenced curriculum, with the learner treated as a passive recipient of knowledge, have been replaced with current state-of-the-art approaches that emphasize the participatory nature of language development. These approaches include opportunities for students to create and manipulate language freely and to engage in complex learning and critical thinking activities while learning English. The ESL lesson in this chapter integrates these ideas.

DEVELOPING LITERACY THROUGH THE FIRST LANGUAGE

For students with little or no English proficiency, literacy instruction takes place in the student's primary language. Research has consistently shown that students acquire common underlying literacy skills most efficiently in the primary language and that, once these skills are mastered, the student can transfer those skills quite easily to English (Cummins, 1989; Ramirez et al., 1991). Thus, those who cannot yet read

English can read books in Spanish. Misunderstanding has occurred in the past because some educators believe that diverse languages and bilingual education are obstacles to literacy achievement producing students who are illiterate in two languages. The research literature does not support this myth. In fact, a substantial amount of research has shown that the fastest route to second language literacy is through the first language (Krashen and Biber, 1988). Empirical evidence has shown that children who are dominant in a language other than English acquire academic language and literacy skills rapidly and better in both the native language and English when they attain literacy proficiency in the mother tongue.

Cummins (1989, 1991) has written extensively on the importance of developing children's literacy skills in their mother tongue. Both on psycholinguistic and sociolinguistic grounds, he argues strongly that, overall, nondominant speakers of English do better in school, in both their native language and English, if they are given ample opportunity to attain literacy proficiency through their native language.

Cummins (1989, 1991), Krashen and Biber (1988), and Ramirez et al. (1991) found that literacy instruction in the native language is the most pedagogically sound way to teach students acquiring English about the relationship between meaning and print in both the native language and English. Literacy in the native language has been found to be the most stable predictor of English literacy. In fact, research shows that those students with high levels of literacy proficiency in the L1 perform better on tasks of academic English than do students with low levels of language and literacy proficiency in their native language (Fischer and Cabello, 1978; Lindholm and Zierlein, 1991; Medina and de la Garza, 1989; Snow, 1990). A recent study by Ramirez et al. (1991) concluded that students acquiring English can be provided with substantial amounts of primary language instruction without impeding their acquisition of English language and literacy skills. A major misconception is that teachers waste time by teaching students to read in their native language. However, a number of researchers (Cummins, 1989; Krashen and Biber 1988; Snow, 1990; Verhoeven, 1991) have found that instruction in the students' native language simultaneously promotes the development of literacy skills in both the native language and a second language. Learning to read in the native language is beneficial, not detrimental, because students apply many of the skills and strategies that they acquired in reading in their native language to reading in English. According to Genesee (1979), "There are certain processes that are basic to reading and that once learned can be applied to reading any or almost any language" (p. 74).

Several studies support the view that the processes involved in the reading act operate equally across languages. Barrera (1978), Silva (1979), Eaton (1979), Miramontes and Commins (1989), and Jimenez et al. (1996) have pointed out the parallel between the skills required to read in Spanish and those required to read in English. They found that children who read in their mother tongue (Spanish in each case) are actively involved in a highly selective, multifaceted conceptual process that is identical to the mental process used to read in English. Thus, children who learn to read well in their native language do not have to relearn how to read in English. The skills needed to read well in their native language are also needed to read well in English. If reading skills are required through learning to read in Spanish—the language students speak and understand—these same skills can later be applied to reading in English (Pardo and Tinajero, 1993).

The linguistic interdependence principle, which Cummins describes as the transfer of language knowledge from an individual's L1 to his or her L2, is useful in explaining why young, native speakers of languages other than English perform well in English when they attain literacy proficiency in their mother tongue (Gonzalez, 1989; Krashen and Biber, 1988; Ramirez et al., 1991). Specifically, when these children learn about the intricacies of print relationships through materials that highlight their own language and social reality, the linguistic interdependence principle predicts that they will be able to extend their repertoire of literacy expertise to a range of language and social contexts in their L2 (Pardo and Tinajero, 1993).

EXEMPLARY PRACTICES IN FIRST LANGUAGE LITERACY DEVELOPMENT

The instructional practices discussed in this section are based on an emergent literacy/holistic approach to language. Such an approach is best summarized by Vygotsky (1962) who contends that "the child is the creator of meaning in life largely by using language and this meaning is learned through social interaction" (p. 32). In such classrooms, children take an active part in their own learning, engage in activities they view as meaningful, build on their own understanding and efforts, and partici-pate in collaborative and socially constructed contexts for learning to read, to write, and to share. Teachers surround children with literature; they make literacy a family affair; they integrate and unify the curriculum and they give the children ample opportunities to engage in all of the language arts (Roser et al., 1989).

Literature-based instruction in both the L1 and L2 deals with the use of authentic, original, unadapted literature—poetry, songs, myths, fables, fantasy, folktale, science fiction, mystery, and adventure—as a way of developing the four modes of language—listening, speaking, reading, and writing. It deals with the use of non-fiction as well—biography, information, magazine articles, newspapers—to provide students with rich language-learning experiences. Literature-based instruction focuses on the teaching of skills using an integrated approach that involves students in activities such as story talk and literature study. It includes discussing story events, talking about genre, themes, and style, reading stories aloud, exploring story ideas and concepts, responding to story events, and acting out and role-playing story plots. In literature-based learning, reading strategies are taught in the context of reading for the purpose of constructing meaning. Strategies that are targeted for instruction and practice are driven by the literature and tied to the purposes for reading.

Literacy through Literature in the First Language

What follows is a sample literature-based literacy lesson in the L1 (Spanish), which integrates some of the instructional practices discussed above. For the readership who may not be bilingual, all explanations are translated. The lesson is based on the literature piece "Triste historia del sol con final feliz" (Sad Story of the Sun with Happy Ending) by Elena Climent, the *Cuentamundos Spanish Reading/Language Arts* Series (Tinajero et al., 1993). The theme and literature focus in "Triste historia del sol con final feliz" is "there is strength in numbers." The unusual aspect of this literature selection is that the main character is the sun; and yet, the human characters are the ones who bring about a happy ending by working together.

The following is a summary of the literature selection. One day, the sun rises with less radiance than usual. The consequences could be catastrophic! Without the sun's warmth, the earth would freeze and every living thing on it would die. How should such a crisis be dealt with? People from every corner of the world convene and, after much debate, decide to send a giant balloon to the sun filled with gifts and gestures of love. The night that follows is a nerve-racking vigil. No one sleeps a wink! At last, a new day dawns and, with it, the beaming, radiant face of the sun! In the story, we never find out what made the sun smile again. Each child will interpret it differently, in the same way that each character in the story speculates which particular gift was the one that cheered the sun up. After reading "Triste historia del sol con final feliz," children realize that any problem can be resolved by working together. There is strength in numbers!

Lesson Cycle Using Literature

The lesson is divided into three main parts: (1) prereading (estrategias previas a la lectura); (2) reading and responding to the literature (leer y comentar sobre el cuento); (3) turning back to the literature—literature-based activities and strategies (otra mirada a la literatura—actividades y estrategias basadas en la literatura). The prereading strategies include previewing activities (vistazo preliminar) using the illustrations, the plot, and characters. This first part of the lesson also includes an assessment of prior knowledge and an introduction to the literature piece to create interest in reading and in setting purposes for reading. The prereading phase of the lesson also includes activities for building background (desarrollo de conocimientos básicos) and for preparing children to read the story. In this case, the children discuss "What good is the sun?" Next, the children participate in an experiment and in a variety of activities designed to develop concepts and vocabulary related to the literature selection.

The second part of the lesson has the children reading and responding (leer y comentar sobre el cuento) to questions about the literature selection. It includes the reading of the literature selection using an interactive approach that integrates the development and use of comprehension strategies. This particular lesson has the children analyzing story elements—characters and plot—using the illustrations.

In the third part of the lesson, turning back to the literature (otra mirada a la literatura—actividades y estrategias basadas en la literatura), the children participate in literature through literacy activities for enrichment and extension of concepts and skills beyond the story. They also participate in activities that integrate the language arts and other curriculum areas including art, social studies, and science. They learn and apply a variety of comprehension strategies in which children summarize the story and relate their personal experiences to the literature piece.

Part I: Prereading Activities (Estrategias Previas a la Lectura)

During the prereading phase of the lesson, the children look closely at the illustrations while the teacher reads the text. Next, the children talk about what they see in the illustrations and discuss what they think is happening in the story. The teacher guides children's discussions and thinking with questions such as: ¿Cómo se sienten los personajes? (How do the characters feel?) ¿Por qué se sienten así? (Why do they feel that way?)

To assess children's knowledge of the sun's importance, the teacher then asks children to imagine what the earth would be like if the sun ceased to exist. If children's responses indicate that they do not understand that all living things on earth—plants, animals, even people—need the sun's warmth and light to live, the teacher may choose to conduct the following activities to build these important concepts necessary to understanding the literature selection.

The first activity involves the children in a book talk activity (charla en grupo). To help children become familiar with sun-related concepts, the teacher uses pictures or illustrations in the story to help children understand how the sun helps plants grow. The children then brainstorm (lluvia de ideas) the different ways that the sun affects the earth while the teacher records their suggestions in a word web as follows:

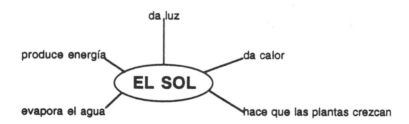

In order to help the children understand the importance of the sun, the children then participate in the following experiment:

- Children find two identical plants.
- They place one plant in a school freezer and leave the other on a windowsill in the classroom.
- After a few hours, children examine the changes in the two plants and check to see if the leaves and branches have wilted.

To build concepts and vocabulary related to the selection, the teacher conducts the following activity to help children understand the descriptions of the sun and the solutions people proposed to solve the problem. The teacher presents the following words and descriptions:

- alumbrar: brillar, llenar de luz (to illuminate)
- consolar: aliviar la tristeza (to console)
- carecer: faltar (to lack, to be in need of)
- impresión: sensación (impression)
- unguento: crema medicinal (ointment)
- remedio: solución; medicina; algo que se hace para reparar un dano (remedy)

The teacher then uses each word in a sentence, in context, which offers clues to its meaning. For example, Hace un mes que no llueve y toda las plantas carecen de agua. (It has not rained for a month and all the plants are in need of water.) Also, the teacher can show children how to use a glossary or a dictionary to find the meaning of new words.

Problem	Solution
Las flores (carecen) de agua.	Las podemos regar.
El Sol no tiene alegría.	Lo podemos (consolar).
La escalera está oscura.	La podemos (alumbrar).
A mi hermano le duele el brazo.	Podemos ofrecerle un (ungüento).
Da la (impresión) de que tu amigo está triste.	Lo podemos alegrar.

The teacher then copies the following chart of problems and solutions on the chalkboard, leaving the spaces in parentheses blank so that children can complete the sentences with words from the story.

Next, the teacher introduces the literature selection. To create interest in reading the story, the children make predictions about what they think will happen in the story. If the children need clues, the teacher mentions some of the most important ideas they discussed in the preview. For example, the children may write: El cuento tiene lugar en la tierra. El Sol está triste. La gente ve que el Sol está llorando. Después de eso mandan un cohete al sol. Un astronauta habla con el Sol y le cuenta algo gracioso. El Sol vuelve a estar contento. (The story takes place on earth. The sun is sad. The people see that the sun is crying. Then they send a rocket to the sun. An astronaut speaks to the sun and tells him a joke. The sun is happy again.)

Working in pairs, the children discuss and record their reasons for wanting to read the story. For example, the children may want to read the story to see if the sun will be happy again or to find out how the people will solve the problem or to find out what the happy ending will be.

Part II: Reading the Selection (Leer el Cuento)

As children read the selection using an interactive approach, the teacher models strategic reading strategies. For example, as the children read the following text the teacher may say:

Pues sí, niñas y niños, (It so happens girls and boys,)
resulta que un día el Sol (that, one day the sun)
salió menos luminoso (wasn't shining as brightly)
que de costumbre. (as usual.)

To model strategic reading strategies the teacher may say: !Fíjense! Parece que el Sol ha salido menos brillante que de costumbre. !Qué triste está! ¿Por qué podrá ser un problema para la gente la tristeza del Sol? Si miran las ilustraciones podrán entender mejor qué pensaba la gente al ver que el Sol no brillaba mucho. Díganme lo que dice el señor que habla aquí . . . ¿Qué piensan las otras personas? ¿Cómo creen que se siente la gente? (Look! It seems like the sun isn't shining as usual today. It must be sad! Why should people worry about the sun's sadness? If you look at the illustrations you can better understand how the people felt when the sun wasn't shining very much. Tell me what the man who is talking here is saying. What do the other people think? How do you think the people feel?) On another page the teacher again models strategic reading by saying: Miren la ilustración en ésta página. Parece que todo el mundo está preocupado. ¿Qué hizo la ilustradora para darnos a entender cómo se siente la gente? (Look at the illustration of this page. It looks as if everyone is upset. How did the artist help us understand the characters' feelings?)

Part III: Turning Back to the Literature
(Otra Mirada a la Literatura)

This part of the lesson has students doing a variety of literature-based activities. The literature selection is then used to teach children critical thinking skills. For example, the teacher has the children notice that only one member of the class panel is discussing the solution to the sun's problem. The teacher explains that on a panel each member presents his or her point of view and everyone tries to come to an agreement. The teacher also mentions the importance of cooperation and then encourages children to form a panel to discuss the following story-related ideas:

- Cada persona tiene algo de valor que puede aportar. (Every person has something worthwhile to contribute.)
- Los aportes de algunas personas pueden ser más importantes que los de otras. (The contributions of some people may be more important than those of others.)

Then the children suggest other situations or problems that the class could address in a panel.

The teacher next uses the literature selection to expand children's vocabulary skills. The teacher explains that in the story they see a great variety of characters and their occupations. To teach terminology related to careers, the teacher invites children to review the story, looking for the different characters' occupations and what each one offers the sun as a gift. The teacher then asks the children to brainstorm a list of other occupations and what the people in those fields could offer to the sun. The teacher records their suggestions in a word web as follows:

The general theme of the sun is then used as a basis for teaching children some interesting facts about the sun. For example:

- Si el globo con las ofrendas pudiera realmente llegar hasta el Sol, tendría que viajar una distancia enorme: 149 millones de km (93 million miles). (If the balloon filled with gifts were really to reach the sun, it would have to travel an enormous distance.
- Si ustedes viajaran al Sol en un auto que viajara a 80 km (50 mi) por hora, tardarían más de 212 años en llegar. (If you could go to the sun in a car that traveled 80 km (50 miles) an hour, it would take more than 212 years to get there.)
- ¿Sabían que nuestro Sol es una estrella? Hay muchas estrellas may-

ores que el Sol, pero están tan lejos que sólo podemos ver un puntito de luz. (Did you know that our sun is a star? There are many stars much bigger than our sun, but they are so far away that all we can see of them is a little dot of light.)
- Un día el Sol sí dejará de brillar de verdad; pero no se preocupen: no empezará a enfriarse hasta dentro de 4,500 millones de años. (One day the sun will actually stop shining; but do not worry; it won't start to cool down for another 4,500 million years.)

The teacher next points out that, in this book, the author is also the illustrator of the story. She explains how Elena Climent used color and details to create the mood for the story. For example, vibrant colors such as yellow evoke happiness. Pale colors, like gray, wilted flowers, and crying show sadness. The children compare illustrations to show the contrast.

In the next activity the children write in their journals where they have the opportunity to express their thoughts, opinions, questions, and concerns about the story. The teacher may prompt children with questions such as:

- ¿Que habrían enviado al Sol? (What would you have sent the sun?)
- ¿Hubo alguna ilustración que les gustó especialmente? (Was there an illustration that you especially liked?)
- ¿En qué pensarán la próxima vez que haga un día lluvioso o nublado? (What will you think about the next time it's cloudy or rainy?)

The teacher can then involve the children in a variety of writing activities related to the story. One activity, for example, involves the children working with a partner to write five questions that they would like to ask the sun. They then exchange their questions with another pair and write the answers to the questions written by the other pair. They later get together with the other pair who gave them the questions and conduct an interview, taking turns being the interviewer and interviewee.

NURTURING SECOND LANGUAGE DEVELOPMENT

Literature is an ideal medium for second language instruction. It captures students' interest, shifting the instructional focus from conscious language learning to the enjoyment of literature. Literature cultivates language and surrounds students with rich, authentic language in meaningful contexts, facilitating natural acquisition of new vocabulary and language patterns. As children listen to rhymes, poems, and patterned/predictable stories they learn new language patterns and idiomatic usages. Children internalize these patterns and use them to express their own thoughts and ideas. Children acquiring English can latch on to the "new" language they have heard, suddenly discovering that their existing vocabulary takes on new dimensions. To support the acquisition of English, teachers surround children with literature. They read a variety of theme-related literature frequently, repeatedly, and with enthusiasm. Reading aloud to children also exposes them to "book language" and demonstrates the communicative nature of written language. It is also important to tell a variety of theme-related folktales, fables, and legends to help familiarize children with their oral heritage.

ESL Approaches, Methods, and Techniques

The following strategies and activities support and promote language and literacy development in the second language by increasing the frequency and variety of interaction among students. Some of these ideas are incorporated in the sample lesson included in this chapter.

- pairing students heterogeneously for activities such as partner "reading" of big books, story retelling, story mapping, illustrating a new ending to a story, or character mapping
- using wordless picture books to elicit language and encourage students to produce longer, more detailed, coherent, and cohesive texts
- incorporating language experience activities to integrate children's ideas, interests, experiences, and natural language
- using shared reading activities to expose children to the written and oral forms of language and to provide them with numerous opportunities to develop listening, speaking, reading, and writing skills
- using songs, poems, stories, games, role-plays, story theater, puppetry tapes, dramatizations, and storytelling activities (which encourage physical, visual, and oral participation) to allow students to use natural English while providing a meaningful, motivating, and enjoyable context for learning
- using authentic literature to nurture children's language development

Selecting ESL Instructional Materials

ESL materials must be carefully selected. Complete, integrated, up-to-date ESL materials that incorporate state-of-the-art methodologies and techniques are best. Look for those that are designed in such a way that they can be used by bilingual, ESL, and mainstream teachers as well as ESL specialists. Special features to look for in selecting these materials include choosing programs that (Tinajero and Schifini, 1997)

- organize the literature and grade-level content into thematic units that teachers can connect to their curriculum
- connect grade-level content with multilevel strategies (to include all students in our diverse classrooms)
- incorporate a wide array of hands-on interactive strategies and include activities designed to build academic language proficiency
- give students access to the core curriculum
- include a simple, effective teaching plan with authentic assessment to organize, manage, and monitor student progress
- incorporate a comprehensive plan for recent immigrants (newcomers)

Literacy through Literature in the L2

An ESL, literature-based literacy lesson would integrate the content areas and some of the instructional practices discussed previously in the lesson done in Spanish. The lesson would be divided into three main parts: (1) language builders—tapping prior knowledge and developing vocabulary; (2) language through literature; (3) language through content. The first part of the lesson would include an assessment of prior knowledge and an introduction to concepts related to the theme of the literature selection. It would also include a variety of activities such as reciting poetry, chants, and singing to develop vocabulary. The second part of the lesson would focus on developing language through the literature selection. This part might include a discussion of the story to help students access the overall idea of the story. Students would also participate in story mapping activities to help them understand the structure and plot of the literature selection. The third part of the lesson would extend children's language proficiency through the content areas. A variety of extension activities related to the literature piece would be implemented to enrich and extend concepts and skills related to the literature piece. For example, the students would participate in journal writing activities, conduct interviews as per the characters in the story, or set up a museum that depicts the theme of the story.

The ESL lesson would parallel the lesson previously presented in Spanish in terms of the variety of activities that are implemented to develop student literacy. The difference in this case would be that students would be developing literacy in the second language, English. In order to facilitate second language development, the teacher would incorporate into the lesson those strategies that provide additional language support for the Potentially English Proficient (PEP) student. These strategies include, for example, use of visuals (graphs, pictures, film, flowcharts, word webs, props, story maps, etc.); paraphrasing to explain/discuss more complex text; use of drama, role-plays, song, and chants; flexible writing/oral activities, which permit the student to respond to language as per his/her level of proficiency; use of cognates; and frequent comprehension checks. In brief, ESL students are not receiving a "watered-down curriculum" but one that is enriched with strategies that assist the student in accessing content through the second language.

SUMMARY

A new view of language and literacy has emerged in the last decade—a view that has revolutionized reading/language arts instruction in mainstream and bilingual classrooms and ESL. This chapter began with a discussion about this new perspective for teaching and learning followed by a discussion on the use of the native language and how it supports optimum literacy development in classrooms for Latino students acquiring English. The chapter also considered what this new perspective implies for teaching language and literacy in both the native language and English (ESL) to young Latino students in bilingual classrooms. Two sample lessons were included: a literacy lesson focusing on the use of the native language in the native language and an ESL lesson that integrates the social studies and science content.

REFERENCES

Barrera, R. B. 1978. "Analysis and Comparison of the First Language and Oral Reading Behavior of Native Spanish Speaking Mexican-American Children." Doctoral Dissertation, The University of Texas at Austin.

California Department of Education. 1990. *Bilingual Education Handbook: Designing Instruction for LEP Students.* Sacramento, CA.

Cummins, J. 1989. *Empowering Minority Students.* Sacramento: California Association for Bilingual Education.

Cummins, J. 1991. "Language Shift and Language Learning in the Transition from Home to School," *Journal of Education,* 173(2):85–97.

Early, M. 1991. "Using Wordless Picture Books to Promote Second Language Learning," *ELT Journal,* 45(3):245–250.

Eaton, J. J. 1979. "A Psycholinguistic Analysis of the Oral Reading Miscues of Selected Field-Dependent and Field-Independent Native Spanish-Speaking Mexican-American First Grade Children." Doctoral Dissertation, The University of Texas at Austin.

Edelsky, C. 1986. *Writing in a Bilingual Program: Había una vez.* Norwood, NJ: Ablex Publishing Corp.

Evans, L. S. 1990. "Storytelling and Oral Language Development in ESL CLassrooms," *TESOL Newsletter.* October, pp. 3, 16, 18, 30.

Fischer, K. and B. Cabello. 1978. *Predicting Student Success Following Transition for Bilingual Programs.* Los Angeles, CA: Center for the Study of Evaluation.

Genesee, F. 1979. "Acquisition of Reading Skills in Immersion Programs," *Foreign Language Annals,* pp. 71–78.

Gonzalez, L. A. 1989. "Native Language Education: The Key to English Literacy Skills," in *Mexican-American Spanish in Its Societal and Cultural Contexts.* D. Bixler-Marquez, G. K. Green, and J. L. Ornstein-Galicia, eds. Rio Grande Series in Language and Linguistics, No. 3, Pan American University at Brownsville, pp. 209–224.

Goodman, Y. 1986. "Children Coming to Know Literacy," in *Emergent Literacy: Writing and Reading.* W H. Teale and E. Sulzby, eds. Norwood, NJ: Ablex, pp. 1–14.

Hudelson, S. 1988. Children's Writing in ESL. ERIC Digest. Washington, D.C.: ERIC Clearinghouse on Language and Linguistics.

Jimenez, R. T., G. E. Garcia, and P. D. Pearson. 1996. "The Reading Strategies of Bilingual Latina/o Students Who Are Successful English Readers: Opportunities and Obstacles," *Reading Research Quarterly,* 31(1):90–109.

Krashen, S. 1985. *Inquiries and Insights.* Hayward, CA: Alemany Press.

Krashen, S. and D. Biber. 1988. *On Course: Bilingual Education's Success in California.* Sacramento, CA: California Association for Bilingual Education.

Lindholm, K. J. and A. Zierlein. 1991. "Bilingual Proficiency as a Bridge to Academic Achievement: Results from Bilingual/Immersion Programs," *Journal of Education,* 173(2):9–20.

Martinez, M. and W. Teale. 1993a. "Emergent Writing," *Teacher's Planning Guide: A New View,* New York, NY: MacMillan/McGraw-Hill Publishing Company.

Martinez, M. and W. Teale. 1993b. "Emerging Readers and Writers," *A New View: A Staff Development Magazine by and for Today's Reading/Language Arts Professionals.* New York, NY: MacMillan/McGraw-Hill Publishing Company, 1:12–13, 16.

Medina, M., Jr. and J. V. de la Garza. 1989. "Bilingual Instruction and Academic Gains of Spanish-Dominant Mexican American Students," *NABE Journal,* 13(2):113–123.

Miramontes, O. and N. I. Commins. 1989, April. "A Study of Oral and Reading Proficiency of Mixed-Dominant Hispanic Bilingual Students." Paper presented at the Annual Convention of the American Educational Research Association, New Orleans, LA.

Pardo, E. B. and J. Tinajero. 1993. "Literacy Instruction through Spanish: Linguistic,

Cultural, and Pedagogical Considerations," in *The Power of Two Languages: Literacy and Biliteracy for Spanish-Speaking Students.* J. V. Tinajero and A. F. Ada, eds. New York: MacMillan/McGraw-Hill Publishing Company, pp. 33–46.

Ramirez, J. D., S. D. Yuen, and E. Ramey, 1991. *Final Report: Longitudinal Study of Structured English Immersion Strategy, Early-Exit and Late-Exit Transitional Bilingual Education Programs for Language Minority Children.* U.S. Department of Education, Contract No. 300-87-0156. San Mateo, CA: Aguirre International.

Roser, N., J. Flood, and D. Lapp. 1989. "Is It Reasonable . . . ? A Photo Essay," in *Emerging Literacy: Young Children Learn to Read and Write.* D. S. Strickland and L. M. Morrow, eds., Newark, NJ: International Reading Association, pp. 80–95.

Roser, N. and J. V. Hoffman. 1993. "Book Talk: Good Discussions about Good Books," *A New View: A Staff Development Magazine by and for Today's Reading/Language Arts Professionals.* New York: MacMillan/McGraw-Hill Publishing Co., 1:8–9.

Silva, A. D. 1979. "Oral Reading Behavior of Spanish-Speaking Children Taught by a Meaning Based Program." Doctoral Dissertation, The University of Texas at Austin.

Snow, C. E. 1990. "Rationales for Native Language Instruction," in *Bilingual Education: Issues and Strategies.* A. M. Padilla, H. H. Fairchild, and D. M. Valadez, eds. Newbury Park, CA: Sage Publications, pp. 60–74.

Strickland, D. S. 1989. "A Model for Change: Framework for an Emergent Literacy Curriculum," in Emerging Literacy: Young Children Learn to Read and Write. D. S. Strickland and L. M. Morrow, eds. Newark, NJ: International Reading Association, pp. 135–146.

Strickland, D. and L. M. Morrow. 1990. "The Daily Journal: Using Language Experience Strategies in an Emergent Literacy Curriculum," *The Reading Teacher.* February.

Teale, W. H. and M. G. Martinez. 1988. "Getting on the Right Road to Reading: Bringing Books and Young Children Together in the Classroom," *Young Children.* November, pp. 10–15.

Teale, W. H. and E. Sulzby. 1989. "Emergent Literacy: New Perspectives," in *Emerging Literacy: Young Children Learn to Read and Write.* D. S. Strickland and L. M. Morrow, eds. Newark, NJ: International Reading Association, pp. 1–15.

Tinajero, J. and S. Long. 1993. *Cuentamundos Teachers' Guide.* New York: MacMillan Publishing Company.

Tinajero, J. and A. Schifini. 1997. *Into English! Teacher's Guide,* Carmel, CA: Hampton Brown Books.

Verhoeven, L. 1991. "Acquisition of Biliteracy," *AILA Review,* 8:61–74.

Vygotsky, L. S. 1962. *Thought and Language.* Translated by E. Hanfmann and G. Vakar. Cambridge, MA: MIT Press.

Willinsky, J. 1990. *The New Literacy: Redefining Reading and Writing in the Schools.* New York: Routledge.

CHAPTER 8

Issues in the Teaching of Math and Science to Latinos

YOLANDA DE LA CRUZ—*Northwestern University*

INTRODUCTION

KNOWLEDGE of mathematics and science is essential for all members of our society. Today, more than ever, our students must be able to understand and apply mathematical and scientific ideas. The achievement levels in these areas among Latino students are cause for concern. There is an ever-growing body of research documenting that the American educational system is differently effective for students depending on their social class, race, ethnicity, language background, gender, and other demographic characteristics (Mullis and Jenkins, 1988; Oakes, 1990; Ogbu and Matute-Bianchi, 1986). This differential effectiveness has been found in mathematics as well as in many other academic subjects among Latino students (Secada, 1992; Secada and De La Cruz, 1996).

This chapter will address how minorities have performed in mathematics and science with respect to the rest of the population. Next, teaching practices that reflect an emphasis on critical thinking, problem solving, and communication will be described. Lastly, changes in roles of teachers, students, and parents will be discussed. Teaching ideas that focus on conceptual teaching methods will be included throughout the chapter.

MATHEMATICS AND SCIENCE ACHIEVEMENT AMONG LATINO STUDENTS

Latinos do not achieve at a level comparable to white children and are underrepresented in mathematics and science careers (Valencia, 1991). Evidence of this underrepresentation is confirmed in the annual analysis of high-school achievement in mathematics and science.

Analysis of the 1990 National Mathematics and Science Achievement results reveals that, by the time U.S. students graduated from high school,

161

they had not mastered advanced skills such as problem solving multistep mathematics problems or analyzing scientific information (Division of Research, Evaluation and Dissemination, Directorate for Education and Human Resources, 1992). Fewer than 10 percent of twelfth-grade students reached an advanced level of science achievement at which they demonstrated the knowledge required to integrate scientific information and draw conclusions. Of this group, fewer than 2 percent were Latino students. Even fewer, less than one percent, achieved a level in mathematics advanced enough to demonstrate the problem-solving skills needed to work in algebra and geometry (Division of Research, Evaluation and Dissemination, Directorate for Education and Human Resources, 1992).

Language and Mathematics

There seems to be some relationship between degree of proficiency in the English language and mathematics achievement. The California Department of Education (1987) found that 42 percent of twelfth-grade Potentially English Proficient (PEP) students—as compared to 13 percent of all other students—failed at least one district mathematics achievement test. Also failing their district mathematics test: 62 percent of PEP students in grades ten and eleven, 45 percent in grades seven through nine, and 28 percent in grades four through six.

Inadequate Student Performance

Mathematics and science education in the United States finds itself in a state of crisis related both to a low rate of student participation and to inadequate student performance in mathematics and science. Data available from national assessments (Dossey et al., 1988; Mullis et al., 1990) indicate that only nine of every hundred graduating high-school students complete four years of college preparatory mathematics or science. For members of ethnic minority groups, the situation is considerably worse (Mullis et al., 1990). In urban schools serving economically disadvantaged communities, four of five students take no mathematics beyond the minimum required for graduation. The related statistics for science do not fare much better. As stated before, large gaps in mathematics and science achievement exist between majority and minority students.

Many worry that the gaps in participation and achievement for minority populations pose a serious threat to the economic and social well-being of the United States. This warning was sounded by the National Research Council in *Everybody Counts* (1989), a report to the nation on the status of mathematics education:

> Because mathematics holds the key to leadership in our information based society, the widening gap between those who are mathematical literate and those who are not coincides, to a frightening degree, with racial and economic categories. We are at risk of becoming a divided nation in which knowledge of mathematics supports a productive, technologically power-ful elite while a dependent, semiliterate majority, disproportionately His-panic and Black, find economic and political power beyond reach. Unless corrected, innumeracy and illiteracy will drive America apart. (p.14)

This report shows the compelling need to improve mathematics for *all* American students, with special attention to students in poor communi-ties, and at all grade levels, since the trajectory for high-school partici-pation and performance in mathematics is set well before the ninth grade (Oakes, 1990).

TEACHING PRACTICES THAT BUILD CONCEPTUAL KNOWLEDGE IN MATH AND SCIENCE

Teaching students to build their conceptual knowledge means teaching in a way that helps them connect new information with things they already know. This requires that opportunities be provided for students to recognize relationships between new information they are learning and ideas that they already understand. Teaching mathematics with the aim of building children's conceptual knowledge can be frustrating and very different for teachers. In 1991, the *Curriculum and Evaluation Standards for School Mathematics* developed by the National Council of Teachers of Mathematics (NCTM) provided teachers with a philoso-phy, direction, and focus for preparing today's youth for our changing world. Young children must, from their earliest school experience, feel a personal success while learning new concepts and making sense of the world.

Teachers face the challenging responsibility of creating long-lasting impressions of mathematics and science that will inspire students to continue building their knowledge. Teachers need to alter the way they think about mathematics and science and their role in teaching them (NCTM, 1991; National Science Committee on Science Education Standards and Assessment, 1994).

Students, through their own experience, come to understand that problem solving is a process, with solutions coming most often as the result of exploring situations, stating and restating questions, and dividing and testing strategies over a period of time. They need to be supported in taking risks to help them realize that it is normal to try ideas and methods that turn out to be unsuccessful in solving the difficult problem, and that by learning from their mistakes, they are able to increase their ability to choose an effective strategy (Urzúa, 1989).

The language of problem solving is the process of thinking—of searching for patterns and regularities. Problem solving is figuring it out—making sense of puzzling or difficult situations. Problem solving does not develop over a few weeks or months. Nor is it a topic that should be taught at a particular grade level. Growth in the ability to solve problems is slow and continuous.

Analytical Reasoning

The development of logical reasoning is closely tied to children's language development. Mathematics and science instruction in the primary grades should help all students—even those who are learning English as a second language—to learn to organize ideas, understand what they are studying, and explain their thinking. Lessons should encourage students to make conjectures, generalizations, and conclusions; to justify them with logical arguments; and to communicate them to others.

Problem-Solving Strategies

Students benefit from learning about problem-solving procedures that are useful in analyzing and solving problems. These procedures are called strategies. Strategies are not specific to particular problems or to particular areas of the mathematics and science curriculum but can be applied alone or in combination with other strategies to solve a wide variety of problems. Students use many strategies intuitively when they solve problems. However, gaining familiarity with a collection of strategies by seeing them modeled, and then by trying to apply them, provides students with useful tools for tackling problems, thus broadening their problem-solving abilities. Problem-solving strategies will be highlighted in the following examples.

Procedures in school mathematics often are rules that prescribe how to manipulate symbols to get correct answers. These are the procedures that students often learn by rote, unconnected to concepts they already understand. Consider an example such as 3 times 8. A drawing of three circles with eight objects inside could connect the written symbols with the quantities. Objects could be used to make three groups of eight. Guessing the answer then checking with objects is another strategy.

Class discussions are useful because they provide opportunities for students to hear other students' points of view and learn of each other's problem-solving strategies. Having a list of problem-solving strategies that emerged during the problem-solving activity posted in the room is helpful. Usually it is possible to solve a particular problem using different strategies or combinations of strategies. The following list presents a partial list of problem-solving strategies:

- Look for a pattern.
- Construct a table.
- Make an organized list.
- Act it out.
- Draw a picture.
- Use objects.
- Guess and check.
- Work backward.
- Write an equation.
- Solve a simpler (or similar) problem.
- Make a model.

Using Problem-Solving Strategies

Problem-solving activities start by stimulating students' thinking about things they already know and expanding those ideas through actual involvement. Following is an example of how the concept of "area" might be taught so that students truly understand what "area" means.

Most textbooks give brief explanations of the concept and a few examples of how to calculate it; then the students apply the concept in a set of exercises. The emphasis is on the *procedure* to calculate the area, and students develop a very narrow understanding of area. "Area is what you get when you multiply the length times the width of a rectangle and say 'square feet' [or inches] afterward." They may get the right answer, but what is their conception of area? Do they really understand what it means?

A meaningful approach would be to start with objects or ideas within students' experiences—for instance, square floor tiles in a rectangular room, such as a classroom. Then a question is posed: "How many tiles would be needed to retile the entire floor?" The task would require students to make a conceptual shift away from one-dimensional, linear measurement to two dimensions, thinking in squares instead of lines (such as inches or feet). They may actually count squares or some might use their knowledge of multiplication to figure out how many tiles would be needed. After this simple introduction, students could be given samples of a new square tile, one foot on each side, made of heavy cardboard. The teacher would then ask, "How many of these new tiles will be needed to retile the classroom floor?" Students could use the cardboard square foot as a measuring device to determine work on the task. The lesson could continue for several days using different materials to measure, such as cardboard boxes of different sizes brought from home.

Next, they would discuss how the linear measure of length and width is related to the number of tiles. The teacher might show them how measuring the length and width of the classroom is easier with a ruler or tape measure. The value of the procedure of length times width will be apparent after these experiences with objects and materials. Students are allowed to make their own discoveries of concepts rather than just learning rules and applying them without really understanding them. This example gives a basic understanding of the concept of area by introducing it in a meaningful way, and by building on students' existing ideas.

Students can be taught to make drawings or models to help them "see" the problem before beginning to solve it. Once they visualize the problem, the path for the solution may become easier. Here is an example of how to use a drawing or model to find a solution: "At a dairy there are both people and cows. There are 22 heads and 64 legs. How many cows are there? How many people are there?" A possible strategy would be to make a drawing or a model of the number of heads. After drawing 22 heads they would draw a pair of legs until there are no legs left. Using the problem-solving strategy of making a model, students would find there are 10 cows and 12 people.

The mathematics reform movement represents using manipulative materials and concrete representations that actively involve the students. Hands-on problem solving that actively involves the students will be much more meaningful to them. They will be able to make connections with prior knowledge. Group discussions will help them hear other points of view that might differ from their own. This is important because they will see that there is not always one correct answer for everything. This is true for science as well.

To know science is not merely to learn the words and their meanings. Science needs to explore different view points that do not have one correct outcome or one correct answer. Math teaching should allow for students to learn more than just the correct answer to math problems. Science teaching should allow students to use the above problem-solving strategies to test principles in new situations that allow them to interpret data intelligently, observe accurately, test hypotheses, evaluate data, and learn what all scientists must know in order to be successful: how to fail and continue trying even after failing.

Students as Language Facilitators

Potentially English Proficient students (PEP) do not have to be separated by language abilities during math and science. They require the same challenges as any other Latino student in order to develop problem-solving strategies (Trueba, 1987). Research has shown that people learn language when they are in real situations where communication is valued. Authentic situations give a purpose for acquisition of another language (Cazden, 1988; Enright and McCloskey, 1985).

PEP students can participate in authentic situations by being placed in small groups where at least one bilingual student can act as an interpreter or language facilitator during some activities. This is not to say that a student's school day should be spent translating. One example of this kind of activity is a box with a hand-sized hole on either end into which interesting objects are placed. The science task would be for two group members to talk to each other about the contents. Other group members could guess, from descriptions, what is in the box. Bilingual students could explain anything not understood by other group members. This situation is one way of actively involving PEP students in interactive participation.

Real-World Connections

Another practice that can bring more active participation is connecting the math and science curriculum to real-world situations. Mathematics and science learning means more to students when it is rooted in real-life problems and situations (Saxe, 1988). With a real-world foundation, students can develop an understanding of mathematics and science as a relevant and purposeful life skill. Mathematics should be an active process in which students explore their own ideas. Isolated facts and skills are not going to be effective if they do not translate into real-life learning. Students should be engaged in their learning and construct their own meaning as they integrate new learning experiences with prior learning. It is important for students to see their everyday actions connected to the school mathematics and science curriculum.

In a possible real-life geometry lesson, the teacher asks each student to name one geometrically-shaped item that we encounter every day—with no repeats. This discussion could be the basis for teaching the geometric shapes. Students could walk around the school to look for geometrical shapes in nature. Then they could draw these shapes and perhaps enter them in their journals. At home, in either English or Spanish, parents could help their children find other shapes in nature and around the house. Drawings of these additional shapes could be added to journals.

In follow-up activities, the children can arrange pieces of yarn on a flannel board to represent polygons and closed curves. Subsequent lessons should focus on the characteristics of geometrical figures, their relationships, their similarities and differences. Three-dimensional figures of the shapes can be taught by having students make their own models.

A real-world science/math unit could involve learning about the human body and having each student make a life-size cutout (Cracchiolo, 1990). The cutout could have life-size organs glued on each time they have studied the functions of that particular organ. Arm and leg measurements could be written on each cutout and later they could be used to find class averages.

Another real-world connection is to involve students in cooking activities after they have learned about fractions. The fraction game, described under Use of Manipulatives in this chapter, could be used as an introduction for understanding the use of measuring cups. Students would have an opportunity to connect the learning of parts in an actual situation. Veitch and Harms (1981) have written a child's cookbook with pictorial single portion recipes that would be useful for PEP students.

CHANGES IN THE TEACHER'S ROLE

The teacher's role is very important in setting the tone for the type of learning environment that includes and values every student. A classroom that values each student will be conducive to learning math and science, fostering positive attitudes, and establishing healthy social interactions. If students are freed from the belief that there is only one right way to go about doing a problem, they will gain more confidence in their own abilities to solve problems. Seeing their teachers trying out different strategies and coming up with new ways to approach problems helps students understand that mathematics is not a "one-way" street they will never find.

Role of Facilitator

The role of the teacher becomes that of the facilitator. This role no longer places the teacher in the center of learning because there are many aspects of the learning process that are opened up for children's input and are not solely under the control of the teacher. Learning to think skillfully, like learning to read fluently, requires substantial time on task. Teachers who want their PEP students to become thinkers must provide them with substantial time on task in higher-order mental functioning. Active participation involves all students. A positive and inclusive classroom atmosphere will be created by valuing the input of all students. PEP students need to interact with others to share their ideas and knowledge. A language facilitator can include them in all discussions.

Mathematics and science instruction that involves students actively and intellectually requires the teacher to assume a different role. Teachers cannot simply tell children how to think or what habits to acquire. Processes and such habits of thought are acquired over time in a community where thinking and such habits are the norm. For students who are learning English as a second language, these types of environments will make learning in English much more meaningful because it is connected to content rather than fragmented and disconnected from everything else in the curriculum.

Students and their worlds must be taken seriously. They must be given many opportunities to think about their conclusions and be allowed to explain how they can come to a particular conclusion and be allowed to explain in any language. Diagrams and visual models can provide a bridge to fill in gaps caused by barriers of language differences. By teaching mathematics and science with reasoning, students will be able to use the ideas they already have to invent new ones and modify old ones.

Many of the changes in the teacher's new role of facilitator make it easier for PEP students to succeed because lessons that emphasize lecture and vocabulary are replaced with student-centered learning involving a high proportion of hands-on experiences. This practice places less of an emphasis on proficiency in English and more of an emphasis on the thought processes.

Changing teacher practices is not easy, but teachers must consider the needs of their students and the importance of their role. The key to growth in teaching is constant, ongoing reflection—about personal beliefs and attitudes, about personal instructional goals, about teaching practices, and about student learning and attitudes.

Use of Manipulatives to Link Understanding

To ensure that instruction is at a level where every student can experience success, manipulatives can be used to demonstrate a concept so that new information can be processed. This also aids comprehension on the part of all students. A check for understanding can be implemented by allowing several students to explain the process or concept in their own words. This can be done in both English and Spanish so that all students benefit from these explanations. This procedure might seem to take up more time but students are learning to cooperate and to share their knowledge while learning different strategies from other students. Students can then work on a group project reinforcing the new concept. Small group processing is important because students might be too shy to speak out during large group discussion. This is especially true for Latino students who might feel less threatened sharing their knowledge in a small group where they have established a close working relationship with some of their peers.

Fraction Game

The fraction game (adapted from Stenmark et al., 1986) is an example of an activity with manipulatives that are easy and inexpensive to make. The main materials needed are strips of 3" by 18" construction paper in five different colors for each student. The teacher could demonstrate the game with larger size strips of paper.

How to make the fraction game:

Take 5 strips of different colors and have students compare strips to be sure they are the same length.

Talk about the fact that the strips each represent *1 WHOLE* and that they will cut them into fractional parts.

Label one strip *1 WHOLE*.

Take another strip and fold carefully in half.

Open and count together.

Label each part 1/2.

Take another strip and fold in half *two* times.

Have students guess how many parts there will be when opened.

Open and cut and count.

Label each part 1/4.

Take another strip and fold in half *three* times.

Have students guess how many parts there will be when opened.

Open and cut and count.

Label each part 1/8.

Take another strip and fold *four* times.

Have students guess how many parts there will be when opened.

Open and cut and count.

Label each part 1/16.

Materials for game: one die labeled: 1/2, 1/4, 1/8, 2/8, 1/16, 2/16.

Start with *1 whole* strip.

Work in pairs and take turns rolling the die.

Take the fraction you roll and place on the *1 whole* strip.

The first player to cover the *1 whole* strip wins.

Manipulatives in the Science Curriculum

Manipulatives in the science curriculum can provide students with opportunities that help children understand concepts of interest. What follows is one example of a science lesson that facilitates children's abilities to focus on beautiful and interesting characteristics of the natural world. This lesson provides more than observation; it provides opportunities for setting up activities that children can really connect with some aspects of their natural world. Some parts of their natural world may be overlooked even though those parts are always there to observe. Sometimes it is possible to be overwhelmed by too many things to observe; sometimes we do not see the forest for the trees. For example, think of children walking on a beach; there is so much to see, so much open space, so many interesting objects, that it is almost too overwhelming to notice anything in detail. Manipulatives such as magnifying tools can help students to observe things more closely. Students could be encouraged to bring in things they collect during family outings and could have family members participate in the hunt for items.

Magnifying Tools

There are both tools and techniques for "tuning in" to the natural world. Tools usually force us to focus on one aspect of the natural world.

A magnifying glass makes us concentrate on a blade of grass, a rock, or a patch of dirt. A magnifying bug container makes us look intensely at one bug. A pair of binoculars lets us look at the bird perched among many birds on the fence. Little magnifying boxes where rocks can be placed permit closer scrutiny and comparison.

Encapsulating Nature

One becomes more in tune with parts of the natural world when they are encapsulated and placed to be watched over time. Small animals in cages, birds, bug houses, ant farms, fish aquariums, and butterfly gardens all permit a closer study of the structure and behavior of animals out of context. They need not involve long-term imprisonment; butterfly gardens, for example, permit children to watch the progression of the butterfly and then release it to the wild. Appropriate uses of bug houses include short-term incarceration for the purpose of studying bugs. By recording nature, sometimes one "sees" things in a photograph, film, or videotape that escapes one's eyes at first glance. Videotaping a field trip to the beach (or a walk around the school) and then using that as a basis for a discussion of all that was seen and done, or using a big poster blowup of a bumblebee can focus attention on details that might otherwise be overlooked.

CHANGES IN THE STUDENTS' ROLE

Teachers need to know how children actually construct knowledge and how they can help children develop this ability. By having students explain the purpose of what they are doing, teachers will be better able to understand their logic and the reasonableness of their solutions (Baroody, 1987).

Teachers should probe children's thinking when they respond to a question. Children are forced to organize their thoughts when asked to explain their thinking. For the students whose first language is other than English, a cultural broker serves as a translator for the rest of the class. In this way, all children can participate in the activity and, at the same time, model for other students that language differences do not have to be an obstacle for these types of activities. All children's comments are validated and their thinking is important for the benefit of everyone. Some questions to use as probes for the students might include: "What do you think of that?" "Why does that make sense?" "How can you prove it?" "Does anyone have a different way to think about the problem?" "Does anyone have a different explanation?"

Students should be encouraged to talk to one another during math and science. Interaction maximizes children's opportunities to talk about their ideas, get feedback for their thinking, and hear others' points of view. The challenge is to have students engage in dialogue and work together to solve problems and bring meaning to ideas in spite of a language difference. This will create further opportunities for students to solve problems and extend the number of interactions and discussions.

Learning Is Different for All Students

Students should not be expected to get the same thing out of the same experience. What students learn from any particular activity depends in large part on their past experiences and level of cognitive development. Cognitive development does not parallel second language learning. By allowing students to share and explain their line of reasoning, they will become aware that there are cognitive differences among the group and that language plays a minor role in this cognitive development.

Understanding is achieved through direct, personal experiences. Students need to validate their own thinking rather than depend on an outside authority to tell them if they are right or wrong. The teacher's role should be that of setting up appropriate situations, asking questions, listening to children, and focusing the attention of the students on important elements.

Teachers should recognize that partially grasped ideas and periods of confusion are a natural part of developing understanding. When a student does not reach the anticipated conclusion, one must resist giving an explanation. Instead, the teacher might try to answer a question or pose a new problem that will give the student the opportunity to contemplate evidence not previously considered.

CHANGES IN THE PARENTS' ROLE

Parents can become partners in their children's education. Teachers can help parents understand and adjust to the new way of teaching mathematics and science by forming a partnership. When talking to parents, teachers need to discuss the following points:

(1) Parents have a great deal of important mathematical and scientific knowledge to share from their everyday experiences.
(2) Children learn best from people who accept and respect them.
(3) Learning is more lasting when it takes place in the context of familiar home experiences.
(4) Children must see that math and science are not just subjects in school, but are used constantly in everyday family life.
(5) The home is an ideal place in which to learn mathematical and scientific problems because the problems encountered there are real, not just textbook examples.

Parents should be encouraged to help in any way they can. Teachers will find that most parents are willing to participate in ways that fit their individual schedules. Some parents might not be able to come during school hours but they can help cut or make materials for classroom use at home. Parents should be encouraged to become active partners in any way they can.

SUMMARY

Virtually every job in today's society requires some knowledge of mathematics and, more importantly, mathematical and scientific thinking. Today's employers are searching for personnel with the ability to solve new and unique problems. Children need to visualize themselves learning to reason and solve problems. All students enter school already understanding a great deal of mathematics and science. This knowledge needs to be integrated into the school curriculum. In order to accomplish this, parents must be made to feel that they are valuable partners in their children's education.

Student populations are becoming more linguistically diverse. Teachers need to problem solve for new ways that can help bridge understanding among students who speak a language other than English. Language can no longer act as a barrier that prevents some students from gaining access to mathematics and science. Educators should not use language as a barrier, if the process of thinking is to be valued. This can certainly be appreciated and developed in any language. We must prepare all children for a future that will require a deeper understanding of math and science in their everyday world.

REFERENCES

Baroody, A. 1987. *Children's Mathematical Thinking.* New York: Teachers College, Columbia University.

California Department of Education. 1987. *Student Achievement in California Schools* (1985–1986 school year). Sacramento: Author.

Cazden, C. 1988. *Classroom Discourse. The Language of Teaching and Learning.* Portsmouth, NH: Heinemann Educational Books, Inc.

Cracchiolo, R. 1990. *Mi Cuerpo.* Huntington Beach, CA: Teacher Created Materials, Inc.

Division of Research, Evaluation and Dissemination, Directorate for Education and Human Resources. 1992. *Indicators of Science and Mathematics Education 1992.* L. E. Suter, ed. Washington, D.C.: National Science Foundation, 1993 (NSF 93–95).

Dossey, J., I. Mullis, M. Lindquist, and D. Chambers. 1988. *The Mathematics Report Card: Are We Measuring Up?* (Report No. 17-M-01). Princeton, NJ: Educational Testing Service.

Enright, D. and M. McCloskey. 1985. "Yes, Talking! Organizing the Classroom to Promote Second Language Acquisition." *TESOL Quarterly* ,19 (3):431–453.

Mullis, I. and L. Jenkins. 1988. *The Science Report Card: Elements of Risk and Recovery.* Princeton, NJ: National Assessment of Educational Progress, Educational Testing Service.

Mullis, I., E. Owen, and G. Phillips. 1990. *Accelerating Academic Achievement: A Summary of Findings from 20 Years of NAEP.* Princeton, NJ: Educational Testing Service.

National Council of Teachers of Mathematics. 1991. *Professional Standards for the Teaching of Mathematics.* Reston, VA: NCTM

National Research Council. 1989. *Everybody Counts: A Report to the Nation on the Future of Mathematics Education.* Washington, D.C.: National Academy Press.

National Science Committee on Science Education Standards and Assessment. 1994, Draft. *National Science Education Standards: An Enhanced Sampler.* Washington, DC: National Research Council.

Oakes, J. 1990. "Opportunities, Achievement, and Choice: Women and Minority Students in Science and Mathematics," in Review of Research in Education, Vol. 16. C. B. Cazden, ed. Washington, D.C.: American Educational Research Association, pp. 153–222.

Ogbu, J. and M. Matute-Bianchi. 1986. "Understanding Sociocultural Factors: Knowledge, Identity, and School Adjustment," in *Beyond Language: Social & Cultural Factors in Schooling Language Minority Students.* Los Angeles, CA: Evaluation, Dissemination and Assessment Center.

Saxe, G. 1988. "Linking Language with Mathematics Achievement: Problems and Prospects," in *Linguistic and Cultural Influences on Learning Mathematics.* R. Cooking and J. Mestre, eds. Hillsdale, NJ: Lawrence Erlbaum Associates, Publishers.

Secada, W. 1992. "Race, Ethnicity, Social Class, Language, and Achievement in Mathematics," in *Handbook on Research on Mathematics Teaching and Learning*. A. Douglas, ed. New York: Macmillan Publishing Co., pp. 623–660.

Secada, W. and Y. De La Cruz. 1996. "Teaching Mathematics for Understanding to Bilingual Students," in *Binational Programs Meeting the Needs of Migrant Students: A Handbook for Teachers and Administrators*. J. Flores, ed. ERIC Clearinghouse on Rural Education and Small Schools.

Stenmark, J., V. Thompson, and R. Cossey. 1986. *Family Math*. Berkeley, CA: Regents, University of California.

Trueba, H. 1987. "Organizing Classroom Instruction in Specific Sociocultural Contexts: Teaching Mexican Youth to Write in English," in *Becoming Literate in English as a Second Language: Advances in Research and Theory*. S. Goldman and H. Trueba, eds. Norwood, New Jersey: Ablex.

Urzúa, C. 1989. "I Grow for a Living," in *When They Don't All Speak English. Integrating the ESL Student into the Regular Classroom*. P. Rigg and V. Allen, eds. Urbana, IL: National Council of Teachers of English.

Valencia, R. 1991. "The Plight of Chicano Students: An Overview of Schooling Conditions and Outcomes," in *Chicano School Failure and Success: Research and Policy Agenda for the 1990s*. R. Valencia, ed. London: Falmer Press, pp. 3–26.

Veitch, B. and T. Harms. 1981. *Cook and Learn*. Menlo Park, California: Addison-Wesley Publishing Company.

CHAPTER 9

Standardized Testing of Latino Students:
A Legacy in Need of Reform

JOZI DE LEÓN—*New Mexico State University*
LINDA J. HOLMAN—*El Paso Independent School District*

INTRODUCTION

ISSUES concerning the uses and abuses of standardized tests with Latino students have been much debated in educational literature (Kretschmer, 1991). This chapter does not intend to revisit those issues, but rather to focus on central points of concern educational administrators and policymakers need to take into account in establishing more equitable practices.

A historical perspective is presented in an attempt to examine where educators have been, where we are now, and where we need to move in the future. Issues in understanding some of the limitations of standardized tests with Latino students are discussed only as they relate to tests that are typically used for decision-making purposes. Assessment issues are examined and have not been restricted to those only relevant to special education placement. Testing as it relates to all forms of decision making is discussed. Finally, the authors provide recommendations for more responsible practices.

HISTORICAL PERSPECTIVES

Concerns about the assessment of Latino students first were noticed during the 1960s. During the Civil Rights Movement, previously "undeserving" citizens voiced their rights to equal opportunity in all sectors of life, including education. There were concerns that Latino and other minority students' needs were not being well-addressed in the educational system. Valencia and Aburto (1991) report that channeling Latino students into "slower ability tracks" and "low-grade vocational education curricula" on the basis of performance on group administered intelligence tests actually dates back to the 1920s and 1930s. It was also

177

not uncommon to find Latino students referred to "development centers" for the mentally retarded if scores on IQ tests were 70 or below. By the 1960s placement of Latino and other minority students into remedial, low-ability tracking programs or special education programs, through the use of standardized ability tests, seemed to be the order of the day. These programs influenced the pace and the type of instruction minority students received and contributed to differences in educational opportunity (Armour-Thomas, 1992; Valencia and Aburto, 1991).

Rueda and Mercer (1985) reported that, although Latino students comprised less than 10 percent of the school population, they constituted 32 percent of the students identified as mentally retarded. Additionally, for over 62 percent of these students, the only symptom of mental deficiency was low IQ test scores. Their study provided the impetus for further investigation into Latino and other minority student overrepresentation in special education and failure in schools. These studies also led to litigation on behalf of students who had been wronged by the system. *Arreola v. Board of Education Unified School District* challenged the placement process. *Covarrubias v. San Diego* also dealt with placement procedures and the consent of parents prior to placement. *Diana v. California State Board of Education* and *Larry P. v. Riles* most directly challenged the misuse of tests in the special education placement process. The use of certain tests was challenged, as was inappropriate administration of tests to students whose primary language was not English. These two cases brought landmark decisions that provided for distinct procedural changes in identification and placement of Latino students. The underlying premise was that access to equal educational opportunity and the elimination of unfair identification and placement practices for low-ability, remedial, and special education programs would solve some of the problems for Latino students in the schools.

In 1970 the Office of Civil Rights issued a memorandum to school districts. It was presented after much documentation and research on how schools were failing minority students. The memorandum was an attempt to enforce action against discriminatory practices leading to segregation or denial of equal access to the full benefits of an educational program to minority children. Gerry (1973) states the following about the mandates addressed in the memorandum:

> School districts must adapt their educational approach so that the culture, language, and learning styles of all children in the school (including but not limited to those of the Anglo children) are accepted and valued. As a result, minority children are not penalized for cultural and linguistic

differences, nor are they asked to bear the unfair burden of conforming to a school culture by the abandonment of their own. (p. 308)

According to Oakland and Laosa (1976), the Civil Rights Act of 1964 and the Fourteenth Amendment address protection under the law against discriminatory practices resulting from disproportionate representation of minority children in low-ability tracking or special education classes, especially since such placement can limit the educational experience. Such legislative and constitutional protection remains in place to date. With the existence of a historical legacy of denial of equal access due to the use of standardized ability testing and placement decisions for Latino and other minority students, one would assume that many of the issues that emerged in the 1960s would now merely be historical fact. One would assume that we would have learned from past mistakes.

Present day consequences of testing with Latino students are best examined by analyzing reports on representation of these students in special education programs. Placement into other types of remedial or low-ability tracking programs is difficult to analyze due to lack of documentation. Recent reports indicate that Latino and other minority students continue to represent disproportionate numbers in categories of disability (Harry, 1994; Ortiz and Yates, 1983; Tucker, 1980) and are underrepresented as gifted (Harry, 1994; McIntosh, 1995). African Americans, Hispanics, and Native Americans are underrepresented in gifted programs by 30–70 percent (Richert, 1987). The primary disability categories overrepresented have now changed from "mentally retarded" in the 1960s and 1970s to "learning disabilities" (Ortiz and Yates, 1983; Tucker, 1980).

In addition to testing of minority students and special education placement, Latino students continue to score lower than other groups on standardized tests that assess competence at all levels (Valencia and Aburto, 1991). The fact remains that appropriate assessment of Latino students continues to be a critical issue.

ISSUES IN THE ASSESSMENT OF LATINO STUDENTS

Central to the problem is Latino and other minority students' performance on standardized tests. Generally, between an 11 to 22 point difference is reported in favor of majority children compared to minority children on certain measures of ability (Palomares, cited in DeBlassie,

1980; Sattler, 1988). The point difference explains the overrepresentation of Latino students in low-ability classes and their inability to meet criteria for placement in programs for the gifted.

Problems with the assessment of these students have been reported in a number of studies and books across three decades (Baca and Cervantes, 1989; Cummins, 1984; DeBlassie, 1980; Johnson, 1979; Oakland, 1973; Oakland and Matuszek, 1976; Samuda; 1975; Sattler, 1988; Valdés and Figueroa, 1994). The problems associated with differences in performance are very complex, and while notions of bias have been debated for decades, the fact remains that Latino students may come out on the losing end educationally. The literature has not led to definitive answers and has too often focused on the problems. In this chapter the authors present some of the main issues in arriving at possible solutions.

Underlying Belief That Latino Students Are Inferior

No one would readily admit to a belief that Latino and other minority students are inherently inferior. Yet, such theories have been espoused in the past (Jensen, 1969), and in the present have received such national attention that they merit consideration as an issue.

Theories espoused by Jensen (1969) bluntly declare that some minorities, as a group, are intellectually inferior to whites. In addition, they attribute social pathologies such as poverty, welfare dependency, illegitimacy, and crime to low IQ. These theorists do not take into account the test construction and norming, as well as factors such as the level of education of the child's parents, family income, family size, and other sociocultural factors, in examining differences in minority student performance on standardized tests (Gould, 1981, 1995; Grissmer et al., 1994).

What does this mean to educators and how does it translate into an educational environment? In the past, the disproportionate placement of minority students in low-ability classes and special education, and the lack of questioning about such practices, has stemmed from a premise that those students belonged in such programs due to their intellectual inferiority. Today, overrepresentation of Latino and other minority students in special education and placement in low-ability tracking programs continues. With the lack of widespread concern about high Latino drop-out rates and overrepresentation in previously mentioned programs, we can only assume that notions of minority student inferiority still prevail.

When students score low on tests, the scores are taken at face value and are interpreted as valid indicators of ability. External factors influencing performance are seldom part of the analysis. When large numbers of Latino and other minority students score low on certain tests, a more subjective examination of student performance needs to take place in determining the validity of the test with those students. It is important to determine whether the test is identifying a deficit in a group of students requiring some form of intervention, or whether the test itself is biased and invalid for that group. A blanket acceptance of the test as valid, despite its overidentification of Latino students as low functioning, may reinforce underlying beliefs by practitioners that a group of students is indeed inferior. The following describes problems with different types of tests when used with Latino students.

Limitations of Standardized Instruments

The majority of standardized tests administered to students can be categorized as either norm-referenced or criterion-referenced. When administered in a standardized format, both utilize uniform procedures for administration and scoring and indicate a student's strengths and weaknesses related to specified subject matter. Both may be "normed" according to a larger student population. One primary difference between the two tests lies in the interpretation of test results.

Norm-Referenced Tests

A norm-referenced test compares individual student performance with that of other students taking the test, usually in the form of standard scores, grade equivalent scores, age equivalent scores, or normal curve equivalents. Norm-referenced tests are designed to evaluate the performance of a particular student in comparison to a national norm or standard (Hieronymus and Hoover, 1986; Overton, 1992). Norm-referenced tests have historically underestimated the abilities of culturally diverse students. Explanations that have been offered include inequities in educational opportunities and resources, problems related to test bias and test validity (American Association of University Women Educational Foundation, 1992), and inappropriate testing of young culturally and linguistically diverse children or those not yet proficient in English. Norm-referenced instruments require the understanding and use of certain language patterns and vocabulary. Often students who have acquired

English as a second language may not yet have acquired such language skills. According to Valdés and Figueroa (1994) norm-referenced tests, especially those assessing intelligence and achievement, present specific problems of language and cultural bias to bilingual children.

Another concern expressed about norm-referenced tests is the inadequate representation of certain culturally and linguistically diverse groups in the norming sample (Sattler, 1988). While most testing companies have been especially sensitive to this issue and have attempted to include norming groups that are representative of the population, some problems still persist. For example, the Stanford-Binet, fourth edition, a commonly used standardized measure of intelligence, includes a disproportionately high percentage of individuals from middle- to upper-middle-class status. Such a norming sample greatly impacts the appropriateness of the test with individuals from lower socio-economic groups. In addition, the test is considered one of the most verbally loaded intelligence instruments, thereby influencing its effectiveness with linguistically diverse groups whose English language skills are not yet developed or who may be less verbal (De León, 1995).

Yet another criticism of norm-referenced tests is the underlying assumption that American society is homogeneous. Comparing all individuals with a single norming group in a pluralistic society in which each cultural group may have its own very distinct norm is considered ludicrous (Valdés and Figueroa, 1994; Watson et al., 1981).

Criterion-Referenced Tests

In contrast, criterion-referenced tests, which compare a child's performance with mastery of a specific criteria or skill, have been touted as less discriminatory because the use of these instruments involves identifying skills children are expected to achieve and assessing them to determine if the skills are present or not. Despite the differences in their use and interpretation, they have not escaped criticism. A major criticism is their format, which may be limiting for students with less test-taking experience and different educational or experiential backgrounds. Multiple-choice items, close-ended formats, and formal rules for determining the meaning of the responses may affect performance and/or interpretation of results (Smith et al., 1989). These tests also require examinees to understand specialized test terminology (Durán, 1989). Therefore, criterion-referenced tests may present many of the same problems as norm-referenced tests for minority students and children from low socio-economic backgrounds. They do not automatically counter discriminatory aspects of norm-referenced measures, such as wording or content (Bailey and Harbin, 1980).

Additional problems are inherent in criterion-referenced testing. They include: (a) selecting and defending the ideas and abilities to be tested; (b) defining the level of test performance that indicates mastery of an objective; and (c) reporting only two levels (mastery and non-mastery) of achievement that may exist at various mastery points (Ebel, 1975). Ultimately, criterion-referenced tests are neither language- nor culture-free and can therefore present as many problems in performance for culturally and linguistically diverse students.

High-Stakes Testing

While mention has been previously made of testing of Latino students and its resultant overrepresentation in special education and underidentification as gifted, there are other testing outcomes that impact Latino children. High-stakes testing is mandated standardized testing that is used to make inferences, decisions, or evaluations of people or schools relative to some domain. Results can be linked directly to sanctions or important rewards or recognition of students, teachers, school districts, or institutions. Examples of such sanctions and rewards include teacher certification, high-school graduation, class assignments, allocation of funds, merit pay, and accreditation of a school or school district (Smith et al., 1989). Although high-stakes tests purport to measure progress toward desirable educational goals, their present use has serious implications for Latino and other minority students. Students who may be presumed to bring down scores and performance evaluations of classrooms or institutions may become ostracized and undesirable. An unintentional push to failure and dropping out may occur as a consequence. In some cases, a teacher who is talented in working with Latino or other students who demonstrate lower achievement levels may not wish to work with such students if merit pay is contingent on high-stakes test performance. Ultimately, serving students who most need help may be at issue when high-stakes testing is a driving force.

These problems have been identified at the national level as well. In a 1978 report to the U.S. Assistant Secretary of Education, the Committee on Testing and Basic Skills of the National Academy of Education stated their belief "that any setting of state-wide minimum competency standards . . . is basically unworkable, exceeds the present measurement arts of the teaching profession, and will certainly create more social problems than it can conceivably solve" (cited in Jaeger, 1989, p. 491). Selection of a passing score is an arbitrary judgment; and if there is not a demonstrated relationship between the passing score and its associated standard of performance, the validity of test score results is very much in question (Kane, 1994).

The emotional impact of high-stakes testing in English for some immigrant high-school students acquiring English as a second language is evident in many U.S.-Mexico border areas. Currently in Texas, students are given a maximum three-year exemption from testing in English, and all students must pass a high-stakes exit-level exam in English to graduate from high school, regardless of their length of time in the United States. One high-school senior, Maria V., who had recently exited the bilingual education program, had classroom grades placing her in the top two percent of her graduating class. Maria left the school in tears, never to return, when she was informed by her high-school counselor that she had not passed the reading portion of the test and, thus, would not be allowed to graduate with her class later that month (K. Korn, Districtwide Test Coordinator, Research & Evaluation, El Paso Independent School District, personal communication, October 10, 1994). Maria's younger sister, having the advantage of living additional years in the United States prior to the end of her high-school career, successfully passed the test (A. Woo, Counselor, Bowie High School, El Paso Independent School District, personal communication, April 3, 1995). Testing of second language learners before they have acquired the English language skills to handle the test is both inappropriate, unethical, and potentially dangerous for individual students. The long-term effects of such testing on students' self-esteem and the high probability that it will lead to erroneous decisions and placements based on the results suggests that school administrators and policymakers should abandon such practices.

Principals and other educational practitioners can reduce the negative impact of high-stakes tests for culturally and linguistically diverse children by:

(1) Understanding the limitations of the different forms of standardized tests
(2) Ensuring appropriate use of test results to the extent possible

(3) Actively educating policymakers regarding the fallacy of implementing a unidimensional measure to evaluate a multidimensional educational experience

(4) Ensuring that Latinos, other minority students, and students from low socio-economic backgrounds do not get unfairly penalized by high-stakes testing

(5) Ensuring that teachers working with lower performing students do not get unfairly penalized

Only through the incorporation of these practices can a more responsible use of high-stakes testing be accomplished. The ultimate question school administrators and policymakers need to ask themselves is what is the intent of such testing practices. Is it to better educational practice and/or offer more educational opportunities for everyone or is it to sift out some of the student population thereby condemning them to less education and a life of reduced opportunity?

Language as a Primary Influencing Factor in Test Performance

Language as a major influencing factor in Latino test performance must be taken into account with most Latino students. Language bias is seen as real for those individuals who have been exposed to Spanish even though they may appear to be fluent in English. Language bias can exist but is not exclusive to the use of regionalism or dialects. Latino student performance can be affected by language bias when subtle differences in English language proficiency, due to Spanish interference or the manner in which English was acquired as a second language, affect the ability to understand or articulate responses. In Spanish, adjectives generally follow nouns while in English, nouns generally follow adjectives or are located opposite a passive verb form. Such structures may affect the performance of bilingual Latino students in testing situations.

The style of writing used in standardized tests also plays a factor in minority students' test performance. Elaborate, stylized English used in most testing situations may prevent the accurate measurement of achievement, ability, or skills of Latino, African American, or other students who use nonstandard English vernaculars (Medina and Neill, 1990). For instance, a study of first-grade bilingual Latino students found substantial differences in performance on problem solving due to the semantic structures of stated problems (Secada, 1991). Such findings point to the possibility of underestimation of knowledge and strengths culturally and linguistically diverse children possess when tests are used as the sole or primary indicators of ability.

Assessing language proficiency prior to an evaluation becomes a very important part of any assessment. Without such an assessment it would be difficult to interpret test scores of Latino students who come from linguistically diverse backgrounds (De León, 1990).

Cummins (1984) contends that there is a definite connection between academic achievement and levels of language proficiency. His theoretical framework conceptualizes two levels of language proficiency. One is the Context-embedded Basic Interpersonal Communication Skills (BICS) level of proficiency that allows individuals to gain meaning and understanding of language from "paralinguistic and situational cues." The Context-embedded level of communication includes typical everyday conversation that is used outside the classroom. The second level of language proficiency is the Context-reduced Cognitive Academic Language Proficiency (CALP) level that involves the type of language skills that would be needed to interact with text or oral cognitively- demanding tasks. Some students who appear to be fluent in English may only have conversational skills, and consequently their performance on tests may be hampered when they cannot perform on tasks requiring Cognitive Academic Language Proficiency. Cummins (1984) contends that the incongruency in language skills students possess and the linguistic demands of certain tests leads to erroneous judgments about student ability. He also views this misinterpretation as one of the major causes of overrepresentation of linguistically diverse students in special education and the labeling of minority students as underachievers. In order to figure out whether test results mean anything for students who have acquired English as a second language, it is important to consider whether they have the level of language proficiency necessary to effectively understand and respond to test items. Not only should language dominance be of concern, but language proficiency in both languages is also important. In assessing language proficiency it is important to determine the level of language proficiency within an academic context.

The building of academic language does not happen automatically. It requires a concerted and deliberate effort by the teacher to ensure that language that will enable learning is incorporated. Often students do not get instruction that builds such skills. These students not only perform poorly in the classroom, but they may also perform poorly on all tests. While they may look disabled according to test scores, they cannot truly be considered disabled. A disability is something a student is typically born with. It does not go away. Students whose academic language skills are limited can appear disabled on tests but proper intervention and a curriculum that focuses on the building of CALP and higher-level thinking skills in the second language can remedy the situation.

Inherent in the administration of any test with Latino students is the understanding that for students who have been exposed to a language other than English or who speak a dialect of English, "every test administered in English becomes, in part, a language or literacy test" (American Educational Research Association, American Psychological Association, and National Council on Measurement in Education, 1985, p. 73). In other words, if an individual is not proficient in the language in which he or she is tested, we cannot truly assess what that individual knows. Therefore, all tests, unless they measure actual task performance, are first a test of language and only secondarily a test of skill or knowledge.

One assumption of many educators is that in testing mathematics skills, language is not as important. They believe that mathematics possesses a universal language of its own that can be taught effectively through the use of rote computation, culturally unbiased numerals, and mathematical symbols. In reality, in assessing mathematical skills, problems arise for potentially English proficient students in the form of language skills and understanding English language syntax (Mather and Chiodo, 1994). Cantini and Tremblay (1979) found that successful mathematics performance required language skills two years ahead of the student's current grade level. Additionally, second language learners unable to adequately manipulate English syntax, prepositions, and semantics may wrongly interpret the language pattern in determining operational order (Richard-Amato and Snow, 1992). The understanding of logical connectors was found by Dawes (1983) to be the one variable differentiating between students who demonstrated successful mathematical reasoning and those who did not. Cognitive Academic Language Proficiency, or the lack thereof, impacts the test performance of potentially English proficient students in the area of mathematics as surely as in language arts. The effect of language background in testing situations may be especially acute for Latino children from homes in which little English is spoken. Verbal tests normally used to measure academic and general aptitude may not accurately assess aptitude in minority youth, as correlations between verbal and performance tasks are likely to be highest in those persons who have had the greatest opportunity to maximally develop traditional verbal skills (Johnson, 1979).

MULTIDIMENSIONAL vs. UNIDIMENSIONAL ASSESSMENT

Testing refers to the use of standardized instruments exclusively in determining functioning levels of students. Assessment requires that the examiner(s) gather all the necessary data to determine the nature of the problem. It involves the use of standardized tests and informal assessment instruments. Assessment evaluates the student, the environment, and significant interactors in the process of learning and analyzes data within the context of culture, language, home and community environments, experiential background, opportunity to learn, and past educational programs. Often, those trained to perform evaluations on students or interpret test data for decision making adhere to a philosophical stance that testing is the most valid form of determining the ability of all students including minority students. In their development they have been trained to use, administer, and interpret test scores as if all students were the same and arrived at the testing situation with similar experiences. These individuals do Latinos and other minority students a disservice. Cummins (1984) postulates that examiners implementing more traditional methods of administering and interpreting test data with minority students has led to the overrepresentation of these students as learning disabled and the labeling of minority students as low achievers. He mentions some underlying presumptions that examiners have which impact test administration and interpretation. These include but are not limited to:

(1) Interpretation of a significant difference between verbal and performance IQs as an indication of a learning disability or communication disorder
(2) Determining that fluency in conversational skills in English indicates that the child can be appropriately tested in English; therefore, when the student receives a low score he/she is considered low functioning
(3) Establishing that English fluency indicates that there is no need to take into account an English as a second language background in the interpretation of test results; therefore, low scores can again lead to erroneous judgments about student ability

There are several reasons to employ multidimensional assessment practices rather than relying exclusively on unidimensional test data. Multidimensional assessment allows for a more complete and global picture of student ability. In addition, this type of assessment circumvents some of the limitations of standardized instruments. If one can think of testing as a snapshot, multidimensional assessment can be viewed as a video recording.

IMPLEMENTING RESPONSIBLE PRACTICES WITH LATINO STUDENTS

Prior to considerations of improving assessment practices, educators need to begin to think about making instructional changes to improve opportunities for Latinos and other minority students. Low-ability grouping, while seeming to provide opportunities for students to pick up skills they may be lacking, can also have a limiting effect on students' overall educational achievement (Valencia and Aburto, 1991). Special education programs should not be used as an alternative for students who have learning difficulties but do not have a learning disability. While differences may be difficult to detect at times, it is important to determine whether the students' learning problems were created by inappropriate instructional programs, lack of learning opportunities, or whether the learning difficulties have always existed in both languages and in all areas of life, not just school.

Practitioners are presented with a heavy responsibility regarding Latinos and other second language learners in their schools. These include, to the extent permitted by federal, state, and local mandates, exerting their influence to accomplish the following:

(1) Empowering minority students through the incorporation of their languages and cultures in the curriculum

(2) Including the parents of language minority students in meaningful activities and decisions

(3) Utilizing instructional models and methodologies proven successful with language minority students in meaningful activities and decisions

(4) Adopting and communicating high expectations

(5) Educating teachers and other school administrators, as well as informing policymakers and the general public, regarding first and second language acquisition so that they can understand some of the difficulties these students may encounter in learning

(6) Establishing a climate of acceptance of different languages and cultures, especially those represented in the school population

(7) Adopting a focus on CALP and literacy development in the native language and in English

In the area of assessment and placement of Latino students, changes in attitude about standardized testing are requisites for changes in practices. Tests should not be viewed as a unidimensional measure of the academic performance of culturally and linguistically diverse students. For Latinos and other minority children, many aspects of learning cannot be adequately assessed through standardized testing; and in our quest for high standards we weigh the value of accountability against possible negative effects for individual groups. As we evolve into an increasingly multicultural and multilingual world, educators and policymakers must guard against the implementation of standards that on the surface appear to demand excellence and accountability but, in effect, restrict opportunity with resultant discrimination against and exclusion of minority groups.

In assessment, more responsible practices can be implemented by educators through incorporating the following:

(1) Examining existing data on Latino and other minority students to make a global judgment about performance by these students
(2) Determining whether test scores are generally low for any culturally and linguistically diverse groups and taking a more analytical look at the causes
(3) Determining the appropriateness of tests used for all groups represented in the schools, i.e., norms, item bias, language bias, etc.
(4) Examining placement patterns in special education and determining if there is overrepresentation in disability categories and underrepresentation in gifted programs by Latinos and other minority students
(5) Using more holistic methods of assessing students rather than relying solely on standardized tests
(6) Redesigning requirements of state-mandated testing programs to exclude testing in English for accountability purposes for any students who are classified, based on district language testing standards, as potentially English proficient
(7) Postponing standardized testing for accountability purposes in English or Spanish until such time as a student demonstrates CALP at the level demanded in standardized testing situations
(8) Scrutinizing high-stakes tests for culturally and linguistically biased items and examining the psychometric properties of tests for consistency across cultural groups

(9) Assessing students who are not native speakers of English in their dominant language or providing dual language assessment
(10) Abstaining from the use of high-stakes testing in English for those students who do not yet have the English CALP to be able to perform well on such tests

The Latino community is actually composed of several groups rather than a homogeneous group sharing many similarities (Hernández and Descamps, 1986). Latino students come to our schools from a wide variety of backgrounds. Some are from families who were original settlers in our country; others, new immigrants from various Spanish-speaking countries with a low degree of familial adjustment to the majority culture. Most of the time, it is the background of a particular Latino that becomes most critical in making sense of test scores and determining what additional data needs to be gathered in obtaining a more holistic picture of that student. Only with additional information can fair and equitable decisions be made.

SUMMARY

There is overwhelming evidence that standardized tests underestimate minority students' abilities. The interaction of language, cultural differences, socio-economic status, acculturation stress, and biases inherent in the test can affect minority student performance and validity of test scores. The responsible interpretation and use of test scores in placement decisions has serious implications for all students, but particularly Latino students who have been victims of abuse by such practices in the past. There is good cause for concern that the American public has lost sight of the fact that tests are only one useful but fallible indicator of ability. School districts need to make progress in areas concerning unfair evaluation of Latino and other minority students rather than adding to the legacy that has existed for several decades.

REFERENCES

American Association of University Women Educational Foundation. 1992. *How Schools Shortchange Girls.* Washington, D.C.: American Association of University Women Educational Foundation.

American Educational Research Association; American Psychological Association; National Council on Measurement in Education. 1985. *Standards for Educational and Psychological Testing.* Washington, D.C.: American Educational Research Association; American Psychological Association; National Council on Measurement in Education.

Armour-Thomas, E. 1992. "Intellectual Assessment of Children from Culturally Diverse Backgrounds," *School Psychology Review*, 21:552–565.

Baca, L. M. and H. T. Cervantes. 1989. "Assessment Procedures for the Exceptional Child," in *The Bilingual Special Education Interface.* Columbus, OH: Merill Publishing Co.

Bailey, D. and G. L. Harbin. 1980. "Nondiscriminatory Evaluation," *Exceptional Children*, 46(8):590–596.

Cantini, G. and R. Trembly. 1979. "The Use of Concrete Mathematical Situations in Learning Second Language: A Dual Learning Concept," in *Bilingual Education and the Professional.* H. T. Trueba and C. Barnett-Mizahi, eds. Rowley, MA: Newbury House, pp. 246–255.

Cummins, J. 1984. *Bilingualism and Special Education: Issues in Assessment and Pedagog.* San Diego, CA: College Hill Press.

Dawes, L. 1983. "Bilingualism and Mathematical Reasoning in English as a Second Language," *Educational Studies in Mathematics,* 14:325–353.

DeBlassie, R. R. 1980. *Testing Mexican American Youth.* Hingham, MA: Teaching Resources Co.

De León, J. 1990. "A Model for an Advocacy-Oriented Assessment Process in the Psychoeducational Evaluation of Culturally and Linguistically Different Students," *The Journal of Educational Issues of Language Minority Students*, 7:53–67.

De León, J. 1995. "Intelligence Testing of Hispanic Students," in *Bilingual Speech Language Pathology: An Hispanic Focus.* Hortencia Kayser, ed. San Diego, CA: Singular Publishing Group, Inc., pp. 223–240.

Duran, R. P. 1989. "Assessment and Instruction of At-Risk Hispanic Students," *Exceptional Children*, 56(2):154–158.

Ebel, R. L. 1975. "Educational Tests: Valid? Biased? Useful," *Phi Delta Kappan*, 57(2):83–89.

Gerry, M. H. 1973. "Cultural Myopia: The Need for a Corrective Lens," *J. of School Psychology*, 11:307–315.

Gould, S. J. 1981. *The Mismeasure of Man.* New York, NY: W.W. Norton & Co.

Gould, S. J. 1995. "Mismeasure by Any Measure," in *The Bell Curve Debate: History, Documents, Opinions,* R. Jacoby and N. Slaberman, eds. New York, NY: Time Books, pp. 3–13.

Grissmer, D. W., S. N. Kirby, M. Brends, and S. Williamson. 1994. *Student Performance and the Changing American Family.* (RAND/MR-535-LE). Santa Monica, CA: RAND's Institute on Educational Training.

Harry, B. 1994. *The Disproportionate Representation of Minority Students in Special Education: Theories and Recommendations.* Alexandria, VA: National Association of State Directors of Special Education.

Hernandez, N. C. and J. A. Descamps. 1986. "Review of Factors Affecting Learning of Mexican Americans." Paper Presented at the Meeting of the National Association of Chicano Studies, El Paso, TX. ERIC, ED 267–946.

Hieronymous, A. N. and H. D. Hoover. 1986. *Manual for School Administrators.* Chicago, IL: Riverside Publishing Co.

Jaeger, R. M. 1989. "Certification of Student Competence," in *Educational Measurement*. R. L. Linn, ed. New York, NY: MacMillan Publishing Company, pp. 485–514.

Jensen, A. 1969. "How Much Can We Boost IQ and Scholastic Achievement," *Harvard Educational Review*, 2:1–124.

Johnson, S. T. 1979. *The Measurement-Mystique—Issues in Selection for Professional Schools and Employment*. Occasional Paper No. 02. Washington, DC: Howard University, Institute for the Study of Educational Policy.

Kane, M. 1994. "Validating the Performance Standards Associated with Passing Scores," *Review of Educational Research*, 64(3):425–463.

Kretschmer, R. E. 1991. "Exceptionality and the Limited English Proficient Student: Historical and Practical Contexts," in *Limiting Bias in the Assessment of Bilingual Students*, E. V. Hamayan and J. S. Damico, eds. Austin, TX: Pro-Ed, pp. 1–38.

Mather, J. R. C. and J. J. Chiodo. 1994. "A Mathematical Problem: How Do We Teach Mathematics to LEP Elementary Students?" *The Journal of Educational Issues of Language Minority Students*, 13:1–12.

McIntosh, S. 1995. "Serving the Underserved: Giftedness among Ethnic Minority and Disadvantaged Students," *The School Administrator*, 4(52):25–29.

Medina, N. and D. M. Neill. 1990. "Fallout from the Testing Explosion: How 100 Million Standardized Exams Undermine Equity and Excellence in America's Public Schools." Cambridge, MA: National Center for Fair and Open Testing (FairTest), ERIC, ED 318749.

Oakland, T. 1973. "Assessing Minority Group Children: Challenges for School Psychologists," *J. of School Psychology*, 11(4):294–303.

Oakland, T. and L. M. Laosa. 1976. "Professional, Legislative, and Judicial Influence on Psychoeducational Assessment Practices in Schools," in *Nonbiased Assessment of Minority Group Children: With Bias Toward None*. B. Bogatz, ed. Lexington, KY: University of Kentucky, pp. 15–34.

Oakland, T. and P. Matuszeh. 1976. "Using Tests in Nondiscriminatory Assessment," in *Non-Biased Assessment of Minority Group Children: With Bias Toward None*. B. Bogatz, ed. Lexington, KY: University of Kentucky, pp. 28–37.

Ortiz, A. A. and J. R. Yates. 1983. "Incidence of Exceptionality Among Hispanics: Implications for Manpower Planning," *NABE Journal*, 4:41–54.

Overton, T. 1992. *Assessment in Special Education*. New York, NY: MacMillan Publishing Co.

Richard-Amato, P. A. and M. A. Snow. 1992. *The Multicultural Classroom: Readings for Content-Area Teachers*. White Plains, NY: Longman Publishing Group.

Richert, E. S. 1987. "Rampant Problems and Practices in the Identification of Disadvantaged Gifted Students," *Gifted Child Quarterly*, 31(4):149–154.

Rueda, R. and Mercer, J. 1985. *A Predictive Analysis of Decision-Making Practices with Limited English Proficient Handicapped*. Report No. 300-83-0273. Washington, D.C.: Department of Education, ERIC, ED 266 590.

Samuda, R. J. 1975. *Psychological Testing of American Minorities: Issues and Consequences*. San Francisco, CA: Harper and Row Publishers.

Sattler, J. M. 1988. *Assessment of Children*. San Diego, CA: Jerome Sattler Publishers.

Secada, W. G. 1991. "Degree of Bilingualism and Arithmetic Problem Solving in Hispanic First Graders," *The Elementary School Journal*, 92(2):213–230.

Smith, M. L., C. Elsky, K. Draper, C. Rottenberg, and M. Cherland. 1989. *The Role of*

Testing in Elementary Schools. Los Angeles: Center for Research on Educational Standards and Student Tests, Graduate School of Education, UCLA.

Tucker, J. 1980. "Ethnic Proportions in Classes for the Learning Disabled: Issues in Nonbiased Assessment," *J. of Special Education*, 14:93–105.

Valdés, G. and R. Figueroa. 1994. *Bilingualism and Testing: A Special Case of Bias*. Norwood, NJ: Ablex Publishing Co.

Valencia, R. R. and S. Aburto. 1991. "The Uses and Abuses of Educational Testing: Chicanos as a Case in Point," in *Chicano School Failure and Success*. New York, NY: The Falmer Press, pp. 203–251.

PART IV

LEADERSHIP PRACTICES FOR SUCCESS AMONG LATINO POPULATIONS

CHAPTER 10

Latinos in the United States:
A Tapestry of Diversity

ALICIA SALINAS SOSA—*The University of Texas at San Antonio*

INTRODUCTION

LATINO children and youth in the United States may share the same language and some similar cultural characteristics, but they differ widely in demographics. Latinos represent a tapestry of diversity. Although government agencies such as the U.S. Bureau of the Census (USBC) have grouped Latinos under the umbrella category of "Hispanics" to distinguish them from Europeans or those of European ancestry, they are not a homogeneous group. The term *Hispanic* is primarily used by governmental agencies in the United States to identify Spanish-speaking persons residing in the United States or its territories who either became citizens at birth or immigrated from Mexico, Central or South America, the Caribbean, or Spain. However, these persons prefer to be referred to as Latino, a self-selected name/label, rather than by the government designation of Hispanic. As in the rest of the book, I will honor their preference in this chapter and use the term *Latino*.

LATINOS IN THE UNITED STATES: DEMOGRAPHICS

According to figures provided by the USBC (1993), the Latino population is large and growing at a tremendous rate in this country. It grew 61% between 1970 and 1980. During the last decade, the Latino population was still experiencing rapid growth; it grew 53% between 1980 and 1990. In 1990, 22.4 million Latinos comprised almost 9% of the U.S. population.

Census data further shows that Latinos are concentrated in a small number of states, mostly in the South and West. In 1990, nearly nine of every ten Latinos lived in just ten states while the largest populations were concentrated in five. More than 34% of all Latinos in the United

197

States live in California, more than 19% live in Texas, almost 10% live in New York, and 7% live in Florida.

Latinos can trace their cultural roots to a variety of countries and locations. Many find their roots in Mexico (61%), but Puerto Rico (12%), Central America (6%), Cuba (5%), South America (5%), the Dominican Republic (over 2%), Spain (over 2%), and other areas are sources of Latino heritage. Nevertheless, nearly 75% of the U.S. Latino population is native born and naturalized.

These figures show that the Latino community is not only large and growing within the United States, it is also internally diverse and complex. Examining this internal diversity reveals some interesting dimensions. For example, about 83% of the U.S. Spanish-heritage Latinos were born in this country, compared to 67% of Mexican-heritage Latinos. Far from being a monolithic segment of our society, Latinos represent a wide variety of subgroups.

VARIETIES OF SUBGROUPS

Mexican Americans

Mexican Americans comprise the largest subgroup of Latinos. Mexican Americans number 13.3 million and make up 61% of this country's Latino population. The Mexican American population nearly doubled between 1970 and 1980, and it nearly doubled again by 1990 (U.S. Bureau of the Census, 1993).

The Mexican American student population is diverse. Students may be immigrants themselves or the sons and daughters of immigrants. Those who are native born may be the second, third, or tenth generation born in the United States. Many trace their ancestry back to historical periods when the land was either an independent republic or under Spanish or Mexican rule.

The family backgrounds and reasons for leaving their native Mexico have varied over time. Some immigrants left Mexico for political reasons during the early 1900s at the time of the Mexican Revolution. Between 1910 and 1930, 10% of the population of Mexico immigrated to the United States; this represented about 685,000 legal immigrants. In many cases, these immigrants had been well connected and politically involved. Many left professional careers and high social positions.

Other immigrants left Mexico during difficult economic times because they were unable to provide sustenance for their families. Another group, perhaps smaller than those previously mentioned, chose to come to the United States in search of better opportunities for themselves and their children. Most Mexican Americans are not new immigrants, however. During the past several decades, far more Mexican Americans (compared with other Latinos) have been native rather than foreign born. The 1990 census showed that almost seven out of ten Mexican Americans were born in the United States (USBC, 1993).

Puerto Ricans

Puerto Ricans represent about 12% of all Latinos, making them the second largest Latino group (USBC, 1993). Puerto Ricans, like the first Mexicans, became U.S. citizens through conquest. Following the brief Spanish-American War, Puerto Rico became a U.S. possession through the Treaty of Paris (National Council of La Raza, 1986). In 1898, when Puerto Rico was annexed by the United States, the island was overpopulated and suffering problems, including an underdeveloped economy, massive unemployment, poverty, hunger, and poor housing (Larsen, 1973).

Problems arose regarding treatment of Puerto Ricans, and their status was finally clarified through the Jones Act of 1917, which made all Puerto Ricans U.S. citizens. According to Larsen (1973), the 1920s marked the beginning of Puerto Rican immigration to the United States. However, large-scale immigration did not occur until after World War II (National Council of La Raza, 1986).

In the 1960s, immigration to the U.S. mainland leveled off. Between 1980 and 1990, the Puerto Rican population grew at a rate at least four times as fast as the rest of the U.S. population. Puerto Ricans are concentrated in central cities and work primarily in the manufacturing and service industries (Carrasquillo and London, 1993). They have a 30% poverty rate, the second highest rate among Latinos (USBC, 1993). Because Puerto Ricans are U.S. citizens and come from a democratic country where English is taught in schools and educational attainment is relatively high (Carrasquillo and London, 1993), the high poverty rate is difficult to explain.

The educational attainment level of Puerto Ricans is affected by the same factors that affect other language minorities. Students are placed at risk when they attend schools where the following obstacles, among others, stand in their way of academic achievement: low expectations, tracking, over-reliance on testing, disregard for language and culture in the instruction, too few minority teachers, and poorly trained teachers who lack the skills to teach minorities (Quality Education for Minorities Project, 1990).

Central and South Americans

In 1990 Central Americans represented 6% and South Americans represented 5% of the total Latino population in the United States. About 20% of the Central American foreign born arrived between 1970 and 1979, and about 70% arrived between 1980 and 1990. Most had left countries experiencing war and extreme poverty. The countries of origin having the highest representation are as follows: El Salvador, 43%; Guatemala, 20%; and Nicaragua, about 15% (USBC, 1993). Central Americans represented the largest proportion of newly arrived Latino immigrants during the 1980s. In general, many of the youth immigrating during this period had little or no prior schooling and lacked literacy skills in their own language. Recent Central American immigration has been tied largely to economic and political conditions in these countries, most notably during the past two decades (National Council of La Raza, 1986). Political instability, typified by the border conflicts between Honduras and El Salvador, has contributed to the growth of a war-refugee class among these immigrants. Since 1979 the number of individuals and families immigrating to the United States from El Salvador, Guatemala, and Nicaragua has grown substantially. Many of these nationality groups have settled in a few cities. Guatemalans have settled predominantly in Los Angeles and Washington, D.C. Nicaraguans have settled primarily in Miami, Southern California, and San Francisco (National Council of La Raza, 1986).

South Americans represent nearly 5% of the Latino population, with the highest breakdowns for country of origin as follows: Colombia, 37%; Ecuador, 19%; and Peru, 17%. Central and South Americans live in large cities and are dispersed across the United States. Some, however, relocate to semi-rural areas (Carrasquillo and London, 1993).

Cubans

Cubans represent 5% of the Latino population and are the third largest Latino group. Many of the Cubans who fled communism in Cuba in the early 1960s were middle class and have been able to transfer their educational and commercial skills to businesses revolving around real estate, clothing, construction, restaurants, television, and newspapers (Carrasquillo and London, 1993). About 46% of the Cuban foreign born came between 1960 and 1969, during the second wave of immigration. Between 1970 and 1980, both the Cuban and the Puerto Rican populations grew at a rate four times that of the rest of the nation (USBC, 1993). A large, third wave of immigration occurred in 1980 during the Mariel evacuations. These immigrants, most of whom came here to start a new life, were not as socially, politically, or economically well off. A few had been in prisons or in mental institutions and others were desperate because of hardships related to a depressed economy and poor nutrition.

Dominicans, Spaniards, and Other Latinos

Dominicans, Spaniards, and other Latinos each represent over 2% of the Latino population. Dominicans have settled, to a great extent, in New York City (National Council of La Raza, 1986). Dominican immigration has occurred in small numbers across several decades (Carrasquillo, 1991). The 1980 census reported that 62% of the Dominicans in New York City had arrived after 1965. In the 1980s many Dominicans immigrated to New York City in search of better living conditions because of economic difficulties in the Dominican Republic (Carrasquillo, 1991). There appears to be a mix in the social class structures and urban/rural representation of Dominicans immigrating to the United States. While Dominican immigrants came to this country in hopes of bettering their life situation, lack of English proficiency and job skills have prevented their attainment of quality employment. A large percentage of Dominican households in the United States are headed by women employed in manufacturing, most typically in the textile industry (Carrasquillo, 1991).

This overview of Latino subgroups reveals variations in reasons for immigrating and dates of arrival. But Latino students also vary in their language proficiency. Some are proficient Spanish/English bilinguals. Some are monolingual Spanish speakers. Within the monolingual Spanish-speaking group, some are literate in Spanish while others are not. Across the Potentially English Proficient (PEP) group, the command of English may range from marginally proficient to very limited. For monolingual Spanish speakers, the PEP group, and even bilinguals, academic success partially correlates with language proficiency.

EDUCATIONAL ATTAINMENT LEVELS

Sosa (1993) reviewed educational attainment levels of Latinos and found that drop-out rates had increased, not decreased, during the period of reform. The data examined showed decreasing levels of achievement for women and language minority students. For example, a study recently released by the American Council on Education (ACE) reported a decline in high-school completion rates, which in 1990 stood at less than 55% for Latinos, 77% for blacks, and over 82% for whites. High-school completion rates for Latinos had not improved significantly since 1970. Rather, the 1990 completion rate had dropped below the 55.2% completion rate reported for Latinos in 1973. An even greater drop had occurred for Latino women, whose completion rate fell nearly 5% between 1989 and 1990 (Carter and Wilson, 1992). Steinberg et al. (1984) reported a similar trend. Among Latinos the drop-out rate rose steadily from approximately 30% in 1974 to 40% in 1979. In 1990, only about half of the U.S. Latino population had a high-school diploma.

Data from the National Center for Education Statistics published in 1976 suggests that language minority status may be an even more important predictor of school achievement than ethnicity. Steinberg et al. (1984) analyzed the data by ethnic background to determine the percentages of students in grades five to eight who were at least two years behind their expected grade level. Their findings showed that for students with an Anglo background, 8% were two or more years behind in school; for students with a non-Anglo, non-Latino background, the figure stood at 10%; and for students with Latino backgrounds, it was 12%. When the analysis was conducted using the classification according to language rather than ethnicity, the differences were far greater. Only 8% of students who usually spoke English were two or more years behind their expected grade level, compared to 25% of non-English, non-Latino language background students and 32% of Spanish-speaking Latinos.

Educational attainment levels become increasingly important as the number of Latinos continues to increase at rates much higher than for any other group. In the fall of 1986 Latino students comprised less than 10% of the total enrollment in public elementary and secondary schools; by the fall of 1992 that total had grown to over 12%. The Latino population continues to grow, and its impact on public education can be expected for many decades to come.

TRENDS AND PROJECTIONS

Latinos represent the largest segment of the language minority population in the United States. Latinos account for 40% of the total PEP population and 64% of the school-age population from a non-English language background (Jeager and Sandhu, 1985). Latinos are a young group with a median age of twenty-five (Hispanic Policy Development Project, 1988), and in 1990 nearly 70% of all Latinos were under the age of thirty-five (USBC, 1993). They are also the fastest growing ethnic group in the nation. From 1980 to 1989 they experienced a population growth of nearly 40%, five times that of the nation as a whole. By the year 2000, the number of Latinos is expected to grow an additional 46%. This dramatic growth can result in students receiving fewer services—especially when one considers that close to 90% of the Latino population is concentrated in nine states, with more than half of them living in California and Texas alone (Quality Education for Minorities Project, 1990).

On several levels, burgeoning numbers work against the Latino student. In states with high Latino student enrollment, segregation is the norm. According to Orfield et al. (1989), 59% of the students in New York and 41% of the students in Texas are enrolled in schools where nearly all (90–100%) of the students are minority. The fact is that many Latinos across the nation attend predominantly minority schools.

Furthermore, 88% of all Latinos reside in urban areas and attend urban schools where high percentages of minority students run a disproportionately high risk of dropping out (Pallas, 1991). A high poverty rate among Latinos places this group at an even greater educational disadvantage. The poverty rate among six- to seventeen-year-old Latino children is over 35%, compared to a rate of less than 14% among whites (Children's Defense Fund, 1990).

These data present shifts in the populations of potentially English proficient students enrolled in American public schools. These students possess varying language competencies and experiences that are seen as obstacles by many educators. These obstacles to achieving educational equity are reflected in the following, which are found in the educational system: low expectations, over-reliance on testing, poorly prepared teachers, a scarcity of minority teachers, tracking, disregard for language and cultural diversity, and inadequate school financing (Quality Education for Minorities Project, 1990).

During the late 1980s and early 1990s, studies of effective bilingual education programs identified major factors that must be addressed in order to meet the instructional needs of PEP students (Cummins, 1986; García, 1987; Hakuta, 1986; Lindholm, 1991; Ramírez et al., 1990). The researchers documented (1) the important role of continued native language development over an extended period of time, (2) strong instructional support that aids students' access to challenging subject matter content, and (3) school-level action that provides validation of students' cultural and national heritage (Sosa, 1993). Effective bilingual programs emphasize each of the major factors, which in turn are reflected in the different models of instruction. The following section briefly explains the components of the most recognized models of bilingual education.

MODELS OF BILINGUAL EDUCATION

Baker (1993) describes ten broad categories of bilingual education programs. He further classifies these into two main forms, weak and strong, based on their aims. The weak forms of bilingual education aim to shift the student from the home, minority language into English. The strong forms attempt to affirm the rights of minority students by fostering the native language and strengthening cultural identity.

The following are some of the existing bilingual program models and their goals. The most commonly used programs are listed first.

(1) Transitional: The goal is proficiency in English. Students are main-streamed into all-English instruction as soon as possible. This model makes use of the native language in the initial stages. Most state and federal laws call for transitional bilingual education programs.

(2) Immersion: The goal is proficiency in English. Children are im-mersed in sheltered English activities with minimal use of the native language.

(3) Maintenance Bilingual Education: The goal is to develop high levels of proficiency in both the native language and English. Instruction is in both languages in all areas of the curriculum, often over an extended period of time (five or more years).

(4) Two-Way (Dual) Bilingual Education: The goal is bilingualism for language majority as well as language minority students. Non-native English speakers develop their English, and native English speakers

develop a second language. Instruction is done in English as well as in the second language.

Program options at the secondary level are more limited. Several states have passed legislation requiring schools to provide English as a Second Language (ESL) classes for PEP students at the middle- and high-school levels. Two main language needs are targeted:

- learning the English language itself, usually through English as a Second Language methodology (ESL)
- opening access to the content subject matter by making the instruction more comprehensible

For students with a low level of language proficiency, the ESL classes initially focus on development of listening and oral language skills, and also develop students' reading and writing skills using methods for teaching a second language. Academic content instruction may be made comprehensible by using sheltered instruction. Sheltered English is an approach for offering content instruction in English to classes composed solely of PEP students not yet fully proficient in English (Minicucci and Olsen, 1992). In sheltered English, the subject matter and the students' attention are focused on the message (the content) and not the English language. Teachers are taught to add support to their instruction through use of: (1) visual cues, (2) language modifications (pauses, repetition, elaboration), (3) interactive teaching where students are actively engaged, and (4) focus on key concepts rather than on details (Edwards et al., 1984).

ACHIEVEMENT IN BILINGUAL EDUCATION

Students in bilingual education programs are able to demonstrate learning gains when tested in the language that they know best. Ramírez et al. (1990) compared the effectiveness of two alternative programs (structured English immersion and late-exit transitional bilingual education) with the early-exit bilingual program, a program most typically funded by the U.S. Department of Education.

Structured immersion programs are used with language minority students in the United States. Baker (1993) labels these as "submersion" programs because the first language is not developed but is replaced by the majority language. The teacher provides some assistance by using a simplified form of the majority language, and, initially, is accepting of some use of the home language in students' responses. The early-exit model calls for placing students into all-English classes within two to three years in the program. The late-exit bilingual program (a form of transitional program) allows for teaching in English and use of the home language for 40 percent of the instructional time. Students learn content and continue receiving instruction and developing proficiency in the home language until the sixth grade.

Researchers found that students learned English in all three program types. However, they found that parents of children enrolled in the late-exit program were better able to help with homework. Because the children were reading or writing in Spanish, their parents felt competent and comfortable in responding to their questions. This support helped students to complete their assignments. Moreover, researchers found that the students in the late-exit bilingual program made great achievement gains after several years in the program. Further analyses revealed that students in late-exit programs—who were provided with substantial instruction in their native language and who were gradually introduced to English as the language of instruction—showed the greatest growth in mathematics, English language skills, and English reading, effectively closing the achievement gap that characterizes the schooling of most language-minority children (Ramírez et al., 1990).

Students in bilingual education perform well when they have access to instruction in the native language as they learn English. It is when students are "transitioned" prematurely to an all-English classroom that they can begin to flounder. When students enter the mainstream, they must interact with teachers and students who do not understand what it means to learn and study in a second language in the context of a new culture.

Exited students face the additional obstacle of encountering instruction that (1) is presented in their newly acquired second language (English) and (2) requires them to read material for the purpose of learning content. In other words, they are required to read to learn instead of learning to read, which they did in the previous three grades. Their reading task shifts from reading narrative text with access to context clues from illustrations and concrete events to reading longer, expository text with language that is decontextualized in the upper grades. At these upper elementary and middle-school grades, students—recently exited from bilingual programs—must suddenly rely extensively on context-reduced language (the words themselves without extra linguistic cues).

Facilitating this transition in reading materials and reading objectives poses an additional challenge for educators of bilingual students.

INSTRUCTIONAL PRACTICES IN BILINGUAL EDUCATION

This section provides brief descriptions of changes in instructional practices within bilingual classrooms during the past twenty years. It lists trends in the education of language minority students within bilingual education classrooms.

Developing Literacy in the First Language

Potentially English proficient Latino students arrive at school with oral language skills (speaking and understanding) in Spanish. They are ready to learn literacy skills in Spanish. Rather than missing this teachable moment and delaying the introduction of reading until after students learn English, educators would do well to consider the role of the first language (L1) in the development of the second language (L2).

The role played by L1 in the development of L2 is found in Cummins' (1979, 1986, 1989) "Interdependence Hypothesis." According to Cummins, the development of L2 is partially a function of the level of L1 proficiency at the time when the student is first introduced to L2 in an intensive manner. Students whose L1 development is disrupted and replaced by L2 will suffer cognitive deficits. Cummins' work provides solid documentation to previously noted phenomena. Educators had long noted that Latino students enrolling in U.S. classrooms after age ten or eleven were quick to pick up the second language and able to complete academic work assignments with success after several years. Latino students whose arrival in the United States occurred prior to acquiring literacy in Spanish (their L1) experienced difficulty in learning English (L2). As the research later pointed out, it was not the age of the student that was critical; it was the student's development of literacy skills in L1 that supported the learning of a new, second language.

Guidelines from various state agencies call for decreasing the amount of instruction in Spanish as the student gains greater English fluency and moves into the upper elementary grades. School personnel need to recognize that state requirements contain minimum behavioral expectations. They should allow opportunities for continued development of literacy in Spanish through the use of children's literature and the fine arts.

While learning English is one of the major goals of bilingual instruction serving Latinos, another equally important goal is to teach content by presenting it in Spanish, a language the students understand. Content material and skills developed in L1 will transfer to English. Teachers should accept code-switching, language alternation between L1 and L2, by the students, but they must carefully plan their Spanish instruction to achieve quality instruction in the native language. When using English, especially during reading or language lessons, teachers need to negotiate their language level so that it is not too elevated. Ideally, the teacher's language level should be only slightly higher than the student's language proficiency level. Teachers need to be aware that students' comprehension exceeds by a small margin their production level. And, as with all effective instructional practices, teacher expectations are not the primary issue; a high level of sensitivity to individual learner characteristics is vital.

Viewing Students as Active Learners

In the 1970s, methods for teaching language focused more on aspects related to the teaching act, i.e., on methodology and materials. Teachers used the audio-lingual method with its emphasis on language learning through habit formation, rote learning and practice (Morley, 1987). In the 1980s natural processes were recognized, and the role of the teacher shifted to that of a facilitator. According to Morley (1987), teachers and teaching materials must adapt to the learner rather than vice versa. Similarly, Wong Fillmore et al. (1985) reported that the development of English production and comprehension was related to teacher responsiveness to student cues. Teachers who adjusted their linguistic interactions in response to student feedback were more likely to produce English language gains. Such adjustments included simplification of syntax, less rapid speech, and repetition. These teachers not only allowed but encouraged student interaction.

Recent research suggests that transmission-oriented teaching does not benefit minority students. Transmission models of teaching see the teacher's task as imparting knowledge or skills that s/he possesses to students who do not yet have these skills. According to Cummins (1989), this model contradicts central principles of language and literacy acquisition. For these students, as well as with language majority students, reciprocal interaction teaching has proven more effective (Cummins, 1986). Reciprocal interaction in teaching requires genuine dialogue between students and teachers in both oral and written modalities, with the teacher serving more as a facilitator and guide. This model emphasizes higher-order cognitive thinking, meaningful language use by students, language integration across the curriculum, and intrinsic motivation. García (1987) reports on instructional strategies used in effective bilingual classrooms. He suggests that student-student interaction discourse strategies are important to enhance cognitive and linguistic development.

Using Holistic Approaches, Themes

In the early 1970s teachers received inservice training on methods for introducing initial reading instruction. Teachers acquired information about three methods for teaching beginning reading in Spanish: the phonetic method, the syllabic method, and the global method (Thonis, 1970). Because Spanish is such a phonetic language, the overwhelming majority of bilingual teachers initially used the phonetic method with its letter-sound correspondence and consonant-vowel combinations. Students were expected to naturally make the transition to reading whole words and even phrases as these were repeatedly encountered. While teachers received inservice training on the use of the language experience approach, they reserved the use of this reading approach for teaching students to read in the second language. Moreover, teachers were asked to delay teaching writing until after a student was reading at a fluent level.

Kline (1988) reports that the most successful reading experts focus on whole language development, integrating the teaching and learning of reading and writing and the use of children's literature to counter skills-driven student basal readers. Holistic approaches and themes can provide additional support for language learners. Bilingual education teachers are now using predictable stories and asking their students to maintain dialogue journals. Students write in their dialogue journals about things that they know and find interesting. By their nature dialogue journals help students link thinking with language, especially with the writing process. Both dialogue journals and predictable books provide for language repetition that is natural (authentic), fun, and supported with visual symbols of language embedded in a social situation.

Educators are also encouraging teachers to use new structures that encourage group work: planning tasks, and discussing and reporting outcomes. Students develop group interaction skills as they learn thinking skills and extend their language skills. This educational practice is recommended for use with PEP students (Calderón, 1989; Enright and McCloskey, 1988). Cooperative learning appears to make use of a previously untapped learning style. Cooperative learning facilitates successful heterogeneous grouping, verbal skills, and higher order thinking.

SUMMARY

The Latino population in the United States grew by 53% between 1980 and 1990, and by 61% between 1970 and 1980 (USBC, 1993). The USBC attributes the tremendous increase to a birth rate higher than that of the rest of the population and substantial immigration from Mexico, Central America, the Caribbean, and South America. Projections are that the Hispanic population in the United States will increase from 24 million in 1992, to 31 million by the year 2000, and to 81 million by the year 2050. The number of PEP students will probably increase in similar proportion. PEP students will require language response programs that meet their unique educational needs.

Bilingual education is a proven program of instruction. When properly implemented, bilingual instruction teaches students how to read in their native language, and it provides access to content via the native language (or sheltered ESL) at the same time that a second language is being learned. Over the past twenty years, several trends have emerged. The most current thinking calls for accepting the diversity among PEP students, facilitating the teaching of ESL through lessons that actively involve students, utilizing cooperative learning strategies, and organizing the learning materials into thematic units.

Research also indicates that time spent mastering subject content and developing literacy skills in the first language will serve as a strong base for learning the second language—not only faster, but better. The implications of the research are clear; if school district personnel wish to increase the PEP student's success in all-English classes, they will extend the student's access to learning in L1 and continue literacy development in the native language.

REFERENCES

Baker, C. 1993. *Foundation of Bilingual Education and Bilingualism.* Philadelphia: Multilingual Matters Ltd.

Calderón, M. 1989. *Cooperative Learning for LEP Students.* IDRA Newsletter, 16(9):1–7.

Carrasquillo, A. L. 1991. *Parents and Children and Youth in the United States.* New York, NY: Garland Publishing, Inc.

Carrasquillo, A. L. and C. B. G. London. 1993. "The Hispanic-American Experience in Family Context," in *Parents and Schools. A Source Book.* New York, NY: Garland Publishing, Inc.

Carter, D. and R. Wilson. 1992. *Minorities in Higher Education.* Washington, D.C.: American Council on Education.

Children's Defense Fund. 1990. *Latino Youths at the Crossroads.* Washington, D.C.: Author.

Cummins, J. 1979. "Cognitive/Academic Language Proficiency, Linguistic Interdependence, the Optimum Age Question and Some Other Matters." *Working Papers on Bilingualism,* No. 19. Toronto, Ontario: Ontario Institute for Studies in Education.

Cummins, J. 1986. "Empowering Minority Students: A Framework for Intervention," *Harvard Educational Review,* 566(1):18–36.

Cummins, J. 1989. *Empowering Minority Students.* Sacramento: California Association for Bilingual Education.

Edwards, H., M. Wesche, S. Krashen, R. Clement, and B. Kruideneir. 1984. "Second Language Acquisition Through Subject-Matter Learning: A Study of Sheltered Psychology Classes at the University of Ottawa," *Canadian Modern Language Review,* 41:268–282.

Enright, S. D. and M. L. McCloskey. 1988. *Integrating English.* Reading, MA: Addison-Wesley Publishing Company.

García, E. E. 1987. *Effective Schooling for Language Minority Students* (New Focus, NCBE Occasional Papers in Bilingual Education, No. 1). Wheaton, MD: National Clearinghouse for Bilingual Education.

Hakuta, K. 1986. *The Mirror of Language.* New York, NY: Basic Books.

Hispanic Policy Development Project. 1988. *Closing the Gap for U.S. Hispanic Youth.* Washington, D.C.: Hispanic Policy Development Project.

Jeager, S. and H. Sandhu. 1985. "Southeast Asian Refugees: English Language Development and Acculturation," *Focus No. 21.* Rosslyn, VA: National Clearinghouse for Bilingual Education.

Kline, L. W. June 1988. "Reading: Whole Language Development, Renewed Focus on Literature Spur Change," *Curriculum Update,* 1(4):9.

Larsen, R. J. 1973. *The Puerto Ricans in America.* Minneapolis, MN: Lerner Publications Company.

Lindholm, K. J. 1991. "Theoretical Assumptions and Empirical Evidence for Academic Achievement in Two Languages," *Hispanic Journal of Behavioral Sciences,* 13(1):3–17.

Minicucci, C. and L. Olsen. 1992. *Programs for Secondary Limited English Proficient Students.* Washington, D.C.: National Center for Bilingual Education.

Morley, J. 1987. "Current Directions in Teaching English to Speakers of Other Languages: A State-of-the-Art Synopsis," *TESOL Quarterly,* 21(2):16–20.

National Council of La Raza. 1986. *Beyond Ellis Island: Hispanics—Immigrants and Americans.* Washington, D.C.: National Council of La Raza.

Orfield, G., F. Monfort, and M. Aaron. 1989. *Segregation, Integration and Public Policy:*

National, State, and Metropolitan Trends in Public Schools. Washington, D.C.: National School Boards Association Council of Urban Boards of Education.

Pallas, A. M. 1991. "Who Is at Risk? Defined Demographics and Decisions," in *Overcoming Risk: An Annotated Bibliography of Publications Developed by ERIC Clearinghouse.* W. Schwartz and C. Howley, eds.

Quality Education for Minorities Project. 1990. *Education That Works: An Action Plan for the Education of Minorities.* Cambridge, MA: Massachusetts Institute of Technology, Quality Education for Minorities Project.

Ramírez, J. D., S. D. Yuen, D. R. Ramey, and D. J. Pasta. 1990. *Final Report: Longitudinal Study of Immersion Strategy, Early-Exit and Late-Exit Transitional Bilingual Education Programs for Language-Minority Children* (2 vols.). San Mateo, CA: Aguirre International.

Sosa, A. S. 1993. *Thorough and Fair: Creating Routes to Success for Mexican-American Students,* Charleston, WV: ERIC Clearinghouse on Rural Education and Small Schools.

Steinberg, L., P. L. Blinde, and K. S. Chan. 1984. "Dropping Out among Language Minority Youth," *Review of Educational Research,* 54(1):113–132.

Thonis, E. W. 1970. *Teaching Reading to Non-English Speakers.* New York, NY: Collier MacMillan International Inc.

U.S. Bureau of the Census. 1993. *We Are the American Hispanics.* Washington, D.C.: U.S. Bureau of the Census.

Wong Fillmore, L., P. Amanon, B. McLaughlin, and A. S. Ammon. 1985. *Final Report for Learning English Through Bilingual Instruction.* Washington, D.C.: National Institute of Education.

CHAPTER 11

Profile of Leadership at the Middle-/High-School Levels: Successful Schools and Their Principals

MARÍA LUÍSA GONZÁLEZ—*New Mexico State Univesity*
ANA HUERTA-MACÍAS—*New Mexico State University*

INTRODUCTION

MOST of the current literature on leadership and the role of the principal has omitted strong mention of dealing with the culturally, ethnically, or linguistically diverse student (Reyes and Valencia, 1993). Furthermore, rescarchers (Noddings, 1992; Reyes and Valencia, 1993) criticize the school restructuring and reform movement for not addressing the leadership that is critical to meet the needs of diverse learners. Both of these issues deserve a closer look given the growing population of ethnic groups in the United States—particularly Latinos. Latinos now number about 27 million and make up well over 10 percent of the nation's population (National Association of Hispanic Publications and U.S. Census Bureau, 1995); and, according to National Center for Education Statistics (1994), Latinos will comprise the largest minority group attending U.S. schools by the year 2050. However, alongside these demographics is the deplorable completion rate for Latinos, which rose from 55 percent to 63 percent between 1993 and 1994, as compared to 89 percent for whites and 84 percent for African Americans. More than one third of Latino students drop out of high school on a yearly basis (National Center for Education Statistics, 1995).

The grim statistics are in large part due to the conditions that researchers have found plague secondary schools: irrelevant course work, fragmented learning due to rigid scheduling, ineffective teaching methods, large class sizes, tracking systems, inequity related to resource allocation, autocratic administrators who discourage shared decision making, and a lack of interdisciplinary teaching and schoolwide communication (Boyer, 1983; Goodlad, 1984; Kozol, 1992; Sizer, 1992). These conditions may further complicate and confuse many Latino students as they struggle to become literate in a new language and meet graduation requirements at the same time (Giacchino-Baker, 1992).

Yet, there are secondary schools that are student centered, equitable, and highly efficient places for learning that take into account the needs of culturally and linguistically diverse students. This chapter highlights three such schools in the border Southwest along with their principals who are continually meeting the challenges of school reform through innovative and creative practice. The chapter emphasizes the role of the principal in each of these schools, for as has been noted in the literature, "leadership is a key feature in successful schools; *strong* instructional leadership has been cited as a key ingredient of effective schools" for Latino, language minority students (Lucas et al., 1990, p. 328). The portrait of a middle-school principal is followed by that of two culturally competent high-school principals. We now turn to our first portrait—Ysleta Middle School.

A CULTURALLY COMPETENT MIDDLE-SCHOOL PRINCIPAL: YSLETA MIDDLE SCHOOL

Remember who you are wherever you go. You represent yourself, your family, your friends, your neighborhood, your city, your country, and Ysleta Middle School. (Motto, Ysleta Middle School)

Background on School and Principal

As one drives to this middle school located in a neighborhood that is a quarter of a mile from the U.S.-Mexico border one is struck by the clean building. Trees are neatly planted along with rose bushes that line the wall facing the street. The outside walls are clean and free of the familiar graffiti that one finds in other middle schools. Walking into the building one is struck by the touches that make this school warm and inviting. The library is color coordinated in tones that reflect the school colors; plants, couches, and posters are all reminiscent of schools in a higher-income bracket. Yet, the essence of the school does not lie in its neat and orderly climate nor in its lovely interiors. The school, with its 500 students, is considered one of the best middle schools in the Southwest region where countless visitors from different areas of the nation visit, eager to learn from the educational practice of both principal and teachers.

With its close proximity to the border one would expect that the majority of the students would be immigrants. However, 94 percent of the students are second and third generation Latinos with a majority living in the Kennedy Apartments (a section of lower-income housing units) or renting small homes in the vicinity. Even with the surroundings that are testimony to the compounding effects of poverty, the school has the lowest failure rate in the district, a distinction that was no easy feat for the principal, faculty, and staff. Two years ago, with the arrival of Barbara Trousdale, the school was literally turned around.

The first time that the principal met with the school staff the meeting went well, with one exception. As the principal rose from her chair, her skirt tore due to the old, broken seat. The incident with the chair was an awakening experience for her. She realized that the physical and academic surroundings were not the best for the students and parents at Ysleta Middle. She saw it as an inequity: because this environment would not be good enough for her own children, why should it be good enough for the children under her charge? This is the filter that she has since used. All the teachers in the school also follow the idea that one needs to provide the best, as if it were for one's own children.

Transforming the School

The school's emphasis is on academics, self-discipline, and decision making. The strength, according to the principal, lies in the area of block scheduling, which the school has adopted. The teachers in teams will meet to discuss and plan instruction for at least seventy minutes. The principal provides a conference room and telephone specifically for this purpose. This facilitates a student-centered focus for each instructional team. When an individual student is having problems, the team can readily meet with the parent and student. All issues are openly discussed and student feedback is solicited, which the principal feels is critical. Every adult is expected to be an active participant in student development, and the students are expected to play an active role in their own development.

Given this positive atmosphere, the former bad reputation of the school has disappeared. In fact, a long list of teachers has requested transfers to this school. Their chances are slim, given that the faculty/staff turnover rate is quite low, with only two openings for the incoming year that were quickly filled. The principal feels that the popularity of her school is built on the reputation for providing the best for all its stakeholders—students, teachers, staff, and parents. Teachers who opt to work in a school with culturally and linguistically diverse students living in a low socio-economic area need to be "way above average." When teachers do not meet these expectations they are placed on a growth plan and/or asked to seek employment in an area where they may feel more comfortable.

The building boasts four computer labs that are fully equipped and fully functional. The principal's goal is for each child to become highly computer literate. In fact, the entire faculty and staff is expected to be computer literate. Every classroom is further equipped with four to six computers. In one situation where a teacher had an aversion to computers, the principal quickly reminded her that she did not have the right to deny students the skill that they absolutely needed for present and future use. She feels technology is a necessity, not an option, to better provide an equitable education. An example of the school's strong commitment toward increasing student technological ability is put into practice when a student group produces a daily announcement program on video for the school. Sheeran and Sheeran (1996) in their discussion of school reform for the twenty-first century cite availability of the latest technology as a component of reform. "Teachers must ensure that the most current technology is used. . . . It is upon such technology that the success of any reforms will be based" (p. 53).

A major difference between this school and other middle schools that may encounter discipline problems is that the lockers have been permanently shut or locked. The principal feels that this takes all excuses away from students getting into trouble and not concentrating on instruction. The students do not have to change between classes. Textbooks are kept in sets in each classroom. Everything that the students need, in terms of supplies, is provided by the school. The students carry an organizer, which is provided at the beginning of each year. They are expected to keep the notebook for the entire year and use it as an end-of-the-year portfolio. The students are taught organizational skills by keeping track of their assignments, each lesson's objectives, and samples of their best work. The notebook further serves to communicate concerns or make parents aware of their child's work. Notes from home to school are easily exchanged via this notebook. Ms. Trousdale's focus on organizational skills is supported in the literature. Chamot and O'Malley (1994) have written extensively on the importance of incorporating learning strategies into our teaching—particularly with those students who are non-native English speakers. This includes teaching students organizational as well as other strategies (self-evaluation, note-taking, inferencing, summarizing, etc.) that help them learn.

The principal's philosophy lies in bringing the best to the school. She uses creative budgeting and grant writing to assist her in the challenge to provide this middle school with all that is available and appropriate for middle-school Latino adolescents. The principal believes that teachers are instructional leaders and promotes a sense of professionalism by encouraging her entire staff to attend professional conferences with financial assistance provided.

The principal's leadership is also evident by her high visibility throughout the school. She moves from hall to hall greeting students, teachers, and staff. She visits every room in the building at least twice daily. When the students leave on a field trip she bids them farewell from the bus and positively motivates them to enjoy the trip by showing their best behavior. The principal's visibility is continuous and consistent.

Advocacy for Latino Students, Parents, Language, and Culture

In a school that is student centered the principal advocates for Latinos in multiple ways. In fact, the personnel and staff are an extension of this advocacy. One such example is the presence of Officer Martinez at the school. The officer is part of an innovative program between the local police department and the school district. This school resource officer works closely with the school to provide a positive image of law enforcement officers to young adolescents. Her role is one of guiding and nurturing the youngsters at the school. This and other programs to promote positive behavior in the school have proven successful, given the few fights on record.

To further promote positive expectations an incentive program is in place. The students' efforts and work are rewarded by books, school supplies, and materials, as well as the opportunity to receive the coveted Sundance Award. The Sundance Award, a handmade, framed gift certificate, is given to one exemplary eighth-grade boy and girl at a formal banquet during the eighth-grade ceremony. The teachers select the award winners.

In keeping with the middle-school concept, the principal wants a climate more similar to that of an elementary school than a mini high school. The principal, for example, expects to see student work posted throughout the building. Further, the students have learned to respect each other and understand that the school belongs to them. There is never a problem with "tagging."

In order to expand the students' horizons multiple field trips are taken each year, making the curriculum more relevant. The principal promotes this idea, for she wants them to dream beyond what they could possibly imagine. This is critical for Latino youth who do not have the opportunity to travel with their families. She wants them to have a taste of a broader world that can be theirs through the attainment of an education. McLeod (1996) found that the schools that she studied emphasized "meaningful connections across academic disciplines," and curricula that reflected "integration, depth, and hands-on approaches" (p. 17). This was often achieved by involving the schools in projects that took them beyond the classroom walls and into the community.

The ability for a principal to communicate with adults at a school is very important. The ability to communicate with adolescents, the major stakeholders in a school, is crucial. Ms. Trousdale is adept with both groups, students and adults. In no uncertain terms the students explain that they especially like their principal because she cares. They believe her strength lies in her ability to understand them and make herself understood; she uses what one student describes as "kid talk." The issue of care in the public schools has been addressed by Noddings (1992, 1995) who asserts that "a morally defensible mission for education necessarily focuses on matters of human caring" (Noddings, 1995, p. 367). She feels that educators need to, first and foremost, instill in students a respect and care for each other and the world around them. Ms. Trousdale's strong belief in the primary importance of communicating with and understanding her students and their families is reflective of the concept of caring as described by Noddings. If educators are to develop caring in their students, they must also model it.

Berla et al. (1991) write that parent involvement in a child's education during the middle-school years is just as important a factor in a child's success as it is in earlier grades. The principal and staff at Ysleta Middle School firmly believe this. From the moment one meets different parents in the school, whether they are drinking coffee in the library or going about the business of volunteering, it is clear that parents are wanted and needed. One parent who completed her degree is now working as a social worker for the school. A grandmother who volunteers in the cafeteria brings her younger granddaughter to show the principal her "diploma" from preschool. The principal drops everything to show respect to the grandmother and pay attention to the young child. She speaks in Spanish to both and applauds the child's efforts in starting her formal education. Another parent enters the office; this parent completed her GED and is now an instructional assistant at the school. These are success stories, yet Ms. Trousdale is striving to engage more parents in different ways at the school. She believes that middle schools make it difficult at times for parents to become more fully engaged in their children's learning. She would like to see parental activities created as part of each department and grade level's curriculum. This type of parental component would get the parents to the schools when it is currently difficult to do so. Further, she believes that the empowerment that her teachers are experiencing in terms of decision making should be extended to parents. Within the next three years she wants the parents to work with teachers in defining what they want for their child's academic development.

Close contact is kept with the parents regarding their child's weekly progress in both English and Spanish. Both languages are valued and they are used throughout the building, not only in classes that teach Spanish. This is critical for both parents and students to feel "at home" while at school. An English-only edict at school negates the culture and language that the students do bring.

Advocacy for culture begins by orienting teachers to the community they are serving. This is important especially for new faculty and staff. Therefore, to promote the atmosphere where parents and teachers work together, home visits are a beginning to this process. Part of her interview questions for prospective faculty members include: Are you willing to work in this neighborhood? Do you have an open mind? Can you lead in a school with Latinos?

To further support an acceptance of language and culture, half of the faculty will be participating in on-site university classes offered in teaching English as a second language. The principal wants the type of program that will not track or segregate children in bilingual or ESL classes. She believes the system of "pull-out" programs is a broken one. The school is planning a new format for ESL and bilingual classes. ESL classes will be scheduled side by side with a mainstream English class. The teachers will work as a team, the bilingual/ESL teacher with non-designated ESL teachers. The importance of instructional collaboration betwen ESL and other teachers has been underscored in the literature (Chamot and O'Malley, 1994; Lucas et al., 1990; Richard-Amato and Snow, 1992). Kaufman and Brooks (1996) write, "It is clear that collaboration between ESOL [English for Speakers of Other Languages] teachers and teachers of other subject areas is imperative for effective education of language minority students" (p. 232).

To understand the sensitivity and acceptance that the teachers have of the culture of the school one need only look at an activity that takes place in sixth-grade science. This activity also follows the exemplary practices that McLeod (1996) found in the schools she studied where school projects take language minority students beyond the classroom walls and into the community. The Ysleta Middle School students study their community as part of science, and the final project is a video documentary. The teacher walks with her students during class time through the community where student-composed surveys are conducted and videos are made. Students interview people, neighbors, and/or family members. This teacher makes a concerted effort to understand the students and their world. One of her students wrote in her journal, "I felt for the first time that someone didn't think the Kennedy projects, where I live, were ugly."

Leadership into the Future

The principal's educational philosophy has not changed over the years. She still believes in self-responsibility. Her style is direct, yet teachers are permitted to be professionals. They make decisions, attend professional meetings, and are empowered to implement substantiated change for the betterment of the students.

The principal is deeply motivated by the idea that each Latino child should be able to have a dream about her/his future. As a result she strives to afford the school community with every opportunity to broaden the students' experiences. She feels that in a community with second- and third-generation Latinos a sense of futility may exist. These parents may have attended the same school and their experiences may not have been as pleasant as those of their own children.

The principal believes that more Latino teachers are needed to serve as role models for the students. The students need teachers who reflect their own background and with whom they can relate. If a teacher agrees to work at Ysleta Middle School the teacher agrees to accept the students unconditionally as the best and the brightest. In order to do this they are expected to learn the culture and respect it. They must also have the highest expectations for the students and believe that they are as capable as anyone else. The principal states most emphatically, "It is a privilege to work here! If you do not see this please go somewhere else!"

In discussing her impact on the school or vice versa Barbara Trousdale recalls that two years ago she was reluctant to accept the assignment as principal. She enjoyed her role as a central office supervisor. However, it just took three days of working with the students at the school when she discovered that "this place put wings on my soul."

A CULTURALLY COMPETENT HIGH-SCHOOL PRINCIPAL: SANTA TERESA HIGH SCHOOL

Students have more need of models than of critics. (Sign posted on principal's door.)

Background on School and Principal

Two years ago Santa Teresa Junior High School was transformed into a high school. The school lies in a unique area that was once rural and is now becoming industrialized. It is sandwiched between two states, two cities, and two countries. There is an affluent country club setting and a lower-income housing area where some people are still living in old travel trailers with no running water or electricity. Although students from both settings comprise the school's population the majority are on free or reduced lunch. Students arrive at school through an opened gate in any of the twenty school buses or in their own vehicles. As they drive on campus other cars speed by to the newly constructed international border crossing on their way to work at one of the Mexico-U.S. twin plants.

The demographics of the school reveal the Latino predominance in the area. Out of a school enrollment of 865, forty-four are Anglo, one is Native American, and the rest are Latinos. A small number, thirty-six students, are enrolled in special education. A total of eighty-four students are served by the bilingual education program and are at different levels of instruction.

Ben Molina has been principal of the two-year high school since its inception. Mr. Molina, at one point, served as mayor of the Sunland Park community. He and others believe that one of his major strengths lies in his internal knowledge of the community. In fact, Mr. Molina lives in the same school community. He feels that even if principals do not live in their school communities they should get to know the community intimately. In fact, he believes that attending church, buying groceries, and visiting the local restaurants all add to further a principal's credibility and knowledge related to parents and students.

Transforming the School

One of the strengths of this school is the collegiality evidenced by the faculty and staff. The principal is fully committed to site-based decision making. The faculty and staff work together to develop an open environment for students to learn. Currently the faculty is working on an articulation project to align the curriculum from elementary to secondary. They want this project to help all the educators involved in their students' instruction to understand the conceptual bases that Latino students bring to secondary.

Webster (1994), in his study of high-school principals, proposes that "site-based management should become a permanent part of how schools and districts are run" (p. 78). He cautions, however, that it must be supported by everyone from the school board to the school staff, if it is to succeed. This type of support is present at STHS; one indicator of this is the collaborative work of the Campus Improvement Committee.

The Campus Improvement Committee (CIC), which is comprised of parents, students, and faculty, works diligently to plan for the school's future. The self-study report that they drafted includes a vision statement that has "Striving Toward Higher Standards" as a slogan. The acronym STHS is posted throughout the building on walls, as well as on floor tiles, and the students have been involved in a contest to see how well they remember their mission and vision statement.

Mr. Molina believes in building a shared vision and team learning. "We want to define Santa Teresa High School as a learning organization," he explains. As part of the site-based management practice at this school each department elects its own department head and CIC members. Every applicant for a position is interviewed by the CIC, where students as well as parents also play an integral role in the selection of school personnel. The principal expects that each applicant spend at least a day observing in the school to see if they feel they are a good match for the school.

Another strength of this school is its size. With a student population at less than a thousand, the faculty and staff get to know all the students well. As a consequence, there is little gang activity within the school environs. Students, parents, and staff feel safe at the school. On campus there is just one gang to which everyone belongs: the Desert Warriors, the school's mascot.

In only two years the principal has created a feeling of community and ownership, where there is no graffiti on any of its walls. The principal feels that the building does not need to be secured from those within but merely to keep trouble out.

The principal feels that this saying describes his philosophy of education: "Each one teach one, each one reach one." He genuinely believes that there is more to education than the content areas. One needs to be aware of what each student does bring to school. He wants the school to offer hope and opportunity for students to see "that there is more to life than Sunland Park" (the tiny community where most students live).

Ayers (1993) supports this vision of hope, which goes beyond the classroom walls. He writes, "We must move away from teaching as a way of attacking incompetencies, . . . we must find a better way . . . that engages the whole person and guides that person to greater fulfillment and power" (p. 32).

The principal is a strong believer in leading by example. The school is clean because the students help keep it clean. He believes that this is so because they see him doing the same. The students at this age are always in need of positive role models; therefore, he has made it his policy to hire people who will provide these. He further believes in positive thinking and systems learning, where all components of an organization work in conjunction to build a better whole by making collaborative decisions.

He believes that the success of any school lies in the hands of principals who immerse themselves in the culture of the school and community. He recommends that principals become engaged in professional development beyond just management-type seminars. A more critical need is to understand the art, literature, music, and contributions of the Latino culture. Respect is a powerful word and part of the principal's modus operandi. To truly show respect for the language and the culture he recommends that principals learn to speak Spanish.

Furthermore, Mr. Molina organizes all major training at his school. He is also planning a workshop for teachers, parents, and students. They will become involved in professional development by applying the Multiple Intelligences Theory (Gardner, 1993) to the secondary level. He further wants parents to understand their own educational role in a process that also takes place in the home. His goal is to create a community of learners. He further feels that all teaching and learning must constantly undergo evaluation. He wants to reach the point where his success is quantified and qualified.

Advocacy for Latino Students, Parents, Language, and Culture

To understand Mr. Molina's advocacy for his Latino student population is to understand his ideals for a good education at a secondary level. He believes that instruction should not be time bound. Scheduling should be flexible, and written material should be adapted to the learning styles of the students. Instruction should support metacognition, reflective thinking, and self-discipline. These are the guiding frameworks that provide relevant instruction to the school's students and that are supported in the literature. McLeod (1996), for instance, found that flexible scheduling was one of the characteristics of successful schools in her study. She writes, "None of the schools in this study follow a traditional time schedule, in which students do the same things every day for a roughly equal length of time. Instead, schools rearrange their daily schedule to fit curricular priorities" (p. 21).

As much as we may hear adults yelling at students and correcting them in public this is not the practice at Santa Teresa High School. The principal will always speak with a student privately as does the rest of the staff. Never is a student to be humiliated in front of her/his peers. Suspensions are minimal at this school because the principal believes that "a student's educational career is in the hands of educators and ten days of suspension weighs heavily against this." He tries to intervene and help students as much as possible and students readily understand this. There is an open-door policy and his office is constantly visited by students sharing different news about their lives, the community, or the school.

All communiques to parents are handled in both English and Spanish. All PTA and school activities are conducted in both languages. Over 70 percent of the students in the first graduation were the first in their families to get a high-school diploma. During the first graduation ceremony held, the speakers as well as the valedictorian and salutatorian addressed the audience in both languages. Lucas (1993) in her study of elements of effective secondary schooling for language minority students emphasizes the importance of placing value on and promoting the students' languages and cultures. She writes that in the exemplary schools which she studied, "The use and development of the students' native languages are supported in a variety of ways inside and outside the classroom" (p. 3).

Parents were also recognized for their contributions in helping their children through high school. At this school parents are requested to offer input and provide recommendations regarding any school concerns. When the principal realizes that a student is in continuous trouble, parental support is enlisted. In one situation a young man was in constant trouble for gang activity. The parent was asked to speak with the principal and teachers. The father thought that the school "was picking on his child." However, the father decided reluctantly to follow the principal's recommendation and shadow his son for three consecutive days in lieu of suspension. At the end of the experience the parent realized that the school was legitimately trying to help his son, yet the son was a difficult student. In fact, he willingly agreed to work with the principal and helped turn the student around from a gang member to a serious student.

Mr. Molina considers every adolescent to be in an at-risk situation. He commonly asks, "Would you want to relive your teenage years?" He believes in interventions and prevention rather than suspension and expulsion. Part of this effort is to have home and school work together to benefit the students.

To further link the home with the school, the school computer labs are open for two hours every evening. Parents and younger children are invited to participate in an after-school community program for computer literacy. In fact, the building is opened to GED, ESL classes, as well as various sports and recreational activities.

Mr. Molina believes that parents are just as interested as educators are in the academic achievement of their children. Although he finds that involving parents at the secondary level poses a greater challenge than at the elementary, parents can be enticed if provided with the right invitation. Students, he feels, can get their parents to school. During staff interviews parents are called to assist. When parents cannot attend due to job constraints they readily identify alternates to serve as their replacements. They are always eager to help out the school. Parent involvement has been identified in the literature as a significant factor in successful schools (Lucas, 1993; Lucas et al., 1990; Romo and Falbo, 1996; U.S. Department of Education, 1995). McLeod (1996) elaborates on the importance of involving parents in the life of the school and in addressing "the social and educational needs of the families of the students" (p. 30). This involves not only communicating with parents in their own language but making home visits, assisting families with obtaining medical care, clothing and other necessities, including them in educational decisions about their children, and providing educational opportunities (GED, ESL, computer literacy, citizenship, etc.) as well.

Students are not perceived as culturally deprived or disadvantaged at Santa Teresa High School. The principal believes that this term reflects a mental model that must be removed from the dominant culture. It is as erroneous as saying a student is linguistically deficient. A child comes to school with language and culture. The principal further believes that the term "alingual" or the concept that students cannot read is a further mistake; the child may simply be a poor reader who can be taught to read better. Every child has language, and it is the school's responsibility to work with the students and what they bring from home.

Educators should have the skills and resources to provide the instruction required for each student. School educators must learn how to use both languages and reflect this in daily education plans. Workshops on cultural awareness are in the planning stages at this school for new faculty. However, the majority of the faculty and staff speak Spanish. Since the staff members are encouraged to take risks and are honored for their innovations, they also feel free to ask for assistance as needed. When two teachers did not feel that they were reaching their PEP students, they revamped their curriculum. To better understand the needs of students acquiring a second language they requested help from the faculty's ESL teachers.

Leadership into the Future

A major challenge for this high-school principal is increasing the "academic self-esteem" of many students. This he feels is tightly connected with the expectations held at home. In many low-income communities students are expected by parents or guardians to become the families' drivers when no one else is licensed or to accompany parents to visit sick relatives in other cities. This creates a cycle of absences that impacts the student's progress adversely. For this reason the principal explains compulsory attendance laws and other legal issues at parent meetings.

Ben Molina's dream for Santa Teresa High School is for the school to become a model in providing the best in bilingual, bicultural, and biliterate education, especially in light of the doors of opportunity that are being opened by the North American Free Trade Agreement. For students with professional aspirations he feels that a college education should be tenable, given the superior instruction received at the school. He wants his students to compete successfully and live a full life. His goal is to attract other students to attend the school as well. He wants to remain in this school at least until his goal becomes a reality. Mr. Molina sums up his commitment with the following statement: "This is the best job ever. What else could be more important?"

A CULTURALLY COMPETENT HIGH-SCHOOL PRINCIPAL: SOCORRO HIGH SCHOOL

Socorro High School will promote the development of life skills for all its students by providing a stimulating educational environment which offers strong academic, social, emotional and physical growth. (Mission Statement, Socorro High School)

Socorro High School was recently presented with a National Blue Ribbon Award for its outstanding achievement. The following sections highlight the school, its principal, and those features that have made the school successful.

Background on School and Principal

Socorro High School is located in the lower valley of El Paso, where much of the area consists of cotton and alfalfa fields and where families are generally of low socio-economic status. The school has an enrollment of 2200 students and is headed by a principal and four assistant principals. The enrollment is 98 percent Mexican American, with over 90 percent of the students on free/reduced lunch. SHS was built in 1965 to house 250 students and was named after the city of Socorro. In 1986, a major renovation added classroom wings, a state-of-the-art computerized media center, a 1,200-seat auditorium, and a 3,000-seat gymnasium.

Socorro High is a comprehensive school offering an alternative program, vocational programs for the whole district, SPED (Special Education) and ESL (English as a Second Language) programs, magnet programs such as COSMOS (Career Opportunities for Students in Math or Science) and HOSA (Health Occupations Student Association), as well as all the regular programs. In all, the school offers ninety-nine extracurricular activities, including civic clubs, sports teams, and instructional programs. The variety of programs offered is credited for the school's low drop-out rate of less than 2 percent; there is something for everyone at Socorro High. The many programs and activities offered at the school are indicative of the school's philosophy, which is expressed in the mission statement presented previously.

Mr. Mike Quatrini, principal of Socorro High School, was born in Pennsylvania. However, his father was in the army and after having lived in various places they moved to El Paso. Mr. Quatrini considers El Paso, where he has spent the last thirty years, to be his home. Upon graduating with a bachelor's degree in criminal justice, Mr. Quatrini attended law school. He soon discovered that was not for him, and subsequently taught in a parochial school in El Paso. He enjoyed this work so much that he returned to school and received teaching certification and a master's degree in educational administration. His professional experiences include teaching as well as being a principal at the elementary, middle- and high-school levels. He arrived at Socorro High School in 1992. At that time the middle-school building and the high-school building were

undergoing construction in order to turn them into one large and reno-
vated high school. The physical changes that the school underwent were
but the beginning of a school-wide process of transformation.

Transforming the School

One of the first things Mr. Quatrini noticed upon his arrival at SHS
was that there was a lack of communication within the school. Thus, he
immediately put up a large calendar board across his office where
program sponsors annotated meetings, games, and all other activities
going on within the school. The objective was to increase awareness by
all staff, parents, and community as to what was going on at the school.
Another change which he initiated in this effort to increase communication within the school was to move the head secretary up to the front of
the school office, to where she could be seen and was accessible to all.
There is now an open-door policy, such that she does not "guard" his
door. Any student, parent, or teacher can walk directly into the principal's
office to speak with him.

This initiative toward greater communication also prompted him to
begin a staff development program where all teachers, on a rotating basis,
were involved in introducing themselves and presenting their programs
to the rest of the staff. This was received very positively by the teachers,
some of whom had been there for ten years without knowing each other,
nor what and how they taught. A strong and relevant staff development
program has continued at the school, supported by a fund specifically for
that purpose. Teachers are provided support so that they can attend
workshops and conferences. They then come back, share their new
understandings with other staff, and integrate them into their instruction.

An example of the positive outcomes of staff development is evident
in the fine arts program. The perception by the principal was that this
program was too loose; there was a lack of coordination of efforts and
activities, such that the program had fallen apart. Mr. Quatrini set out to
create a new program and started by sending a group of teachers to visit
schools in a district where exemplary art programs existed. They came
back with excitement and ideas about creating a new program, recruited
students from the middle schools who enrolled in the program, and now
have a strong fine arts thematic block. In this block, the students take the
usual required courses for their levels, but additionally take elective
courses specific to the fine arts area. (Likewise, students in other thematic

blocks take their elected courses within that specific area of study, e.g., health care or math.)

These changes have ultimately led to a team effort among everyone. Mr. Quatrini now notes that the teachers "see themselves as part of the school, as part of a team. . . . It's a team effort, everybody cares for kids around here, and the kids give you reason to care for them."

Changes in the programs were also initiated by the new principal. A major change—block scheduling—took place as a result of his experiences at the middle school, which he applied to the high school. Mr. Quatrini notes that when he arrived at the school, "What they had here was a typical high school where kids were scattered, no ownership of kids by teachers. There was no linkage; there was no connection between teachers." Now every teacher is hooked up to an instructional block, and he indicates, "What we're doing is making it smaller because we have a school within a school concept, with our blocks; it's like they are families within those blocks. . . . You've got umbrellas within the school and all of these nets fit in case the students fall; there's someone to pick them up."

Some blocks in grades nine and ten overlap with blocks in the eleventh and twelfth grades; some don't. HOSA, for instance, is a four-year block such that if a student gets in there in grade nine, s/he can have basically the same teachers until the twelfth grade. There are also four-year vertical blocks in regular programs, so that students do not have to go into a new block once they move up a grade but can continue with the same basic group of teachers. Incoming students can go into a thematic block or a basic ninth-grade block, the difference being that, in the thematic (COSMOS, for instance) block, the electives are geared toward that theme—the rest of the curriculum is the same.

The concept of block scheduling and creating programs, or schools within schools, has been identified in the literature as a key factor in successful secondary schools for Latinos. Romo and Falbo (1996) write, "We recommend that secondary students be grouped into schools within schools. . . . Subgroups of these schools would take courses together so that the same students are together most of the day. In this way, schools would be creating peer networks that are integrated into the school structure" (p. 237).

Likewise, the U.S. Department of Education (1995) in its report of promising secondary school practices states, "Working together in houses, whose membership is usually stable over the whole period of a student's enrollment, enables teachers and students to get to know and understand each other better" (p. 29).

Another major change that has positively impacted the school is year-round scheduling where school is in session for twelve weeks and then off for four weeks. This, the principal feels, has been very rewarding and has worked particularly well at Socorro High because they are on a single track. This allows staff the opportunity to remediate or enrich students during the off time. In the traditional model if a student failed the first six weeks, she would have to wait until the summer to make it up, and she would return to school for the second six weeks already feeling bad about her grades.

Students are currently recommended to attend intersession programs, which are conducted like mini summer schools. A student can participate and earn a passing grade that replaces a failing grade. Students then are motivated to try harder because they know they have the opportunity to pass; in this manner, intersessions function as safety nets. The implementation of intersessions is but one way in which Mr. Quatrini advocates for students.

Advocacy for Latino Students, Parents, Language, and Culture

Mr. Quatrini recalls that when he first arrived at the school he found an old lecture-type routine in the classes where "everyone was doing their own thing . . . and teachers were only concerned about their subject area . . . as if they had blinders on . . . with tunnel vision." That type of philosophy was dropped and was replaced with one that states, "The buck stops here." This philosophy is one that puts the responsibility for graduating every student on the entire school staff. To this end, "There's a lot of camaraderie, lots of communication, and a lot of helping one another and the focus is on the success of students."

This success has partly been achieved by the implementation of active learning in the classroooms where the instruction includes hands-on activities and is thus motivating for the students. A science class, for example, may have the students making ice cream, reflecting on the effect of salt on the ice-cream-making process, analyzing the caloric count for each serving, analyzing the nutritional contents of the ice cream, and finally eating the ice cream. There are other incentives that are provided throughout the year as a way to motivate students—for example, rewards such as ice cream, frisbees, caps, and other items that are earned by students for their various accomplishments, including attendance. The principal thus advocates for students by providing the paths whereby all can succeed at Socorro High, regardless of whatever level the student was at upon arrival at the school.

Mr. Quatrini does not see language or culture as barriers to success and explains that he does not actually do anything differently for Latino students that he wouldn't do for all students—regardless of their background. He is aware that many students come with "a different language that may disallow them to initially perform at a level that an English-speaking student does" and "that they have to take tests in English without having had the experiences that will allow them to do well on standardized tests." Nonetheless, he feels these students are better off than those who are monolingual because they have better job opportunities. He himself speaks limited Spanish and feels apologetic with the bilingual students and their families because they can speak some English but he cannot speak their language. However, he communicates with them and has a working knowledge of Spanish.

Latino students, including ESL students, are winning at Socorro High. The school has a very strong ESL program, the program that best exemplifies what is going on in the entire school by way of curriculum, instruction, and parent involvement. About 10 percent of the students at the school are enrolled in the ESL program. There is a great sense of unity, belonging, and ownership in the department. Approximately twenty mainstream teachers who are ESL-endorsed work with those students acquiring English. There are five full-time ESL teachers working in the program as well as a coordinator who splits her time between Socorro High and another school.

All the teachers working with the ESL students get together for monthly and weekly meetings to share, collaborate, and update each other on their activities. These teachers help each other and support each other's work through reinforcement in their respective classrooms, collaborative implementation of activities, and/or support with planning and organization. The program has provided the means for endorsement in ESL for all of those teachers working with the students in the program, an initiative that strengthened relationships between teachers across the entire campus.

The importance of staff development and a schoolwide team effort to serve language minority students more effectively has been highlighted in the literature on high schools that successfully promote achievement for Latino students. Lucas et al. (1990) noted that in the schools which they studied, "*All* teachers and professional staff were encouraged to participate in professional development . . . not just those who taught specific classes for this [Latino] special student population . . . all staff took responsibility for teaching these students" (p. 330).

The ESL program brings in over 100 parents for their meetings—an uncommon achievement at the high-school level. At these meetings the parents are provided with information that is relevant to their needs. At their request, for instance, the staff has provided them with "immigration information nights" where they are given personalized help, with community assistance, on issues related to citizenship and residency. The program also provides a freshmen orientation for the families of incoming ESL students. Great care is taken to greet them during their first school visit and to personalize the incoming process, a factor that the department feels is critical to establishing linkages with the families. As the ESL lead teacher indicated, "The induction process is a 'big deal'; parents are offered coffee, hospitality, shown a video, given pamphlets, lots of personal attention. . . . This is done for every parent who is new to the school." Romo and Falbo (1996) affirm the importance of making schools accessible to parents and creating, maintaining, and nurturing partnerships with them: "Before schools can build partnerships with parents, they will have to learn how to communicate with parents in respectful and meaningful ways" (p. 224).

According to the ESL coordinator, Mr. Quatrini listens carefully to the teachers in her department and he "buys into the ideas of the teachers; teachers are given lots of space by the principal. . . . He rarely rejects any idea that is presented to him as long as he sees that it is well thought out and that teachers have done their homework. . . . It is not a rigid environment." His advocacy for these students is thereby seen in his support for the program, support that ranges from providing staff development funding to the teachers to buying T-shirts for the ESL students.

Leadership into the Future

Mr. Quatrini's formulas for success led Socorro High School to receive national recognition by the U.S. Department of Education in 1996. It was one of 266 schools in the nation to receive this award. Yet he feels that there is still much to be done. The staff, with his leadership, sets goals every year and participates in site-based management. These goals and objectives are revisited by the individual departments and teachers during the year and re-evaluated—always with a focus on the students. The main question is, "Are the goals of benefit to the students?" When an idea hasn't worked, it is thrown out and replaced with something different, a process that Mr. Quatrini feels has brought much growth among the staff. Change is implemented when change is needed; the teachers do not allow themselves to fall back but rather continue to work hard and go even further in their achievements every year. Their work has been reflected in the achievement of their students not only during their stay at SHS, but in the years following. Hispanic students at Socorro High, for example, have continued their studies at Ivy League and other highly reputed institutions. This, perhaps, is the highest recognition for the efforts of the students and staff at the school.

SUMMARY

This chapter has presented portraits of three successful principals and their schools. These portraits have introduced principals at the middle and high school levels who provide us with exemplary models of leadership in schools with high Latino student enrollments. The philosophies and practices that are implemented at these schools are, moreover, supported by the research literature in the area of exemplary middle and high school education. The studies presented herein, as well as the literature, identify those characteristics found in schools that provide Latino students with the highest probability of schooling success. The following highlights these characteristics.

- Schools place value on students' home languages and cultures, and teachers integrate their culture, language, and experiences into their instruction (Howe, 1994; Lucas, 1993; McLeod, 1996; Saravia-Shore and Garcia, 1995). Included in this is an effort by teachers and staff to acquire, at least, a basic command of the Spanish language, as well as teachers constructing lessons "in ways consistent with students' home-community culture and language to take advantage of students' cognitive experiences and to allow students opportunities to engage in behaviors conducive to achievement" (Saravia-Shore and Garcia, 1995, p. 59).
- High expectations are set for Latino students (Howe, 1994; Lucas et al., 1990; Romo and Falbo, 1996; Saravia-Shore and Garcia, 1995; U.S. Department of Education, 1995). Teachers and staff explicitly communicate these expectations to students and help them to meet the expectations. Lucas et al. (1990) write, "The six schools we visited not only held high expectations of their students but had also

taken concrete actions to demonstrate those expectations and to help students accomplish what was expected" (p. 327).

- Professional development is provided to assist all teachers and staff working with Latino students—not only the designated ESL teachers. Training is comprehensive and includes, for instance, methodology in sheltered English instruction, the implementation of instruction that actively involves students, and the cultural dynamics of the Latino population (Howe, 1994; Lucas, 1993; Lucas et al., 1990; McLeod, 1996; Romo and Falbo, 1996). As Romo and Falbo (1996) state, "Before all teachers can become good teachers, they must be trained and retrained to have the teaching skills necessary to promote learning in all students" (p. 221).

- All school faculty and staff shared a strong commitment to help their students succeed (Howe, 1994; Lucas et al., 1990; McLeod, 1996; Romo and Falbo, 1996). Saravio-Shore and Garcia (1995), in their study of the literature on successful teaching approaches for diverse populations, found that a key element was that teachers were "personally committed to achieving equity for all students and believe that they are capable of making a difference in their students' learning" (p. 49).

- The organization of the schools allows for flexibility in scheduling, includes block scheduling, and incorporates "schools within schools" in order to (1) promote increased learning time for students, (2) allow teachers and students to become more familiar with each other, their needs, their families, and their interests; and (3) provide students with the opportunity of focusing on that subject matter which is of most interest to them. McLeod (1996) found that exemplary schools "create larger, more stable, and more flexible groups that incorporate students at all ability levels and all levels of English language proficiency" (p. 19).

- Parents are actively involved in their children's education in exemplary schools (Howe, 1994; Lucas, 1993; Romo and Falbo, 1996; Saravio-Shore and Garcia, 1995; U.S. Department of Education, 1995). Parents at these schools are involved not only in fund-raising events, but in assisting with instruction in and out of the classroom and in decision-making processes. McLeod (1996) writes, "The schools in this study make significant efforts to involve parents in their children's education and in the life of the school, and to address the social and educational needs of the families of their students" (p. 30).

The principals portrayed herein have led their schools in creating a vision that promotes success for all students, regardless of language, culture, socio-economic status, or formal educational background. This vision is always kept in mind as staff struggle on a daily basis to meet their goals and objectives, and most of all, to caringly look at each student as an individual full of potential and energy who can achieve high levels of success in all aspects of life.

As Lucas (1993) writes in her study of secondary schools that she calls "bright spots," "so while I present some hope, I acknowledge that what I describe is not typical, and that we cannot simply apply these features to school and hope to solve all the problems" (p. 2). Through this look at culturally competent administrators one finds three more bright spots to add to the educational horizon. One clearly sees that each struggles to compete with an inequitable system imposed from outside their school buildings. They do not tire of striving to bring educational attainment to the Latino students whom they serve. They are culturally committed and culturally cognizant that this educational attainment is within their reach.

REFERENCES

Ayers, W. 1993. *To Teach: The Journey of a Teacher.* New York, NY: Teachers College Press.

Berla, N., A. T. Henderson, and W. Kerewsky. 1991. *Parent Involvement at the Middle School.* Washington, D.C.: National Committee for Citizens in Education.

Boyer, E. 1983. *High School: A Report on Secondary Education in America.* New York, NY: Harper and Row.

Chamot, A. and J. M. O'Malley. 1994. *The CALLA Handbook: Implementing the Cognitive Academic Language Learning Approach.* Reading, MA: Addison Wesley.

Gardner, H. *Multiple Intelligences: Theory into Practice.* New York, NY: Basic Books.

Giacchino-Baker, R. 1992. "Secondary Education: Equity and Quality Issues for Language Minority Students." In L. T. Diaz-Rico and K. Z. Weed, *The Crosscultural, Language, and Academic Development Handbook.* Boston, MA: Allyn & Bacon.

Goodlad, J. 1984. *A Place Called School: Prospects for the Future.* New York, NY: McGraw-Hill.

Howe, C. K. 1994. "Improving the Achievement of Hispanic Students," *Educational Leadership,* 51(8): 42–44.

Kaufman, D. and J. G. Brooks. 1996. "Interdisciplinary Collaboration in Teacher Education: A Constructivist Approach," *TESOL Quarterly,* 30(2): 231–251.

Kozol, J. 1992. *Savage Inequalities: Children in America's Schools.* New York, NY: Crown.

Lucas, T. 1993. *Applying Elements of Effective Secondary Schooling for Language Minority Students: A Tool for Reflection and Stimulus to Change.* Washington, D.C.: National Clearinghouse for Bilingual Education.

Lucas, T., R. Henze, and R. Donato. 1990. "Promoting the Success of Latino Language Minority Students: An Exploratory Study of Six High Schools," *Harvard Educational Review,* 60(3):315–340.

McLeod, B. 1996. *School Reform and Student Diversity: Exemplary Schooling for Language Minority Students.* Washington, D.C.: National Clearinghouse for Bilingual Education.

National Association of Hispanic Publications and U.S. Census Bureau. 1995. Cited in *Hispanic,* November, p. 12.

National Center for Educational Statistics. September 1995. In *Dropout Rates in the United States,* 1994, Washington, D.C.: U.S. Department of Education.

Noddings, N. 1992. *The Challenge to Care in Schools: Alternative Approaches to Education.* New York, NY: Teachers College Press.

Noddings, N. 1995. "A Morally Defensible Mission for Schools in the 21st Century," *Phi Delta Kappan,* 76(5):365–368.

Reyes, P. and R. R. Valencia. 1993. "Educational Policy and the Growing Latino Student Population: Problems and Prospects," *Hispanic Journal of Behavioral Sciences,* 15(2):258–283.

Richard-Amato, P. A. and M. A. Snow. 1992. *The Multicultural Classroom: Readings for Content-Area Teachers.* New York, NY: Longman.

Romo, H. and T. Falbo. 1996. *Latino High School Graduation: Defying the Odds.* Austin, TX: University of Texas Press.

Saravi-Shore, M. and E. Garcia. 1995. "Diverse Teaching Strategies for Diverse Learners," in *Educating Everybody's Children: Diverse Teaching Strategies for Diverse Learners.* Alexandria, VA: ASCD.

Sheeran, T. J. and M. F. Sheeran. 1996. *Schools, Schooling and Teachers: A Curriculum for the Future.* NAASP, Vol 80:580.

Sizer, T. 1992. *Horace's School: Redesigning the American High School.* Boston, MA: Houghton Mifflin.

U.S. Department of Education. 1995. *Raising the Educational Achievement of Secondary School Students: An Idea Book. Volume 1: Summary of Promising Practices.* Washington, D.C.: U.S. Department of Education.

Webster, W. E. 1994. *Voices in the Hall: High School Principals at Work.* Bloomington, IN. Phi Delta Kappa Educational Foundation.

PART V

EXEMPLARY PRACTICES FOR LATINOS IN MIDDLE SCHOOLS

Middle Schools for Latinos: A Framework for Success

REBECCA BENJAMIN—*University of New Mexico*

INTRODUCTION

JESSICA and Antonio are middle-school students at Madison Middle School. Like them, the majority of students at Madison are Latino, roughly 94%. In the past, the school had a more varied enrollment, which included greater numbers of African Americans and whites. However, like many schools serving Latino students, Madison has become increasingly segregated (Dryfoos, 1990; Simons et al., 1991). Achievement scores for thirteen-year-old Latino students at Madison closely mirror national trends. In reading, 34% of the Latinos are scoring at the expected proficiency level as compared to 63% of whites and 39% of African Americans, nationally. In math, Latinos are faring a little better with 55% scoring at the expected proficiency levels as compared to 78% of whites and 49% of African Americans. In science, Latinos once again are the lowest achievers, with only 20% achieving expected levels of proficiency as compared to 61% of whites and 27% of African Americans, nationally (Simons et al., 1991).

White teachers make up the majority, 78% of the teaching staff at Madison Middle School. Most of them, though well-meaning, are unfamiliar with Latino cultures and the needs of Latino students. This, and the high teacher turnover rate, also reflect the experiences of Latinos across the nation (Dryfoos, 1990; Simons et al., 1991; Sleeter, 1993; Weinberg, 1994). Although there are no drop-out rates specifically for Madison, the school district reports an 18% drop-out rate for Latinos, as compared to 5.5% for African Americans and 6.8% for whites. As in the case of the achievement levels reported here, these drop-out levels reflect national trends. In 1975, when Latino drop-out rates first became available, nationally, 13.2% of Latino sixteen- to seventeen-year-olds were leaving school. In 1988, that rate had climbed to nearly 20%.

The picture presented here of Madison Middle School, and of the schooling experiences of Latinos nationally, underlines the severity of problems facing many Latino middle-school students. The stance taken in this chapter is that it is not these children who have failed, but, rather, it is the schools that have failed to meet the needs of Latino students (Simons et al., 1991). In this chapter, a profile of Latino middle-school students and their experiences will be developed. Reflections on their developmental and identity needs will be included, as well as an examination of some possible solutions in light of those needs. But the term Latino tends to obscure some significant differences, which become evident as soon as we take a closer look at them and their communities.

Jessica, an eighth grader, was born and raised in East Alamo, the Madison Middle School neighborhood. Her parents also attended this school when they moved to East Alamo from a rural area with their parents. The neighborhood has a long and important Latino history. Many of the local and regional Latino leaders claim their beginnings in East Alamo, often commenting how the "tough life" in East 'Mo prepared them for the struggles they now face.

However, East 'Mo has changed in some significant ways since those adults were growing up. As the neighborhood has become more urbanized, many of the employment possibilities that were once plentiful, such as the railroad, heavy industry, and stable, agriculturally-related jobs, have moved out of the area, or all but disappeared. In the days of better job opportunities, Mexicano migrants coming to East Alamo and their Spanish-speaking Chicano neighbors were able to form bonds, despite their differences. However, as jobs have become scarce and the children of both Chicanos and older Mexicano migrants have lost the ability to speak Spanish, there is a growing distance between the native born and those who are newly arrived from Mexico and Central America.

There are additional changes in East Alamo. The growth of a young urban underclass, coupled with the availability of guns and drugs has meant an escalation in gang activity and violence in the neighborhood. Despite these changes, Jessica is very proud to be from East 'Mo. It is an important part of her identity. For that reason, she has adopted the clothes, hair style, and ways of speaking of many young females from East Alamo. In addition, she is sometimes resistant to authority, especially in school. These behaviors often lead her to be "typecast" as a *chola*, or gang member, by some of her teachers and some of the people she meets outside of East Alamo.

Antonio, Jessica's schoolmate, is in the seventh grade. Antonio's family moved to East Alamo to join his mother's sister who has lived in the neighborhood with her family for the past twenty years. Antonio and his younger siblings were born in East Alamo. His older brother and sister were born in northern Mexico, in the general area where his parents are from. While Antonio's parents don't speak English, they are very familiar with some aspects of life in the United States, having been migrant workers during a better part of their childhood. In elementary school, Jessica and Antonio would often work together in the reading buddies program, where they read to younger students. At that time, they were both good students, especially in the area of language arts and reading. Since then, Jessica has become a mediocre student, often failing to turn in assignments and spending a great deal of class time socializing with her friends.

For Antonio, the change to being considered a mediocre student has been more dramatic. In elementary school, Antonio spent most of his time working: in class; in the cafeteria student work program; in the crossing guard program; and in the library. While Antonio did enjoy a social life with a few close friends, his contacts were mostly limited to other children who, like Antonio, self-identified as Mexicano. They also continued to use some Spanish in their social interactions. When Antonio first entered Madison Middle School, he and Jessica were initially able to call on their reading buddy experience to have some casual conversations. Soon, however, the tensions at Madison between Chicano and Mexicano students began affecting Jessica and Antonio's relationship. Both of them were getting a great deal of pressure from their respective group of friends to sever any ties they might have had with those who were considered "unacceptable." Not surprisingly, they both succumbed to this pressure. In Antonio's case, he also began to distance himself from his teachers and consequently from school work as well. At the end of sixth grade, he had had so many absences that he was forced to attend summer school to pass to seventh grade.

MIDDLE-SCHOOL LATINOS AND THE SEARCH FOR AN IDENTITY

As adolescent Latinos begin this search, they must sort out their identity at various levels. Not only must they come to terms with their sexuality, their interest groups, and their families, but also with their identity as members of a particular ethnic group.

The Importance of Group

Jessica and Antonio, like most young adolescents, are in the beginning stages of trying to define who they are. Much of this process involves defining oneself as a member of a particular group (Santrock, 1993; Sue and Sue, 1990). As their bodies begin to change in significant ways, these young people start to question all of the assumptions they came to have in childhood, particularly regarding those closest to them, in an effort to begin to see their "new" selves (Erickson, 1963). Adolescents are, in Erickson's view, in the Identity vs. Role Confusion stage during which time they must experiment with different solutions to the roles they will play as adults (Erickson, 1963; Santrock, 1993). This experimentation often gets played out by gauging oneself through others' eyes. For this reason, the adolescent's peer group quickly becomes important, and those who are different help a young person test similarities between oneself and one's group.

The Search for an Ethnic Identity

Minority adolescents, and in this particular case Latino adolescents, must also begin a search for an ethnic identity, as they enter the Identity vs. Role Confusion stage (McAdoo and McAdoo, 1985; Phinney and Rotheram, 1987; Sue and Sue, 1990). This can be a difficult process, depending to a large degree on the student's personal and family background and on his/her experiences with racism and prejudice (Gibbs and Huang, 1989; Sue and Sue, 1990; Tatum, 1992). Some adolescents are aware early on of the need to identify with one's own ethnic group. In Antonio's case, as previously discussed, some of this is due to his family's close ties to Mexico and to personal experiences he has had with racism. Others, like Jessica, may begin this process by identifying with the group closest to them in their neighborhood.

Much of the work that has been done on ethnic identity comes from research conducted on and by African Americans in this field (Cross, 1991; McAdoo and McAdoo, 1985; Tatum, 1992). Several different stages of ethnic identity development have been identified by these and other researchers (Sue and Sue, 1990). The *preencounter* or *conformity* stage is characterized by a denial of the existence of racism, a valuation of white culture and a devaluation of the individual's own culture. Statements like "there's no prejudice at this school" are typical of this stage. In the *encounter* or *dissonance* stage, it is usually some personal experience with prejudice that leads the individual to question the beliefs and assumptions she/he held during the previous stage. This involves acknowledging the existence of racism and one's membership within a particular ethnicity. It also involves a growing admiration for the values and traits of one's own group. At the same time, persons in this stage may begin to feel negatively about the dominant culture, some for the very first time. In the *resistance* or *immersion* stage, individuals totally immerse themselves in their own culture and history and reject the dominant culture. Just as they feel pride and admiration for their own group, they feel a corresponding sense of anger against the dominant group. In the *introspection* stage, individuals are often bothered by the rigid or unilateral beliefs of some people within their own group. In this stage, they begin to question some of the beliefs that they whole-heartedly adopted in the previous stage, which may create some distance between them and those they were closest to before. In the final stage, the *integrative* or *internalization* stage, individuals are able to move to a more realistic appraisal of their own ethnicity and corresponding groups in the society including the dominant one (Cross, 1991; McAdoo and McAdoo, 1985; Phinney and Rotheram, 1987; Sue and Sue, 1990; Tatum, 1992).

For Jessica and Antonio, several processes are occurring at the same time, each one attempting to resolve particular developmental needs. In Jessica's case, we can see how her conformity in dress, speech, and behavior is a way for her to experiment with her role as a young Chicana from East Alamo. Both Antonio and Jessica are rejecting their previous roles as good students, in part to test their own self-images as good students and perhaps in response to district expectations of Latino students (Fordham and Ogbu, 1986; Weinberg, 1994). In Antonio's case, he may also be immersing himself in his own culture so as to work out ethnic identity issues. Other considerations for understanding both Antonio's and Jessica's behaviors may lie in understanding the importance of the family in the development of a personal identity.

Latino Adolescents, Personal Identity, and the Family

As was mentioned previously, adolescents test their previous assumptions by experimenting with the varied roles they may play in early adulthood (Erickson, 1963; Santrock, 1993). By casting those closest to them as adversaries and reacting against them, adolescents are often able to test these assumptions. Unfortunately, these "adversaries" can frequently be their parents, which can cause some tension in the families of adolescents. For many years, the traditional view of adolescents and their families was one of a constant struggle between the adolescents, who intently focused on achieving independence and autonomy, and their parents' active resistance of such efforts (Santrock, 1993). More recently, there has been a realization by researchers in this field that while achievement of independence is an important part of adolescence, young people continue to need a close and supportive relationship with their families, which reassures adolescents of their assumptions and their "testing" efforts (Santrock, 1993). Further, there is an acknowledgment of the role that culture plays in the move toward autonomy (Erickson, 1963; Meade, 1928; Santrock, 1993). There are some cultures where intense conflict between parents and adolescents may not exist (Meade, 1928). In Latino families, one will find a wide variety of responses to an adolescent's need for growing independence, depending on the family's nativity, place of residence, configuration, and socio-economic status.

Many Latino families may experience little conflict between their teenage children and themselves. There are several possible reasons for this. In many Latino families, regardless of socio-economic status, the extended family is a reality. This means that adolescents have relationships with several adults other than their parents, who can often help to diffuse tensions that exist. Adolescents, or their parents, will often turn to these other adults (grandparents, aunts, and uncles) when conflicts arise, thus gaining the assistance of a "third party." Another common trait among many Latino families, particularly those who are poorer or from more rural backgrounds, is the primacy of the family as a unit (Benjamin, 1993; Valdés, 1989). Children, and in particular adolescents, learn to subordinate their needs to the needs of the family. In Valdés' study, children of all ages were expected to behave in ways that would contribute to the good of the entire family. Staying in school, getting excellent grades, or excelling in sports were secondary to the needs of the family. For adolescents, this often means taking a part-time job so as to contribute income to the family, baby-sitting younger siblings while parents work, or taking care of the elderly (Benjamin, 1993; Valdés, 1989).

There are times, however, when intense struggles can arise between Latino parents and adolescents. These often involve cultural conflicts between younger Latinos who are more acculturated to mainstream American values and those who are older and less acculturated to American society. This can be especially difficult for young Latinas whose life and work expectations as young women may be in direct conflict with those of their parents (Tinajero et al., 1991; Weinberg, 1994). Some may react by rejecting the influence and support of their families. Given proper support, some may opt for a different role by preparing for a career. The Mother-Daughter Program co-sponsored by the University of Texas, El Paso, the YWCA of El Paso, and several area school districts works to maintain the close ties between Latinas and their young adolescent daughters by introducing them to university career options and assisting them to plan for these careers together (Tinajero et al., 1991).

Older siblings can also play important roles in helping middle-school-aged Latinos develop a sense of identity. In the case of Jessica, much of her assertiveness and her style has been heavily influenced by her older sister who is in high school and works part-time as a clerk in a social service agency. For Antonio, his early awareness of ethnic identity has been fostered by his older brother who experienced a great deal of racism in school, dropped out, and joined an exclusively Mexican gang.

CONGRUENCE BETWEEN MIDDLE-SCHOOL STUDENTS' DEVELOPMENTAL NEEDS AND SCHOOL OFFERINGS

Jessica and Antonio, like many Latino middle-school students are in the beginning stages of finding out who they are: who they are as students and future workers; who they are in terms of their gender and sexual orientation; who they are as Latinos, each with their own definition; and who they are in terms of their present and future families. These are not easy issues to deal with, not for young people nor for the adults with whom they interact. Many middle schools may not be prepared to handle all of these developmental aspects. Middle schools have sometimes been accused of treating their students as little high schoolers, ignoring the special needs of young adolescents (Santrock, 1993).

When a new student enters middle school for the first time, she may encounter several new elements. In the first place, the size of the school, which is often fed by several elementary schools, dramatically increases. Secondly, while in elementary school, a student is oriented to her teacher and classmates; in middle school, she must now orient herself to several different teachers, differing expectations, and several sets of classmates. In essence, she must now orient herself to the entire school (Anderman and Maehr, 1994). Thirdly, there is a stronger emphasis on achievement and assessment (particularly on standardized tests), which often results in more formalized tracking of students (Anderman and Maehr, 1994; Slavin, 1991). Fourthly, new students are now in contact with greater numbers of other students who may reflect increased heterogeneity, both in terms of groups and ethnicity. Lastly, the curriculum rarely addresses the identity needs of minority adolescents.

These encounters can create a great deal of stress for a student who is at the same time dealing with the complex issues of self-identity. Several of the aforementioned elements, the new orientation to the whole school and the increased emphasis on achievement, often through tracking, may contribute in large part to the drop in academic motivation that is seen in middle-school students (Anderman and Maehr, 1994). According to these authors, middle-school students develop the cognitive ability to differentiate between effort and ability in achievement. For those middle schools that emphasize achievement and where tracking is found, students see very little reason for exerting any effort, especially when they are in lower tracks (Anderman and Maehr, 1994; Braddock, 1990). Moreover, even when individual teachers may be exhorting their students to try their best, if the school as a whole defines success in terms of achievement test scores, the students' perceptions of the school's climate will outweigh an individual teacher's expectations.

For Latino middle-school students who are more likely to be at least two grades behind their white counterparts, individual effort in school may make little sense (Braddock, 1990; Simons et al., 1991). These and other factors may put Latinos at considerable risk of school failure and other possible dangerous behaviors.

LATINOS IN AT-RISK SITUATIONS: SOME DEFINING CHARACTERISTICS

In 1990, Dryfoos conducted an exhaustive review of studies and programs focused on adolescents involved in high-risk behaviors, that is, behaviors that could prevent young people from becoming responsible adults. Six common characteristics were found to predict high-risk behaviors (Dryfoos, 1990, pp. 94–95):

(1) Age: Early initiation or occurrence of any behavior predicts heavy involvement in the behavior and more negative consequences.
(2) Expectations for education and school grades: Doing poorly in

school and expecting to do poorly in school are associated with all of the problem behaviors.

(3) General behavior: Acting out, truancy, antisocial behavior, and other conduct disorders are related to each of the problem behaviors.

(4) Peer influence: Having low resistance to peer influences and having friends who participate in the same behaviors are common to all of the behaviors.

(5) Parental role: Having insufficient bonding to parents, having parents who do not monitor, supervise, offer guidance, or communicate with their children, and having parents who are either too authoritarian or too permissive are all strongly associated with the behaviors.

(6) Neighborhood quality: Living in a poverty area or an urban, high-density community is predictive of these problems.

For many Latino middle-school students, two of these factors are likely to be present, through little fault of their own: attending schools that expect little of them, which often results in doing poorly in school; and living in urban, high-density, poor communities. In 1989, 34.6 percent of Latino children ages six through fifteen were living below the poverty level (Simons et al., 1991). This was the case in spite of the fact that almost two thirds of Latino adolescents live with two parents (Simons et al., 1991). The issue of social class is often ignored in discussions on troubled adolescents, confounding ethnicity with socio-economic status. However, as Dryfoos (1990) points out, it is important to keep the effects of social class in mind when reviewing the literature on high-risk behaviors.

High-risk behaviors can be divided into four general categories: school failure, delinquency, substance abuse, and early childbearing (Dryfoos, 1990). In the following sections these behaviors will be discussed as they relate to Latino youth. This discussion will begin with a consideration of school failure since it frequently precedes other high-risk behaviors.

School Failure

The problem of school failure for Latino students is a complex one involving issues of language, ethnicity, racism, and poverty. The preceding section entitled the "Congruence between Middle-School Students' Developmental Needs and School Offerings" indicated some of the difficulties Latino middle-school students can experience in school: the new orientation to the whole school rather than to a single classroom and teacher; an increased emphasis on academic achievement; the introduction of a formalized tracked curricula; a developmental change in motivation; and a lack of focused study on Latino cultures.

In addition, many native Spanish speakers continue to have difficulties with English that may not be obvious to some of their teachers, counselors, or principals. Although the Council of Chief State School Officers (1992) has recommended that English learners be assessed with multiple measures (i.e., an English language test that includes listening, speaking, reading and writing sections, achievement test scores, teachers' observations, and student interviews), many schools continue to rely on a narrow, English-assessment instrument to promote students into "regular" classrooms where little to no language assistance is available. These language tests often fail to detect language difficulties, particularly where literacy is concerned. When these English learners are placed with teachers who do not understand the language acquisition process, they are left to struggle on their own. As a result, many Latinos continue to fall behind their white and African American counterparts.

This persistent lag frequently means that Latinos are placed in the low or vocational tracks in a school (Braddock, 1990; Wells, 1989). These less-academic-oriented programs are often characterized by low expectations, the development of discrete skills through repetitive drill, and generally poor teaching (Oakes, 1990; Riccio, 1985; Wells, 1989). Moreover, students in these tracks are more likely to be retained from one grade to another (George, 1988; Wells, 1989). The long-term effects of these practices commonly lead to alienation, resistance, and eventually, school desertion (Dryfoos, 1990; George, 1988; Wells, 1989).

This discussion on high-risk behaviors has begun with school failure because schooling is one of the central concerns of this chapter. Moreover, it is important to keep in mind the role that school failure may play in several of the behaviors that are described below. While it may be difficult to determine cause and effect, "It appears that school failure begins to occur at very early ages, and that once failure occurs, other events seem to take place" (Dryfoos, 1990, p. 105). In many cases, school failure is the antecedent to many other high-risk behaviors, such as delinquency, which is the subject of the next section. This being the case, it is incumbent on educators to take every step necessary to ensure school success.

Delinquency

Delinquency is defined by a wide range of behaviors that can run the gamut from truancy or curfew violations to serious illegal acts, such as robbery or assault. For this reason, it is difficult to determine just how many adolescents are involved in these behaviors. Differences in penal codes across states further complicate a determination of the exact violation in each case (Dryfoos, 1990).

Several surveys conducted across the last twenty years indicate that adolescents report committing more illegal acts than are reported. It is not until a young person is actually arrested that they are considered, officially, to be delinquent (Dryfoos, 1990). Given this difficulty, Simons et al., 1991, report that in 1987, out of 3,096 committed juveniles eleven to fourteen years old, 313 were Latino. Generally this means that roughly 10 percent of young Latinos were involved in more serious offenses, such as arson and burglary (Dryfoos, 1990; Simon et al., 1991).

Despite the lack of more specific data, there is growing public concern with youth and delinquency, especially as it relates to violence and gang affiliation. Much of the research that is available on adolescents and delinquency goes far beyond the scope of this chapter. For this reason, this section will be limited to a review of some of the antecedents of delinquency and a brief discussion on Latinos and gangs.

As is the case for school failure and dropping out, it is difficult to determine the causes of delinquency. However, there are several variables that are more likely to predict delinquent behavior in adolescents. The first of these is a discontinuity or lack of fit between the school and the child's home. For example, a failure to behave as expected by a first-grade teacher can often lead to poor achievement which can reinforce misbehavior or "acting out." If these behaviors are reinforced over the years, they can result in antisocial behavior in adolescence. For many Latino children, who come from homes with different expectations and a different language, their inability to fit in quickly may lead to misperceptions on the part of teachers that can have serious consequences for the children throughout their school careers (Diaz et al., 1986; Valdés, 1989). This is especially true for males across all populations (Dryfoos, 1990).

Secondly, Latino youth often live in urban areas with high crime. This can put them at high risk of victimization; that is, where they will be the victims of crime or of becoming involved in criminal activity themselves (Dryfoos, 1990; Simons et al., 1991). With little to no support for alternative activities, young people living in highly populated, high-crime areas will often turn to what they see around them (Simons et al., 1991; Weinberg, 1994). Given their developmental needs, i.e., the search for an identity, often through an oppositional strategy, their possible involvement in crime is not surprising. This risk is especially high when their peers are involved.

Research on gangs follows several traditions: those that are focused on gangs and their relation to delinquency, those that are concerned with the relationship between gangs and low-income ethnic communities, and those that focus on the role of the underclass and gangs (Weinberg, 1994). Weinberg's study on Central American middle-school students and their possible relationship with gangs is similar to other studies that acknowledged the marginality many Latinos suffer at multiple levels (Padilla, 1992; Vigil, 1988, Weinberg, 1994). While they clearly see the dangers of violence in gang life, they also analyze the role that gangs can play in the development of a personal and ethnic identity. As middle-school students turn away from adults and more to their peers for confirmation of their identity, they can be especially susceptible to peer influence. In particular, for many Latino youth, the subculture of a gang can be one way to combine elements of mainstream culture and their own home culture (Vigil, 1988; Weinberg, 1994).

Another variable in delinquency is unsupportive families. These can be either very authoritative and repressive families or those that are overly permissive and negligent (Dryfoos, 1990; Santrock, 1993). In some cases, Latino parents may be judged as overly authoritative because of the cultural differences that exist between parents' roles in Latino culture versus those that are present in mainstream families. Care must be taken to keep these cultural differences in mind so that hasty decisions are not made about parents' supportiveness. On the other hand, in cases of negligence, many antisocial youth may have parents or siblings who also have a history of illicit activity (Dryfoos, 1990).

Substance Abuse

In many respects the antecedent behaviors found in those adolescents who abuse specific substances closely parallel those found in delinquency: early initiation, school problems, family problems, and peer influences. In addition, researchers also point to certain personality traits, such as being nonconformist, rebellious, or strongly independent, as possibly contributing to substance abuse when the other factors are also present. While most young people have experimented with alcohol, cigarettes, and illicit drugs, researchers are especially concerned with those who are heavy users.

In early adolescence, Latinos and whites are more likely to abuse drugs than their African American counterparts (Dryfoos, 1990; Simons et al., 1991). Later, after the age of eighteen, African American and white substance abuse levels become higher than those of Latinos (Dryfoos, 1990; Simons et al., 1991). This statistic would indicate that middle school is an especially critical time for young Latinos. Middle school is also a time when sexual experimentation may begin. As will be seen in the following section, more research is needed in this area as it relates to young Latinos.

Teenage Pregnancy

Every year, roughly one-half million unmarried teenagers become mothers in the United States—the highest rates in the world for developed nations (Dryfoos, 1990; Santrock, 1993; Simons et al., 1991). Of these, 16.4 percent are young Latinas (Simons et al., 1991). While these are lower rates than for whites and African Americans, they still point to a serious problem with unprotected sex among young Latinos.

Although there is a lack of research on the sexual behaviors and attitudes of young Latinas specifically, those who become teenage mothers are generally girls with very low educational skills and those from poor families (Darabi et al., 1985; Dryfoos, 1990; Simons et al., 1991). For example, 21 percent of Latinas who had below-average basic skills and were from below-poverty-level families were mothers as compared to only 5 percent who were above-average students and came from families above the poverty level (Dryfoos, 1990). Becoming a mother at this early age, without any preparation, often ensures that these young women will remain poor and underemployed. In 1988, 36.4 percent of single Latina mothers, ages eighteen to twenty-four, had never graduated from high school. Once again, as in the cases of delinquency and substance abuse, school attainment is both an important antecedent and consequence of teenage pregnancy (Dryfoos, 1990).

RESPONSES TO DEVELOPMENTAL NEEDS OF LATINO ADOLESCENTS

As the previous sections have demonstrated, it appears that many of the needs of Latino middle-school students are not being met. The research cited here points to the critical role that schools can play in the prevention of more serious problems. In this section the need for better human relationships and services within and outside the school will be considered.

Access to Adults: The Need for Advisors

In many middle schools, the ratio of school counselors to students is frequently one to one hundred. This ratio makes it impossible for counselors to deal with little else but superficial academic issues. When they do work with children on emotional problems, it is usually only after a student has experienced serious, often legal trouble.

There is a need to change this ratio, so that Latino middle schoolers can have easy and continuous access to adults in the school. Some schools have addressed this need by assigning groups of middle-school students to individual members of the teaching staff in an advisory program. Each teacher works with ten to fifteen students during the year, meeting with the group bimonthly to talk about academic and personal issues. The advisory time period allows the students to talk with their peers and advisor about issues that concern them, such as getting along with family members, peers, or teachers. At the same time, advisors can provide important information to their advisees; for example, study skills, conflict resolution, or safe sex practices. Moreover, the advisor has the responsibility for keeping track of each advisee's academic progress. When school difficulties arise, other teachers can approach a student's advisor, who in turn, can alert parents. Similarly, when parents have concerns, the advisor can assist them within the school.

These advisory programs can be very successful when teachers/advisors know and understand the developmental needs of their students. In the case of Latino middle-school children, it also requires that advisors learn about the Latino cultures and the particular communities their students represent. It is also necessary that teachers understand their students' need for developing an ethnic identity and the difficulties their students can face in this process, particularly with existing racist attitudes. This can often be a difficult issue for teachers, especially when they have not resolved these issues for themselves. Therefore, when considering the implementation of an advisory program, it is a good idea to first develop these understandings in the faculty and the school leadership.

It is also important that young Latinos have the opportunity to interact with Latino teachers who can serve as important role models.

Personal characteristics of middle-school teachers/advisors are also important. These individuals need to be fair and consistent in applying any given criteria to their advisees, i.e., for grading, infractions, consequences, etc. They should also be respectful of the student, her/his culture, family, and peer group (Weinberg, 1994). At the same time, teachers/advisors need to require respect from their students. Some teachers confuse this with being standoffish or rejecting. In their efforts to have closer relationships with students, they may forget their responsibilities to their students and their students' needs for consistency. As in the case of parenting styles, it is best to encourage independence and communication, but place clear and consistent limits on students' actions (Santrock, 1993).

Parental Involvement through Empowerment

As was mentioned previously, although adolescents are in the process of developing autonomy, they continue to need strong relationships with their parents and families. This is especially true for middle-school students, who have often come from schools where a great deal of effort was expended to get parents involved in their children's school lives. For Latino middle-school children, who often come from extended, close-knit families, the continued need for a connection to family is vital.

The term parental involvement most often means that parents participate by attending individual and group meetings at school, assist teachers by donating their time or skills for specific events, and help their children with school work. These are all activities that cast parents as helpers or assistants to the teachers and the school (Valdés, 1989). These are tasks that make many Latino parents uncomfortable. For many Latino parents, there is a clear distinction between their responsibilities to teach their children values and life skills, and teachers' responsibilities to teach their children academic material (Benjamin, 1993; Valdés, 1989).

There are few opportunities, however, for parents to define for themselves or for school personnel what involvement means to them. This is especially the case for Latino and other minority parents. When parents fail to become involved in the ways that schools have defined, they are labeled uncaring or irresponsible, despite the fact that they may have provided their children with valuable skills (Benjamin, 1993; Goldenberg and Gallimore, 1992). For example, in interviews with several working-class Mexican families, it was discovered that the parents had taught their children to read in Spanish, a fact that went unnoticed by their children's teachers (Benjamin, 1993). These Spanish literacy abilities benefitted the children in their overall literacy development, a fact that has been well-established by other researchers (Cummins, 1991; Diaz et al., 1986).

Given this scenario, if schools desire parental involvement, they must first ask parents how they would like to participate. For those parents who wish to assist their children with their school work, schools must consider the financial struggle many parents face, holding two and three jobs at a time, while caring for children and extended family. After a serious analysis of their own and the parents' resources, together with parents, they can then consider the most appropriate ways to meet the needs of their middle-school children (Moll et al., 1990).

In order to build on parents' strengths, school leaders and teachers must first know what those strengths are. Unless there are persons in the school who know parents well, it may be difficult to obtain this information. When this is not the case, it would be helpful for parents to meet monthly in small groups (perhaps in the advisory groups in which their children meet) to talk in general about middle-school development and their own adjustments to a middle schooler. As the group of parents comes to know each other and the teacher/advisor, the group can devise ways in which they can support their children, using their strengths. At the same time, teachers can learn a great deal about the strengths of Latino families. For example, in the interviews mentioned previously, parents were very aware of their children's need for Spanish-language abilities, for continued communication with their families, and for their identity development (Benjamin, 1993). They had therefore devised several ways to reinforce their children's Spanish. By providing these opportunities for their children, the parents were supporting, in significant ways, their children's language growth, in both languages. Their development of new tenses, new phrases, and new vocabulary in Spanish allowed the children to develop new concepts about language and the world, which could then be transferred to English (Cummins, 1991; Diaz et al., 1986; Wong Fillmore, 1991).

As schools come to recognize the valuable skills and teaching that parents provide, parents themselves will begin to appreciate their own contributions (Moll et al., 1990). Parents will feel better able to participate in school-based activities, such as English as a Second Language (ESL) classes, presentations on school-related issues, parent association meetings, etc. At this point, parents should be encouraged to share with other groups of parents in the school, exchanging ideas and strategies that help their children and help to empower them to deal with an educational system that has often rejected and alienated them. This process is neither easy nor quick. It requires that the school as a whole, administrators, teachers, and others, expend a good deal of time and effort getting to know the parents of the school. It also requires that schools provide the resources, such as baby-sitting, Spanish-speaking personnel, counselors, and ESL teachers to encourage parents' presence in the schools. Research has born out the importance of parental involvement in children's academic success. Given the present statistics on Latino school failure, real partnerships between middle schools and Latino parents must be formed.

The Full Service School

There is growing recognition of the complex social, physical, and educational issues facing many public school children and their families. In response, some schools have explored the possibilities of providing their students with the health and social services they often need.

In the area of health care, Latino students are less likely to have any source of regular health care than either whites or blacks (Simons et al., 1991). Therefore, when schools are able to provide some basic health care, it may be all the health care that some Latino students will get. Some schools have entered into partnerships with public hospitals in establishing medical clinics on campus for students. These clinics can provide such primary care services as physical exams, prescriptions, preventive care, and contraceptive counseling (Dryfoos, 1990). When these services are accessible and confidential, focused on adolescents' problems, linked to the school and its curricula through medical and school personnel, and non-judgmental, they can be an important support service for Latinos and other adolescents (Dryfoos, 1990). Moreover, these services can be especially helpful to young Latinos in educating them about sexual development and contraception, topics that may be very difficult for their parents to discuss.

Several model programs or organizations have been established that have experienced some success with Latino and other minority students. The Teenage Pregnancy and Parenting Project in San Francisco helps pregnant or teen parents with educational, social, health, or employment issues. Couples or single parents are assigned to a counselor who follows their case and is the liaison to other concerned institutions. There is a particular effort to recruit teenage fathers and help them to become more responsible parents (Simons et al., 1991). The state of New Jersey has established school-based youth service centers that offer adolescents health screening and referral, mental health or family counseling, and some employment services (Carnegie Council on Adolescent Development, 1989). El Puente in New York City offers health, social, and educational services to Latino adolescents (Simons et al., 1991). The key to the success of each of these programs seems to be the following: (1) having knowledge and respect for adolescents' needs, (2) incorporating health, social, and educational services in one place, and (3) working to meet both present and future needs. With the help of other agencies or individuals, schools are considered to be the best option for meeting these needs (Carnegie Council on Adolescent Development, 1989).

Several administrators have also brought social workers into their schools. These social workers can provide a variety of services including family and employment counseling, assistance with social and legal agencies, and peer group counseling. These services provide valuable assistance for schools, for their students, and for their families, thus avoiding an often confusing social service system. An added benefit is that in coming to see the social worker, some parents will visit the school site more often, thus bringing school personnel and parents in closer contact. This means that, together, social workers, administrators, and parents can work together in more efficient ways to solve complex problems.

THE ACADEMIC PROGRAM

Over the last ten years, there has been a great deal of concern over the large gap that exists between the achievement levels of mostly white, middle-class students and those of mostly Latino and African American, poor children. As the movement for educational excellence has gained momentum, several researchers have focused their attention on the educational opportunities Latino and other minority children have available to them in public schools. What has come out of this research is an indictment of the present system that places the majority of Latino and African American students in fixed lower-ability groups, with teachers who have less professional preparation than in the higher-ability classes and who place little emphasis on higher-order thinking. Moreover, in these classes, there is less access to the schools' resources such as laboratories and other materials (Braddock, 1990; George, 1988; Oakes, 1990). While it is doubtful that educators planned for such effects, the reality is that the practice of ability grouping and tracking has resulted in unequal access to quality education for most minority students (George, 1988; Goodlad et al., 1988; Oakes, 1990; Slavin, 1991).

Academic Expectations and Latino Students

With large numbers of Latino middle-school students in the lower academic tracks there is little opportunity for them to develop the kinds of skills that would allow them to move out of lower tracks. Much of this is due to low expectations that teachers hold for students in these tracks. There is an overemphasis on drill and rote memorization of basic skills, and little attention to problem solving and critical thinking (Braddock, 1990; Oakes, 1990; Wells, 1989).

The results of such practices can be devastating to young Latinos and other minorities. For example, Braddock found that tracking contributed significantly to low minority achievement in literacy, as defined by the National Assessment of Educational Progress (NAEP) Young Adult Literacy Survey. Students did not have the skills and strategies necessary for understanding and using information in community-type texts, such as newspapers, or for understanding non-textual materials, such as graphs or tables, or for applying computational skills to such tasks as balancing a checkbook. The Oakes study (1990) found that many middle schools did not offer minority students the opportunity to take and learn algebra, a gate-keeping course for further study in mathematics.

In an effort to move away from these harmful practices, the California Task Force on Middle Grade Education recommended three basic changes for middle schools: defining a core curriculum for all students within a school; assuring equal access to educational opportunities within the school and the school district; and preparing students for the broadest possible options in future high-school work (Carnegie Council on Adolescent Development, 1989). In particular, it urged middle schools to do away with a tracked system so that all students, regardless of language, ethnicity, or academic skills, can have access to a rich and challenging curriculum (Goodlad et al., 1988). Some schools have taken these recommendations a step further by establishing a tutoring program where their own students, who are having academic difficulties, become the tutors for elementary-school programs. The results have been increased academic achievement for both elementary- and middle-school students, and increased interest and participation by middle-school tutors in their own school work (Dryfoos, 1990; Simons et al., 1991).

Homogeneous Grouping and the
Issue of Equal Access

Moving to homogeneous groups, however, does not ensure equal access to educational opportunities in and of itself. Teachers must also change many of their teaching practices so that the curriculum is available to students with different ethnic and language backgrounds. For teachers of Latino students, who have wide variations in their use of Spanish and English, homogeneous grouping means that all the teachers in the school understand language development among both monolinguals and bilinguals, and accept their responsibility for its development.

In the teaching of literacy, the focus must change from a restricted view of information processing to one where students are taught to read critically. Within this latter focus, students are empowered to change by using what they know about themselves and the world and allowing them access to information about themselves, their communities, and their place in the world (Cummins, 1991; Freire and Macedo, 1987). This will require that teachers and administrators discuss openly and explicitly their expectations of students and their grading criteria. If other criteria are also used, as in the case of standardized testing, teachers need to be sure that students understand and know the appropriate skills or strategies that are needed for success. Open and honest discussions of curricular and assessment issues allow the students to demystify many schooling experiences. For example, if there is a district-wide writing assessment that expects a five-part essay, then teachers should discuss both positive and negative reasons for this kind of writing with their students, and then assist them with appropriate practice (Delpit, 1988; Reyes, 1992).

Scheduling

The move away from a tracked curriculum has offered varied opportunities for changing the way in which classes are scheduled in middle schools. A major effort has been made to create smaller units within middle schools, or schools within schools. In these heterogeneous groups students are not forced to move every hour and teachers can develop closer relationships with students, as described in the following sections.

Alternative Groupings: Reinforcing Peer
and Teacher-Student Relationships

Several different ways of grouping students have been developed to better meet middle-school students' developmental needs. The idea behind the family concept is to group clusters of students with several teachers for the majority of the school day. Teaching configurations may differ. There may be team teaching, or one teacher teaching related subjects. The students, however, remain together, thus allowing for closer ties between teachers and students and among students themselves. Moreover, students usually remain within the same general physical space, which reduces anxiety about moving through a large school. These smaller groupings often reduce disciplinary problems as well.

In the block concept, a similar attempt is made at keeping groups of students together, but for less periods of time. Here, teachers of related subjects may either team teach or plan together to cover related topics. Students remain with these teachers for a block of time and then move on to another block with another pair of teachers. Typically, one can find social studies and language arts teachers in one block and math and science teachers in another. The advantage in this arrangement is that teachers can teach their specialized fields. The disadvantages are that teachers see many more students, cutting down on the quality of the attention they can give individual students.

The aforementioned scheduling changes are attempts to create more supportive environments for middle-school students. With the many changes that Latino middle-school children experience in personal and ethnic identity, it is helpful for them to have a group identity within the school, i.e., within a family or block. It is also very important for them to have access to adults in the school. For those Latino students who have not done well in school, it is especially important for them to develop positive relationships with teachers at a time when they may be feeling less motivated. Furthermore, if families, or blocks are formed that are not substitutions for tracking, students may be able to orient themselves to teacher expectations, rather than to the definitions of achievement set by standardized tests.

Having closer relationships with teachers and a stable group of peers may also be more culturally congruent for many Latino students, who often come from large, extended families.

The Curriculum

Much has been said in previous sections about the kinds of teaching one finds in the lower-track classes that Latinos are forced to take. In this section, the content of the curriculum will be considered. Additionally, some of the better practices used in teaching this content will be considered.

The Content

There has been a great deal of controversy surrounding the core curricula in public schools (Hirsch, 1983). The California Task Force on Middle Grade Education has recommended that rather than using particular texts, events, or facts as the starting point for the curriculum, teachers should instead select primary topics or themes of study that can be used as the basis for the development of an integrated curriculum across different disciplines, including for instance, social studies, language arts, math, and science (Carnegie Council on Adolescent Development, 1989). This allows teachers opportunities for better communication with their peers and to make the necessary connections between subject matter for students.

These recommendations help to create a more cohesive structure for Latino middle-school students who, because of linguistic or cultural differences, may not be familiar with some of the material that is covered in their classes. Seeing the same themes represented in different ways in various classes will reinforce learning across classes. Latino students, like students from other groups, need to learn about the historic events, inventions, literary texts, and great works of the many groups that make up the United States and the world. They have a concurrent need, however, to learn about the historic events, inventions, literary texts, and great works of their own ethnic group, especially during the middle- and high-school years, as they develop an ethnic identity. For this reason, it is critical that each of the subject areas in the curriculum—language arts, social studies, Spanish, math, science, art, music, and physical education—include related information on Latino cultures. While younger middle schoolers may not always be aware of this need, it is often the focus of alienation from school in the last years of middle school and the first years of high school (Benjamin, 1993; Herr and Anderson, 1993).

The Adults in the School

Given these needs, the adults in the school (teachers, advisors, para-professionals, social and health workers, counselors, and administrators) must understand the particular stresses in Latino adolescent development. Furthermore, they must be committed to learning more about the communities and cultures of their students, and to finding better ways of teaching them. Whenever possible, it is also desirable to recruit Latino teachers to the school who have similar commitments to learning about their students and teaching in more effective ways.

The kind of curriculum described here also demands individuals who are flexible and open to learning themselves. There are few, if any, prepackaged curricula similar to the one described above. This means that teachers and administrators will have to work hard, looking for materials and designing appropriate activities. This kind of work often places too many demands on teachers, a fact too often ignored in many restructuring efforts.

Administrators must find ways of relieving teachers of some of their demands, so that important work like curriculum design can be completed. Bilingualism is another important skill for the adults in a pre-dominantly Latino school. It is helpful if most of the staff, including the administrators, have at least a passive knowledge of Spanish, so that they can understand what students and parents say. However, there must be teachers in the school whose knowledge of the language is such that they can read, write, and teach through this language at appropriate middle-school levels. Additionally, as mentioned previously, all school personnel should have an understanding of first and second language development.

The Language of Instruction

Bilingual programs in middle schools are relatively new to the field of bilingual education. There are several models or kinds of programs that can be found in middle schools, each with different levels of success.

Generally, those programs that are least successful are those where paraprofessionals are made responsible for teaching Spanish-speaking students in the content area. For the most part, paraprofessionals have only the language competence, but little content or pedagogical knowledge to teach subject matter (Wong Fillmore et al., 1985). Moreover, the teachers in many of these classrooms do not know how to develop English-language competence in their students, and students are left almost on their own to learn English. The sad results are that they learn little content material and only what little English they can pick up from classmates.

The most successful bilingual programs for middle-school students are those where teachers are able to deliver content instruction through Spanish at age-appropriate levels. This is not an easy task. Teachers need to know the specialized vocabulary in both oral and written forms for their subject matter, something few universities prepare them for. The most successful of these classrooms are where teachers use English and Spanish separately, for example, by using each language on different days. By separating the languages, and using language development techniques for content teaching, students and teachers must struggle to communicate, thus further developing language capabilities (Wong Fillmore, 1985). Below is a list of appropriate practices for the development of English and of Spanish best suited to middle schools, adapted from the *Excellence in Leadership and Implementation Guide* developed by Meyer (1985) for the San Francisco Unified School District.

- Teachers should place language development as one of their central concerns in their daily teaching, no matter what subject matter they teach.
- The activities teachers plan should get students actively involved in listening to the language and in using it, in meaningful ways, within the subject matter that is taught.
- Grouping practices should be varied so that students are given opportunities to take different roles and to use their languages appropriately in those roles. For example, an English learner can benefit from working with peers who can lead an activity in English, but he/she also needs to have the chance to lead English speakers in other tasks.
- Teachers need to have high expectations of their students, regardless of language abilities, while having patience with the language learning process. In other words, teachers need to provide students with cognitively challenging work, but understand that their students will need time before they can express themselves clearly.

The Teaching of Spanish and Its Importance for Middle-School Latinos

Many middle-school-aged Latinos come to middle school with either native abilities in Spanish or with several years of Spanish instruction in an elementary bilingual program. Too often, these experiences are ignored when they get to middle school. These children are frequently confronted with a Spanish language curriculum that requires memorization of vocabulary, conjugation drills, and literacy activities that involve pattern practice, activities that are inappropriate for Latino adolescents who already have some proficiency in Spanish. As a result, many Latino children lose interest in Spanish study, and never take up formal study again. By making changes in the curriculum and methods, middle-school Spanish classes can play a critical role in reversing this trend.

As mentioned previously, Spanish teachers need to involve native speakers in meaningful activities that require them to use Spanish in a variety of contexts and in both oral and written modes. There are several important books written on the teaching of Spanish to native Spanish speakers; for example, *El Español para el hispanoparlante: Noción y Función,* (Blanco, 1987) or *Composición: Proceso y Síntesis* (Valdés et al., 1984). Most of these texts, however, are written with the adult learner in mind. The middle-school Spanish teacher must incorporate suggestions about the development of literacy, or more formal registers, into learning activities that are appropriate for middle-school children's developmental needs. Some of these activities might include inviting Latino writers into the class, conducting oral histories of children's relatives and developing written texts from these, participating in community service activities where Spanish-language use is required, or researching the histories of different Latino communities (Weinberg, 1994). At this point in their development, students are more interested in those things they see as most immediate—their surroundings, their families, and communities—than in a particular period of history in one or another of the Spanish-speaking countries. Therefore, the curriculum of the Spanish class should utilize what is most immediate, i.e., families' oral histories, the geography and the physical surrounding of the community, a scientific study of traditional foods, and a historical view of the community's customs or music, to reflect the themes that form the basis for other content classes.

Physical Education and Latino Middle-School Children

Little has been said, thus far, about the physical development of middle-school children. However, it is important to remember that many of the emotional and cognitive changes that occur in middle school are often the result of physical growth. Schools can do a great deal to ensure that middle-school students are healthy and physically fit. The establishment of a nutritious food program, consistent physical education classes, and a preventive health education program are all elements that can contribute to a healthier school. These can be made more effective when students and the adults in the school can work at them together.

Some Latino middle-school students are less healthy than they could be because of poverty and the lack of resources in their communities. When they go home after school, they may not have safe places to exercise and play, or they may be needed at home to help with family responsibilities. The more that physical and health education can be incorporated into the school day, the better their chances will be for maintaining their health.

In the past, many young Latinos did not have the opportunity to participate in extracurricular sports programs, because they did not excel in school. For the most part, these programs were open only to those who either maintained a certain grade point average, or who took the higher track courses. While some middle schools have done away with a tracked curriculum, the opportunities to participate in these programs have actually diminished. In an attempt to bring their budgets under control, some school districts have done away with intramural sports programs. It seems that the administrators responsible for such cuts have not realized how badly needed these programs are at the middle level, especially by poor children or by those who are having difficulty in school. Some model academic programs, such as "Midnight Basketball," have used sports as a way to keep young people off the streets and in school. They are allowed to play a sport, in this case basketball, so long as they attend tutoring classes and stay out of trouble (Simons et al., 1991). The results are often positive, helping those with academic or personal problems to remain in school. Middle schools should utilize these models to experiment with programs that can provide healthy alternatives to negative behavior.

SUMMARY

Middle-school Latino students begin a complex and often confusing journey as they enter middle school, searching for a personal, ethnic, and sexual identity, as they struggle with physical changes. Statistics on school achievement, drop-out rates, and high-risk behaviors indicate that, at present, too many middle schools are failing to meet their responsibilities to Latino children. When middle-school administrators and teachers understand and accept the developmental, cultural, and linguistic needs of young Latinos, they can create a curriculum and environment that nurtures Latino children and fosters their growth.

REFERENCES

Anderman, E. R. and M. L. Maehr. 1994. "Motivation and Schooling in the Middle Grades," *Review of Educational Research,* 64(2): 287–310.

Benjamin, R. 1993. "The Maintenance of Spanish by Mexicano Children and Its Function in Their School Lives." Ph.D. diss., U. of California, Berkeley.

Blanco, G. 1987. *El Español para el Hispanoparlante: Función y Noción.* Austin, TX: Texas Educational Agency.

Braddock, J. H. II. 1990. "Tracking: Implications for Student Race-Ethnic Subgroups." Report No. 1. Baltimore, MD: Center for Research on Effective Schooling for Disadvantaged Students, Johns Hopkins University.

Carnegie Council on Adolescent Development. 1989. *Turning Points: Preparing American Youth for the 21st Century.* New York, NY: Carnegie Corporation of New York.

Council of Chief State School Officers. 1992. *Recommendations for Improving the Assessment and Monitoring of Students with Limited English Proficiency.* Alexandria, VA: Council of Chief State School Officers, State Educational Assessment Center, Resource Center on Educational Equity.

Cross, W. E. 1991. *Shades of Black: Diversity in African-American Identity.* Second edition. Philadelphia, PA: Temple University Press.

Cummins, J. 1991. "Empowerment through Literacy," in *The Power of Two Languages.* J.V. Tinajero and A. F. Ada, eds. New York, NY: McMillan McGraw-Hill, pp. 9–25.

Darabi, K. E., J. Dryfoos, and D. Schwartz. 1985. *The Fertility-Related Attitudes and Behaviors of Hispanic Adolescents in the United States.* New York, NY: Center for Population and Family Health, Faculty of Medicine, Columbia University.

Delpit, L. 1988. "The Silenced Dialogue: Power and Pedagogy in Educating Other People's Children," *Harvard Educational Review,* 58:280–298.

Diaz, S., L. Moll, and H. Mehan. 1986. "Sociocultural Resources in Instruction: A Context-Specific Approach," in *Beyond Language: Social and Cultural Factors in Schooling Language Minority Students.* Bilingual Education Office, ed. Los Angeles, CA: Evaluation, Dissemination and Assessment Center, California State University.

Dryfoos, J. 1990. *Adolescents at Risk: Prevalence and Prevention.* New York, NY: Oxford University Press.

Erickson, E. 1963. *Childhood and Society.* Second edition. New York, NY: Norton.

Fordham, S. and J. Ogbu. 1986. "Black Students' School Success: Coping with the Burden of Acting White," *The Urban Review,* 18(3):176–206.

Freire, P. and D. Macedo. 1987. *Literacy: Reading the Word and the World.* Boston, MA: Bergin & Garvey Publishers Inc.

George, P. S. 1988. "Tracking and Ability Grouping. Which Way for the Middle School?" *Middle School Journal,* September: 3–10.

Gibbs, J. T. and L. N. Huang. 1989. *Children of Color.* San Francisco, CA: Jossey-Bass.

Goldenberg, C. and R. Gallimore. 1992. "Local Knowledge, Research Knowledge and Educational Challenge: A Case Study of Early Spanish Reading Improvement," *Educational Researcher,* 20(8):2–14.

Goodlad, J., J. Oakes, and P. Swartzbaugh. 1988. "We Must Offer Equal Access to Knowledge," *Educational Leadership,* 45(5):16–23.

Herr, K. and G. L. Anderson. 1993. "Oral History for Student Empowerment: Capturing Students' Inner Voices," *Qualitative Studies in Education,* 6(3):185–196.

Hirsch, E. D., Jr. 1983. "Cultural Literacy," *The American Scholar,* Spring: 159–169.

McAdoo, H. and L. McAdoo 1985. *Black Children.* Beverly Hills, CA: Sage.

Meade, M. 1928. *The Coming of Age in Samoa.* New York, NY: Morrow.

Meyer, L. 1985. *Excellence in Leadership and Implementation Guide.* San Francisco, CA: San Francisco Unified School District.

Moll, L., C. Vélez Ibañez, and J. Greenberg. 1990. *Community Knowledge and Classroom Practise: Combining Resources for Literacy Instruction.* Technical Report. Washington, D.C.: Innovative Approaches Research, Department of Education.

Oakes, J. 1990. "Excellence and Equity: The Impact of Unequal Educational Opportunities." Paper presented at the *American Educational Reseach Association Conference.* April, 1990. Boston, MA.

Padilla, F. M. 1992. *The Gang as an American Enterprise.* New Brunswick, NJ: Rutgers University Press.

Phinney J. and M. J. Rotheram. 1987. *Children's Ethnic Socialization, Pluralism and Development.* Newbury Park, CA: Sage.

Reyes, M. de la Luz. 1992. "Challenging Venerable Assumptions: Literacy Instruction for Linguistically Different Students," *Harvard Educational Review,* 62(4): 427–446.

Riccio, L. L. 1985. "Facts and Issues about Ability Grouping," *Contemporary Education,* 57(1):26–30.

Santrock, J. W. 1993. *Adolescence: An Introduction.* Dubuque, IA: Brown & Benchmark.

Simons, J. M., B. Finlay, and A. Yang. 1991. *The Adolescent & Young Adult Fact Book.* Washington, D.C.: Children's Defense Fund.

Slavin, R. E. 1991. "Ability Grouping in the Middle Grades: Effects and Alternatives." Paper presented at the *American Educational Research Association Conference.* April, 1991. Chicago, IL.

Sleeter, C. 1993. "How White Teachers Construct Race," in *Race Identity and Representation in Education.* C. McCarthy and W. Crichlow, eds. New York, NY: Routledge, pp. 157–172.

Sue, D. W. and D. Sue. 1990. *Counseling the Culturally Different: Theory and Practice.* New York, NY: John Wiley.

Tatum, B. 1992. "Talking about Race, Learning about Racism: The Application of Racial Identity Development Theory in the Classroom," *Harvard Educational Review,* 1(62):1–24.

Tinajero, J. V., M. L. González, and F. Dick. 1991. *Fomentar las Aspiraciones Profesionales entre Las Jóvenes Hispanas.* Bloomington, IN: Phi Delta Kappa Educational Foundation.

Valdés, G. 1989. "Individual Background Factors Related to the Schooling of Language

Minority Students." Spccech delivered at *Education of Language Minority Students Conference.* Oakland, CA.

Valdés G., T. Dvorak, and T. P. Hannum. 1984. *Composición: Proceso y Síntesis.* New York, NY: Random House.

Vigil, J. D. 1988. *Barrio Gangs: Street Life and Identity in Southern California.* Austin, TX: University of Texas Press.

Weinberg, S. 1994. "Where the Streets Cross the Classroom: A Study of Latino Students' Perspectives on Cultural Identity in City Schools and Neighborhood Gangs." Ph.D. diss., U. of California, Berkeley.

Wells, A. S. 1989. *Middle School Education–The Critical Link in Dropout Prevention.* New York, NY: Eric Clearinghouse on Urban Education Digest.

Wong Fillmore, L. 1991. "When Learning a Second Language Means Losing the First (for the No-Cost Research Group)," *Early Childhood Research Quarterly,* 6:323–346.

Wong Fillmore, L., P. Ammon, B. McLaughlin, M. S. Ammon, and M. Strong. 1985. *Learning English through Bilingual Education* (final report). Washington, D.C.: National Institute of Education.

CHAPTER 13

Literacy Instruction for Middle-School Latinos

KARIN M. WIBURG—*New Mexico State University*

INTRODUCTION

CLASSROOMS in the United States are a microcosm of the world's diversity. In the year 2010, one third of the nation's children will live in just four states—California, Texas, New York, and Florida—with "minority" Latino children becoming the majority in these school populations (Hodgkinson, 1992). By the year 2020, one half of the nation's school children will be non-European American (Au, 1993), and one quarter will be Latino (Darder et al., 1993). Some sources predict that these national "minority" majority schools will occur even sooner within the next decade (Carter and Wilson, 1992).

Our classrooms reflect this changed world; yet the curriculum used in most public schools is based on materials and instructional strategies developed in the first half of the twentieth century, when nearly three fourths of all students were European Americans (Pallas et al., 1989) and the country's human resource needs were the product of an industrial rather than an information age. This curriculum is inappropriate in both content and activities for today's and tomorrow's Latino student populations and is often in direct conflict with many students' cultures and community lives (Darder et al., 1993). For Latino students, the problem is compounded by an often unrecognized diversity within the population. For example, in New Mexico many Latino students are the descendants of families who lived in their current locations for many years before European Americans arrived in this part of the world. Linda Ronstadt, the well-known singer, was once asked when her family moved to Tucson from Mexico. She replied that they didn't move, the border did. While children from well-established Latino families have instructional needs different from the standard, Eurocentric curriculum, they do not have the same needs as immigrant children, such as Carmen and Victor, whose following

269

story illustrates the growing gap between home and school experienced by many Latino children.

THE GROWING GAP BETWEEN HOME AND SCHOOL

Carmen and Victor: An Example

Carmen rose early on Friday morning anxious to see her relatives who had arrived late the night before to begin preparations for her sister's quinceañera celebration to be held this weekend. Even though the sun was just beginning to shine through the window over the sink, the kitchen was alive with talk of the latest events in Ciudad Juárez, Mexico, and hands were busy preparing coffee and chocolate, menudo, and tortillas for the day's meals. It was hot in El Paso even in May, and the early morning was the best time to do the cooking. Carmen hugged Tia Norma, her favorite aunt, and her cousin María Teresa, who had turned fifteen only last year. It was important in her family to celebrate this coming of age for young women, and they discussed the origins of the ceremony in the Aztec culture and its later modification by the Catholic community. Carmen took a bowl of menudo and a fresh francesito and sat down at the kitchen table, lifting her little brother Carlos onto her lap while engaging in animated conversation with María Teresa as she ate.

Too soon, it was time to leave for school. She rushed down the block to pick up her cousin Victor, who had only recently arrived with his family to El Paso, and they walked together to the middle-school. Even though half the students at the school spoke Spanish, as soon as Carmen entered her first-period classroom her culture disappeared. She had worked hard to learn English, but she had more trouble than usual since they were studying Shakespeare and much of the language didn't look like English to her. Her teacher did not show pictures or even encourage acting out scenes, as her English teacher had done last year in fifth grade. Since she was a girl who was quiet and well behaved, she was largely ignored and managed to survive. She knew it was harder for Victor. Speaking English every day was difficult for him, and in the social studies class they took together the teacher paid more attention to the boys. She could feel his embarrassment when he didn't know the right answer and her stomach tensed as she thought of this class scheduled for later today.

Lunch was better. Carmen had made friends in her new community and could relax and share her excitement at having her relatives here for the weekend, speaking Spanish in order to share all she knew about the celebration to be held on Saturday. Then it was time for American history. Carmen sat down in the back of the room behind Victor and took out her textbook, reading the unfamiliar phrases over and over and thankful for the pictures that helped her to understand something of American history.

They had been studying the early history of the United States and the teacher was engaged in the traditional recitation often found in class-rooms (asking low-level questions to which the student already knew the answer). He turned to Victor and asked, "Who is the father of this country?" Victor, who had been trying hard to decipher the meaning of U.S. history from parts of the textbook and lectures, had been able to understand the concept of the Pilgrims and the Mayflower as a first, important event. Victor answered the teacher by suggesting that the first president must have been "the person who built the big boat" (the Mayflower). Of course, the students roared with laughter, and Victor was ashamed and embarrassed. Carmen and a couple of the other Latino kids who were "making it" in the regular history class looked down, uncom-fortable and ashamed for Victor. The teacher did not seem to notice.[1]

Carmen invited Victor to come over to her house after school. She knew a visit with their relatives would cheer him up. Aunt Norma's husband, Robert, was in the kitchen along with her mother and aunt and two of the younger children. They were making *sopaipillas* for supper, a New Mexican fluffy pastry. Victor knew that Robert was running for a city office in the neighboring border city of Juárez, and the two men and Carmen were soon engaged in deep and meaningful conversation about a current political situation in Mexico.

THE NEED FOR A NEW DESIGN TO PROMOTE LITERACY

Victor and Carmen have a deep and rich understanding of history, culture, and political science, yet their teachers and many of their classmates have no concept of their abilities. The dichotomy between their lives in their warm and rich community at home and their daily struggle to survive at school is clear. Teachers lack strategies for incor-

[1] The story of Victor, a boy who misunderstood his social studies teacher, is common among Teachers of English to Speakers of Other Languages (TESOL) and was first told to me by Ann Campbell, a TESOL instructor at Pima Community College in Tucson, Arizona (May, 1994).

porating the resources available within diverse cultures to build, rather than stifle, student learning (Au, 1993). They are unaware of the need to provide sheltered instruction that emphasizes the concepts to be learned while protecting students from excessive language barriers. Many still possess attitudes that consciously or unconsciously see students like Victor and Carmen as either dumb or lazy, rather than kids whose knowledge and skills are hidden behind linguistic difficulties. Educators have characterized the at-risk student as lacking a broad range of learning abilities; yet it could be argued that it is the curriculum that is deficient, providing only very limited avenues for learning to which some students may not have access (Joyce et al., 1992).

There are instructional strategies that can assist educators in designing learning environments for literacy, supportive of Latino students, which provide the means for these students to share their own rich experiences and knowledge. This chapter focuses on such strategies for middle-school Latinos, although the ideas are, of course, adaptable to other grade levels. The proposed design for literacy is expanded through the following four approaches: (1) use of sheltering techniques for students learning English; (2) strategies for drawing on culturally relevant content; (3) creating an active learning environment; and (4) uses of technology that support literacy development for Latino middle-school students.

Use of Sheltering Techniques

Two personal experiences of the author set the stage for looking at sheltering techniques for Latino students learning English. Recently, I was with a group of colleagues visiting schools in Juárez, Mexico. I was the only member of this group not fluent in Spanish. After a morning of catching only a few words in Spanish, entering a preschool room was like discovering paradise. Suddenly words had context and meaning. Color words were next to the appropriate colored papers, days of the week were printed in order on a familiar calendar; words for window (*ventana*), door (*puerta*), and library (*biblioteca*) were taped to the appropriate objects. Of course, the intention was to help the young student learn to read and write Spanish for the first time, but the same approach worked for this second language learner. I am an experienced user of colors and calendars, and language tied to relevant experiential learning worked. There was just enough support that I could begin to build on my previous knowledge of calendars, colors, and the names and functions of objects. Later that hot summer day, we were traveling in a crowded van when several people shouted "*sombra, sombra.*" The driver then moved our crowded van under the inviting shade of a large tree. I knew at that moment that I would always know that *sombra* means shade in Spanish. The contextual support in these instances was critical to my comprehension of the language.

The second experience involves a class I am taking at our university to learn Spanish. While the class is offered at a beginning level, the teacher speaks almost completely in Spanish and has designed the literacy environment so that it is totally comfortable and comprehensible to the beginning Spanish speaker. The teacher uses the same strategies to teach Spanish to second language learners as would be helpful for Latino students learning English as another language. New words are introduced together with pictures, cartoons, or role-playing by the teacher. Literacy in Spanish is supported by an integrated approach that emphasizes listening, speaking, reading, and writing. Phrases related to classroom management and procedures are used daily so that students know that *preguntas* means questions, *hablen con su compañero o compañera* means practice phrases with a partner, *escribe* means to write in your notebook or on the board. There are frequent opportunities to create one's own sentences through speaking and writing using the topic and words being studied. The following discusses specific strategies that can be used to provide support for students developing literacy in ESL (English as a Second Language).

Zehler (1994) suggests that teachers can make language and content more comprehensible to students by:

- restating complex sentences as a sequence of simple sentences
- avoiding or explaining the use of idiomatic expressions
- restating at a slower rate if necessary, but not so slow as to be abnormal or interfere with the natural flow of instruction
- pausing to allow students time to process instructions
- providing specific examples of key words and technical vocabulary using pictures, props, videos, or role-playing
- using pictures, film, posters, and other media to help ensure understanding
- using charts, graphs, tables, Venn diagrams, and other visuals to help explain content and process
- checking comprehension frequently through questioning, retelling, or reteaching

Students can be given notes or an outline with the key words to be used in the day's lesson. Words relating to class lessons can also be put on posters and signs around the room with appropriate pictures or drawings that illustrate the meaning. There is no reason why students can't create these posters, providing additional practice with language and hands-on opportunities for activities that middle-school students enjoy. Even though students are new to a language, they benefit by generating their own sentences, stories, essays, and even illustrations related to what is being studied. Asking students to copy meaningless phrases does not support literacy.

As mentioned above, growth in literacy is supported by opportunities to practice language that involve all forms of communication—listening, speaking, writing, and reading—within each lesson. Pairing and grouping students for these types of communicative activities is also an important sheltering strategy. Students need the maximum number possible of opportunities to speak and listen to English. The more opportunities there are for social interaction the faster literacy can be gained. The teacher should try to group students so that each small team contains members with varying levels of English proficiency. Bilingual students can help each other. For example, middle-school students can develop a project together in their native language and/or English, practice presenting it in English in their small groups, and then present it again to the entire class in English. The following classroom vignette illustrates these strategies.

In Shiela Hill's class at Sierra Middle School in Las Cruces, New Mexico, a fourth of her students spoke only Spanish, a fourth spoke only English, and the other half, as is typical of this border community, spoke both Spanish and English; yet all of her students spoke a common language—multimedia. Juan, who had only arrived at the middle school yesterday, sat with his new friend Jorge and two other students from Mexico who had been in the sheltered program for several months and now had a pretty good grasp of the English language.

Groups of students gathered around one of the four computers in the classroom. Their task was to use a computer-based authoring program called "Point of View" (1993) to develop an original presentation on the first president of the United States. The program provides access to many images of Washington's childhood, his growing up, his years fighting in the revolution, and the early history of the government. Fortunately, the principal of this middle school had ensured that all language arts classrooms had four computers. Because Ms. Hill taught both language arts and social studies, she was able to provide students with convenient access to computers for group project work. However, this same project could also be done without computers by using magazines, cutout pictures, and relevant documents and photographs, and allowing students to assemble these into a non-computer-based multimedia exhibit.

Juan and the three other students in his group browsed through a variety of images related to presidents and government. They had to decide what images to use and then assemble them in some kind of order. Two of the students typed text in English. Because the school supported bilingual approaches, students who were more comfortable writing in Spanish also typed in Spanish into a second text box on each page of their presentation.

They had a couple of days to complete their assignment and then they would present it to the many newcomers to the United States in their class. Juan was really excited to be able to learn so much about American history after having only been in school in the United States for a few days.

The next three sections focus on additional strategies for creating a classroom environment that is supportive of Latino students.

Creating Culturally Relevant Curricula

Recall that Carmen and Victor, characters from the scenario that opened this chapter, possessed a rich social network that could be supportive of learning but remained largely untapped in their school. Their knowledge and aptitudes were hidden behind cultural, ethnic, and linguistic barriers. Researchers who have studied students in Latino communities have found vast "funds of knowledge" related to science, mathematics, and social studies (Moll and Greenberg, 1992); yet these funds of knowledge remain untapped. This is very clear in New Mexico where one can see children engaged in raising animals and crops, building shelters, and repairing swamp coolers; yet none of this knowledge finds its way into the classroom. All children need to see people from their culture valued in the materials they work with in schools. A new kind of curriculum is needed that is grounded in an instructional approach that considers the students' languages and cultures as valuable sources of knowledge.

Given the need for multicultural resources, how does one decide what to use? One of the guidelines is to focus on universal themes: survival, justice, conflict resolution, friendship, or betrayal. Such themes are universal and provide a way to connect children across cultures while enjoying and respecting the different perspectives within each group. Multicultural literature also provides a rich resource for the Latino middle-school classroom. However, caution is needed in selecting literature. One way to decide what materials to use in the curriculum is to look at the latest standards developed by professional organizations including TESOL (Teaching English to Speakers of Other Languages), NABE (National Association of Bilingual Education), and NCTE (the National Council of Teachers of English). Sometimes the best literature is that which is created by the students themselves after interviewing people in their own community or studying their own traditions and experiences.

Creating a Knowledge Base in the Community

Students themselves can play a valuable role in creating culturally meaningful text for use in the school and larger community. In the Nuestra Tierra Project at Oñate High School in Las Cruces, New Mexico, students are learning about their local history and environment. John Sandin, a doctoral student and history teacher at New Mexico State University, has been working with Latino students who are considered at risk of school failure and who have experienced little previous success in history classes. John knows the Hispanic history of the area, speaks Spanish, and is a great storyteller. He has been successful in engaging these students in conversations about what really happened in New Mexico in the last 100 years, the cowboy and Indian fights, the conflicts between Mexico and the U.S. government, and the battles over borders and rivers. As the kids became interested in local history, they all chose an area to research using both traditional print resources and the Internet access, which is available in their classroom. When the students discovered that there was very limited information on local history, they decided to make their own publication of the history of Mesilla, an old town near Las Cruces. John arranged a walking tour for the students. They interviewed people, took photos, discussed issues, and were sometimes overheard saying things like "I didn't know history could be so interesting." The result of their work became a multimedia essay developed in "Hyperstudio" (1993) and then imported into Oñate High School's Home Page on the World Wide Web. The students are so excited about their work that they want to continue by composing a Southern New Mexico history book for students in the area. The same activity could again be implemented using a combination of print materials (pictures, magazine clippings, drawings, etc.) even when computer programs are not available. The important concept is capitalizing on the richness found within the local community.

Creating an Active Learning Environment

The third strategy relevant to the design of instruction for Latino middle-school students is the creation of an active learning environment. This strategy is based on what we know about the social construction of knowledge, the use of cooperative learning, and expanded definitions of literacy and intelligence. Victor, in his social studies classroom, suffered from an instructional strategy that is all too common in classrooms and limiting to all students—not just second language learners. The instruction in Victor's scenario involved presenting students with limited facts and concepts and then asking them to memorize those facts and give them back to the teacher. In this case, students have not been provided with opportunities to construct meaning from comprehensible input. The power structure requires that they respond in specific limited ways, rather than become engaged with the materials and ideas themselves.

Tharp and Gallimore (1990) describe the recitation they believe is very common in American schools:

> What is this ubiquitous recitation? It consists of a series of unrelated questions that require convergent factual answers and student display of (presumably) known information. Recitation questioning seeks predictable, correct answers. It includes up to 20% yes/no questions. Only rarely is recitation or teacher questions used to assist student production. (p. 14)

Tharp and Gallimore then suggest that there is really very little teaching occurring in schools. Rather, teachers, the administrators who supervise them, and the education professors who teach them engage in a process of assigning and assessing. Daily activities consist primarily of assigning activities, monitoring to be sure students are on task, and then grading these activities. This recitation model can be contrasted with a different view of teaching based on the work of Vygotsky (1962). Vygotsky and his followers, who make up the neo-Vygotskian movement, theorize that learning is not the result of isolated, individual activity but is based on social interaction. Within this framework, teaching becomes a process of assisting performance rather than controlling and testing. Learning occurs as a result of specific types of social interactions, interactions that must be designed by the teacher to assist students in creating meaning.

Those who believe that students learn best when they are supported in constructing knowledge through guided interaction with ideas, resources, tools, and other learners generally follow a constructivist philosophy. Fosnot (1989) describes four principles of constructivism in her excellent book, *Enquiring Teachers, Enquiring Learners*. These principles are summarized briefly below, although a more complete reading of her book is recommended.

(1) Knowledge consists of past constructions. We can only know the world through our mental framework that transforms, organizes, and interprets our perceptions. This mental framework is constructed and evolves through development as we interact with our environment and try to make sense of our experiences. It is the teacher's role to assist students in making sense of the input in the classroom. The teacher must structure the environment and the learner must structure his/her own understanding of it.

(2) Constructions come about through assimilation and accommodation. This is based on Piaget's theory that we assimilate information based on our existing mental framework. When our assimilation frame is found insufficient we accommodate; that is, we develop a higher-level theory or logic to encompass the information.

(3) Learning is an organic process of invention, rather than a mechanical process of accumulating facts. The learner must be provided with experiences of hypothesizing and predicting, manipulating objects and data, researching answers, imagining, investigating, and inventing in order to construct knowledge.

(4) Meaningful learning occurs through reflection and resolution of cognitive conflict that negates earlier, incomplete levels of understanding. The teacher can only mediate in this process.

The process of helping students to learn within a constructivist approach is challenging for teachers who have been trained in the information delivery model dominant in industrial-age schools. Vygotsky's concept of the Zone of Proximal Development (ZPD) might be helpful. What the ZPD suggests is that all students have a zone of development, which ranges from being able to do something with assistance to being able to do something alone. The teacher cannot expect students to learn above their level of development, e.g., a child who knows no Spanish could not suddenly converse in Spanish. At the same time, a child who comprehends English, probably at one or two higher grade levels than she or he speaks, should not be required to spend hours filling out worksheets with simple words. For Vygotsky and the neo-Vygotsky movement, intellectual development and social interaction are inextricably interrelated.

A second strategy for creating an active learning environment is to utilize a cooperative learning structure as much as possible. Cooperation is at the heart of family life, government, and even the evolution of the human species. Diamond (1989), a biologist, writes that if there were any single moment when we could be said to have become human, it was at the time that Homo sapiens learned to cooperate. It can be seen as naturally occurring within the family and in early agricultural societies, but seems to be often missing in schools. Cooperative learning is also an important aspect of the Latino culture. Carmen's younger brothers and sisters are learning how to make *sopaipillas* in a natural and comfortable way as they sit on their older siblings' laps in our opening scenario.

There has been extensive research on cooperative learning both from a scientific and a practitioner's perspective. The research is reviewed by both Johnson and Johnson (1994) and Joyce et al. (1992), and results are generally very positive, especially for students who have not done well in the classroom previous to becoming engaged in cooperative learning. In general, cooperative learning stimulates cognitive complexity (seeing different perspectives and alternative solutions) and provides a positive social climate. Students like it and classroom management is easier. However, just putting students together in a group and asking them to interact does not constitute cooperative learning. A true cooperative learning group must: (1) have a common purpose; (2) support both group goals and the learning of each individual; (3) complete real tasks (not just share information); and (4) be able to evaluate their group work in terms of both academic and social support, and strive to continuously improve these abilities.

A third strategy for creating an active, participatory environment is to provide additional ways for students to learn and to demonstrate what they know. For the sake of Latino students and all learners, we must expand the definitions of literacy and intelligence. Eisner (1994) suggests that one of the major aims of education should be the development of multiple forms of literacy. By literacy he does not mean just print, but rather the ability to communicate and comprehend meaning in any of the forms of representation used in the culture. Eisner suggests:

> What we ought to develop, in my view, is the student's ability to access meaning within the variety of forms of representation that humans use to represent the contents of their consciousness. These forms are no less

important in the fine arts than they are in the sciences; they are no less important in mathematics than they are in the humanities. Further, the provision of opportunities to learn how to use such literacies ought to contribute to greater educational equity for students, especially for those whose aptitudes reside in the use of forms of representation now marginalized by our current educational priorities. (p. x)

Related to this expanded notion of literacy is the work by Gardner (1985) that suggests a greatly expanded definition of intelligence. He defines intelligence as "the ability to solve problems, or to create products, that are valued within one or more cultural settings" (p. x). His definition of multiple intelligence builds on biological and anthropological evidence that reflects the differential values placed on diverse human abilities in different cultures. We live in a culture that places high value on only some of these intelligences, specifically linguistic and logical/mathematical skills. Yet in other cultures, other types of intelligence are often of more value. Gardner gives the example of the Puluwat sailor who is considered intelligent only if he can sail by the stars. Whether or not he can read the printed word is not relevant to being considered intelligent in his culture. His literacy is measured by his ability to read the stars.

Schools have focused primarily on the transmission of knowledge via print. Our minds are capable of comprehending and expressing ideas using a variety of forms of representation including visual, musical, and spatial. Limiting communication primarily to print and words has literally limited the development of students' minds to a single dimension. It is also particularly devastating to the Latino student who has extensive knowledge, feelings, and experience, but is blocked from expression in the classroom by an overemphasis on print.

The design of learning activities that supports literacy for middle-school Latinos requires the use of a variety of media as channels for students to both receive information and to be able to show what they know and think. Students can demonstrate their understanding of a certain historical period by writing, drawing pictures, putting together a series of video images, or making a radio show from the period. For example, if students are studying the Civil War they should be able to choose from a variety of assignments including: writing a play or creating a simulated newspaper (linguistic intelligence), creating a pantomime or dance to demonstrate conflict (kinesthetic intelligence), drawing a map to show where certain battles took place (spatial intelligence), writing a song about the conflicting needs of the North and South (musical intelligence), engaging other students in a discussion of the causes of the Civil War (interpersonal intelligence), demonstrating the economics that caused the defeat of the South using spreadsheets (mathematical intelligence), or writing or telling an original story about what might have happened if the South had won the war (intrapersonal intelligence).

These enlarged understandings and applications of instructional strategies support what is emerging in the critical pedagogy literature as an expanded view of literacy (Freire, 1970; McLaren, 1993). Students need to be assisted not just to read textbooks and answer limited questions, but also to use reading, writing, and speaking as critical tools for their own school and life success.

Uses of Technology That Support Literacy Development

While technology can be liberating and can provide the tools needed for Latino students to succeed in school, technology has not been used well with this population. Skelle (1993) wrote that less frequent educational computer use by groups other than white males or high-ability-level students has been noted in the research for some time. She suggested that it was "indisputable that the classroom computer is not shared equally" (p. 15). Drouyn-Marrero (1989) found that white students were given significantly more access to computers in schools than Latino and African American students. In addition, Dutton et al. (1987) compared the uses of computers by poor students and richer students in schools, and concluded that richer students direct the computer while poor students are directed by it. Many researchers (Connell, 1993; Linn, 1992) agree that students learn best with technology when using computers as tools under their own direction; however, Latino students are often not provided with the same opportunity to explore with technology as many non-minority students.

Hunt and Pritchard (1993) have been studying the use of technology with Latino students and report that fewer than 25 percent of teachers currently teaching these students use technology in their classrooms. Although half of the teachers participating in the study ($N = 177$) had regular classroom access to computers, 60 percent of these teachers who used technology regularly with their students reported never using computers with language minority students. The other 40 percent who did use computers with their Latino students had them doing drill and practice programs in language arts and mathematics, a practice that researchers have found may be more harmful than helpful (Hativa, 1988).

According to Mergendoller and Pardo (1991), Latino students do as well or better than mainstream students when taught with effective instructional strategies and appropriate uses of technology. Technology-based cooperative learning is truly an instructional model that values diversity rather than sameness. A variety of different skills are required in a group multimedia project using technology. For example, in order to complete a multimedia presentation on a subject from the curriculum, one student can be asked to design an outlined presentation using software, another to conduct the research needed to complete the project, a third to illustrate the concepts being presented, and a fourth student can scan in the pictures and connect each presentation card. In the process, each student becomes the expert at something and is valued for her/his unique talents by the rest of the group. The following scenario illustrates this process.

Ms. Gómez worked in a middle school and her class had been studying myths. They wanted to study not only Greek myths but also stories and fables from many of the cultures represented in her multicultural school. At a recent staff development workshop she had been given a computer program that provided a template for the development of a presentation of a literature story on the computer. The computer program provided a "HyperCard" (1993) template with a page for characters and cards already linked to the cover page with a space for both text and pictures.

Ms. Gómez had shared several different stories from various cultures with her class. She then assigned them to different cultural myth groups and provided them with a pile of books and stories. Each group had to decide which story they wanted to turn into a computer presentation. A group facilitator and a recorder for votes had been assigned, and each group was told to use a simple democratic process to decide on the story it wished to present.

Ms. Gómez had used cooperative learning for many years and knew this was not a simple task. She had worked on developing group skills since the beginning of the year and used groups throughout the curriculum. In the first week of school she had engaged the groups in simple tasks, such as all agreeing on movies and food they liked and disliked as a way to build group process. The students were accustomed to working in small groups and generally enjoyed the process.

Once each group decided on a story, the four members were given the opportunity to each take one of four tasks needed to complete the computer presentation. If they had trouble, the teacher helped them divide up the tasks. One person who was comfortable with using the computer organized the presentation, planning out the sequence of cards and then programming the computer to make this work. A second student summarized the text for each page and asked the rest of the group to give their feedback on how it sounded. After quite a few changes, he typed the text into the computer. A third student drew some pictures to illustrate the myths. He drew the first one with felt pens and scanned it into the computer. Then he used the paint tools with the computer program to create some additional illustrations. Several other students in the group added drawings under the direction of the illustrator. A fourth student, the library researcher, had, as directed, found a similar story to the myth they had chosen from another culture and typed the summary for this story on a new page in the presentation.

Ritchie and Wiburg (1994) have written elsewhere about schools such as this one that incorporate technology with teaching. There are a number of variables that seem to be essential if this integration is to be successful. These include: (a) the support and leadership by the principal in using technology, (b) an interest in innovative pedagogy, (c) high-quality professional development opportunities for teachers, and (d) alliances with other institutions and organizations such as higher education and businesses. The following example from another project in a bilingual school, also in California, will serve to illustrate the building of community around the integration of technology.

Ms. García had worked with schools in California for several years to help teachers integrate computer use with the curriculum. Knowing how busy teachers are, she organized a student group of computer tutors. The students filled out applications and told why they would be good tutors for other students. They also had to ask for and receive their teacher's approval before joining the tutoring group. They had to be willing to give up several lunch recesses during the week in order to learn the programs they would teach to their peers. In this bilingual school, the students knew that being bilingual could help you get a position as a computer tutor.

After working with Ms. García for several weeks on very kid-oriented software sessions, the students went on duty for several hours a day in the classroom. They taught specific groups of children, assigned to them by their teachers, how to work on the basic programs that would be used in social studies, writing, and science during the next few months. The rooms were soon alive with writing in both Spanish and English on the "Bilingual Writing Center" (1992) and with graphs of their latest science experiments. At the same time, teachers and the principal began learning the same software. Soon all sorts of original and colorful signs and instructional materials started showing up. Parents became interested and demanded training too, and many of them started volunteering to help in the computer-enriched classrooms.

The schools were electronically linked to the local bank and to the teacher education program at the nearby college. Teachers coordinated with the bank to design lessons for their math classes. Students could send class questions to volunteer bank officers, who would then respond via e-mail. Some students were paired with Spanish-speaking student teachers in order to develop their writing skills by writing to this real and interested audience in Spanish. Technology, which is often considered a cold and even scary tool, became a factor in creating a collaborative, multicultural learning community.

Another way in which technology can be used to support development for Latino middle-school students involves using technology to support literacy in the content areas, especially in science and mathematics. It is important for Latino students to gain literacy not just in English but in the formal vocabulary used in the sciences, in mathematics, and in the social sciences. Problems that minority language learners have in these disciplines are often the result of language differences and are not thinking or conceptual problems. With technology support, students will find it easier to gain scientific and mathematical literacy as well as demonstrate their understanding of the concepts and processes involved. Science and math can even provide bridges across language and cultural barriers if they are project-based, invite experimentation, involve the manipulation of numbers and data, and use calculators and/or computers. Science is a process in which everyone can participate. The heat retention of sand and water is the same in any language. One possible technique is to ask Latino students to share the words for different objects and operations in their language and culture and let them assist in translating words and concepts for other students. The following scenario illustrates the role of technology in supporting literacy in the content areas.

Ms. Barreras attended the summer institute on technology, mathematics, and science that centered around the arid lands curriculum. She then returned to her fourth-grade classroom and began a unit on plants. She wanted her students to realize that, contrary to popular myth, there are many varieties of plants and animals that live in the local desert. She asked her students to each adopt a square meter of land at home and out in the fields that are close to the school. She also asked them to interview their families and relatives about any local plants that might be useful as medicine and food.

Her students were given time during the school day to carefully observe their land twice a week for several weeks. They were helped to note the changes in plants and to observe any traces of animals. They were allowed to use a camera to take pictures of their land both at home and at school during the project. In addition, they took notes and drew pictures of everything they saw on the land, especially the plants and animals. They reported on what they had discovered, consulting with members of the community about plants. When the children found an especially rich source of information about desert plants in the local community, the teacher and a small group of children interviewed this person, taking along the camera and a tape recorder.

The teacher and students created a database about plants that included both printed information and pictures. Either photographs or children's drawings were scanned into the computer database. Audio capabilities allowed them to record what they knew about plants into their database. The children also used a new graphing program for kids to enter data about temperatures and plant growth into the computer. They then experimented with different kinds of graphs and used a variety of formats and colors. One boy discovered a way to show the extreme differences in temperature between early morning in his home land and afternoon at the school by charting the afternoon with a red line and the early morning in blue.

These learning activities using technology are only a few examples that reject old ideas about the need to teach facts first and then engage students in problem solving. It is often more effective to put the problem first and then assist students in searching for information, generating hypotheses, finding additional information, and modifying their first hypotheses as they become proficient in the work of solving problems. The problem-centered thematic curriculum approach suggested in this chapter will assist Latino middle-school students in participating and thinking about content while gaining literacy.

SUMMARY

This chapter was concerned with the development of literacy instruction for Latino students at the middle-school level. It began by showing the urgent need to change our classrooms to reflect the increasing diversity of the population in the United States, and to meet the needs of

Latino students. A variety of strategies were suggested including the development of sheltered instruction, the development of culturally relevant curricula, the creation of an active learning environment, and the expansion of our definition of literacy. Technology tools were explored as a means of expanding opportunities for students to demonstrate their knowledge through the use of images, sound, and video, as well as print. Finally, it was suggested that technology be used to develop interdisciplinary learning activities that tie the school more closely to the community.

REFERENCES

Au, K. H. 1993. *Literacy Instruction in Multicultural Settings.* Fort Worth, TX: Harcourt Brace College Publishers.

Bilingual Writing Center v.1 [Computer software]. 1992. Freemont, CA: The Learning Center.

Carter, D. J. and R. Wilson. 1992. *Minorities in Higher Education: Tenth Annual Status Report, 1991.* Washington, D.C.: American Council on Education, Office of Minorities in Higher Education. (ERIC Document Reproduction Service No. ED 354 834).

Connell, M. 1993. A Constructivist Use of Technology in Elementary Mathematics. In *Technology and Teacher Education Annual* pp. 579–582. Charlottesville, VA: Association for the Advancement of Computing in Education.

Darder, A., Y. R. Ingle, and B. G. Cox. 1993. *The Policies and the Promise: The Public Schooling of Latino Children.* Claremont, CA: Thomas Rivera Center.

Diamond, J. 1989. The Great Leap Forward. *Discover,* 10 (5):50–60.

Drouyn-Marrero, M. A. 1989. Computer Access, Social Interaction and Learning in a Bilingual-Multicultural Setting (Doctoral dissertation, University of Massachusetts, 1989). *Dissertation Abstracts International,* 50: 3871A.

Dutton, W. H., M. E. Rogers, and S. Jun. 1987. Diffusion and Social Impacts of Personal Computers. *Communication Research,* 14 (2):219–250.

Eisner, E. W. 1994. *Cognition and Curriculum Reconsidered* (2nd ed.). New York, NY: Teachers College Press.

Fosnot, C. T. 1989. *Enquiring Teachers Enquiring Learners, a Constructivist Approach for Teaching.* New York, NY: Teachers College.

Freire, P. 1970. *Pedagogy of the Oppressed.* New York, NY: Continuum.

Gardner, H. 1985. *Frames of Mind.* New York, NY: Basic Books.

Hativa, N. 1988. Computer-Based Drill and Practice in Arithmetic: Widening the Gap between High-Achieving and Low-Achieving Students. *American Educational Research Journal,* 25 (3):366–397.

Hodgkinson, H. L. 1992. *A Demographic Look at Tomorrow.* Washington, D.C.: The Institute for Educational Leadership. (ERIC Document Reproduction Service No. ED 359 087).

Hunt, N. and R. Pritchard. 1993. Technology and Language Minority Students: Implications for Teacher Education. In *Technology and Teacher Education Annual 1993,*

25–27. Charlottesville, VA: Association for Advancement of Computers in Education.

Hypercard 2.2 [Computer software]. 1993. Cupertino, CA: Apple Computer.

Hyperstudio 1.0 for Windows [Computer software]. 1993. El Cajon, CA: Roger Wagner.

Johnson, R. and D. Johnson. 1994. *Learning Together and Alone* (3rd ed.). Boston, MA: Allyn & Bacon.

Joyce, B., M. Weil, and B. Showers. 1992. *Models of Teaching* (4th ed.). Boston, MA: Allyn & Bacon.

Linn, M. 1992. Science education reform: Building on the research base. *Journal of Research in Science Teaching,* 29 (8):821–840.

McLaren, P. 1993. *Schooling as a Ritual Performance: Towards a Political Economy of Educational Symbols and Gestures* (2nd ed.). London, England: Routledge.

Mergendoller, J. R. and E. B. Pardo. 1991. *An Evaluation of the MacMagic Program at Davidson Middle School.* Novato, CA: Beryl Buck Institute for Education. (ERIC Document Reproduction Service No. ED 351 143).

Moll, L. and J. B. Greenberg. 1992. Creating Zones of Possibilities: Combining Social Contexts for Instruction. In L. Moll (Ed.), *Vygotsky and Education: Instructional Implications and Applications of Socio-Historical Psychology,* pp. 319–348. New York, NY: Cambridge University Press.

Pallas, M. M., G. Natriello, and E. I. McDill. 1989. Changing Nature of the Disadvantaged Population: Current Dimensions and Future Trends. *Educational Researcher,* 19(5):16–22.

Point of View 2.0 [Computer software]. 1993. New York, NY: Scholastic.

Ritchie, D. and K. Wiburg. 1994. Educational Variables Influencing Technology Integration. *Journal of Technology and Teacher Education,* 2(20):143–153.

Skelle, R. 1993. Technology and Diversity: Resolving Computer Equity Issues through Multicultural Education. In *Technology and Teacher Education Annual 1993,* 14–18. Charlottesville, VA: Association for Advancement of Computers in Education.

Tharp, R. and R. Gallimore. 1990. *Rousing Minds to Life: Teaching, Learning, and Schooling in Social Context* (2nd ed.). New York, NY: Cambridge University Press.

Vygotsky, L. S. 1962. *Thought and Language.* Cambridge, MA: MIT Press.

Zehler, A. 1994. *Working with English Language Learners: Strategies for Elementary and Middle School Teachers* (Program Information Guide No. 19). Washington, D.C.: National Clearinghouse for Bilingual Education. (ERIC Document Reproduction Service No. ED 381 022).

PART VI

EXEMPLARY PRACTICES FOR LATINOS AT THE HIGH-SCHOOL LEVEL

Transforming High Schools to Meet the Needs of Latinos

JULIA ROSA EMSLIE—*Eastern New Mexico University*
JUAN A. CONTRERAS—*Ysleta Independent School District*
VIRGINIA R. PADILLA—*Ysleta Independent School District*

INTRODUCTION

EDUCATORS must come to realize with a passion that they are educational architects of the future. They must visualize that if their own children are to be academically, socially, and economically successful, then all children must be successful as well.

Yet the reality is that even though our students are increasingly more culturally and linguistically diverse, the number of qualified bilingual, bicultural teachers that might best help these students achieve success is disproportionately low. The issue then becomes that of assisting monolingual teachers to better meet the needs of their diverse students (Ramirez, 1996).

Students enter U.S. schools at different ages with a wide variety of fluency levels in English and with all varieties of educational backgrounds; nonetheless, Latino students, despite their diverse backgrounds, have several common needs. Many need to build their oral skills, as well as their reading and writing skills in the English language, while maintaining a learning continuum in the content areas (e.g., mathematics, science, and social studies). Potentially English Proficient (PEP) students have other needs that make learning more challenging. Some arrive from countries where schooling is quite different from that of the United States. Some may have large gaps in their schooling or no formal schooling at all; others may lack important native language literacy skills for students of their age (see Lucas, Chapter 15).

Latinos are also diverse in their economic backgrounds. They may have financial as well as medical problems. These students may need support from health and social service agencies, or they may simply need an understanding about some of the special circumstances that they are experiencing when parents work long hours and cannot help with homework. Students may be required to baby-sit brothers and sisters until late each evening, making it difficult to complete all of the assigned homework (Zehler, 1994).

The important point to remember is that each individual student presents a profile of abilities in subject areas and skills, which is true for ESL students as much as for native English speakers. Latino students bring unique backgrounds, experiences, and perspectives that can provide many resources for the entire classroom including (Zehler, 1994):

- information about other countries, together with beliefs, cultures, and customs
- new perspectives about the world and society
- opportunities for exposure to other languages, for sharing ways of thinking and doing things that might otherwise be taken for granted

Teachers often make the error of thinking that Latinos are proficient in English because they hear them expressing themselves clearly in informal situations; however, this is not the case. Although social conversational skills are important, they are not sufficient for classroom-based academic learning. In fact, a student who is fluent in social conversational English is likely to require four to seven years in English language development in order to acquire the level of proficiency needed for successful academic learning. There is also a belief that young children learn a second language faster than an adolescent or young adult. However, this is far from the truth; older children and adults have already developed strategies that assist them with learning a second language. Through the strength of their primary language, they have knowledge of language rules and structures that can help them in learning a second language (Collier, 1995).

This chapter will focus on the following themes in the education of Latino high-school students: (1) going beyond curriculum and instruction; (2) school and personal commitment for Latinos including ESL students; and (3) community and parental involvement at the high-school level.

GOING BEYOND CURRICULUM AND INSTRUCTION

Educators need to develop a greater appreciation for and understanding of the diverse populations they teach. They must be able to make use of a multiplicity of teaching techniques and strategies that reflect an appreciation of cultural diversity (Kuykendall, 1992). In turn, these instructional methods lead to a stronger academic program. Interdisciplinary team teaching and design of curriculum, cooperative learning, block scheduling, and sheltered English are some techniques and strategies that integrate Latino students into the total school community.

Interdisciplinary Team Teaching

Interdisciplinary team teaching involves a grouping of teachers who usually present four or five subjects to several sections of students. The teachers meet as a block during the same planning period. The number of students involved ranges from 50 to 150. Generally, an interdisciplinary program consists of English, social studies, mathematics, science, and reading or foreign language, and features cooperative planning of lessons for this common group of students.

Interdisciplinary teams provide several advantages, such as the following:

- Students have subject matter specialists for each content area who also coordinate the total program.
- Special interdisciplinary units and activities are provided by teachers; these units integrate the content areas.
- Planning periods are used for pupil and parent conferences as well as for coordinating the instructional program.
- Flexible scheduling allows for 45 minute, 60 minute, or 90 minute class periods.

When implementing interdisciplinary teams, the time needed for planning must come from the regular work day. A block of time for planning on a daily basis is a high priority. Once interdisciplinary team teaching grouping has been established, the teams can begin work on an interdisciplinary design.

Interdisciplinary Design

An interdisciplinary design is an approach used where each teacher in a team or individual teachers make connections for the student through the development of general learning experiences across disciplines that support conceptual themes and related skills. Broad-based issues, problems, and themes serve as the organizing element. Teachers determine common generalizations and concepts to be developed across disciplines. When a major theme is selected, such as "change," the development of the theme takes place. Generalizations about change are first derived, such as change is constant and change may lead to growth. A goal is developed for the theme, for example "to lead students to understand that changes impact cultural values, social and economic progress, and vice versa." The teachers next outline the focus for each content area as related to the goal. This is done with all populations. The following is an example of such an outline:

(1) Social Studies
  • Changes occur in social systems.
  • Changes occur across and within cultures.
  • Changes occur when diverse people interact in certain time periods.
(2) Mathematics
  • Changes occur in numeration as needs of culture evolve.
(3) Language Arts
  • Changes in characters' actions and attitudes occur due to conflict, events, and/or choices.
(4) Science
  • Changes occur in medicine from early herbs to genetic engineering.

All broad-based themes and generalizations are developed across disciplines (Crain, 1995). The following vignette discusses a culturally relevant activity developed through interdisciplinary design.

In a classroom composed of newly immigrated Latino students, Mrs. Payne's ninth-grade vocabulary development class for PEP students, the following took place. The theme selected was *culture.* To generate discussion, generalizations were made with regards to culture. The discussion was mainly in English with some reinforcement in the native language (Spanish). Students were asked as a homework assignment to interview and gather three definitions of culture from three different people representing a different ethnicity. The next day the students read and discussed their definitions. The students agreed that culture meant different things to different people.

Using a technique called mind mapping, the students developed their own interpretation of culture. For mind mapping, the students were asked to put their heads on their desks while keeping only a paper and pencil on their desks. Mrs. Payne asked the students to listen to soft music and write or sketch whatever came to mind as they listened to the music.

Mrs. Payne walked around the room posing different questions about culture using the five senses. The technique was initiated by giving culture a color. Questions such as the following were used. What color is culture to you? Is it brown like the dirt? Is it white like the clouds? How does culture feel? Does it feel soft like a rose petal or fuzzy like a peach? How does culture sound? Does it sound like laughter? Does it sound like rain? This continued until all the senses were addressed.

The following day the students created their *mind map*. They took a sheet of drawing paper and wrote "Culture" in the center. Then, using their notes from the prior day, they created pictures and wrote words around the word "Culture" that encompassed their thoughts and feelings with regard to culture during the mind mapping technique. The students colored and elaborated their mind maps, which were exhibited on the bulletin board and around the classroom.

After the mind maps were completed, culture was again discussed and the class as a whole decided that "folk medicine" was a concept within their definition of culture that was unique to them. The students decided to research folk medicine and did the following activities:

- interviewed parents as to folk medicines utilized in the home
- compared and contrasted the different herbs/folk medicines used in their homes
- created charts with information relevant to the different herbs
- created medicine books with remedies for specific ailments
- gave oral presentations on herbal medicine and steps in the development of their medicine books

The students responded positively to this activity mainly because it made sense and was relevant to their daily lives. Through the use of interdisciplinary design, the Latino students were made part of the integral school curriculum, since all other content areas were also working on "Culture" as a theme. They also explored the areas of social studies and science through the various activities that were implemented.

This vignette demonstrates how interdisciplinary designs and cooperative learning can be encouraged in secondary settings for PEP students. They promote positive feelings of mutual appreciation, support, and respect among Latinos and all other students (Calderón, 1992).

Cooperative Learning

Cooperative learning may be defined as a technique whereby students work together in partnerships and teams, helping one another become strategic learners. Emphasis is placed on equal opportunities for success, individual accountability, common goals, and rewards (Slavin, 1993). Cooperative learning is an instructional strategy that helps the teacher with classroom management for grouping students. It provides a manageable structure for cooperative peer interaction, crucial for natural second language acquisition (Faltis, 1993; Wong Fillmore, 1989, 1991). This is true for all students and especially Latino students who are learning English as a second language.

Cooperative learning begins when students are grouped, preferably in groups of four. Each group then selects a recorder, timekeeper, materials manager, and reporter. The students may be asked to create a poster with (1) the name for their group, (2) a picture to represent the group name, and (3) a logo that makes reference to the group name. Each student presents their poster and the rationale for choosing the group name, picture, and logo. The teacher may ask students to make the posters relevant to education. The groups are kept together for a specific amount of time and then new groups can be formed. As the students work on the different assignments, each of the students in the different groups must show accountability for the completion of the assignment. Cooperative learning at the high-school level is important for Latino students and other English language learners. Sheltered instruction for Latinos who are acquiring English can be implemented via cooperative learning. This approach is discussed later in this chapter under "The Sheltered Instructional Approach."

Block Scheduling

Block scheduling is increasingly being used around the country in middle and high schools. This type of scheduling involves setting aside large blocks of time for different subject areas (usually one and a half hours to two hours) and meeting less often per week. A science block, for instance, might meet from 8 to 10 A.M. on Mondays and Wednesdays, while a language arts block might meet at the same time on Tuesdays and Thursdays. Special activities would take place on Fridays, as well as other classes. This type of scheduling brings several advantages, such as creating larger blocks of time for instruction, permitting students to enroll in one additional class each year, and increasing the time available for professional development (Hackman, 1995). Block scheduling is thought to be one of the characteristics of successful schools (see González and Huerta-Macías, Chapter 11, this volume).

The Sheltered Instructional Approach

One of the most successful approaches to teaching content in English to non-English speakers is sheltered or comprehensible English. This approach uses English as the medium for providing content area instruction. It provides content area instruction while emphasizing the development of English language skills. Teachers explain complex concepts in content areas using instructional strategies that include simplification of teacher's speech and prolific use of visual aids and other nonverbal clues. The key is to provide comprehensible input so that students understand the content. Yet they are careful not to simplify things to the point where the students notice and feel patronized. Competent teachers keep the PEP students in mind as they plan their lessons and anticipate difficulties that the students may encounter with the material. Sheltered English teachers can identify key concepts in the lesson and provide an understanding of key vocabulary words that represent these concepts before implementation of the lesson (Constantino, 1994).

Peregoy and Boyle (1993) suggest that teachers in sheltered English instruction do the following: (1) organize instruction around content and provide access to the core curriculum; (2) modify language used during instruction by speaking clearly in simple terms as well as limiting the use of idiomatic expressions; (3) use Total Physical Response (TPR), which includes gestures, facial expressions, actions to dramatize meaning, props, concrete materials, graphs, pictures, visuals, and maps; and (4) explain the purpose of the activity by building on students' prior knowledge in order to prepare them for information and to provide vocabulary development in advance. Working with PEP students requires not only knowledge of teaching strategies, but a strong commitment as well.

SCHOOL AND PERSONAL COMMITMENT TO SCHOOLING FOR LATINO/ESL STUDENTS

Educators today face a redefined agenda that must address issues of race, ethnicity, culture, history, gender, and technology to include linguistic and social sensitivity. No school can successfully educate its students unless key instructional support and administrative staff are committed to and fully participate in the programs and services designed to educate students (Lucas, 1993). In the long run, this commitment to education can only reap rewards of quality. Staff members in successful

schools demonstrate their commitment through their actions, their beliefs, and dedication to the programs and services provided to Latino and
PEP students. They dedicate extra time, energy, and effort to work with
these students at school. They excel in their efforts to guarantee their
success.

Lucas (1993) writes that:

> Some staff members who excel in their work demonstrate that they place
> value on students' languages and cultures; devise ways to incorporate
> students' native languages in schooling; hold high expectations of stu-
> dents; design, promote, and attend staff development activities; encourage
> families to participate in schooling; design and provide support services
> and extracurricular activities; and design and implement curricula. (p. 8)

Lucas (1993) elaborates on these issues and emphasizes that even
though a school entity is made of different parts, all the parts must work
together for the benefit of all students. Principals must promote staff
development focusing on issues relevant to the education of Latinos and
PEP students. They must work with district bilingual staff and find ways
to bring families to join the school. As advocates for the Latino and
English language learner, principals must actively support and develop
programs and services for these students and their families, while also
engaging faculty and staff in professional development related to building the home/school connection.

Schools should provide counselors who can communicate effectively
and in the students' native language or provide someone who can
facilitate communication. Counselors should be knowledgeable about
students' cultural values, experiences, and issues. They also influence
Latino students' behavior and learning.

To implement changes, those people directly involved must work
together setting realistic goals and strategies for effective success that
make sense within their communities.

COMMUNITY AND PARENTAL INVOLVEMENT

There is overwhelming evidence from formal as well as informal
sources that a strong relationship between the community and the school
strengthens the academic performance of students. However, there is an
extensive set of myths regarding parents/families of Latino students and
their views and beliefs about education. Unfortunately, once certain
pronouncements are made through the media, it is very difficult to change

people's perceptions. In an attempt to dispel existing myths, the Intercultural Development Research Association (IDRA), an independent nonprofit advocacy organization dedicated to improving educational opportunity, has devoted time and energy to the subject of parental involvement and Latino students. Some of the pervasive misconceptions are that Latinos do not value education, will not talk to school personnel, blame the system for the students' failure, and are not able to help students at home (Symonds, 1994).

Research by IDRA and other educators and institutions has revealed that Latino parents are truly concerned about their children's future and hold high aspirations for their educational attainment. Thus, parents must be brought into the educational and academic world of the school. A parent-school relationship must be built to make parents aware of their own voice in their children's schooling, even though schooling may be conducted in a language that the parents may not speak. Parents do have constraints that limit their attendance at school functions: many parents hold two jobs; others may feel intimidated with unfamiliar school situations; students may not be living with their parents; and some parents have had genuinely unfavorable experiences with schools.

The most effective ways to attract parents to workshops and meetings have been through personal contacts from bilingual school personnel and from their own children. Parents should be telephoned individually to explain the importance of attending meetings; in some cases, meetings become family affairs when students are encouraged to attend alongside their parents (Chamot, 1995). Some teachers conduct home visits, either during their conference hours or after school.

Schools in the Ysleta Independent School District in El Paso, Texas, provide various activities that directly engage parents in school activities. For example, parent centers, with money to pay parent liaisons are provided. At the parent centers parents meet others and participate in different activities with teachers as well as other adults.

Another innovative approach engages all parents by providing free summer school for students. The summer school program has one major requirement: that parents contribute two hours of volunteer work weekly during the summer sessions. This applies to retainees as well as students who want to advance in the academic programs. Activities for parents are provided, such as mini health fairs, training in parenting skills, computer training, tours to the local university, etc., depending on the needs of the parents and the resources of the community. This program was instituted four years ago by the district, and due to its success the legislature has allocated funds providing for free summer school statewide.

The same district has also established an entrepreneur center. Parents, students, and teachers work together to create assorted art work that is sold through the entrepreneur center. On a monthly basis the entrepreneur center holds a *mercado* (market) where teachers, students, parents, and community join efforts to celebrate and sell their arts and crafts. During *mercado* the festivities include singing, ballet *folklorico* dancing, and *mariachi* bands. Businesses join hands to celebrate student efforts in entrepreneurial endeavors. Moneys generated from sales are then used for school and student needs.

In the classrooms parents are also welcomed with open arms. They are invited to enhance instruction as storytellers or historians, who are called upon to share their knowledge and expertise with the entire student population. The effect of these joint parent and student activities is to provide additional avenues of communication between parents and teachers, between students and parents, and between students and teachers and the community. An example of this type of involvement took place in Mr. Carr's classroom.

During a thematic unit on patterns, parents were invited to come into the classroom to share stories of folklore and family histories with the class. Some parents shared stories, while others brought in artwork they had created that represented a significant time in their lives. Needless to say, the students were happy to see their parents as fully contributing educational partners.

After this, students were given a homework assignment to interview other adults to relate stories, history, or even writings that were part of their lives. The following day everyone shared their experiences. The teacher then explained the value of folktales and their impact on storytelling and writing. The students were next given an additional assignment of writing a poem involving their five senses that described the sharing of time with their parents. This type of poem used the five senses to describe what they see, hear, touch, taste, and smell. Examples of this task were:

> *I see life engraved upon your face,*
> *I hear the roar of thousands in your place,*
> *I touch tomorrows with love,*
> *I taste victory over trials and tribulations,*
> *I smell yesteryears of struggle.*

The impact of this activity was in seeing parents and students spending instructional, quality time together and valuing each other's contributions.

There are no quick recipes for parent and family involvement, especially at the secondary level. We do know that some schools are successful with parent orientations in which presentations and videos in Spanish are given to parents with faculty, students, and staff serving as facilitators to answer questions. The relationship must be established and the initiative for increased parent involvement must be on the part of the school. Part of the effectiveness of teachers will be a measure of their involvement with Latino communities. The transformation of the high school must take into consideration the need for secondary schools to make strong connections with the home. It will happen in the case of very dedicated staff alongside administrators who make time to strengthen home-school partnerships.

SUMMARY

In this chapter, issues related to the high-school instruction to meet the needs of Latino students have been discussed. Descriptions of Latino students, teachers with quality instructional practices, and features that are characteristic of positive relationships have been addressed. The importance of family and community involvement and ways of improving this relationship were presented.

The processes and the practices presented in this chapter are necessary in transforming high schools to meet the needs of Latino students, including those who are learning English.

Educators are always searching to answer questions related to the how and why of secondary instruction. As a nation we cannot afford to stop seeking answers and looking for solutions that may be directly before us. Educators must be open and receptive to Latinos, their families, and communities, which add to the beautiful tapestry of diversity.

REFERENCES

Calderón, M. 1992. *Sheltered Instruction Through Cooperative Learning*. El Paso, TX: Educational Psychological and Special Services at The University of Texas at El Paso.

Chamot, A. U. 1995. Implementing the Cognitive Academic Language Learning Approach: CALLA in Arlington, VA. *Bilingual Research Journal* 19 (3–4): NABE.

Collier, V. P. 1995. *Promoting Academic Success for ESL Students: Understanding Second Language Acquisition for School.* NJTESOL-BE. Elizabeth, N J.

Constantino, R. 1994. "A Study Concerning Instruction of ESL Students Comparing All-English Classroom Teacher Knowledge and English as a Second Language Teacher Knowledge," *The Journal of Educational Issues of Language Minority Students* 13:37–57.

Crain, J. A. 1995. Address before Ranchland Hills Middle School. Staff development on Interdisciplinary Design. El Paso, TX.

Faltis, C. J. 1993. *Joint Fostering: Adapting Teaching Strategies for the Multilingual Classroom.* New York, NY: Macmillan.

Hackman, D. J. 1995, November. "Ten Guidelines for Implementing Block Scheduling," *Educational Leadership,* 53(3):24–27.

Kuykendall, C. 1992. *From Rage to Hope: Strategies for Reclaiming Black and Hispanic Students.* National Educational Service. Bloomington, IN.

Lucas, T. 1993. "Applying Elements of Effective Secondary Schooling for Language Minority Students: A Tool for Reflection and Stimulus to Change." NCBE 14 Program Information Guide Series.

Peregoy, S. F. and O. F. Boyle. 1993. *Reading, Writing, and Learning in ESL: A Resource for K–8 Teachers.* White Plains, NY: Longman.

Ramirez, J. D. 1996. Address before Secondary Education for Limited English Proficient Students in Texas: A Call for Action. State meeting, Austin, TX, July 1996.

Slavin, R. 1993. *Cooperative Learning and Success for All.* Baltimore, MD: Center for Research on Effective Schooling for Disadvantaged Students.

Symonds, M. 1994. "Hispanic Parents and Successful Schooling: Dispelling Misconceptions in the Information Age," *International Development Research Association* 21(6):3–17.

Wong Fillmore, L. 1989. Teachability and Second Language Acquisition. In R. Schiefelbusch and A. Rice (Eds.), *The Teachability of Language,* pp. 311–332. Baltimore, MD: Paul Brookes.

Wong Fillmore, L. 1991. Second Language Learning in Children: A Model of Language Learning Social Context. In E. Bialystok (Ed.), *Language Processing in Bilingual Children,* pp. 49–69. Cambridge, MA: Cambridge University Press.

Zehler, A. 1994. "Working with English Language Learners: Strategies for Elementary and Middle School Teachers." NCBE 19 Program Information Guide Series.

CHAPTER 15

Aspects of Successful Programs for Unschooled Latino Immigrants/Recent Arrivals at the Secondary Level

NANCY J. LUCAS—*John F. Kennedy Middle School, Riviera Beach, FL*

INTRODUCTION

ACCORDING to a National Assessment of Educational Progress (NAEP) report (1987), many American school children have mastered reading and writing fundamentals but have not learned how to analyze, evaluate, and extend the ideas they read and write about. If most American school children suffer from these academic and literacy gaps, what about our unschooled Latino youth? What does the term unschooled mean in the context of American life? How does this condition affect the adolescent children of Latino immigrants in public secondary schools in the United States, which have often failed to provide the needed remedies? What factors impact the quality of efforts made to meet the educational needs of these students? The purpose of this chapter is to provide educators and educational leaders with new insights to better develop and influence the quality of programs designed to meet the educational needs of Latino youth without formal schooling backgrounds.

Many of the nation's recent arrivals from other countries are of Latino origin. These immigrants do not fit into a single mold, but come with diverse backgrounds. As Gonzalez and Darling-Hammond (in press) state:

> Immigrant children and youth do not share a common "immigrant experience." . . . They include those who have been traumatized by the ravages of famine and persecution as well as those who come from the privileged oligarchies of the world. Immigrants come to the U.S. schools with varying degrees of prior schooling or no schooling at all. While some have suffered more than others prior to coming here, all experience some level of trauma and change in adjusting to a new culture, a different language, and even a world view that may be distinct from their own. (p. 13)

Many Latinos come with strong academic skills and years of formal education, which they have received in their own countries. Many, however, do not come with these experiences. Upon arrival to the United States, these Latino immigrants find themselves in another country where survival depends upon the skills of the formally educated. The need to more adequately acquire these skills requires the development of comprehensive educational programs that teach these competencies to recently arrived immigrant children without formal schooling backgrounds.

CHARACTERISTICS OF UNSCHOOLED IMMIGRANT ADOLESCENTS

The most recent influx of immigrants who for various reasons are limited in academic and literacy skills comes primarily from Mexico, Central and South America, and the Caribbean (U.S. Department of Education: Office of Policy and Planning, 1993). Latino children who arrive as adolescents, in particular, seem to meet with great difficulty when trying to complete high school in the United States. In 1991, 35.3 percent of Latinos between 16–24 years of age had not completed high school compared to 8.9 percent of non-Hispanic whites. Drop-out rates from 45 to 65 percent for Hispanic students have been reported in several states. Unresolved literacy problems at the secondary level seem to only magnify at higher levels. In 1990, only 6 percent of the nation's undergraduate college students were Latinos (The Tomas Rivera Center, 1993). A closer look is needed to better understand the obstacles facing Latino immigrants who come to us without formal schooling backgrounds.

Definitions of Unschooled

"Unschooled" is one of many descriptors found in the literature to indicate that certain groups or individuals lack formal education. Most definitions include a number of forces that have come together to build this educational gap. Educational backgrounds, geographical settings, economic conditions of the native country, and political situations have been posited as reasons for an apparent lack of literacy skills. Terms such as *unschooled, low-schooled, non-literate, illiterate, less prepared, semi-literate, preliterate, borderline literate, academically delayed,* and *functionally illiterate* have been coined to describe those with limited formal education. Regardless of the descriptor, individuals may well find themselves struggling to meet the literacy demands for surviving in the United States, and especially for succeeding in our secondary schools.

To more fully understand and better serve these students, it is important to first examine the reasons for this lack of formal schooling. For one, Latino students' formal schooling has frequently been interrupted due to civil war, terrorism, or torture in their native countries, as in the case of children from El Salvador, Guatemala, and Nicaragua (First and Carrera, 1988). Once here, unschooled immigrant children may also become part of a highly mobile and transient family structure. Their academic and literacy skills may continue to suffer as a result of their interrupted schooling.

Many even lack literacy skills in Spanish (Romo, 1993). Often students have less than an eighth-grade education and some less than five years of formal education (Valdez-Pierce, 1987). Others are described as those whose "native language literacy rates are low and there has often been little or no exposure to an urban setting" (Bliss, 1986, p. 19). These recent Latino arrivals are often those "from rural areas with little or no contact with western culture or with a technologically advanced society" (Bensinger-Lacy, 1986, p. 25).

Adolescent Latino students may enter American schools with limited abilities in reading and utilizing textbooks or other instructional materials, or in need of literacy skills related to their own personal and individual situations and responsibilities in life (de Felix et al., 1993). Others with limited ability to read and write effectively in English may have previously participated in ESL programs that have concentrated on predominantly oral English skills and have neglected reading comprehension and writing development (Garza and Orum, 1982).

Although the backgrounds of our recent Latino immigrant communities may reflect large gaps in education and varied literacy abilities, these individuals bring many strengths and skills to our society that can help them build new and productive lives. If the strengths and talents of these unique populations are untapped and their literacy concerns left unaddressed, our nation runs the risk of never discovering the rich contributions they bring.

Strengths Brought by Unschooled Latinos

Building upon the existing strengths of recently arrived Latino adolescents can help them in mastering the skills needed to succeed in a new culture that demands competence in literacy. One of the strengths these students often demonstrate is a surprising degree of leadership ability. This results from students having to accept major responsibilities within the home, such as caring for younger relatives and friends; providing an income for basic necessities, such as food and clothing; or making the decision for the family to migrate. Although encouraging the involvement of recently arrived parents in the educational process and helping them to realize the importance of schooling in the United States is indeed a worthy goal, the children of the immigrant family may be capable of improving their own education and helping one another early in the process. As immigrant families begin to acculturate, the children often learn English and adjust to American culture more quickly than their parents. They are at times forced to assume a parental role by becoming the language brokers, representatives, and communicators for the family in daily affairs of the new culture (Bliss, 1986). These leadership skills should be fostered and encouraged in the public schools, since leadership is a trait admired and sought after in American culture.

Latino adolescent immigrants are also one step ahead of most American-born youth in reaching the national education goal of bilingualism. Goals 2000, the federal Educate America Act, dictates that "By the year 2000 all American students will leave grades 4, 8, and 12 having demonstrated competency in challenging subject matter including English, mathematics, science, *foreign languages*, art, history, and geography" (U.S. Department of Education, 1993). As schools recognize the Latino immigrant youth's growing ability to communicate in both Spanish- and English-speaking worlds, they should tap into these gifts by encouraging and heralding bilingualism.

Many Latino families who come with little formal education bring a rich oral tradition by way of music, folklore, and the Spanish language. The rich descriptive vocabulary and oral expression already developed in the native language serve to provide the framework for concepts needed to successfully acquire proficiency in English. Students can build on these skills to help achieve academic success in American schools. In a similar manner, social skills can also be transferred to the new culture. Latinos tend to value personal relationships and socialization. These skills are motivators for students to quickly develop conversational English. Many times Latino adolescents exercise strong social competence and mature problem-solving capabilities and are able to take on adult-like responsibilities (Williams and Newcombe, 1994).

Regardless of the terminology used to indicate the lack of literacy skills in English or the native language, the singular point is to identify the many untapped resources inherent in the cultures of Latinos. All immigrant students new to the United States have a right to a free and quality public education, even those who may come ill-prepared to succeed in American schools. The Equal Protection Clause of the Fourteenth Amendment of the U.S. Constitution and the 1982 Supreme Court ruling of *Plyler v. Doe*, 457 U.S. 202, 102 S. Ct. 2382, 72 L. Ed. 2d 786 (1982) establish that fact. But it takes effort to adequately build upon the strengths that immigrants bring to ensure that these newly arrived, unschooled adolescents learn the skills required to achieve in American schools.

New Cultural Knowledge and Academic Needs

The need for new cultural knowledge and academic skills adds to the difficult literacy challenges already facing unschooled Latino youth. In American culture, for example, it is assumed that if parents are concerned about their children's education, they will be significantly involved with the educational process. Latino parents, on the other hand, sometimes view education as belonging to educators who know what is best for their children. The idea of taking a responsible role in their children's education has often not occurred to them. This may be due in part to the lack of successful efforts by mainstream schools to appropriately "invite" Latino parents into the educational setting and value them as contributing members of the school system.

Many Latino immigrant youth share academic and cognitive gaps from not having formal schooling experiences. In order to work through secondary school curricula, recent arrivals are expected to have mastered basic English literacy and academic knowledge. Early on, this academic gap is so large that it takes more than an ESL course to fill it (Minicucci and Olsen, 1993). The problem is compounded by the fact that educators are not in agreement concerning the nature of these literacy or academic skills. Some secondary educators argue that literacy refers to functional literacy skills required for specific types of social roles or job responsibilities. Others contend that literacy is the ability to use an academic text and to correctly use syntax, word structure, punctuation, and spelling (de Felix et al., 1993). In the following passage, Bliss (1986) speaks of the multidimensional functional literacy dilemma many new immigrants share from the outset of their new lives in a relatively unknown world.

Predictably enough, the usual definitions of literacy refer to the literacy needs of the nation's English-speaking population: the need to read, write and compute enough to be able to function in the community and on the job. We're aware though that many Americans manage to *get by* without these skills by using spoken language or the assistance of friends, co-workers or family members. The limited-English speaker doesn't have this capacity to *get by* because he doesn't possess the ability to listen to, comprehend and produce the spoken language necessary to meet basic survival needs of everyday life. (p. 20)

Many educators have worked diligently to develop and identify program factors that have proven to enhance the quality of services for immigrant students specifically dealing with a secondary curriculum and related requirements for success. Implementing program factors proven to be successful for unschooled secondary immigrant students allows these adolescents not only to get by in school, but to also build upon their own strengths to become competent and productive members of a literate society.

FACTORS THAT INFLUENCE PROGRAMS FOR UNSCHOOLED LATINOS

Developing successful programs for Latino immigrant youth who have limited formal education requires a holistic look at cultural, attitudinal, and academic factors that may influence a program's effectiveness. These factors include building on the strengths of students and their families; exhibiting positive attitudes toward immigration, using the native language, and literacy; and insisting upon the highest quality in intake and assessment procedures. Of utmost importance to successful literacy programs for unschooled immigrant youth is the quality of leadership and support of the school administrators responsible for their implementation.

Building on Student and Family Strengths

Building upon student and family strengths is a crucial factor in the development of supportive and successful programs for Latino youth with limited schooling. In relation to cultural factors, school leaders and staff must become knowledgeable and supportive of the unique cultural values and strengths recently arrived secondary school immigrants and their families bring to the school culture. Recognizing and utilizing these strengths along with other positive attributes of Latino youth, such as leadership, responsibility, and cooperation, will accelerate the development of their academic and literacy skills. It is doubtful, however, that knowledge of cultural factors can have a significant impact on the quality of services without a realization that the attitudes of those in the school community toward new immigrants will determine the true value of the efforts put forth.

Attitudes toward Immigration, Using the Native Language, and Illiteracy

The attitudes of the local school community toward immigration issues will reflect whether new immigrants make a positive difference in American society. In a recent poll conducted in 1993 by *Time* magazine, 61 percent of the respondents indicated they would like to see it made more difficult for people from other countries who claim they are victims of persecution in their countries to enter the United States. Eighty-eight percent of those surveyed stated they were a great deal or somewhat concerned with the presence of illegal aliens in this country. Forty-seven percent of the respondents felt that the nation should stop providing government health benefits and public education to immigrants and their children (Nelan, 1993). The recent passing of California (i.e., Proposition 187) legislation regarding the unavailability, for the first time, of public health care to immigrants without legal documentation substantiates the intolerant mood of some communities in the United States today.

Negative attitudes in a community toward immigration could affect not only the climate but the programmatic issues of local school efforts. These attitudes have a ripple effect upon students, parents, faculty, and staff. When ambivalent or negative attitudes prevail, decisions detrimental to learning may result. A school may place special classes for students in portable classrooms isolated from the main campus. Schools may also neglect to include immigrant students in elective courses and extracurricular activities, although their free and public education is guaranteed (*Plyler v. Doe,* 1982).

In the absence of positive attitudes, other problems may arise. The use of one's native language as a medium for socialization and instruction in the American classroom may become a sore spot for some. Although using the primary language for instruction has been shown to be an effective strategy for learning and teaching English, this practice can also be controversial. One formal outcry against using the primary language not only in the educational setting but in the larger societal context is the "English Only" movement. Supporters fashion legislation that declares English as the "official" language. Some researchers claim a lack of documentation supporting the effectiveness of using the bilingual approach. According to one study, "research reports on programs for linguistically diverse students lack documentation of the classroom environment and teaching processes used" (de Felix et al., 1993, p. 357).

Proof of just how effective the use of the primary language really is in teaching academic and functional literacy is abundant, however. National research has found considerable evidence in support of the bilingual approach. These successful programs share a strong support of native language instruction using a variety of methods (Flores, 1990). Teachers have knowledge about how children come to learn and comprehend written language. They use the native language to check comprehension, translate a lesson, explain an activity, and provide instruction. Written language is learned and used for social interaction with real dialogue. Students use the primary language to assist and tutor each other, to ask and answer questions, to use bilingual dictionaries, and to write in their native language. In successful literacy programs for unschooled youth, the native language is also utilized in the larger school context. Library books, communication with parents, and content instruction are found to be in the primary language (Lucas, 1993).

Accepting attitudes toward the social and academic use of the native language has positive effects. The success of Dade County's (Florida) bilingual education programs in the public schools and the private ethnic schools run by Cuban educators has helped in gaining greater economic power for the Spanish-speaking community in Dade County (Garcia and Otheguy, 1985). At Elgin High School in Elgin, Illinois, a bilingual program with a strong native language and literacy component has found success. Content courses are taught in several different languages using integrated thematic instruction [National Coalition of Advocates for Students (NCAS), 1994b]. A part-time counselor and community liaison speak the native language of many of the students. In this program, the students' entry assessment process, which is, for the most part, conducted in the native language, is a major strength of the program.

Quality of Intake and Assessment Procedures

Clearly, accurate assessment of Latino students who are unschooled gives them a much better chance to succeed in their new educational surroundings. An extensive entry assessment, as at Elgin High School, makes all the difference. Use of oral interviews and tests to evaluate oral and written proficiency in English, ability in mathematics, and reading ability in the student's home language are essential components of successful programs for secondary unschooled youth.

Crucial to the intake process of newly arrived adolescent immigrants is an immediate determination of the fluency of oral/aural English. This is extremely important for the preliterate student who has mastered basic listening and speaking skills in English (Friedlander, 1991). The student's oral language can serve as the basis for the content of a literacy curriculum tailored to meet his/her unique needs.

Reading and writing proficiency in English and the native language must also be correctly assessed to determine at which levels the student can be most effectively taught. As an integral component of programs with intake and assessment procedures of quality, parents are carefully listened to for determining the characteristics and scope of the student's prior educational experiences. Formal or informal evaluation of the level of mastery in mathematics is also beneficial in identifying the extent of the newly arrived immigrant student's formal education.

The National Coalition for Advocacy of Students (NCAS, 1988) reiterates integral components of a comprehensive intake plan for unschooled immigrant adolescents. Among them are the components of orienting parents to the U.S. educational system, assisting with the enrollment process, assessing the child's academic skills in both English and the child's first language, and assessing the child's English language proficiency. The organization strongly suggests developing a process to identify obstacles that could undercut the child's chance for academic success, ensure access to needed physical and mental health services, and keep consistent track of local demographic changes as they occur.

Utilizing the results of these informal and formal assessments from initial intake, educators are in a better position to accurately diagnose individual student's academic needs and answer important questions concerning program design. Which language will be primarily used to begin instruction? Can both languages be used in some manner? Can the student be mainstreamed into mathematics? Is the student capable of fluent writing in his or her native language?

Recognition That Success Comes in Many Forms

Another factor that influences programs for Latino students is how success is defined. When academic skills are the sole measure for success in public schools, large segments of the adolescent population are excluded from achieving. The far-reaching "Learning A Living: A Blueprint for High Performance, A SCANS Report for America 2000" (U.S. Department of Labor, 1992) outlines skills essential for success at our nation's worksites. Thinking skills, such as creative thinking, decision making, problem solving, and reasoning are several of the foundational skills defined in this report. These competencies are mastered cognitively and should be measured apart from English language ability.

Progress assessments and performance evaluations should rely on multiple ways to measure success for Latino immigrant students (see Chapter 16). Teachers of successful students use observations and notes, student portfolios, checklists and inventories, tests with open-ended questions, and student service projects and products as part of the testing process. In this way, educators can identify and build upon the cognitive skills so vital to achievement in American life today (NCAS, 1993). Every student has a better opportunity to excel when curricula, support services, and programs also include strategies for identifying and utilizing leadership abilities, social skills, and school and community services.

Successful training programs that prepare the students for entry into the U.S. workforce, for example, teach and simulate the skills outlined in the SCANS Report. These skills include the know-how to find and use resources, the ability to work productively as a team member, and the ability to understand and work within larger systems (U.S. Department of Labor, 1992). Opportunities for learning these skills provide recently arrived immigrants with numerous avenues for success. Career, vocational, and on-the-job programs designed specifically for Latino immigrants help to ensure that their success is not solely dependent upon performance of academic competencies or school-related literacy skills in English, but also related to their cognitive skills and abilities.

Administrative Support and Participation

Without the support of school administrators in developing a safe and accepting multicultural and language-sensitive climate, programs for immigrant youth are in danger of failing. First, school leaders must challenge any existing educational myopia that would prevent them from taking more risks in experimenting with programmatic innovations. Secondly, by providing staff development opportunities and receiving training in immigrant and literacy issues themselves, school administrators learn to model the needed instructional leadership. Finally, educational leaders of today should inspire an organizational vision that carefully considers the cultural, attitudinal, and academic factors as new and innovative programs are cultivated (McGee Banks, 1992).

PROGRAM MODELS FOR UNSCHOOLED IMMIGRANTS

Molnar (1993), in "Facing the Racial Divide," expresses his fear that poor race relations may have something to do with failure rates of many secondary students in our nation today. Garcia and Pugh (1992) state that "our schools, our programs, and our teachers should reflect the changing population patterns of our nation. Schools of education can either exercise leadership in this effort or continue on their current course and risk obsolescence" (p. 214). Some educators have decided to exercise their leadership and have made significant strides in creating viable alternatives to traditional educational approaches. In recent years, multicultural education programs have been created as instructional alternatives.

Providing a Positive Climate through Multicultural Education

The beneficial features of multicultural education programs are those which foster positive interaction among varied cultural groups, require a multicultural approach to instruction, and demonstrate cultural sensitivity in the delivery of supplemental, non-instructional services to students. Culturally sensitive programs insist that instructional materials treat cultural differences sensitively and realistically, embrace and utilize the accepted behavior and learning styles of cultural groups within the local school, and encourage and recruit a culturally diverse staff (Florida Department of Education, 1993).

Sound multicultural programs are created to foster positive interaction among varied cultural groups and are generally marked by powerful prejudice-reduction strategies. For unschooled Latino students, school programs that promote the acceptance and tolerance of differences among those with varied cultures increase chances for acceptance and success. The establishment of a student advisory board, representative of the school population, for school discipline and policy matters, and a conflict mediation student group, who helps to promote understanding and ethnic harmony, for example, are among the strategies incorporated into such programs.

In addition, programs that promote a positive multicultural school climate often include a system for pairing multicultural students with new arrivals, especially those from the same country of origin (Ramírez, 1992). Clearly, these efforts to orient new arrivals to the school culture and to allow multiple perspectives when dealing with cultural issues can greatly improve the unschooled secondary student's opportunities to achieve.

Other programs assume a multicultural approach in the area of classroom instruction. These programs allow the curriculum to be transformed into that which more closely reflects the history, values, and contributions of the cultures the students represent (Diaz, 1992). Lesson plans and instructional materials that exhibit the history and values of minority students in the classroom are in developing stages in school districts across the United States. In cities such as Portland, Oregon, Atlanta, Georgia, and Fort Lauderdale, Florida, unschooled immigrants knowledgeable of the history and values of their own countries become the experts to their teachers and fellow students in these aspects of the curriculum. This new role enhances their self-esteem and further opens doors for language development and personal growth.

In Broward County, a South Florida school district, school-based pilot programs are implemented and materials and teaching strategies developed to emphasize one particular ethnic group each year. The Rochester City School District in New York State is developing comprehensive curricula with a multicultural perspective. The structure of the language and the roots of words in literature, for example, serve as rich environments for discussing differences in geography, language variation, and attitudes toward such differences (Swartz, 1989). When given the opportunity, unschooled youth offer their world views to classroom discussion. These new perspectives add a rich and dynamic dimension to student dialogue, helping to set a natural context for real-life application of the subject being taught.

Great strides have also been made in enhancing cultural sensitivity through the arts. A unique idea that began as a classroom art project in a New York City school has now become a worldwide exemplary program for teaching collaboration across cultural differences. The "Human Mosaic Project" began as a series of student discussions about ethnicity and cultural differences. These culturally diverse students were then introduced to the concept of the mosaic in which each student would draw individual tiles of familiar faces and glue them to a large cardboard background. From the visual cues, discussion was initiated related to personal and cultural backgrounds and values. The idea has spread throughout the nation and to several foreign countries, teaching the spirit and practice of collaboration and tolerance (Gura, 1994). The strength of these types of programs involving the visual arts allows unschooled youth opportunities for expression and success based on skills other than academic. This art project shows the importance of integrating multicultural aspects throughout a school's curricula.

Other schools are at the starting point of integrating multicultural perspectives into their subject areas. They have just begun by celebrating multiculturalism at different times of the year. For example, at B.M.C. Durfee High School in Fall River, Massachusetts, the entire school celebrates an annual multicultural awareness week with lectures, workshops, presentations, and discussions by students, faculty and community representatives. Topics regarding racism, customs of specific cultures, and refugee experiences are samples of the pertinent topics for the week. According to surveys completed by the participants and workers, the week-long event brings increasing awareness of culture and allows all to participate. In such an event, unschooled secondary students may use their public speaking skills or show videos or slides to share their information. In this program, the skills required for achievement are of a communicative and integrative nature rather than purely academic (NCAS, 1994a). Using this approach, unschooled youth are better able to demonstrate their skills and share their strengths.

The look of traditional classroom culture has been transformed in some imaginative programs to reflect the learning styles and accepted cultural behaviors of student populations within the school. In secondary classrooms, teachers integrate cooperative learning, minimize teacher talk, extend teacher wait-time, change turn-taking rules to a less formal activity, and enrich traditional academic assessment and evaluation practices in the classroom (Gay, 1992). Unschooled Latinos find opportunities for success increase in the American secondary classroom when these strategies are implemented. Just as multicultural ideas have taken root in a number of American schools, creative instructional techniques have advanced to meet the academic and literacy needs of Latino immigrant youth.

Success in Academic and Literacy Skills
Using L1 and L2

The nation's educators have long realized that inventive programming is required to adequately serve unschooled Latino youth. The key features of these approaches encompass using both the first language, Spanish, and the new language, English. The two languages are used to provide formal orientation to American schools and culture. The bilingual approach is also used to develop specialized curricula, provide access to a variety of support services, and supply individualized or small group attention to students in need.

In California, Illinois, New York, Texas, Pennsylvania, and Massachusetts, a constructive approach to assisting in the transition to American school culture is in full swing. Newcomer programs at the secondary level have been established to serve the educational needs of the newly arrived. Using this comprehensive and innovative approach, newcomer programs are housed within a regular school or as a separate educational facility, and help newly arrived students in a sheltered or pre-mainstreamed environment to learn English as they acquire basic academic skills. The newcomer concept also strives to help students through the difficult period of cultural adjustment as they face unfamiliar cultural norms in school and in society at large (Friedlander, 1991).

The newcomer model is structurally different from traditional public schools in that it may consist of a school within a school or a self-contained and separate site, a full-day or half-day program, and monolingual or multilingual programs. "Most newcomer programs set a one-year limit on participation to minimize the period of isolation from a mainstream program" (Friedlander, 1991, p. 9). Added benefits for students unfamiliar with a school setting are access to resources, such as trained bilingual teachers who have the skills to provide native language and/or English literacy instruction; a supportive environment, in that all students are in various stages of adjustment; a family atmosphere because of the shared experiences and common circumstances of all of the students in the program; and a *sheltered* school climate during the students' adjustment period. Sheltered instruction relies on teachers knowing and utilizing "aspects of language learning in a natural context, levels of proficiency in language acquisition, the role of primary language literacy and second language learning, and the connection between conversational and academic English" (Castañeda, 1993, p. 445). Using this type of instructional approach facilitates cultural and school adjustment, as well as successful second language and academic skill acquisition (Friedlander, 1991).

Some secondary schools have met the needs of their recent immigrants by designing dual language instructional programs. These programs allow the students to learn subject matter in their native language while developing literacy in English (Hewlett-Gomez and Solis, 1995; Marsh, 1995). Other schools have enjoyed the benefits of instructional programs that help immigrant students meet the mathematics and science academic goals of the U.S. Department of Education's Goals 2000. One school district was funded to develop a comprehensive middle-school program that integrated the mathematics and science curricula into a class designed as a two-hour block. The principal components included interdisciplinary classes, hands-on approaches to instruction and assessment, a process-oriented curricula, career education opportunities, and the native language used in the transition to English.

The field of educational technology has recently developed literacy and language instructional materials using the native language as the medium of instruction. Multimedia instruction is being developed and piloted in Spanish and English that provides reinforcement in listening, speaking, reading, and writing in English. Spanish is used to establish meaning for low-level or nonreaders as students listen, read, repeat, and tape their responses to the exercises on the CD-ROM and other electronic instructional materials. Secondary Latino students can learn at a comfortable pace and participate in a variety of communicative activities in English. They are also learning to use the technology that is of great help in holding and keeping a job.

Student-centered instruction is also finding success. Communicating in both English and the primary language, educators conducted a study that sought selected immigrant students' opinions regarding the academic settings of their schools and how well they accommodated the students' experiences as new arrivals (Guild, 1994). The youth surveyed felt that their schools demonstrated marginal, if any, interest in their personal lives or their diversity in language and culture. The students overwhelmingly saw the educational system as unwilling to accept them if they did not perform academically at grade level. Instructional approaches were then implemented to try to counteract the system's perceived weaknesses. In both English and their home languages, they were encouraged to talk, theorize, and write about the contexts and content of their lives in and out of school. One instructional activity, for example, was the creation of a photonovel about a teenage boy's problems. Providing a forum for true communication and expression for our newly arrived students related to their real-life experiences may help to set a climate conducive to more successful achievement for them in academics, basic literacy, and their future employment (Walsh, 1991).

Teaching Success for the U.S. Workforce

Higher education as preparation for the world of work has been virtually out of reach for secondary immigrant youth arriving with limited education and literacy. The University of Wisconsin, however, has made a commitment to double the number of minority undergraduates, hire minority faculty, require ethnic studies courses, and create financial aid plans for minorities with low incomes. The institution has decided to focus on reaching out to local high schools to encourage and identify potential minority students, as well as continue to encourage minority students after the undergraduate years toward graduate studies (Action Council on Minority Education, 1989).

In the past, large numbers of Latino students were disproportionately tracked into vocational programs, thus creating an inequitable system whereby Latinos were discouraged from seeking university degrees. While university degrees should be strongly promoted, there may still be a place for vocational education. Secondary immigrant students who are unschooled, for example, may find preparation for future employment in vocational programs that have strong program components. First of all, students in successful job training programs are actively recruited into courses best fitting their backgrounds, interests, and skills. Secondly, as in other effective program models for Latino youth, an accurate assessment of literacy skills in the primary language is used to develop beneficial employment training classes (Bradley and Friedenberg, 1988).

Additionally, vocational education that truly meets the needs of those limited in literacy skills provides career education, job shadowing events, and business and industry field trips. Local corporations sometimes provide opportunities for students to follow or *shadow* selected employees for the day. Unschooled youth spend a day in real-life interaction rather than the traditional world of the academics and textbooks. On the job, they learn firsthand about varied cultural contexts in their new country. Sheltered vocational courses are also available for unschooled youth. Vocational instructors of these courses complete comprehensive training programs in immigrant and literacy issues, as well as multicultural and second language education. Their classes include students with similar educational backgrounds. Mentoring and volunteer programs from local businesses also provide the one-on-one assistance and attention needed to adequately serve these unschooled secondary students.

Vocational English as a Second Language classes, career counseling services, ethnic career fairs, cultural training for the world of work, and technology skills training are all innovative efforts to teach and encourage use of literacy and interpersonal relations skills as they relate to the world of work. A pilot program, BABS (Bilingual Academic and Business Skills), was implemented at two high schools in Brooklyn that included occupational education (food management), survival skills mathematics, career awareness, and extracurricular activities such as field trips and career conferences. The students also received instruction in English as a Second Language (ESL), native language arts (NLA), and career education. Students learned to successfully complete mock job interviews and experienced job shadowing at local corporate sites.

A district-funded program for secondary immigrant students that is thriving in South Florida provides access to vocational elective courses by utilizing a bilingual teacher assistant, adapted and translated bilingual materials, and extensive training for the teachers and assistants. One of the most successful components includes strong partnerships with local business that provide immigrant students with opportunities to job shadow, tour company plants, and even secure part-time employment. Students organize service projects at their schools according to the vocational discipline (Broward County Public Schools, 1994).

Programs That Enrich Family Involvement

Schools are missing out when they fail to involve the rich heritage and cultures of the new student populations and their families in their schools. One key element of successful parent and family involvement programs for immigrant students is when the lines of communication between U.S. schools and ethnic cultures are strengthened by newsletters, meetings, and orientation programs provided in the primary language of the families. Another essential feature is to educate recently arrived family members regarding the values and expectations of American school culture and simultaneously teach the academic and literacy skills necessary for success. Thirdly, educational systems willing to change their school climate, language, intake and assessment procedures, support services and staff as necessary to meet the educational needs of their immigrant families find that their efforts are richly rewarded (NCAS, 1994a).

Many excellent parent involvement programs demonstrate such flexibility and commitment to meeting the needs of their local populations. Their services include native language assistance for recruiting parents into the school's traditional community, offering informative training programs regarding school procedures and expectations, and providing literacy courses for all ages. In the Trinity-Arlington Teacher and Parent Training for School Success Project 1985–86 Final Evaluation Report (Kaiser and Raupp, 1986), program components such as developing home lessons in which parents and children work together were found to be fruitful. According to the participating families, they learned new information about school procedures and requirements in this unconventional manner and increased their participation and confidence while interacting with the school. Many family literacy programs are directed toward parents and their young children. As new projects are developed, there is a need to include secondary students as the targeted participants with their parents and other family members in program designs.

Simply gaining a better understanding of the characteristics of unschooled immigrant adolescents and being able to identify components of successful programs targeting them is not enough. Educators must commit to applying their existing resources, creativity, and entrepreneurship to better equip the unschooled adolescent for the world outside the classroom.

IMPLICATIONS FOR EDUCATORS

Educators are often primarily concerned about funding when conceptualizing new instructional programs for youth with special needs in their schools. To more effectively serve unschooled immigrant students, however, creativity, entrepreneurship, and training on the part of school administrators are factors just as important to consider.

Developing Programs with Existing Resources

Using a little creativity to budget and organize, educators can utilize existing programs and resources to meet the needs of the unschooled. Within existing after-school programs, for example, immigrant students can provide peer tutoring to students taking Spanish courses, especially in listening and speaking skills, in exchange for receiving tutoring in English and the content areas. The same group of students, both English and Spanish speaking, can provide tutoring services at the local elementary schools to immigrants and other young children needing academic assistance. As Latino adolescents provide help, they are also receiving help by getting reinforcement and practice in literacy skills.

Staff Development Priorities

School leaders are in need of learning new skills to reach children of changing demographics who may also be affected by war, poverty, crime, and drug abuse. Hallinger and Murphy (1991) emphasize that society is becoming increasingly populated by people from linguistically different groups. The authors underscore the "need for leaders of tomorrow's schools to address the rapidly changing complexion of society" (p. 129). Garcia and Pugh (1992) indicate that schools should show courage in addressing and confronting multicultural issues.

Fortunately, efforts are being made to include multicultural education training in the formal education of school administrators. School administrators may be in the best position to lead efforts to bring about multicultural reform. State governments must be sharing these same thoughts. To earn a Professional Administrative Services Credential in the state of California, for example, a course dealing with cultural and socio-economic diversity is required. The course content includes the general ethnic, racial, and religious composition of California and the local community, concepts of cultural values and language diversity, instructional programs and procedures for Potentially English Proficient (PEP) students, and principles of effective parent involvement in school activities to reach academic goals (Bartell and Birch, 1993).

The State of Florida has also made considerable strides in establishing guidelines for a similar type of training concept. The Florida Department of Education has developed curriculum frameworks for courses designed to teach English as a new language, which include Florida legislation related to PEP student issues, English for Speakers of Other Languages (ESOL) and Multicultural Education program selection and evaluation guidelines, suggestions for teacher evaluation, activities to enhance a positive school climate, and strategies for successful parent/community involvement (Florida Department of Education, 1993). As training requirements dealing with immigrant issues increase for educational leaders, services will hopefully improve for new linguistically diverse populations with literacy needs.

Recruiting Latino Teachers

Yet how many educators across the nation can relate to the backgrounds and cultures of our Latino immigrants? The Latino population in the United States has doubled in the past twenty years from 11 million in 1970 to 22.4 million in 1990. According to the U.S. Bureau of Labor Statistics and the U.S. Department of Education, 3.7 percent of the teachers in K–12 public schools in the United States in 1991 were Latino. In sharp contrast, Latino children made up 11.8 percent of student enrollment (Castro and Ingle, 1993). There is a great need for teachers who clearly understand and have high regard for the cultures of Latino children. Colleges and universities need to take a comprehensive role in recruiting and educating Latinos for careers. In Project: TEACH in San Antonio, Texas, local schools and universities are brought together to recruit and support Latino students in teacher education and to provide assistance in academics, study skills, and test-taking development (Gonzalez, 1992).

The Need for New and Innovative Strategies

Congress continues to require bilingual education programs to assist children who are PEP. These programs are typically transitional or maintenance-oriented as attempts are made to better serve secondary students with literacy needs. Further research is needed in alternative teaching methods, language constructs, cultural factors, beginning reading and writing, and testing and evaluation as areas for new invention and innovation (Golub, 1980).

Educational policymakers must not be exempt from needing to understand the unschooled immigrant populations in the United States. In turn, politicians will see the need for funding strong literacy programs that help to build a productive society. Efforts to strengthen literacy skills should begin in the early years of schooling. Teachers and administrators should be required to have adequate training in literacy, English as a Second Language, and bilingual and multicultural strategies. Dropout prevention and intervention strategies, such as peer tutoring and study skills seminars, should be implemented during the elementary and middle-school years. Most importantly, educators should provide abundant and varied opportunities for secondary students with limited literacy skills and academic experience to gain the skills they so desperately need (Orum, 1986).

Despite the many successful secondary programs to combat the limited literacy skills of unschooled immigrants, other programs have been found to be ineffective. Due to the trauma and interruptions in the backgrounds of unschooled youth, the lack of attention to their strengths and skills by school personnel, and the weaknesses in many educational programs designed for them, many secondary programs for immigrant youth are still in need of improvement. In December of 1993, the Andrew Mellon Foundation awarded grants specifically targeted for immigrants at the secondary level to several organizations across the country. These grants are in the developmental stages to improve English language and literacy development, improve mastery of academic content and skills, and improve transitions to postsecondary educational programs or employment for secondary immigrant students (National Clearinghouse for Bilingual Education, 1994).

SUMMARY

Much is known about factors that positively influence the quality of programs for unschooled students at the secondary level in the United States. What is needed, then, are programs that contain these factors. Programs across the nation for recently arrived secondary students should identify and build upon their students' strengths and skills, provide opportunities for multiple forms of success, and extend opportunities for involvement in the learning process to the family and the total school community. To the extent that these program components are implemented, there will be proportionate progress made in increasing the literacy skills of unschooled Latino youth. Reflection and application by our nation's educators of the factors presented in this chapter can help to move the nation forward in preparing our immigrant populations for productive and successful new lives for the twenty-first century.

REFERENCES

Action Council on Minority Education. 1989. *Education That Works: An Action Plan for the Education of Minorities.* Cambridge, MA: Massachusetts Institute of Technology.

Bartell, C. and L. Birch. 1993. *An Examination of the Preparation, Induction, and Professional Growth of School Administrators for California.* Sacramento, CA: State of California.

Bensinger-Lacy, M. 1986. "Elementary Literacy Materials," *Proceedings of the Symposium held at Trinity College.* June 6–7, 1986, Washington, D.C., pp. 25–28.

Bliss, B. 1986. "Literacy and the Limited English Population: A National Perspective," *Proceedings of the Symposium held at Trinity College.* June 6–7, 1986, Washington, D.C., pp. 17–24.

Bradley, C. and J. Friedenberg. 1988. *Teaching Vocational Education to Limited English Proficient Students.* Bloomington, IL: Meridian Education Association.

Broward County Public Schools. 1994. An Annual Publication Produced by the Title VII BEAMS Project. *The Satellite*. 1(Summer, 1994).

Castañeda, L. 1993. "Alternative Visions of Practice: An Exploratory Study of Peer Coaching, Sheltered Content, Cooperative Instruction and Mainstream Subject Matter Teachers," *Proceedings of the Third National Research Symposium on Limited English Proficient Student Issues: Focus on Middle and High School Issues*. Washington D.C.: U.S. Department of Education, pp. 431–467.

Castro, R. and Y. Ingle. 1993. *Missing Teachers in the Southwest: The Supply and Need for Latino Teachers*. Claremont, CA: The Tomas Rivera Center.

de Felix, J., H. Waxman, and S. Paige. 1993. "Instructional Processes in Secondary Bilingual Classrooms," *Proceedings of the Third National Research Symposium on Limited English Proficient Student Issues: Focus on Middle and High School Issues*. Washington, D.C.: United States Department of Education, pp. 355–382.

Diaz, C. 1992. *Multicultural Education for the 21st Century*. Washington, D.C.: National Education Association.

First, J. and J. Carrera. 1988. *New Voices: Immigrant Students in U.S. Public Schools*. Boston, MA: National Coalition of Advocates for Students.

Flores, B. 1990. "Literacy in a Second Language," *Proceedings of the First Research Symposium on Limited English Proficient Issues*. Washington, D.C.: U. S. Department of Education, pp. 281–320.

Florida Department of Education, Multicultural Education Review Task Force, The 1993 Report. 1993. *Multicultural Education in Florida*. Tallahassee, FL: Florida Department of Education.

Friedlander, M. 1991. *The Newcomer Program: Helping Immigrant Students Succeed in U.S. Schools*. Washington, D.C.: National Clearinghouse for Bilingual Education, Program Information Guide Series.

Garcia, J. and S. Pugh. 1992. "Multicultural Education in Teacher Preparation Programs: A Political or an Educational Concept?" *Phi Delta Kappan*, 74(3):214–219.

Garcia, O. and R. Otheguy. 1985. "The Masters of Survival Send Their Children to School: Bilingual Education in the Ethnic Schools of Miami," *Bilingual Review*, 12(Jan–Aug):3–19.

Garza, F. and L. Orum. 1982. "Illiteracy in the Latino Community," Statement of Francisco Garza, Legislative Director, *National Council of La Raza*, before the Subcommittee on Post Secondary Education of the House Education and Labor Committee. ERIC, ED 242 826.

Gay, G. 1992. "Effective Teaching Practices for Multicultural Classrooms," *Multicultural Education for the 21st Century*. Washington, D.C.: National Education Association, pp. 38–56.

Golub, L. 1980. *Literacy Development of Bilingual Children*. ERDS. ERIC, ED 202226.

Gonzalez, G. 1992. *The 21st Century: A Futuristic Look at Recruitment and Retention in Teacher Education Programs for Hispanic-Americans*. ERDS. ERIC, ED 343 900.

Gonzalez, J. and L. Darling-Hammond. In press. "Professional Development for Teachers of Immigrant Youth," *Topics in Immigrant Secondary Education*. J. K. Peyton and D. Christian, eds. Washington, D.C.: Center for Applied Linguistics.

Guild, P. 1994. "The Culture/Learning Style Connection," *Educational Leadership* 51(May):16–21.

Gura, M. 1994. "The Human Mosaic Project," *Educational Leadership*, 51(May):40–41.

Hallinger, P. and J. Murphy. 1991. "Developing Leaders for Tomorrow's Schools," *Phi Delta Kappan*, 71(7):514–526.

Hewlett-Gomez, M. and A. Solis. 1995. "Dual Language Instructional Design for Education—Recent Immigrant Secondary Students on the Texas-Mexico Border," *Bilingual Research Journal*, 19 (3 & 4): 429–452.

Kaiser, J. and M. Raupp. 1986. *Trinity-Arlington Teacher and Parent Training for School Success Project*. Andover, MA: The Network.

Lucas, T. 1993. "What Have We Learned from Research on Successful Secondary Programs for LEP Students? A Synthesis of Findings from Three Studies," *Proceedings of the Third National Research Symposium on Limited English Proficient Student Issues: Focus on Middle and High School Issues*. Washington, D.C.: United States Department of Education, pp. 81–111.

Marsh, L. 1995. "The Spanish Dual Literacy Program: Teaching to the Whole Student," *Bilingual Research Journal*, 19 (3 & 4): 409–428.

McGee Banks, C. 1992. "The Leadership Challenge in Multicultural Education," *Multicultural Education for the 21st Century*. Washington, D.C.: National Education Association, pp. 204–213.

Minicucci, C. and L. Olsen. 1993. Educating Students from Immigrant Families: Meeting the Challenge in Secondary Schools. *Proceedings of CABE* (California Association of Bilingual Education), October 22–24, 1992, Santa Cruz, CA, pp. 1–107.

Molnar, A. 1993. "Facing the Racial Divide," *Educational Leadership*, 50(8):58–59.

National Assessment of Educational Progress. 1987. "N.A.E.P: Students Aren't Literate Enough," *American School Board Journal*. 174:14.

National Clearinghouse for Bilingual Education. 1994. *Forum*. 17. Washington, D.C.: George Washington University.

National Coalition of Advocates for Students. 1988. *The Good Common School: Immigrant Students in U.S. Public Schools*. Boston, MA: NCAS.

NCAS. 1993. *Achieving the Dream: How Communities and Schools Can Improve Education for Immigrant Students*. Boston, MA: NCAS.

NCAS. 1994a. *Looking for America: Volume I*. (April) Boston, MA: NCAS.

NCAS. 1994b. *Delivering on the Promise: Positive Practices for Immigrant Students*. (June) Boston, MA: NCAS.

Nelan, B. 1993. "Not Quite So Welcome Anymore," *Time*, 142(21):10–12.

Orum, L. 1986. *The Education of Hispanics: Status and Implications*. Washington, D.C.: National Council of La Raza, pp. 1–83.

Plyler v. Doe, U.S. Supreme Court. 1982. 457 U. S. 202, 102 S. Ct. 2382, 72 L.

Ramírez, B. C. 1992. "Can We All Get Along? Examining Our Capacity for Diversity," *Educational Record*, 73(4): 42–46.

Romo, H. 1993. *Mexican Immigrants in High Schools: Meeting Their Needs*. Washington, D.C.: ERIC Digest. ERIC, ED 357 905.

Swartz, E. 1989. *Multicultural Curriculum Development: A Practical Approach to Curriculum Development at the School Level*. Rochester, NY: Rochester City School District.

The Tomas Rivera Center. 1993. *Resolving a Crisis in Education: Latino Teachers for Tomorrow's Classrooms*. Claremont, CA: The Tomas Rivera Center.

U.S. Department of Education, Office of Policy and Planning. 1993. *New Land, New*

Knowledge: An Evaluation of Two Education Programs Serving Refugee and Immigrant Students. Washington, D.C.: U.S. Department of Education.

U.S. Department of Labor, The Secretary's Commission on Achieving Necessary Skills (SCANS). 1992. *Learning a Living: A Blueprint for High Performance.* Washington, D.C.: U.S. Department of Labor.

Valdez-Pierce, L. 1987. "Language and Content-Area Instruction for Secondary LEP Students With Limited Formal Schooling: Language Arts and Social Studies," NCBE 3, from *Curriculum Guides—Teacher Resource Guide Series.* Washington, D.C.: National Clearinghouse for Bilingual Education.

Walsh, C. 1991. *Engaging Students in Their Own Learning: Literacy, Language, and Knowledge Production with Latino Adolescents.* Adjunct ERIC Clearinghouse on Literacy Education. ERIC, ED 346 750.

Williams, B. and E. Newcombe. 1994. "Building on the Strengths of Urban Learners," *Educational Leadership,* 51(8):75–78.

PART VII

RESPONSIBLE ASSESSMENT FOR LATINOS AND THEIR SCHOOLS

CHAPTER 16

Alternative Assessment for Latino Students

ANN DEL VECCHIO—*New Mexico Highlands University*
CYNDEE GUSTKE—*New Mexico Highlands University*
JUDITH WILDE—*New Mexico Highlands University*

INTRODUCTION

IN determining how best to assess Latino students, several issues must be kept in mind. First, as described by the Joint Committee of the American Educational Research Association, American Psychological Association, and American Council on Measurement (referred to hereafter as Joint Committee), there are at least thirteen standards for testing bilingual persons. As a basic premise, these standards state that a test that relies solely on the English language is confounded (Joint Committee, 1985); it is impossible to know whether the score reflects content area knowledge or English language knowledge. In addition, the Joint Committee standards specifically:

- prohibit the translation of a test from one language to another
- encourage testing in the primary language[1] as well as English
- suggest that "several dimensions" of language proficiency must be assessed
- point out that when testing bilingual students, testing time, home culture and language background, and training for those administering the test must be considered

Obviously, these standards speak about the bilingual or Spanish-speaking Latino student. However, even for English-speaking Latino students the importance of culture and language background must be remembered. Clearly, then, all of these factors emphasize the need for assessment that is more culturally and linguistically fair to Latino students.

Gardner (1993) contends that currently used testing formats (specifically, NRTs) are decontextualized. This seemingly objective format does

[1] Primary language refers to the student's first language. "L1," "native language," and "home language" are similar terms. For Latino students, the primary language usually is Spanish or English.

not benefit students because it is so unlike real-life situations. He adds that testing in the past involved an apprentice-like situation, in which students were expected to demonstrate the skills necessary to become a master in the field. Gardner suggests a return to more performance-based approaches that are apprentice-like in order to provide students with greater opportunities to demonstrate their strengths (Gardner, 1993).

This chapter will suggest ways to assess Latino students in a manner that will benefit them and their school systems. In such a format, students will show their abilities and skills in the best possible light. Different types of alternative assessments and possible scoring mechanisms will be described. In addition, collecting and managing alternative assessments within a portfolio system will be suggested.

Alternative assessments and portfolios are unique because when designed appropriately they can be used with preliterate, biliterate, and monoliterate (English or Spanish) Latino students. These measures actively involve and empower students and educators. They can be modified easily to meet the needs of students with different linguistic abilities and cultural backgrounds. Furthermore, many alternative assessments can be used as part of the curriculum, without the necessity for a specific testing period.

ALTERNATIVE ASSESSMENT

Gardner (1993) describes assessment as the obtaining of information about the skills and potentials of individuals, with the dual goals of providing useful feedback to the individuals and useful data to the surrounding community. The competency of students can be determined by a variety of strategies. All of these are characterized as "nontraditional" measures (Baker et al., 1993), as opposed to "traditional" paper-and-pencil tests. Many educators who work with Latino students and communities find that they can assess students more effectively with alternative measures that allow them to document growth within the context of meaningful instruction. Alternative assessment tasks are designed to resemble real-life or real learning activities. They focus on what students actually can do, as opposed to focusing on students' deficits. Other benefits of alternative assessments include:

- information gathered over time from a range of classroom experiences
- assessments that indicate a student's broad progress in basic skills,

conceptual understanding, problem solving, and reflective thinking, as well as motivation toward learning and attitudes toward school

- a focus on the process involved in learning or mastery, not on drill and practice
- measurements based on an understanding of diversity in backgrounds, learning styles, and developmental learning
- active student, teacher, and family reflection, ownership, and involvement in assessments of growth and needs
- a climate of trust with strong partnerships between teachers and students and families

The need for alternative assessments generally is agreed upon by some theoreticians (for example, Gardner, 1993) and practitioners [such as, Teachers of English to Speakers of Other Languages (TESOL) Standards, in appendix, p. 353]. The nontraditional nature of alternative assessments is agreed upon (Baker et al., 1993), as are the various benefits of alternative assessments (Navarrete et al., 1990). What remains is to understand exactly what these assessment strategies are and how they are to be used.

Types of Alternative Assessments

There is a great deal of variety in both the design and purposes of alternative assessments. The content (reading, writing, math, art, social studies, etc.) and the purpose (diagnostic, evaluation, grading, self-reflection, etc.) will of course determine the form an alternative assessment takes. The forms of alternative assessment range from simple checklists to week-long performance-based assessments. More complex alternative assessments may require students to show evidence of specific skills and to produce written, graphic, dramatic, or other kinds of products.

Anecdotal Records

A common informal method used to capture evidence of cognitive processes and behaviors is an *anecdotal record*. Teachers, parents, educational assistants, and/or others who work with a group of students simply record their observations of students. These observations may document student growth or student needs. This process can become more formal when observations are recorded on a given time schedule, for individual students, for a specific behavior or purpose. An example anecdotal record is provided in Figure 1.

| Student: | | Grade: | |
| Observer: | | | |
Area	Date	Language	Comment/ Observation
Reading			
Writing			
Math			
Oral			
Coop Learning Groups			
Play			

FIGURE 1 Example alternative assessments.

Checklists

A more formal method for observation involves the construction and use of *checklists*. Checklists can be developed with as few or as many items as necessary to capture progress in a specific area. The checklist consists of a series of expected behaviors that can be scored to indicate whether or not the behavior is present. It can also be scored with a more elaborate rating scale that allows the observer to indicate the degree to which a task is completed or a behavior is evident. A sample checklist is located in Figure 2.

Check the box for "yes" or "no" whether the
student uses each of these strategies as s/he
reads through a familiar passage.

Name
Language   Date
Teacher
Book Title

	Yes	No
Uses picture clues Comments:	☐	☐
Uses context to get meaning Comments:	☐	☐
Substitutes another meaningful word Comments:	☐	☐
Uses phonics Comments:	☐	☐
Backtracks to get meaning Comments:	☐	☐

FIGURE 2 Sample checklist.

Classroom Products

Classroom products may be used to measure student achievement, attitudes, and proficiency levels. These may include journal entries, writing samples, video productions, collaborative and/or individual work reports, essays, debates, reading lists, problem solution descriptions, artistic media, storytelling, and read-alouds. A sample writing process rating scale for use by teachers is presented in Figure 3. Other instruments that may be used to assess students include questionnaires, Cloze reading tests, miscue analysis reading assessments, criterion referenced tests, self-assessments (see Figure 4), peer reviews, and parent questionnaires (see the sample parent questionnaire in Figure 5). These methods are

Name and grade of student

Teacher _____ Language(s) _____

Circle the number that most closely indicates the student's use of skills. Use the following rating scale:

1 Always or almost always   2 Sometimes   3 Rarely or Never

Does the student

write during designated time?	1	2	3
use constructive strategies for getting drafts started?	1	2	3
show growth in understanding the differences between revising and editing?	1	2	3
use the support systems in the classroom (manuals, spelling aids, resource books)?	1	2	3
participate in peer conferences seriously?	1	2	3

Modified from Goodman, Goodman, & Bird, 1992.

FIGURE 3 Sample writing process rating scale.

```
Name
Date

Complete the sentences below.

■ Today in science I


■ I learned more about


■ I still have the following questions


Overall, I would rate my performance in science as
                        ☐ excellent
                        ☐ satisfactory
                        ☐ poor
```

FIGURE 4 Sample student self-assessment.

```
Nombre del estudiante
Fecha                    Grado
Nombre del adulto en la familia

Mi hijo/hija          siempre   a veces   poco
  le gusta hablar        ☐        ☐       ☐
  hace preguntas         ☐        ☐       ☐
  le gusta contar cuentos
     favoritos           ☐        ☐       ☐
  le gusta hablar en inglés ☐     ☐       ☐

  le gusta hablar en español ☐    ☐       ☐
  le gusta escribir de
     mentiritas          ☐        ☐       ☐
  hace preguntas tocante a lo escrito
     que ve en el ambiente ☐      ☐       ☐

  le gusta que alguien le lea
     cuentos             ☐        ☐       ☐
  le gusta jugar a leer  ☐        ☐       ☐
  tiene cuentos favoritos ☐       ☐       ☐
```

FIGURE 5 Sample early childhood parent questionnaire.

described more fully in Bratcher (1994), Del Vecchio et al. (1994), Goodman et al. (1992), Holt (1994), Navarrete et al. (1990), and various materials developed by Stiggins (1990) at the Northwest Regional Educational Laboratory.

Although many of these assessments emphasize student achievement, they can also be used to assess language proficiency in any language. The Council of Chief State School Officers (1992) suggests that all four modalities (reading, writing, speaking, and listening) should be assessed to determine language proficiency. With alternative assessment, a single well-designed instructional activity can generate measures of language proficiency across all four modalities (Del Vecchio et al., 1994).

Methods for Scoring Alternative Assessments

There are many types of alternative assessments. In addition, there are many ways to assign scores to alternative assessments and products. The type of scoring method used is dependent upon the purpose of the assessment. Some of the more common methods are described briefly below; examples are provided in the accompanying figures.

Holistic rating scales are used to judge the whole product or performance. Specific criteria are identified with holistic "rubrics" or rating scales. Generally, these are scored with symbols (e.g., +, ✓ or –), letters (e.g., A to F), or numbers (ranging from a minimum of 1 to 3 to a maximum of 1 to 10). An example holistic rubric for math is included in Figure 6.

If it is desirable to examine particular parts of a performance or product, *primary trait scoring* can be used. For a written product, a primary trait rubric might be applied to the organization, mechanics, voice, and creativity of the piece. Each part or trait of the piece (e.g., organization) has specific criteria upon which to base the score. The ratings for each part then can be either summed to provide a total score for the piece or left as separate parts. As with holistic scoring, the range of scores generally is between 1–3 and 1–10. A sample primary trait scoring rubric for writing is presented in Figure 7.

Analytic Scoring

The most complex type of scoring procedure is the *analytic*. In this variation of primary trait scoring, particular traits are considered more important than others and are weighted accordingly. For instance, the

An individual paper or portfolios is likely to be characterized by some, but not all, of the descriptors for a particular level. The overall score should be the level at which the appropriate descriptors are clustered.

Novice
- Indicates a basic understanding of problems & uses strategies
- Implements strategies with minor mathematical errors but without observations or extensions
- Uses mathematical reasoning & appropriate mathematical language some of the time
- Uses few mathematical representations
- Indicates a basic understanding of core concepts; uses few tools

Apprentice
- Indicates an understanding of problems & selects appropriate strategies
- Accurately implements strategies with solutions, with limited observations or extensions
- Uses appropriate mathematical reasoning & language
- Uses a variety of mathematical representations accurately & appropriately
- Indicates an understanding of core concepts with limited connections; uses tools appropriately

Proficient
- Indicates a broad understanding of problems with alternate strategies
- Accurately & efficiently implements & analyzes strategies with correct solutions, with extensions
- Uses perceptive mathematical reasoning & precise & appropriate math language most of the time
- Uses a wide variety of mathematical representations accurately & appropriately
- Indicates a broad understanding of some core concepts with connections; uses a wide variety of tools appropriately

Distinguished
- Indicates a comprehensive understanding of problems with efficient, sophisticated strategies
- Accurately & efficiently implements & evaluates sophisticated strategies with correct solutions; incudes analysis, justifications, & extensions
- Uses perceptive, creative, & complex mathematical reasoning; sophisticated, precise, & appropriate mathematical language throughout
- Uses a wide variety of mathematical representations accurately & appropriately
- Indicates a comprehensive understanding of core concepts with connections throughout; uses a wide variety of tools appropriately & insightfully

Modified from the Kentucky Instructional Results Information System, Kentucky Department of Education, 1993.

FIGURE 6 Sample holistic scoring for math.

organization of a written piece might be three times as important as mechanics, and twice as important as voice. These weightings might be based on recent topics within the curriculum, the weaker areas in a student's products, or other factors. An example of changing a primary trait rubric to an analytic scoring method is indicated in Figure 7 by italicized print.

Although these methods for scoring alternative assessments do not include all possible techniques, they reflect the practices used commonly today. These methods can be extremely useful for working with culturally and linguistically diverse students. They are flexible and can be used with instruments developed in any language. The most important points to remember in using any of these methods are:

- to set well-defined standards for what is to be assessed
- to describe these standards clearly and completely
- to provide instructional opportunities that match the assessments

Trait Weight	Score	Criteria
Content	1	Topic & purpose unclear; limited reflection of own thinking
x 4	2	Topic basically understood; some supporting detail & reflection of own thinking
	3	Topic & purpose clearly understood; includes a variety of supporting detail & strongly reflects own thinking
Organization	1	Limited use of process, sequence illogical, purpose unclear
x 3	2	Completed most steps of writing process; final lacks either introduction, body, or conclusion
	3	Writing process completed; well organized, includes introduction, body, & conclusions; is well developed, coherent
Sentence Structure	1	Limited use of logical sentences, several problems with sentence structure
	2	Sentences contain few errors, are logical, & vary somewhat in length
x 1	3	Sentences are complete, with little or no errors, vary in length, are logical, concise, & energetic
Voice	1	Sense of awareness of audience or voice is not evident
x 1	2	Sense of awareness of audience & author is somewhat evident; language is natural
	3	Strong sense of audience & author's presence; strong flavor & tone of task completed

Note: weights are used only with analytic scoring and may be adjusted as appropriate.

FIGURE 7 Sample primary trait and analytic scoring rubric for writing.

It is important to keep in mind that alternative forms of assessment should reflect actual teaching practices, with students, families, and teachers understanding how the assessments will be used. Students should be informed of the criteria used to determine grades, and may be involved in the actual development of the criteria.

Creating and Modifying Assessments

Few NRTs and alternative assessments have been developed to assess Latino students' knowledge in content areas. Therefore, it is important to understand the process involved in creating and adapting instruments. Ramírez (in press) has outlined a set of guidelines for developing assessment procedures for Potentially English Proficient (PEP) students. These guidelines involve an eleven-step process, strongly encourage a planning team, and are appropriate for developing materials for all Latino students. They can be summarized into four general areas: (1) deciding about the curriculum framework; (2) determining the frequency of assessment; (3) creating methods and procedures for assessment; and (4) planning professional development about the curriculum framework and the assessment process.

Although all the steps in these guidelines are not essential to developing a specific assessment measure for Latino students, Ramírez's (in press) guidelines provide a broader framework within which to consider any assessment development. They also ensure the generalizability of the assessment to contexts outside the school setting by providing a standardized process for development.

The essential elements necessary to develop or modify alternative assessments are to: (1) identify the purpose for the assessment, (2) generate or find ideas for the assessment that fit with the curriculum, (3) design a prototype instrument and field-test it; and (4) modify the instrument based on the results of the field test. This process is not as linear as it may appear and is iterative; that is, some steps may need to be repeated several times before a good instrument is developed. The procedure is described in more detail in the next section, with Figure 8 providing a brief example of the development of an instrument.

Identify the Purpose for the Assessment

Assessment purposes fall into several broad categories and usually are linked closely to the audience(s) that will use the results of the assessment. Stiggins (1993) suggests that users, as well as uses, of assessment results can be categorized into three levels:

- instructional—including teachers, students, and parents
- leadership/support—including principals, counselors, program directors, support teachers, and curriculum directors
- policy-making—including superintendents, schools, state departments of education, federal and state education agencies and funding sources, community members, and legislators

The purpose of assessment is different for the individuals within each of these levels. As an example, teachers need information about student progress in a particular content area. They can also evaluate their own instructional methods and content coverage, assign grades, and/or identify the need for special programs or instructional methods. On the other hand, students and parents use the results of assessments to inform themselves about the student's academic progress. Superintendents and

Basic Steps	Detailed Process
Identify the Purpose for the Assessment	1. Who is the audience? Who will use the assessment? 2. Will the assessment be used to inform instruction? for diagnostic purposes? to evaluate a program? other purposes?
Find the Idea	1. Consult the students first for ideas. 2. Ask colleagues. 3. Consider the curriculum content and identify real-life community problems and issues related to the curriculum. The newspaper, local news, and community groups sometimes have problems that can be used as the basic idea for an assessment. 4. Make sure the idea is culturally relevant -- asking the students allows them to include aspects of their culture and language in the assessment.
Design the Assessment	1. Define your objectives (refer to your curriculum). 2. Draft a plan including the objectives, the type of task, instructions to the students, a timeline, and possible problems to be addressed. 3. Consider response formats such as written exercises or reports, presentations, group discussions, experiments, etc. 4. Keep notes on the development process so that others could use your ideas. 5. Determine who will judge the assessment (teacher, students, parents, a committee). 6. Develop a method to score the assessment. This could be a rubric, a checklist, or some other method for identifying the quality of the students' efforts. It should be related closely to the curriculum objectives and the standards or evaluation criteria the students are expected to reach should be clearly defined. 7. Furnish the students with information about the evaluation criteria. 8. Consider attitudes and attributes you hope to see (motivation, group cooperation, interest). 9. Identify a method to establish reliability for the task. Can it be used or scored by other teachers with the same results?
Modify the Assessment	1. Try the task out. Do not attach stakes (grades) to it during the pilot test. 2. Use feedback from the students and other teachers to modify the assessment. 3. Revise the task and/or the system for scoring it as necessary. 4. Document revisions in your notes. 5. Try it out again.

FIGURE 8 Example instrument development.

state departments of education use assessment results to identify schools or districts in need of additional resources.

Defining the purpose of the new assessment (or the revised assessment) is a critical step that must be completed early in the development process. In addition, identifying purposes and designing assessments can help educators, communities, and students raise their awareness of what they see as important goals and priorities for education.

Find the Idea for the New Assessment

The idea for an assessment can come from a variety of sources including state competencies, instructional activities, textbooks, newspaper articles, the evening news on TV, another teacher, conversations with friends and family, student interests, or life in general. Some of the best ideas are generated by the students themselves; these are more likely to be meaningful for them and to include aspects of their own language and culture. There generally are three steps to this phase of development: (1) talking about the idea with colleagues, (2) thinking about the language of assessment, and (3) considering whether or not this idea can be transposed into a measurable assessment that matches instruction and has meaning and merit in the community. For Latino students, English- or Spanish-language assessments might be appropriate. If Spanish is used, a determination of the "type" of Spanish (vernacular from a geographic area or "standard") in which to write items and directions, as well as in which to accept responses, must be made.

Design and Field-Test the Assessment

There are four steps to this phase of instrument development: (1) refining objectives to include how and when the instrument will fit into the curriculum; (2) drafting a plan that includes a description of the task, the purpose (objectives) for it, directions for the students, possible formats, scoring guidelines, and nondirective questions to encourage students to find solution strategies; (3) creating a rough draft of the instrument, including scoring, and sharing the draft with colleagues; and (4) revising the draft and using the instrument in a field test. The field test should include students' feedback about the assessment; there should be no stakes (grades) attached to performance at this time. Notes taken throughout the process will allow replication in the future.

Modify the Instrument

If the instrument already exists, but is not fully appropriate for current students, this phase will be used to revise the instrument. The instrument can be shared with colleagues, including the purpose(s) for which it was designed originally, and then a revised version can be drafted. This draft should be field-tested with students, still asking for their feedback and not grading it.

After the field test, the instrument should be modified based on the feedback from students and colleagues and from student performance. The final step in the development process is to evaluate the assessment based on notes and a personal judgement about how it worked. Things to consider at this time are the cost-benefit ratio—perhaps the assessment provided valuable information but it took too long to administer and/or to score. All available information should be considered at this point and the instrument revised as necessary. It may be necessary to repeat these two steps, field-testing and modifying the instrument, several times before the instrument meets the program's needs.

PORTFOLIO ASSESSMENT

Once alternative assessments are selected as the means for assessing student performance, how they can be combined and utilized in the best possible fashion must be considered. One of the more popular and powerful methods is through the *portfolio*. The most common definition of portfolio comes from the Northwest Evaluation Association: "A portfolio is a purposeful collection of student work that exhibits the student's efforts, progress, and achievements in one or more areas" (Northwest Evaluation Association, cited in Arter, 1992, p. 2). The portfolio is an organizational structure that allows the systematic accumulation of various types of assessments. The portfolio may include any of the alternative assessments defined in the previous section, NRTs, CRTs, audio/video tapes, and more. How the portfolio is framed is based on its purpose.

Purposes for a Portfolio

Gottlieb (1992) has proposed six specific purposes for portfolios: to collect, reflect, assess, document, link, and/or to evaluate. Using the first letter of each word, this becomes the CRADLE approach to portfolios.

(See Figure 9 for a fuller definition of each term.) If the full approach is used, a teacher (or a program, school, or school district) might begin at stage one, collecting, and gradually move toward stage six, evaluating. Another person might identify where she/he wants to be on the CRADLE continuum and begin directly at that point.

Another approach to portfolio assessment is to view the portfolio as monitoring either a product or a process. In looking at products, a series of "best" works is selected by students and teachers to include in the portfolio. These best works, across a school year, show the progress and achievement of the student. In looking at a process, a series of draft materials and notes leading to one final product would be collected in the portfolio. These materials show the student's growth as she/he researched, studied, drafted, and refined a particular project or assignment. The portfolio also might contain both works-in-progress and best efforts.

Whatever the purpose of the portfolio, a procedure for planning and organizing it is essential. According to EAC-West (1993), a portfolio of student work should contain, at a minimum

- the criteria or guidelines for selecting and judging students' work
- the student's own selection of work
- evidence of the student's self-reflection

Portfolios can be used to ...

Collect	Encourage an open-ended selection of entries Provide a working repository for individual students Allow for experimentation
Reflect	Emphasize metacognitive and affective learning Focus on the process of acquiring knowledge Represent student-centered activities
Assess	Include primary and secondary evidence Specify criteria for authentic tasks and projects Rely on systematic data collection
Document	Evidence from multiple sources (including NRTs) over time Maintain a record of student achievement Comply with designated regulations
Link	Bridge communication among home, school, community Facilitate connections among teachers Show relative language and cognitive development of students
Evaluate	Assign a value to tasks and projects Summarize and make meaningful assessment findings Serve as a system of accountability at many levels

FIGURE 9 Gottlieb's (1992) CRADLE approach to portfolios.

For large-scale or group assessment, this collection also should articulate clearly (1) the schedule and management plan for collecting students' work; (2) measurable and specified criteria that can be used fairly and without bias for all students; and (3) reasonable procedures for summarizing students' portfolios for grading and/or reporting purposes. Other components that frequently are included in a portfolio are input from teachers, parents, and peers as well as district information such as local or national test information.

Planning and Organizing a Portfolio

Portfolio assessment systems allow the user to track the progress of an individual student over the course of an entire school year or more. Valencia (1990) suggests that assessment must be a continuous, ongoing process in order to chronicle development. Portfolio assessment allows us to observe and collect information continuously. In this way a student's progress is documented, rather than just the outcome of learning (the product). Valencia feels that this sends a very different message to students and parents: learning is never completed, instead, it is always evolving and changing. As an example, a project in New York collects three documents from students each year from the first grade to the seventh grade. The portfolio follows the student from one grade to the next. At the end of seventh grade, the student's portfolio has a total of twenty-one documents showing growth (Keene, 1994).

Scoring the portfolio has become a major issue. Four choices generally are available: (1) using the portfolio as a collection point without grading either papers or portfolio, (2) grading papers within the portfolio (either all or some papers), (3) grading the portfolio as a whole (without grading specific papers), or (4) grading the portfolio as a whole based on the scores of some specific papers. The type of scoring and the extent to which papers/portfolios are scored are based on the purpose of the portfolio. Thus clearly defining the objectives for portfolio assessment is imperative.

Portfolios can be used within one content area (e.g., math, English language arts) or can be used to link two or more content areas (e.g., combining language arts with science and history in a paper on the use of water along the Rio Grande). Because portfolios can include such a variety of assessments, a table of contents that lists the items to be included and the timeline for collecting the information is essential for any portfolio. Figure 10 provides tables of contents for two portfolios

KIRIS Writing Portfolio Assessment
Grade 4

1. Table of Contents
   Include the title of each portfolio entry, the study area for which the piece was written, and the page number in the portfolio.
2. One personal narrative
3. One poem, play/script, or piece of fiction
4. One piece of writing, the purpose of which is to
   a. present/support a position, idea, or opinion or
   b. tell about a problem and its solution or
   c. inform.
5. One piece of writing from a study area other than English/Language Arts. Any of the other portfolio entries may ALSO come from other study areas.
6. A "Best Piece"
7. A Letter to the Reviewer: a letter written by you discussing your "Best Piece" and reflecting upon your growth as a writer.

From the Kentucky Instructional Results Information System, Kentucky Department of Education, 1993.

KIRIS Math Portfolio Contents
Grade 4

1. Table of Contents
   A listing of the titles of the pieces in your portfolio, with page numbers.
2. Letter to the Reviewer
   A letter you write to the person who will read your portfolio. In it you might write about what you've learned from keeping a mathematics portfolio, explain which entry is your best and why, tell about your favorite piece and why it's your favorite, and/or tell from which entry you learned the most and why.
3. 5-7 Best Pieces
   Pieces that show many ways of doing mathematics; involve lots of topics such as estimation, geometry, patterns, and graphs; include the many ways you represent numbers; use mathematics to solve real world problems; and use different mathematical tools.

From the Kentucky Instructional Results Information System, Kentucky Department of Education, 1993.

FIGURE 10 Example Table of Contents from two portfolios.

currently in use for school, district, and state-wide assessment. As can be seen from these examples, the purpose, depth of description, type of materials, and number of materials within portfolios is quite diverse. For example, the purpose of the Kentucky (KIRIS) writing and math portfolio is state-wide accountability (see Figure 10).

Not only are portfolios across programs diverse, but portfolios within a program need not be the same. The grading system, amount of work, and types of work can be adapted (Krest, 1990), as well as the language of the work. Students can be encouraged to take risks and experiment with their language skills as well as with their content skills. As such, portfolios are an ideal method of assessing various linguistically/ethnically diverse groups. In particular, they are ideal for assessing groups such as Latinos who speak the same general language (Spanish and/or English), but with different cultural backgrounds and vernaculars.

USE OF ALTERNATIVE ASSESSMENT/PORTFOLIOS IN EVALUATION

Assessment and evaluation clearly are related. Assessing student achievement across a period of time allows teachers to evaluate their work as a whole and to assign grades. Aggregating students' scores and grades allows the evaluation of a program, school, or district. Because alternative assessment procedures are relatively new, there tends to be confusion over their role within the school assessment process. Given that alternative assessments provide teachers, parents, students, and other key stakeholders with important information about student achievement, methods for including the results of these measures in a grading system and in program evaluation must be considered.

Technical Standards

When thinking of "standards," most people think of standardized tests. But, in order to have confidence in a measuring tool, be it an NRT or an alternative assessment, the procedure must be standardized. What is meant by a *standardized procedure*? Basically, the instrument must be presented and scored in the same manner for each administration. More specifically, a standardized testing procedure is one in which:

- written and oral instruction
- specific items

- length of testing and time of testing
- method of scoring
- purpose for the assessment

are the *same* each time the instrument is used. Only with a standardized procedure can the results of the instrument be compared from one administration to the next, from one group of students to the next.

There is no guarantee that an instrument will be "good." In fact, there is no specific definition of what constitutes a "good" instrument. To be sure, everyone agrees that an instrument must (1) be trusted and (2) provide information that describes how well a student really is doing. As the stakes become higher, the quality of the instrument becomes more important. For instance, a teacher may want immediate feedback about whether students have conquered particular content. The assessment needs to provide only broad-based information; its quality may not be of great concern. Another teacher might want to assign grades based on the alternative assessment. The stakes for the students are higher in this example. A "better" set of alternative assessments is needed. Finally, the stakes are higher still in program evaluation. If an administrator wants to know how well students in a specially funded program are doing, the instruments must be the best possible. Some authors recommend that validity, reliability, and inter-rater criteria are essential to ensuring that an instrument is valuable. These characteristics can be applied to NRTs, alternative assessments, and portfolios.

Linn et al. (1991) suggest that the *validity* of an assessment is tied closely to its use. Validity should include the context in which the assessment is used and whether or not that use has unintended consequences; teaching to the test is an example of an unintended consequence. Validity is described as the degree to which an assessment actually measures what it claims to measure and whether appropriate inferences can be drawn from the student's performance (Messick, 1989; Navarrete et al., 1993). To increase validity, results from an alternative assessment should:

- provide an accurate picture of how well that student knows the targets of achievement proficiency
- be based on at least five different tasks measuring similar skills
- be generalizable to other tasks to infer "real" mastery

Reliability refers to the likelihood that a score would be the same if the assessment were taken again at another time or if it were rescored by someone else. It is a measure of the consistency or stability of an assessment. Reliability also refers to the extent that overall performance can be generalized from a single or small number of performances. To increase reliability in alternative assessments:

- Design multiple tasks that lead to the same outcome.
- Use trained judges, working with clear criteria, from specific anchor papers or performance behaviors.
- Monitor periodically to ensure that raters use criteria and standards in a consistent manner.

Establishing inter-rater reliability for alternative assessments is an essential and straightforward task. The following steps are involved: (1) agree on the criteria that will be used to assess the student's work or behavior; (2) select student work as sample scoring materials; (3) practice scoring the samples of work using the same criteria and the same rating or scoring form; (4) compare the scores to determine the extent of agreement on the scoring criteria; and (5) score independently with frequent reliability checks to avoid inconsistencies in the rating process.

Two people working together will allow a review of reliability by comparing the ratings. Then, any misunderstandings or uncertainties about the criteria can be clarified. Disagreements about the criteria and ambiguities in the criteria can be resolved by implementing the procedures of inter-rater reliability. Well-established inter-rater reliability should ensure accuracy in the rating of students' performances.

Grading with Alternative Assessments

Methods for scoring individual alternative assessments were described earlier. Scores, in a given content area, are combined to create a grade. Thus, grades are summary measures of aggregated scores. As such, they provide a measure of student progress or achievement in a specific content area. How, though, can a grade be created when there are many different ways to score alternative assessments?

First, the instructor must consider the purpose of the grade. As defined by Bratcher (1994), grading is "communication between teacher and student that is designed to enhance the student's [skills]" (p. 9). The teacher must consider how the grading procedures can be used best to work with students, as well as provide information to other teachers, decision-makers, and parents.

The traditional method for grading involves the simple *averaging* of scores—numbers of checks, holistic scores (changing symbols such as +, ✓, – to numbers such as 3, 2, 1), and others—to create a grade. Typically, 90% of the total points possible or above is an *A*, 80–89% a *B*, and so on. According to Bratcher (1994), this method of grading often is referred to as the "common value system" (p. 81). Such converting of scores to letter grades is a method used by a majority of teachers, up to 82% of classrooms at some grade levels (Robinson and Craver, 1989).

Another method for grading is to utilize a *checklist of traits* and characteristics to record student progress. Rather than maintaining the scores on individual assignments, the teacher creates a list of skills that s/he expects students to achieve during the grading period. When a student successfully demonstrates a skill (by achieving a set score on an assessment, through the use of other checklists, or on materials in the portfolio), that skill can be checked off the list. At the end of the grading period, the grade is based on the number of skills actually demonstrated by the student. This type of grading can be considered a criterion-referenced method, since the skills the students are to demonstrate, and the degree of accuracy or proficiency, are determined in advance. Robinson and Craver (1989) refer to this as a method of "nonscale alternatives" that provides "more detail of strengths and weaknesses than other methods of grading" (p. 16). The checklist is used across all grade levels, but is seen most in kindergarten and lower elementary classrooms (Robinson and Craver, 1989, p. 29).

A third option is to create a *contract* for each student. Within the contract, students indicate what work they intend to do, and the grade that the successful completion of that work merits. Such an approach can be especially useful (1) in a class of culturally diverse students, such as Latinos, in which different types and amounts of work might be appropriate for different students or (2) when using portfolios, for which different tables of contents could be developed, each one representing the contract for that student.

Finally, Stiggins (1990) suggests combining these three methods to form a bandwidth methodology. The instructor can develop grades based on percentages. However, since all grading is somewhat subjective, and since students might do poorly on any individual assignment for a variety of reasons, a bandwidth or "gray area" can be established. For instance, if 90% is the breaking point between an *A* and a *B*, the gray area might be between 88% and 92%. Students whose average score falls within this gray area are either given a grade such as *A/B*, or further questions can be asked to determine which grade should be assigned. How many ungraded homework assignments were completed? Did the student start the semester poorly, but then show greatly increased skills as the semester progressed? Did the student attempt extra work to practice skills? These and other sources of data can help determine whether the bandwidth grade should be raised to *A* or lowered to *B*.

Grading "*on the curve*" is not a recommended practice. This procedure is based on grading students relative to one another. The best students receive *A*s and the weakest students receive *F*s, regardless of their actual performance. When grading on the curve, it would be possible for a student with an average of 75% to receive an F. Grading on the curve is appropriate only with a large number of students (some authors suggest at least 150), when relative grading is acceptable.

Another method *not* recommended is the *descriptive grade*. Rather than giving specific grades, descriptive grades include anecdotal records, written letters, and/or other comments by teachers. While some proponents argue that information pertaining to student achievement is more fully and individually communicated in this manner, others argue that descriptive grading increases the influence of teacher biases and provides no systematic and cumulative record of student progress toward school goals (Robinson and Craver, 1989).

Also, assessments of attitude, interest, and motivation should not be included in grading procedures. These assessments do not measure skills or proficiencies. Although they may be helpful in planning curricula, the information is not of a type to be important in grading.

Some school districts are using other methods for reporting student progress to families, the district, and the community. These methods are based on alternative assessments of student achievement; they are not traditional grade report cards. Such changes in the traditional grading system require re-education, careful planning, and "buy-in" from teachers, families, administrators, and others in the educational community. While they may be a promising practice for the future, it is difficult to define guidelines for them at this point.

Program Evaluation with Alternative Assessments

The use of alternative assessment and portfolio assessment to document student progress for the purpose of accountability to funding sources has a number of advantages. It allows the student, teacher, and program to provide a clear picture of progress when the assessments are well designed to clearly specified and meaningful standards. This kind of assessment allows students to show what they know and how they know it because the assessment can be designed in the students' native language to include facets of their cultural background, values, and beliefs. For Latino students who are not familiar with the mainstream concepts and values that form the foundation of many of the current NRTs, this may be the only opportunity they have to show what they know.

Traditionally, evaluation has been defined as formative or summative. *Formative* evaluation is utilized early in a program and leads toward modifications and refinements to improve the program. *Summative* evaluation generally is the final, year-end report that summarizes information for the program and determines whether the program's objectives have been met. A newer methodology is the *dynamic evaluation*, which is a more ongoing process (Figueroa, 1990). Dynamic evaluation allows the program to "keep tabs" on students to determine their progress and make modifications in the program as the need is identified.

Funding agencies generally require an annual evaluation of programs that they fund. Evaluation requirements often include documentation of technical standards for all measures of student achievement/progress. When using alternative assessment to meet funding agency evaluation requirements, it is important to report:

- the process used to develop the assessments
- methods and kind(s) of reliability established for the measure
- the context and validation process for the assessment

This chapter has outlined the manner in which alternative assessment procedures can be standardized while developing alternative assessments. Although it may seem like a costly and time-consuming enterprise, the return on this investment is usually substantial in terms of the rich information they can provide about student progress.

SUMMARY

Psychometricians and educators are beginning to recognize that a single assessment cannot provide an adequate measure of students' capabilities; multiple measures are needed. Concomitantly, there is increased knowledge and awareness of the problems and limitations inherent in standardized tests. This has led to the growth in popularity of alternative assessments, sometimes referred to as authentic assessments, performance-based assessments, or curriculum-based assessments. Educators are discovering that alternatives are empowering to them and to their students. These alternative forms of assessment are ongoing, reflect instruction, are sensitive to individual differences and developmental considerations, and, most importantly, actively involve students. Alternative assessments also can inform instruction by providing valuable information as to the effectiveness of the instructional activities being implemented in a classroom. Culturally and linguistically diverse Latino students can benefit greatly from the opportunities available with alternative assessments to demonstrate growth and competency within the context of meaningful learning.

The way alternative forms of assessment are designed, used, and graded depends greatly on the specific purpose for their use. As with standardized tests, issues of validity, reliability, and inter-rater reliability are important to consider when designing or using alternative forms of assessment. Although establishing technical standards for alternative assessments can be a time-consuming and labor intensive process, the benefits to be derived from alternative measurements are substantial. They can be developed in the native languages of the students to include elements of the students' culture and background. This makes for assessment that is meaningful and more fair for Latino students who may have values and background experiences different from those of the traditional mainstream population that are embedded in many of the current NRTs.

Just as alternative assessments allow a broader and more in-depth view of the student, so do the evaluations that are based on alternative assessments. A formative, dynamic, or summative evaluation should include both NRTs and standardized alternative assessments. In this way, the view of the program will provide the greatest information.

The greater needs of Latino students cannot be met solely through the use of alternative assessments; they must be met within the context of the whole school. A whole-school program that incorporates effective practices for Latino students must be more than an "add-on" to the school's core curriculum. Assessment that looks at what students actually can do (as opposed to what they cannot do) and creates an environment where students are comfortable taking risks is an essential component of meeting the needs of diverse students in whole-school programs. In such schools will we find successful Latino students.

APPENDIX: TESOL STANDARDS[2]

Access to a Positive Learning Environment

(1) Are the language minority (LM) students' schools safe, attractive, and free of prejudice?

(2) Is there a positive whole-school environment? This is defined as one in which the administrative and instructional policies and practices create a positive climate, there are high expectations for all students, and learning experiences are linguistically and culturally appropriate for LM students.

(3) Do teachers, administrators, and other staff receive professional development related to the needs of LM students?

(4) Does the school environment welcome parents of LM students? This includes recognizing parents as at-home primary teachers of their children and as important participators in the life of the school.

Access to Appropriate Curriculum

(5) Do LM students have access to appropriate instructional programs? These programs must support second language development and match the full range of instructional services offered to majority students.

(6) Does the core curriculum designed for all students promote (a) sharing, valuing, and developing both first and second languages and cultures and (b) higher-order thinking skills?

(7) Do LM students have access to the instructional programs and related services that identify, conduct, and support programs for special populations in a district?

Access to Full Delivery of Services

(8) Are the teaching strategies and instructional practices used with LM students developmentally appropriate, attuned to students' language proficiencies and cognitive levels, and culturally supportive and relevant?

(9) Do students have opportunities to develop and use their first language to promote academic and social development?

2 Modified and adapted from TESOL (1994). For a fuller statement of the standards, see the original document.

(10) Are support services (such as counseling, career guidance, and transportation) available to LM students?

(11) Do LM students have equal access to computers, computer classes, and other technologically advanced instructional assistance?

(12) Does the school have institutional policies and procedures that are linguistically and culturally sensitive?

(13) Does the school offer regular, nonstereotypical opportunities for native English-speaking students and LM students to share and value one another's languages and cultures?

Access to Equitable Assessment

(14) Are LM students assessed for language proficiency and academic achievement in the content areas using measures that are appropriate to students' developmental level, age, and level of oral and written language proficiency in the first and second languages? Are these measures reliable, valid, and appropriate? Are the results of such assessments explained to students and their families in their home language?

(15) Are LM students' special needs assessed appropriately? Again, access is further defined by using measures that are nonbiased and relevant, the results of which are explained to the family in their own language.

REFERENCES

Arter, J. A. 1992. "Portfolios in practice: What is a portfolio?" Paper presented at the *Annual Meeting of the American Educational Research Association,* April 1992, San Francisco, CA.

Baker, E. L., H. F. O'Neil, and R. L. Linn. 1993. "Policy and validity prospects for performance-based assessment." *American Psychologist,* 48(12): 1210–1218.

Bratcher, S. 1994. *Evaluating Children's Writing: A Handbook of Communication Choices for Classroom Teachers.* New York, NY: St. Martin's Press.

Council of Chief State School Officers. 1992. *Recommendations for Improving the Assessment and Monitoring of Students with Limited English Proficiency.* Alexandria, VA: Council of Chief State School Officers.

Del Vecchio, A., M. Guerrero, C. Gustke, P. Martínez, C. Navarrete, C. Nelson, and J. Wilde. 1994. *Whole School Bilingual Education Programs: Implications for Sound Assessment.* Program Information Guide #18. Washington, D.C.: National Clearinghouse for Bilingual Education.

Evaluation Assistance Center-West (EAC-West). 1993. *A Brief Guide to Using Student Portfolios in Title VII.* Albuquerque, NM: Evaluation Assistance Center-West (EAC-West).

Figueroa, R. A. 1990. "Best practices in the assessment of bilingual children," in *Best Practices in School Psychology—II*. A. Thomas and J. Grimes, eds. Washington, D.C.: National Association of School Psychologists, pp. 93–106.

Gardner, H. 1993. *Multiple Intelligences: The Theory in Practice*. New York, NY: Basic Books.

Goodman, K. S., L. B. Goodman, and L. B. Bird. 1992. *The Whole Language Catalog Supplement on Authentic Assessment*. Santa Rosa, CA: American School.

Gottlieb, M. 1992. "Portfolios." Paper presented at the *Meeting of Title VII Developmental Bilingual Education Grantees*. December, 1992. Los Angeles, CA.

Holt, D., ed. 1994. *Assessing Success in Family Literacy Projects: Alternative Approaches to Assessment and Evaluation*. Washington, D.C. and McHenry, IL: Center for Applied Linguistics and Delta Systems.

Joint Committee of the American Educational Research Association, American Psychological Association, and American Council on Measurement. 1985. *Standards for Educational and Psychological Testing*. Washington, D.C.: APA.

Keene, D. 1994. "Performance-based assessment and evaluation in developmental bilingual education," a panel presentation at the Developmental Bilingual Education Pre-Institute Conference, National Professional Development Institute. October, 1994. Washington, D.C.

Kentucky Instructional Results Information System. 1993. *KIRIS Math Assessment Portfolio, Grade 4, 1993–1994*. Frankfort, KY: Kentucky Department of Education.

Kentucky Instructional Results Information System. 1993. *KIRIS Writing Assessment Portfolio, Grade 4, 1993–1994*. Frankfort, KY: Kentucky Department of Education.

Krest, M. 1990. "Adapting Portfolios to Meet the Needs of Students." *English Journal*, 79 (2): 29–34.

Linn, R., E. Baker, and S. Dunbar. 1991. "Complex Performance-Based Assessments: Expectations and Validation Criteria." *Educational Researcher*, 20(8):15–21.

Messick, S. 1989. "The Once and Future Issues of Validity: Assessing the Meaning and Consequences of Measurement," in *Test Validity*. H. Wainer and H. I. Braun, eds. Hillsdale, NJ: Lawrence Erlbaum, pp. 33–46.

Navarrete, C., J. Wilde, A. Del Vecchio, R. Benjamin, M. Guerrero, P. Martinez, and C. Nelson. (In press). A New Framework for Assessing Students in Bilingual Education.

Navarrete, C., J. Wilde, C. Nelson, P. Martínez, and G. Hargett. 1990. *Information Assessment in Educational Evaluation: Implications for Bilingual Education Programs*. Program Information Guide #3. Washington, D.C.: National Clearinghouse for Bilingual Education.

Ramírez, D. (In press). *Assessment of Limited English Proficient Students: Program Guidelines for Teachers and Administrators*. Sacramento, CA: Bilingual Education Office.

Robinson, G. E. and J. M. Craver. 1989. *Assessing and Grading Student Achievement*. Arlington, VA: Educational Research Service.

Stiggins, R. 1990. *Classroom Assessment Training Program: Trainer's Instructional Package*. Portland, OR: Northwest Regional Educational Laboratory.

Stiggins, R. 1993. "Users and uses of assessment results." Paper presented at the Large Scale Assessment Conference of the Council of Chief State School Officers. June 1993. Albuquerque, NM.

TESOL. 1994. *The TESOL Standards: Ensuring Access to Quality Educational Experiences for Language Minority Students.* Alexandria, VA: Teachers of English to Speakers of Other Languages.

Valencia, S. 1990. "A Portfolio Approach to Classroom Reading Assessment: The Whys, Whats, and Hows." *The Reading Teacher*, 43(4):338–340.

CHAPTER 17

Creating a Climate for Critical Systemic Assessment

CHRISTOPHER NELSON—*New Mexico Highlands University*
CECILIA NAVARRETE—*New Mexico Highlands University*
PAUL MARTÍNEZ—*New Mexico Highlands University*

INTRODUCTION

IT is difficult to recall a time in recent history when the United States has been confronted by so many of its citizens to improve education for all students. The American public, including significant numbers of parents, members of legislative and business sectors, policymakers, and representatives of hundreds of special interest groups, have reached consensus on the need to fix a system in dire need of repair. The challenge is especially profound for millions of linguistically and culturally diverse students as local school districts, state departments of education, and the federal government struggle with the issue of meeting the unique strengths and needs of these learners. The major response to these and other challenges is systemic educational reform, which attempts to reconstruct and reorganize all parts of educational systems in more coordinated ways. August et al. (1994) suggest that conscious planning, coordination, and leadership in all instructional components including curriculum, professional development, governance, assessment, and accountability are requisites of systemic reform.

Increasingly, standards and assessment are viewed by many educators as the essential elements of systemic reform. At the center of the systemic reform debate are the issues of how student assessment is organized and documented and what it means for all students and schools (Bond et al., 1994). Responding to these issues has forced educators, including those who work with Latino students, to reexamine and therefore redefine assessment to ensure that it embodies more completely the elements and thrust of systemic reform.

During the past several years, the country has witnessed a movement at the local, state, and national levels to establish higher academic, content, and performance standards along with assessments that are

357

closely correlated to those standards. That movement led educators and others to call for systemically reforming our educational system. The major impetus behind this systemic reform effort is a comprehensive and ambitious piece of legislation known as the *Goals 2000: Educate America Act* (Congressional Record, 1994), which provides resources to states and local communities to develop and implement comprehensive education reforms aimed at helping all students meet these new standards. Among numerous initiatives outlined in the legislation, the following components are significant and demonstrate the proposed link between federal, state, and local activities:

- Codify into law the original six National Education Goals and add two more goals that encourage parent participation and professional development of teachers.
- Establish the National Education Goals Panel to oversee and report on the nation's progress toward meeting the goals as well as authorizing grants to support development of assessment systems aligned to state content standards.
- Authorize grants to states through Title III that support, accelerate, and sustain local improvement efforts so that students reach the new academic standards.
- Authorize state planning panels to develop systemic reform plans that, among other things, outline strategies for the development of student performance standards and assessments.
- Allow local school districts to develop or implement improvement plans that require strategies for ensuring all students meet academic standards developed by their respective states.

Of specific interest to those interested and/or involved in the education of Latino children are the changes in several of the programs authorized under the Improving America's Schools Act. Most notably, Titles I and VII contain sweeping statutory changes that will no doubt impact program design and implementation, assessment, teacher preparation, and provision of technical assistance. Implicit in all of the legislation, proposed changes, coordinated efforts, and strategic initiatives is the intention to create and foster a climate for critical systemic reform. As a result of these changes, it is imperative that language minority educators and parents across the country involve themselves not only in local education programs that provide direct services to their children but also in statewide reform efforts (Escamilla, 1994).

CURRENT STATUS OF SCHOOLING FOR LATINO STUDENTS

The increasing attention given to the need to systemically reform American schools has once again pointed to the glaring inequities in and quality of schooling provided to Latino students. García (1994) asserts that continual problems faced by Latino students and their families such as high drop-out rates, lower levels of academic achievement than Anglo students, and serious under-funding of schools with high concentrations of Latino and other minority students, are indicators of increasing educational vulnerability. Darder (1993), in summarizing studies that focus on the academic development of Latino students in public schools, identified numerous barriers associated with under-achievement. Several of the most pressing barriers include:

- significant conflicts between the culture of the teacher or school and the culture of the students
- language differences that are ignored or inadequately addressed
- mainstream teachers of Latino students who often lack knowledge and training on the pedagogical needs of language minority students
- infrequent communication between the school and Latino parents about the education of their children
- a lack of support for the development of bilingualism in Latino students despite the evidence amassed over two decades, which supports the positive effects of maintenance programs on academic achievement
- forms of testing and assessment, at all levels, that reflect both class and cultural biases
- serious inadequacies in teacher preparation programs which contribute to the existence of many of these barriers

Failure to address these conditions and inequities is damaging to the very fabric of American education and society. Systemic reform can be true to its mandate only when fundamental changes occur that reduce and eliminate the barriers and inequity Latino students continue to confront.

However, it is imperative to note that, despite these major obstacles, higher levels of educational attainment and success for Latino students are very much a reality. Numerous studies have identified elements of successful schools and effective program features for linguistically and culturally diverse students, especially Latinos. According to Carter and Chatfield (1986), effective bilingual schools are characterized by: (1) a comprehensive schooling system that develops a school social climate that results in positive student outcomes; and (2) characteristics such as effective leadership and governance, high expectations, strong academic focus, and a school climate conducive to learning. Garcia (1987) identified six critical factors integral to the success of language minority students, including:

- strong school leadership and processes
- positive social climate
- a curriculum that promotes higher-order thinking
- instruction characterized by high expectations, interactive teaching, and an emphasis on authentic communicative learning situations
- adequately prepared staff who are innovative and have a high sense of self-efficiency
- assessment that is conducted when appropriate in the native language, that focuses on targeting help for students, and where teachers and principals monitor students' progress

We want to underscore that the effective program and instructional features identified for Latino students are closely correlated to the characteristics associated with systemic reform. In fact, there is a strong link between both. This link is of particular significance in attempting to identify the characteristics necessary to create a climate for critical systemic assessment.

DEFINING SYSTEMIC ASSESSMENT

A review of the literature indicates that there are multiple definitions and frameworks of systemic assessment. Not surprisingly, however, a similar definition or framework appropriate to Latino students and their special needs has been virtually nonexistent until recently. Del Vecchio et al. (1994) have proposed a systemic assessment framework for language minority students that is based on effective schools and instructional practices research. Their framework revolves around the relevant characteristics and supporting features of school context, program implementation, and student outcomes. This framework, in turn, serves to describe those factors and conditions that researchers and practitioners alike agree are central to creating a climate where systemic assessment not only informs good instruction for Latino students but also catalyzes other reform initiatives which have direct links to school success.

The significance of the framework developed by Del Vecchio et al. (1994) is that it is germane to language minority students, especially Latino students. The framework is also predicated on effective schools and practices theory as it relates to Latino students and provides a blueprint that assists schools to function more effectively and equitably. Equally as important, the framework can be used as a guide for: (1) developing a favorable learning climate; (2) identifying expectations for teachers, administrators, and students; (3) informing good instructional practice; and (4) assessing school reform efforts.

KEY FEATURES OF SYSTEMIC CHANGE

What do I need to know in order to plan and assess the effectiveness of our improvement efforts for Latino students? This question is asked by teachers and administrators alike who want to be informed about the determinants needed for enhancing schools and classroom operations for Latino students. Fortunately, over the last decade several indicators of successful practices targeted for language minority students have been identified (e.g., Lucas et al., 1990; Ramirez et al., 1991; Tikunoff, 1985, 1991). From a whole-school perspective (Del Vecchio et al., 1994), these indicators can be placed into three categories: (1) school context; (2) school implementation; and (3) student outcomes. Figure 1 (page 367) summarizes the key indicators by the whole-school categories.

These indicators are not new. In fact, many are based on earlier studies of effective schools and instructional practices. However, the characteristics of these indicators differ from the mainstream literature in terms of distinct cultural and language-related qualities identified in schools with large populations of language minority, especially Latino, students.

School Context and Environment

According to recent research (Faltis and Merino, 1992; Garcia, 1987; McCollum and Russo, 1993) key determinants of a healthy and successful school context for language minority students are: a prevalent culture or ethos in the school that actively supports learning for *all* its students; how the administration supervises and integrates effective programs for its staff and Latino students; and how assets of the school and its staff are utilized to support student learning.

Ethos

Latino schools with a strong sense of ethos have a well-defined social organization with clear rules and standards. A climate of respect and affirmation by all staff exists regarding the use of Spanish, its dialectal variations, and diverse Latino cultural expressions by students. Knowledge of student background and culture is integrated into instruction and assessment, and students' families are included in all school events and communicated with on a regular basis in Spanish and/or English depending on their level of comfort and proficiency. High expectations are developed and maintained by providing opportunities to develop literacy skills in English as well as Spanish. Academic and behavior expectations are concrete and enforced equitably. Students are involved in mainstream classrooms and extracurricular activities, and their accomplishments are celebrated in a public manner.

Successful Latino schools are committed to building and maintaining a strong morale for staff and students, as well as ensuring an equitable representation in student government and in the teaching staff. In addition, positive attitudes are expressed by students, staff, and parents, and attendance at school events is high and representative of the student population.

Management

Effective management is viewed as a system of supervision that incorporates the monitoring of effective practices for all students across key elements of the school environment. This form of dynamic management ensures: (a) effective practices for both English and Spanish language learners across all parts of the curriculum; (b) staff training that is focused on multicultural education and awareness of community needs; and (c) parent, student, and staff involvement in all planning and restructuring efforts. Other essential features include regular monitoring of assessment procedures, placement, and instructional practices to ensure that they are fair and effective for all students.

Resources

This indicator is measured by the "tangible" and "not-so-tangible" commodities that are used to serve a school including: reallocation of administrative support and resources that are fairly distributed to students and staff; creative strategies (financial and nonfinancial) to sustain and expand effective services including a guiding mission statement; inclusion of all key stakeholders; and regular meetings for planning, training, and implementing school programs. A last, but critical, resource is the time and opportunity set aside to conduct comprehensive needs assessments and to plan effective programs for Latino students and their teachers.

School Implementation Systems

Our review of the literature on effective schools and instruction indicates that the implementation of curriculum and instruction, staff development, the role of the administrator, and family/community involvement can have a positive impact on Latino student behavior and achievement. In a sense, the implementation indicators are an additional means of examining the school context, the difference being that implementation indicators focus on the ongoing, day-to-day execution of effective school and classroom practices rather than the prevailing ambience of the school.

Curriculum and Instruction

There are several key factors that influence the success of instruction and the use of curriculum models for Latino students. The curriculum, first and foremost, is based on national, state, and local standards. Latino students are expected to achieve at the same levels as their non-Latino counterparts. In addition, the curriculum is based on the experiences, interests, and needs of Latinos. Courses are varied, they are presented in a culturally and ethnically sensitive manner, and offered in Spanish and in English. In addition, Latino students are vigorously recruited and involved in extracurricular activities. Community members are also actively involved in planning and supporting the school curriculum and instruction.

Staff

Four general staff qualities are critical for carrying out effective programs for Latino students, including: broad and varied knowledge and experience related to Latino students; awareness and ongoing involvement in identifying training needs based on Latino students and inservice training; a sense of autonomy or feeling of empowerment to make decisions at the classroom and school level; and the ability to collaborate by sharing knowledge and materials, lending support, and working within and across teams.

Administrators

Administrators play a pivotal role in coordinating and facilitating program implementation to ensure Latino student needs are addressed. In managing this role, effective administrators exhibit the knowledge and understanding of student and staff needs, of research and effective practices for Latino students, of students' culture, and of cross-cultural communication strategies. Additional indicators of an effective administrator include the ability to collaborate and support teachers' teaming efforts, training management, and decision making. The administrator also successfully manages relationships with local, state, and federal groups and agencies.

Parents

To address the diverse needs of Latino families a multifaceted framework of outreach, collaboration, and support must be established. For example, long-term and short-term needs of families must be identified and served. Parents and community leaders should be actively involved in collaborations and decision making that impacts Latino students, parents themselves, and other community members. Also, parents are supported vis-à-vis a broad array of activities and services as well as communication in Spanish, where required, for comprehension and participation.

Student Skills

Critical elements of effective classrooms typically include measurement of the amount of time students are actively engaged on academic tasks, the amount of content covered by students during a year, and student outcomes that are based on daily assignments and tests indicating mastery of academic content (Squires et al., 1984). In effective bilingual education programs with large concentrations of Latino students, additional factors such as acquisition of learning and communication processes, skills, and strategies are directly linked to student academic success of Latino students. Performance is also influenced by Latino students' opportunity for self-enhancement as well as by the link between assessment and instruction.

Learning Strategies

Effective learning strategies for Latino students consist not only of opportunities to develop higher-order thinking skills such as inquiry and problem solving, but opportunities to process information, reflect, transfer, and communicate what they are learning in a variety of learning situations. Integrated into these opportunities is time to use and receive feedback on students' communication strategies (listening, speaking, reading, and writing) in Spanish and English in order to assist them in the transfer of skills to the particular learning activity. Through practice and active involvement in meaningful learning tasks, students are able to effectively develop process skills and strategies.

Self-Enhancement

To succeed in school, Latino students must have useful social skills, a positive ethnic self-concept, and motivation to learn. Self-enhancement occurs when language and culture are validated and included in all aspects of the school. Latino students see themselves as an integral and constructive part of the learning environment. Training on prosocial skills is provided to enhance interactions with their peers and teachers. In addition, instructional materials, methods, and content are designed to have meaning to the students in terms of their values, beliefs, customs, and language.

Overall, the research on effective and exemplary schools for Latino students clearly indicates schools can do much to foster positive achievement and performance. The elements for creating success can be identified in the school context, its implementation of programs for students, staff, parents, and administrators, as well as in the learning, communication, and self-enhancement strategies needed to facilitate high student outcomes. When these elements are developed in concert, schools are likely to become self-regulating institutions, creating a climate for continuous improvement and advancement for Latino students.

THE NEED FOR A SYSTEMIC ASSESSMENT OF SCHOOL IMPROVEMENT

As schools go through the process of systemic change, ongoing assessment can serve to focus stakeholders' efforts and provide a way to monitor progress. School staff, students, administrators, and parents should all have input into the systemic change process. While these groups may be working toward the same general goal, their respective concerns and priorities for change may differ. An assessment on which they can independently and anonymously provide their input helps ensure that each stakeholder group has a voice in the change process.

Change within an institution such as a school is multifaceted. Different components may change at different rates and some changes may be more subtle than others. While some changes are obvious (e.g., hiring Latino staff), others may prove difficult to document (e.g., improvement in school morale). An assessment designed to be sensitive to the different components involved in systemic change can, over time, provide a way to document the degree to which desired changes have occurred.

Description of the Systemic Improvement Assessment Instrument (SIAI)

Teachers, administrators, and other stakeholders have numerous responsibilities during the school day. They have little use for meaningless surveys or for activities that do not contribute to what happens at the classroom or school levels. For any assessment to be used successfully in a school, it must be relatively easy to complete and summarize, and it must provide information that can be used by teachers and others. In proposing an assessment designed to measure the need for and to document systemic change, these concepts are kept in mind as well as the need to provide a means to give all stakeholders a voice in the process.

The SIAI in Figure 1 is built on the whole-school program components that are desirable in school context, program implementation, and student outcomes. The SIAI breaks down these three general categories into their components and provides a descriptor for each one. There are two four-point response scales for each component. The first asks respondents to rate the degree to which the component is in place at the school: *Not in place, Partially, To a great degree, Fully in place*. The second response scale asks respondents to rate the importance of taking action to address the component during the next twelve months: *Not important, Somewhat important, Important, Very important*. This second scale sets the stage for prioritizing corrective actions identified by the community and school respondents.

The SIAI is intended for use by all the groups that are school

The purpose of this instrument is to get feedback from you on the effectiveness of our school. Your information is valuable to us, therefore we will keep your responses confidential and use them as part of other school and community input. Please answer two questions for each item:

1. To what degree does this item characterize your school?
   1 = Not in place   2 = Partially   3 = To a great degree   4 = Fully in place
2. How important is it that the school takes action on this item during the next 12 months?
   1 = Not important   2 = Somewhat important   3 = Important   4 = Very important

---

Person completing questionnaire (*Circle all that apply*)
Administrator   Teacher Paraprofessional Community Parent

Date questionnaire completed:

Part A: School Context	To what degree does this characterize your school?	How important is it to take action?
Ethos 1. *Climate*: In our school the student's language and culture is learned, supported and valued by all school staff	1 2 3 4	1 2 3 4
2. *Expectations*: High expectations are maintained and made concrete for all staff and students.	1 2 3 4	1 2 3 4
3. *School Morale*: Commitment is expressed and carried out to build and preserve high staff and student morale	1 2 3 4	1 2 3 4
Management 4. *Integration*: Elements of effective schooling for LM students permeate entire school environment. Staff, parents and students are included in planning and restructuring.	1 2 3 4	1 2 3 4
5. *Supervision*: Equitable assessment procedures, placement, and instructional practices are consistently monitored.	1 2 3 4	1 2 3 4
Resources 6. *Administration*: Reallocation of administrative support and resources are marshalled to assist students and teachers.	1 2 3 4	1 2 3 4
7. *Capacity*: Creative strategies (financial & nonfinancial) are used to sustain and expand service capacity.	1 2 3 4	1 2 3 4
8. *Time*: Time & opportunity are provided to conduct comprehensive needs assessment and planning of effective programs for LM students and teachers.	1 2 3 4	1 2 3 4

FIGURE 1 The Systemic Improvement Assessment Instrument (SIAI).

367

Part B: School Implementation	To what degree does this characterize your school?	How important is it to take action?
Curriculum & Instruction 9. *Cultural and Ethnic Sensitivity*: School curricula, support services, and extracurricular activities are adapted to be culturally relevant and of interest to LM students.	1 2 3 4	1 2 3 4
10. *Flexibility*: National, state, and local standards are adapted in the curricula for LM students to demonstrate learning and language development in a variety of ways.	1 2 3 4	1 2 3 4
11. *English Teaching Strategies*: Instruction is designed to promote active and purposeful use of English. Teachers communicate clearly and effectively. Students are provided immediate feedback to obtain successful task completion.	1 2 3 4	1 2 3 4
12. *Native Language Teaching Strategies:* Pedagogical approaches along with Native language and culture are promoted across content areas. Native language materials are used to develop native literacy skills.	1 2 3 4	1 2 3 4
Staff 13. *Knowledge & Experience*: All staff are knowledgeable of the community and culture of students. A balance of qualifications exists among staff.	1 2 3 4	1 2 3 4
14. *Training*: Staff development is explicitly designed for teachers and other staff to serve LM students.	1 2 3 4	1 2 3 4
15. *Autonomy*: Teaching staff are actively involved in planning and making decisions in the school and in their classrooms.	1 2 3 4	1 2 3 4
16. *Collaboration*: School staff and community members actively work together to promote programs and services for all students.	1 2 3 4	1 2 3 4
Administrators 17. *Understanding & Knowledge*: Administrators have an understanding of student and staff needs, the theory and practice of effective practices for LM students, and cross-cultural communication skills for managing bilingual education programs.	1 2 3 4	1 2 3 4
18. *Collaboration*: Collaboration is fostered with diverse agencies, groups and organizations.	1 2 3 4	1 2 3 4
19. *Support:* Administrators advocate support of bilingual education programs through recruitment, staff development, community, and central office undertakings.	1 2 3 4	1 2 3 4

FIGURE 1 *(continued).*

Part B: School Implementation (Cont'd)	To what degree does this characterize your school?	How important is it to take action?
<u>Parents</u> 20. *Outreach:* Efforts are made to expand family involvement and participation in the school. Attention is paid to "immediate" needs of parents.	1 2 3 4	1 2 3 4
21. *Collaboration:* There is collaborative educator-parent-child involvement central to school-home communication and literacy development.	1 2 3 4	1 2 3 4
22. *Support:* Use of home language and varied forms of home visits are used to nurture school-home relationships.	1 2 3 4	1 2 3 4

Part C: Student Outcomes	To what degree does this characterize your school?	How important is it to take action?
<u>Learning Strategies</u> 23. *Practice:* Students are provided with opportunities to practice, to exhibit high levels of successful task engagement, and to apply learning and test-taking skills in a variety of situations.	1 2 3 4	1 2 3 4
24. *Information Processing:* Students actively integrate new information and skills to each other and to prior knowledge.	1 2 3 4	1 2 3 4
25. *Higher-Order Thinking:* Higher-order thinking skills including metacognitive and metalinguistic skills, are enhanced through use of native language and opportunity to transfer those skills.	1 2 3 4	1 2 3 4
<u>Self-Enhancement</u> 26. *Cultural/Ethnic Identity:* Native language instruction is used to give students a greater sense of cultural identity, culturally appropriate interaction, discourse patterns, and metalinguistic awareness.	1 2 3 4	1 2 3 4
27. *Motivation & Confidence:* Effective school experiences are used to develop ability, confidence, ethnic identity, and motivation to succeed academically.	1 2 3 4	1 2 3 4

Additional areas that need to be addressed in creating an effective school:

_____

_____

_____

_____

FIGURE 1 *(continued).*

stakeholders (i.e., parents, students, teachers, non-teaching school staff, and administrators) and provides space for group identification so that the responses of these different groups can be compared.

Tailoring the SIAI to Meet School Needs

The components identified in constructing the SIAI are based on what research says should be in place in whole-school programs that are effective for Latino and other language minority students. While these findings are represented in the SIAI, school stakeholders may feel additional issues are important as well and should not be limited to looking at only those components we have identified. In the same vein, there may be some components that are not applicable for a particular school community.

For these reasons the SIAI may be tailored to a school's needs by deleting some components from, or adding components to, those that are listed in Figure 1. If one response group is to be compared to the others, though, people from the different groups should respond to the same set of items.

Hypothetical Example

Figure 2 contains hypothetical data representing responses of several teachers on Items 4 and 5 on the SIAI. The following steps demonstrate how the teachers' responses are determined and summarized.

(1) Compute the sum of "In Place" ratings for each item. In Figure 2, the sum for Item 4 is 29 and that for Item 5 is 32.
(2) Compute the mean (arithmetic average) "In Place" rating by dividing each "Total" by the number of people who responded to the item. This can change from one item to another because some people may not answer all the items. In Figure 2, the mean "In Place" rating for Item 4 is 2.9 (29/10) while it is 3.2 for Item 5 (32/10).
(3) Compute the "Total" of the "Importance" ratings for each item. In Figure 2, the "Total" for Item 4 is 40 and that for Item 5 is 35.
(4) Compute the mean "Importance" rating by dividing each "Total" by the number of people who responded to the item. In Figure 2, the mean "Importance" ratings are 4.0 for Item 4 (40/10) and 3.5 for Item 5 (35/10).

The mean scores of the teachers can then be plotted on the profile sheet

Teacher	Item 4		Item 5	
	In Place	Importance	In Place	Importance
1	3	4	4	4
2	3	5	3	3
3	4	3	3	2
4	2	3	4	4
5	2	4	3	3
6	3	4	3	3
7	4	5	3	5
8	2	4	4	3
9	4	4	3	4
10	2	4	2	4
Total	29	40	32	35
Mean	2.9	4.0	3.2	3.5

FIGURE 2 Sample summary of SIAI data from ten teachers on items 4 and 5 of the SIAI.

shown in Figure 3 by indicating the appropriate points on the 1 to 4 rating scales for "In Place" and "Importance." Figure 3 also shows what a profile sheet might look like if the mean values of the teachers' responses were plotted for the twenty-seven items. This information can be used to determine which components are relatively more in place and which are relatively more important for change. For example, the two columns in Figure 3 show some components (Items 1 and 13) to be somewhat in place and rated as important elements to take action for school improvement. Several other components are rated as being characteristic of the school (Items 4, 6, 9, 17, 20, and 23), yet will need some attention over the school year.

FOSTERING AND MONITORING SYSTEMIC CHANGE: CREATING A CLIMATE FOR SCHOOL/COMMUNITY PARTICIPATION

A favorable climate for school and community participation in systemic change efforts can be fostered by giving each stakeholder group an opportunity to have input into the systemic change process. The SIAI we are proposing can serve as the basis for stakeholders to provide this input.

	Degree in Place				Need for Action			
Part A: School Context	Not in Place 1	2	Fully in Place 3	4	Not Important 1	2	Very Important 3	4
Ethos 1. *Climate*	□	■	□	□	○	○	●	○
Management 4. *Integration*	□	□	■	□	○	○	○	●
Resources 6. *Administration*	□	□	■	□	○	○	○	●
Part B: School Implementation								
Curriculum & Instruction 9. *Cultural and Ethnic Sensitivity*	□	□	■	□	○	○	●	○
Staff 13. *Knowledge & Experience*	□	□	□	□	○	○	○	●
Administrators 17. *Understanding & Knowledge*	□	□	■	□	○	○	●	○
Parents 20. *Outreach*	□	□	■	□	○	●	○	○
Part C: Student Outcomes								
Learning Strategies 23. *Practice*	□	□	■	□	○	●	○	○
Self-Enhancement 26. *Cultural/Ethnic Identity*	□	□	□	□	○	○	○	●

FIGURE 3 Sample of an effectiveness profile using the SIAI.

At the beginning of a systemic change process, the SIAI can serve as a needs assessment. Representatives from a school's different stakeholder groups can participate in filling out the instrument, with responses tallied separately for each group. Using the procedures described in the previous section, response profiles could be created along the instrument's two dimensions (i.e., "In Place" and "Importance"). These stakeholder profiles might then be used as the basis for a meeting of stakeholder representatives in which concerns of different groups would be identified and out of which a listing of priorities for action could be developed. This activity serves as a means of outreach to community members and school staff. It also would help set the stage for collaboration among stakeholder groups in the systemic change process. Del Vecchio et al. (1994) suggest that outreach and collaboration are important components of involving communities in school initiatives in diverse language communities.

Monitoring Improvement

Once needs have been identified and prioritized, schools and community members must work together to ensure that systemic change proceeds. It is sometimes difficult, though, for school staff or community members who are involved in institutional change to recognize when change has occurred. For this reason, the SIAI should also be administered while school change is taking place.

Recent treatments of student assessment have suggested that, rather than a pretest/posttest approach to monitoring student progress, a dynamic assessment strategy be employed in which assessment is more continuous and informs the teaching/learning process (Lidz, 1987). The approach is similar in intent to formative evaluation (Scriven, 1972). The proposed SIAI could be used to monitor progress in two related ways. One, the instrument could be used to keep the focus of stakeholder groups on components that are desirable as systemic change moves forward. Informal progress checking based on the instrument could serve as a means to keep awareness high of needed changes and could provide a basis for stakeholder groups to communicate and collaborate toward their common objectives. Regular communication and collaboration might center around specific aspects of a school that need to be improved to provide a higher quality education for Latino students, and might help to focus such things as teacher inservice topics.

Secondly, the SIAI could be administered to stakeholders at regular intervals (e.g., every spring) to determine if mean ratings on the two response dimensions ("In Place" and "Importance") had changed. Responses could be broken down by stakeholder groups and examined across years to determine if a greater number of desired components were in place and to indicate whether systemic change priorities had changed over a one-year time period. This would also reveal whether different stakeholder groups agreed on the status and importance of systemic change initiatives. By graphing or displaying in tables mean ratings from successive years, it would be possible to determine quantifiably whether stakeholders felt the school had systemically changed over a period of time. Used in this way, the instrument could serve to document progress toward bringing about systemic change as well as to identify needs for the next school year.

SUMMARY

Spurred, in part, by the *Goals 2000: Educate America Act*, and as part of the evolution of school reform efforts through the effective schools movement and efforts directed toward school restructuring, the systemic change initiative has gathered momentum within education. Researchers have identified characteristics of successful and effective schools for Latino and other minority students, and we have grouped these characteristics into three categories—school context, school implementation, and student outcomes or skills. As systemic change efforts proceed, it is very important for the welfare of Latino students that these efforts take into account what we know works for language minority students.

Systemic change that is sensitive to the needs of Latino students must create a school context that recognizes students' culture and native language as attributes and not as detriments. This means that Latino culture and the Spanish language are integrated into both instruction and assessment, and that students' families feel welcome to participate in school activities and decision making. This can be enhanced by school staff who are knowledgeable of Latino culture and speak Spanish as well as English.

Systemic change appropriate for Latino students means that the school curriculum incorporates experiences and interests of Latino students even as it addresses local, state, and national standards. Because such a curriculum would vary from what has been the norm for many years, this means further that teachers and school administrators must be active in promoting the use of native language where appropriate, must encourage and model integration of culture into the curriculum, and must participate in or promote training for all staff where necessary.

Systemic change initiatives must hold Latino and non-Latino students to the same high performance standards, and schools should be able to provide alternate paths toward meeting those standards. Students should be provided the opportunity to achieve these standards in both Spanish and English through active engagement in instructional tasks that will help them meet these goals.

In an atmosphere of change driven by such efforts as *Goals 2000* and the reauthorization of the Improving America's Schools Act, the time is ripe to shape programs that serve Latino and other minority students. These programs must meet the needs of a student population that is growing more culturally and linguistically diverse. In developing the programs that help define systemic change, though, we need to carefully continue documenting and evaluating effects of our efforts (Baker, 1993).

The instrument we have developed for this chapter is meant to provide one way to assess the status of systemic change initiatives along dimensions that reflect best practice for Latino students. With the input of stakeholders from the school and community, the SIAI can provide information useful in the change process. It can serve as a catalyst to engage different stakeholders in communicating with each other about the need for change in specific areas. Further, the SIAI can help them prioritize school components that need change.

Used over time, SIAI's results can help document whether change is occurring in desirable directions, and can reflect the views of all interested parties. The instrument has the potential to be sensitive to multidimensional change in school context, program implementation, and student outcomes, not just to the unidimensional change too often represented by over-reliance on standardized achievement test scores. If our goal is systemic change appropriate for Latino students, then it is important that we have ways to show clearly whether this goal is being achieved.

REFERENCES

August, D., K. Hakuta, and D. Pompa. 1994. *Limited English Proficient Students and the Implemtation of Goals 2000. Discussion Draft.* Stanford, CA: Stanford University, pp. 1–13.

Baker, C. 1993. *Foundations of Bilingual Education and Bilingualism.* Bristol, PA: Multilingual Matters Ltd.

Bond, L., L. Friedman, and A. Van der Ploeg. 1994. *Surveying the Landscape of State Educational Assessment Programs*. Washington, D.C.: Council for Educational Development and Research, pp. 1–52.

Carter, D. J. and M. L. Chatfield. 1986. " Effective Bilingual Schools: Implications for Policy and Practice," *American Journal of Education*, 95(1): 200–232.

Congressional Record. March 21, 1994. Conference Report on House Rule 1804, *Goals 2000: Educate America Act*. Washington, D.C.: U.S. Congress (Public Law 103–227).

Darder, A. 1993. Public Schooling and Latino Students: A Brief Overview. Paper presented at the Tomas Rivera Center/Exxon Education Forum. Georgetown University, Washington, D.C.

Del Vecchio, A., M. Guerrero, C. Gustke, P. Martinez, C. Navarrete, C. Nelson, and J. Wilde. 1994. *Whole School Bilingual Education Programs: Implications for Sound Assessment*. Washington, D.C.: National Clearinghouse on Bilingual Education.

Escamilla, K. 1994. "Message from the President," *NABE News,* 17(7).

Faltis, C. and B. Merino. 1992. "Toward a Definition of Exemplary Teachers in Bilingual Multicultural School Settings," in *Critical Perspectives on Bilingual Education Research*, P. Padilla and H. Benavides, eds. Tempe, AZ: Bilingual Press.

Garcia, E. 1987. "Effective Schooling for Language Minority Students." *New Focus: Occasional Papers on Bilingual Education*, No. 1. Wheaton, VA: National Clearinghouse for Bilingual Education.

Garcia, E. 1994. *Understanding and Meeting the Challenge of Student Cultural Diversity*. Boston, MA: Houghton Mifflin Co.

Lidz, C.S. 1987. "Historical Perspectives," in *Dynamic Assessment: An Interactional Approach to Evaluating Learning Potential,* C. S. Lidz, ed. New York, NY: Guilford Press, pp. 3–32.

Lucas, T., R. Henze, and R. Donato. 1990. "Promoting the Success of Latino Language Minority Students: An Exploratory Study of Six High Schools," *Harvard Educational Review*, 60(3): pp. 315–340.

McCollum, H. and A. Russo. 1993. "A Conceptual Framework on Learning Environments and Student Motivation for Language Minority and Other Underserved Populations," in *Proceedings of the Third National Research Symposium on LEP Students' Issues: Focus on Middle and High School Issues*. Washington, D.C.: U.S. Department of Education, pp. 1–140.

Ramirez, J. D., S. A. Yuen, and D. R. Ramey. 1991. *Final Report: Longitudinal Study of Structured English Immersion Strategy, Early-Exit and Late-Exit Transitional Bilingual Education Programs for Language Minority Children* (Contract No. 300-87-0156). Washington, D.C.: U.S. Department of Education.

Scriven, M. 1972. "The Methodology of Evaluation," in *Readings in Curriculum Evaluation*, P. A. Taylor and D. M. Cowley, eds. Dubuque, IA: Wm. C. Brown Company, Publishers, pp. 28–48.

Squires, D. A., W. C. Huitt, and J. K. Segars. 1984. *Effective Schools and Classrooms: A Research-Based Perspective*. Alexandria, VA: Association for Supervision and Curriculum Development.

Tikunoff, W. J. 1985. *Applying Significant Bilingual Instruction Features in the Classroom*. Rosslyn, VA: National Clearinghouse for Bilingual Education.

Tikunoff, W. J. 1991. *Working with Diverse Student Populations* (Working paper). Larkspur, CA: Southwest Regional Education Laboratory.

Index

Biographies

EDITORS

MARÍA LUÍSA GONZÁLEZ earned her doctorate from New Mexico State University where she is currently serving as the academic department head in the Educational Management and Development department. She has worked as an evaluator-researcher and as the principal of an inner city school that received congressional recognition as one of fifteen exemplary schools in the nation for homeless and at-risk populations.

ANA HUERTA-MACÍAS received her doctorate in foreign language education from the University of Texas at Austin in 1978. She is currently a faculty member in the department of curriculum and instruction at New Mexico State University. Her research interests and publications are in the areas of bilingual education, sociolinguistics, family literacy, and Teaching English to Speakers of Other Languages.

JOSEFINA VILLAMIL TINAJERO is currently professor of bilingual education and assistant dean at the College of Education at the University of Texas at El Paso. An authority on the education of linguistically and culturally diverse students, Dr. Tinajero is a noted author, researcher, and featured speaker in the field of bilingual education.

AUTHORS

ALMA FLOR ADA directs the Program of International and Multicultural Studies at the University of San Francisco. Her research centers on the pedagogical interrelation between school and home, participatory research, and critical pedagogy.

REBECCA BENJAMIN is an assistant professor of bilingual education and English as a Second Language in the College of Education at the

University of New Mexico. Her research has focused on the continued uses of minority languages by school-aged students and their families.

JUAN CONTRERAS, who has taught for twenty-three years, is a published author, poet, and lecturer of Latino issues. He is currently an education change agent with Project Mariposa in the Ysleta Independent School District. He holds a master's degree in bilingual education.

YOLANDA DE LA CRUZ is an assistant professor of mathematics education at Northwestern University in Evanston, Illinois. Her teaching and research interests are in mathematical achievement among underrepresented groups, parent and teacher education, and teaching strategies that work among students speaking diverse languages.

JOZI DE LEÓN is an associate professor in the department of special education/communication disorders at New Mexico State University. Her professional interests have focused on culturally and linguistically diverse exceptional students.

ANN DEL VECCHIO is a senior research associate with the Evaluation Assistance Center-Western Region at New Mexico Highlands University. She has designed a variety of attitude and knowledge instruments for use with diverse populations.

JULIA ROSA EMSLIE is associate professor of bilingual education and director of bilingual multicultural education at Eastern New Mexico University. She has committed her time and efforts to the improvement of teacher preparation to meet the needs of linguistically and culturally distinct populations.

CECILIA ESPINOSA is a multiage bilingual teacher at Wm. T. Machan Elementary School in Phoenix, Arizona. She earned a bachelor of arts degree in early childhood education and a master of education degree in bilingual education from Arizona State University.

M. CRISTINA GONZÁLEZ has had extensive experience in teaching, curriculum development, training, and consulting in child development at the local, state, and national level. She is currently a faculty member in child development at the El Paso Community College in El Paso, Texas.

CYNDEE GUSTKE is currently a research associate with the Evaluation Assistance Center-Western Region at New Mexico Highlands University. Ms. Gustke has fifteen years of experience as an elementary teacher and administrator in bilingual education programs in New Mexico and Alaska.

LINDA HOLMAN holds a doctorate in educational management and development and is principal at Hillside Elementary in El Paso, Texas. The focus of her research has been the appropriateness of high-stakes testing of Latino students.

SANDRA HURLEY is an assistant professor of reading education at the University of Texas at El Paso. Her research interests include literacy for linguistically and culturally diverse students, social and cultural influences in literacy development, and qualitative research.

ELIZABETH VARELA LOZANO completed her M.Ed. in curriculum and instruction with a specialization in bilingual education at the University of Texas at El Paso. She currently coordinates a teacher preparation program for undergraduate students who are working in bilingual education with a concentration in math and science.

NANCY J. LUCAS is assistant principal and magnet school coordinator at John F. Kennedy Middle School in Riviera Beach, Florida. She has worked with language and ethnic minority students and their families for over twenty-one years.

PAUL MARTÍNEZ is currently director of the Evaluation Assistance Center-Western Region at New Mexico Highlands University. His professional career spans over sixteen years and includes both public school and university-level teaching and administrative experience.

KAREN MOORE is a multiage bilingual teacher at Wm. T. Machan Elementary School in Phoenix, Arizona. Prior to earning her teaching certificate in early childhood education from Arizona State University, she taught in Head Start programs in Arizona for many years.

CECILIA NAVARRETE is currently assistant director of the Evaluation Assistance Center-Western Region at New Mexico Highlands University in Albuquerque, New Mexico. With over twenty-two years in the field of education, she is an experienced bilingual and migrant education teacher, administrator, curriculum designer, and university instructor.

CHRISTOPHER NELSON is an assistant professor in the School of Education at New Mexico Highlands University. His interests include assessment within diverse student populations, program evaluation, and educational research.

VIRGINIA R. PADILLA has worked with the bilingual/ESL department in the Ysleta Independent School district for nineteen years. She is currently an education change agent with Project Mariposa, a bilingual education project which is being implemented in several elementary schools in the district.

ELIZABETH QUINTERO is an associate professor of early childhood elementary education at the University of Minnesota at Duluth. She has had teaching experiences in several countries and has enjoyed working with Latino, Hmong, and Laotian students in family literacy programs.

IRENE ALICIA SERNA received her Ph.D. from the University of New Mexico in 1989 in curriculum and instruction with an emphasis in education. Her research interests focus on bilingual children's literacy development in Spanish and English.

NANCY JEAN SMITH directs the Resource Center for Bilingual Education sponsored by Title VII in San Joaquin Valley. She has taught migrant children in California for the past 3 years. She obtained her B.A. and M.A. from Eastern Michigan University and, as a Title VII fellow, her Ed.D. from University of San Francisco, California.

ALICIA SALINAS SOSA is an educator with twenty-five years of experience in bilingual education. She is currently a faculty member in the Division of Education at the University of Texas at San Antonio.

KARIN M. WIBURG currently coordinates the learning technologies specialization in the College of Education at New Mexico State University. Her research and publications involve the design, implementation, and evaluation of technology-mediated learning environments. Prior to her work in higher education, she spent fifteen years in public school teaching and administration.

JUDITH WILDE is a senior research associate with the Evaluation Assistance Center-Western Region at New Mexico Highlands University. She has worked as a program evaluator with diverse groups in the western states.